Using Javelin®

David Paul Ewing

Joseph-David Carrabis

Que™ Corporation
Indianapolis, Indiana

Using Javelin®

Copyright© 1986 by Que Corporation

Library of Congress Catalog No.: 85-63877
ISBN 0-88022-199-2

89 88 87 86   8 7 6 5 4 3 2 1

Interpretation of the printing code: the rightmost number of the first series of numbers is the year of the book's printing; the rightmost number of the second series of numbers is the number of the book's printing. For example, a printing code of 86-1 shows that the first printing of the book occurred in 1986.

Dedication

To my parents,
Bob and Rita Ewing

—D.P.E.

To Susan,
for her patience

—J-D C.

About the Authors

David Paul Ewing

David Paul Ewing is Training Products Director for Que Corporaton. He is coauthor of Que's *Using Symphony* and *1-2-3 Macro Workbook* and author of Que's *1-2-3 Macro Library*, *The Using 1-2-3 Workbook*, and the *Using 1-2-3 Workbook Instructor's Guide*.

Mr. Ewing received his B.A. from Duquesne University and his M.A. from North Carolina State University. He is presently completing his Ph.D. at Purdue University. Prior to his position at Que, he was the Assistant Director of the Business Writing Program at Purdue University, where he developed course materials and trained instructors. For eight years, Mr. Ewing taught college-level writing and business communications courses. He has published articles in leading business communications books and journals and given numerous presentations at national conferences on writing and business communications.

Joseph-David Carrabis

Joseph-David Carrabis has been involved with computers for 15 years. His acquaintance with them began at Lincoln Labs, a government institute near Lexington, Massachusetts. In 1980, he founded JDI, Inc., a business consulting and software design firm specializing in large-scale business systems. His clients have included several Fortune 500 companies.

Mr. Carrabis is the author of *dBASE III Advanced Programming* and is a regular contributor to *IBM PC Update*, both products of Que Corporation. He has worked as a product line director for Que Corporation. He has also designed tutorials for Lotus 1-2-3, dBASE II, and WordStar and has developed computer products for handicapped persons.

A man of diverse interests, Mr. Carrabis has studied Old Testament theology and languages, applied mathematics and physics, and gravitational physics, as well as sign language. He has enjoyed being a "designated hugger" for the Special Olympics. He holds a Black Belt in karate and is a member of the Computer Writers' Association and Science Fiction Writers of America.

Table of Contents

2   Getting Started with Javelin   45

10 Creating Graphs

11 Printing Reports 325

12 Javelin Macros 357

Acknowledgments

The authors thank the following people for their assistance in completing this book:

Chuck Stewart, Que Corporation, whose incredible skill was invaluable managing the editing of this text and managing the many individuals involved in this project

Ann Holcombe and Lois Sherman, Que Corporation, for their dedication to assuring quality in the final manuscript

Tim Stanley, Que Corporation, who spent many extra hours producing the hundreds of figures in this book and checking and advising the authors on technical content

Tom Carlton, CF Industries, who critiqued all chapters, contributed text to Chapters 7 and 11, and developed Appendix C, "A Javelin versus 1-2-3 Comparison"

Bob Bush, Eli Lilly & Co., who masterminded many of the book's financial applications and assisted with the design of the book's approach

Jon Waldron and Ellen Brout, Javelin Corporation, for their critique of the book's chapters and recommendations on book content

Trademark Acknowledgments

Conventions Used
in This Book

A number of conventions are used in *Using Javelin* to help you learn the program.

References to keys are as they appear on the keyboard of the IBM Personal Computer. Function keys, however, are defined by the Javelin program. Function-key names appear in uppercase and precede the key number in parentheses: EDIT (F2), GO TO (F5), MACRO (F7).

Direct quotations of words that appear on the screen are printed in a special typeface.

Information within text that you are asked to type is printed in *italic*. Any indented material you are asked to type is set off from the text in ordinary type.

Boldface letters indicate that the word is a Javelin command and that you can select the command by typing the boldface letter. For example, /**W**orksheet **I**mport **W**KS indicates that you type /*IW*. Any command elements that you must select with the cursor will not be in boldface. For example, to select /**D**efine **W**orksheet Column width you would type /*DW* and then use the cursor to select the Column width option.

Names of variables appear in *italic* with the initial letter of each element capitalized: *Total Revenue*, *Blender Units*, *Operating Expense*. Items on settings sheets are also shown in italic, such as the *Name* setting on the Worksheet settings sheet.

Words printed in uppercase include the names of Javelin views (DIAGRAM), status indicators (READY), and Javelin functions (AVG).

Javelin's macro commands appear in uppercase letters preceded by the @ symbol: @READ, @PROMPT, @JUMP. Single-character macros activated by pressing the Alt key appear as Alt-(keyname): Alt-V, Alt-G, Alt-K. Macro names appear in italic: *Autoexec*, *Grapher*, *Pregrapher*. Single letters representing Javelin commands appear in macro lines in lowercase. For example, /**V**iew **T**able is represented as vt in a macro line.

Ctrl– → indicates that you press the Ctrl key and hold it down while you also press the Right-arrow key. Other hyphenated key combinations, such as Ctrl–Home, are performed in the same manner.

Editorial Director

David F. Noble, Ph.D.

Product Director

David Paul Ewing, M.A.

Managing Editor

Gregory Croy

Editors

Charles O. Stewart III, M.A.
Bill Nolan
Ann Campbell Holcombe, M.S.Ed.
Lois Sherman
Virginia Noble, M.L.S.
Jeannine Freudenberger, M.A.
Katherine Murray

Technical Editor

Timothy S. Stanley

Introduction

Javelin®, the most sophisticated, complete business analysis tool for microcomputers, has capabilities that no other single business application program provides. Javelin goes far beyond powerful programs like Lotus® 1-2-3®, Symphony®, and Enable™ by combining their best features with the capabilities of add-on and utility packages. The capability to check errors in your model, display a diagram of your model's structure, produce many types of business reports, display and print professional graphics, and show data in many different ways makes Javelin superior to any other PC business applications program!

Using Javelin

Using Javelin will help you learn the full power of the program and develop the skill to apply this tremendous program to your business' most complex analysis tasks. *Using Javelin* is a complete, comprehensive introduction to what Javelin is and how it can help with business analysis. The book will also help you develop skills by teaching you how Javelin is applied to everyday business problems. And for your reference, *Using Javelin* contains a complete summary of commands and functions.

Who Should Use This Book?

If you own Javelin, you should own this book. *Using Javelin* covers both the basics and the fine points of the program. Every chapter includes clear explanations and examples. And to help you really understand the power of Javelin, the book contains hundreds of figures showing Javelin in action solving realistic business problems. The explanations and examples in this book help put the full power of Javelin at your fingertips.

If you do not own Javelin but are considering purchasing the program, this book is also for you. Chapter 1, "An Overview of Javelin," will help you understand the unique features of this powerful program in relation to other business applications software. If you presently use a conventional spreadsheet program, this book will especially help you understand the differences and advanced capabilities Javelin brings to financial analysis. In particular, *Using Javelin* pays special attention to 1-2-3 users making the transition to Javelin. Throughout the book and in Appendix C, "1-2-3 and Javelin," are references to 1-2-3 to help you see how Javelin's capabilities go beyond those of 1-2-3.

About This Book

Using Javelin contains 13 chapters and is divided into 7 sections:

1. Understanding and Getting Started with Javelin (Chapters 1 and 2)

2. Building a Javelin Model (Chapters 3-7)

3. Checking Your Javelin Model (Chapter 8)

4. Analyzing and Presenting with Javelin (Chapters 9-11)

5. Javelin Macros (Chapter 12)

6. A Comprehensive Javelin Model (Chapter 13)

7. Javelin Reference Guide (Appendixes A-C)

Chapter 1, "An Overview of Javelin," introduces beginning users to Javelin by presenting a complete description of Javelin, explaining Javelin's capabilities, giving examples of its use, and presenting the history that led to its development. Chapter 1 also compares Javelin with 1-2-3 for those 1-2-3 users making the transition to this incredible program.

Chapter 2, "Getting Started with Javelin," describes how to prepare the Javelin disks for your system, including instructions for making backup copies of the original Javelin disks, installing Javelin on your computer system, and starting the program. Chapter 2 also introduces the general program features that new users will need to know before beginning to tackle Javelin for their own applications. Special features of the Javelin screen, an overview of Javelin's command menu system, and an explanation of special uses for function and cursor keys are all covered in Chapter 2.

Chapter 3, "Using the DIAGRAM, FORMULAS, TABLE, and NOTES Views," explains how to begin developing Javelin models. This chapter introduces you to those parts of the program most valuable for creating formulas, entering data, and keeping track of the structure and assumptions of your model as you build it.

Chapter 4, "How Javelin Handles Time," introduces the concepts and program features related to how Javelin automatically links your model formulas and data to time. In Chapter 4, you'll learn how Javelin can automatically calculate values by month, by quarter, or by year and mix data for different time periods in the same formula.

Chapter 5, "Using the CHART, QUICK GRAPH, and WORKSHEET Views," continues to illustrate Javelin as a tool for model building, explaining the special graphic capabilities that allow you to enter and change data by using cursor keys to redraw bar charts and line graphs. Chapter 5 also covers the power of Javelin's worksheet and the range of worksheet functions. This chapter shows how Javelin can automatically display data in a worksheet and emphasizes how different it is to work with a Javelin worksheet instead of a conventional spreadsheet program.

Chapter 6, "Importing and Consolidating among Javelin Models," presents a comprehensive introduction to Javelin's capabilities for importing and consolidating between models you have created in different files. In this chapter, you'll discover how Javelin goes far beyond conventional spreadsheet programs in its capabilities for importing and consolidating.

Chapter 7, "Using the Time Delay, Lookup Table, and Curve Building Blocks," covers the concept of Javelin Building Blocks, explaining how this feature represents complex relationships among variables in your model without requiring that you enter complex formulas. Aging of Accounts Receivable and creating a tax lookup table are two of the applications for building blocks described in this chapter.

Chapter 8, "Using the FORMULAS and ERRORS Views for Model Checking," demonstrates those features of Javelin that help you analyze a model's logic and check for errors. The chapter introduces the numerous command options for checking relationships between formulas and parts of formulas, checking for circular references, and checking for problems with formulas. Chapter 8 explains how Javelin eliminates the need for utility packages to audit the formulas and data in your models.

Chapter 9, "Business Analysis and Presentation with Views and Building Blocks," discusses how you can take advantage of Javelin's options for displaying data to help you think through a business problem and make decisions. Chapter 9 also illustrates Javelin's capabilities for electronic presentation by demonstrating how Javelin displays graphs, tables, diagrams, and worksheets to support your analysis.

In Chapter 10, "Creating Graphs," you'll learn to use the full range of Javelin's graphic capabilities. This chapter gives examples of the types of graphs you can create, explains the options available for producing professional graphs, and lists the commands used to create, display, and print these graphs.

Chapter 11, "Printing Reports," covers the commands and options for printing in Javelin, including the types of print output and print settings. Chapter 11 in particular shows you how to produce professional reports from Javelin's WORKSHEET view.

Chapter 12, "Javelin Macros," explains the step-by-step operations for creating and modifying macros. Chapter 12 also contains sample macros that you can easily duplicate for your own Javelin files.

Chapter 13, "A Comprehensive Javelin Model," integrates all of Javelin's main elements introduced in preceding chapters. The chapter shows how Javelin can be used to develop a corporate model that illustrates Javelin's most powerful features, including capabilities for model building, options for viewing data, building blocks, and macros.

Appendix A, "Javelin Function Summary," and Appendix B, "Javelin Command Summary," will be valuable references as you develop skills using Javelin for your business applications. Appendix A groups all Javelin functions by purpose so that you can easily understand and find the functions you need. Appendix B will help you understand all options available through Javelin's command menu and provides tips on using Javelin commands.

Appendix C, "A Javelin versus 1-2-3 Comparison," is written for those who are making the transition from 1-2-3 to Javelin.

## Part I

Understanding and Getting Started with Javelin

1

An Overview
of Javelin

What Is Javelin?

Javelin is an incredibly powerful software program for business analysis, a complete tool for creating, analyzing, and presenting business models. Unlike any other popular business analysis program, Javelin works the way you think instead of requiring you to think the way it works. Javelin stores formulas and values in a central data base so that they're available instantly—available when you want them for business models. Furthermore, Javelin displays these formulas and values in keeping with your needs instead of requiring that you conform to the limitations of the software. Javelin gives you a precise view of your business models and data in order to ensure accuracy and to help you make the right decisions.

This chapter introduces you to Javelin's powerful capabilities, gives examples of its use, and presents a brief history of the development of spreadsheet software. And if you're moving to Javelin from a conventional spreadsheet program such as Lotus 1-2-3, the comparison of 1-2-3 and Javelin at the end of the chapter will make your transition smoother.

What Can Javelin Do?

For model building, Javelin helps you keep track of the logic of your models and formulas. With Javelin, there's no need to supplement your software investment with utility packages that show the "invisible" relationships in models so that you can audit formulas and data. In Javelin, all relationships are visible, and error checking is simple. You use plain English to build formulas, which Javelin will list or diagram whenever you need to analyze relationships, check for formula errors, or check for circular references.

Model building becomes easy because Javelin understands time. Sales information, for example, can be grouped by month, and operating expenses by quarter. When you build a report displaying results by month, Javelin automatically converts all variables to monthly values. Asked for a year-end report, Javelin combines all values into year-end values. And if you need Javelin to do more than simply add or divide when converting values to new time periods, you can specify techniques such as averaging, interpolating, or repeating constant values.

For analysis, Javelin provides many views of your model's data without the complexity of integrated packages like 1-2-3 and Symphony. Javelin displays data in tables, graphs, worksheets, or diagrams, allowing you to combine two views of data on-screen at once. And when you change the data, Javelin instantly reflects those changes in all the other ways the data can be viewed—in a worksheet, table, line graph, or bar graph, for instance.

Javelin lets you change data in numerous ways: by editing formulas, by changing data in tables, and by redrawing graphs using your computer's cursor keys. Creating a Javelin worksheet is as easy as changing data, involving practically none of the manual entry of formulas, labels, and data required in conventional spreadsheet programs like 1-2-3.

For presenting data to others, Javelin is a state-of-the art tool for electronic presentations as well as for printed graphs and reports. Displaying data in a table, worksheet, diagram, or graph is as simple as selecting a few commands. And because you can redraw graphs by simply pressing the cursor keys, Javelin instantly answers "What if" questions when you're asked to show the effects of changes in data. Javelin can also produce professional printed reports and graphs. Powerful worksheet capabilities display Javelin models in conventional spreadsheet form and let you print professional reports easily.

Javelin is truly revolutionary; it has the flexibility to fit your thinking and your needs for building, analyzing, and presenting business models.

Javelin at a Glance

Published by	Javelin Software Corporation One Kendall Square Building 200 Cambridge, MA 02139 (617) 494-1400
System requirements	IBM® PC, IBM PC XT™, Personal Computer AT or 100% compatible including COMPAQ®, COMPAQ PLUS®, COMPAQ Deskpro®, COMPAQ Deskpro 286®, COMPAQ PORTABLE 286®, COMPAQ PORTABLE II™
	512K of memory
	Two floppy disk drives or one hard disk and one floppy drive
	DOS 2.0 or later
Javelin also supports	IBM Color, Monochrome, and Enhanced Graphics Adapters
	Hercules Graphics Card™
	Intel Expanded Memory Specification
	8087 and 80287 math coprocessors

How Does Javelin Help with Business Analysis?

Javelin fits the way you think by providing 10 separate views of any business model. With these 10 views, Javelin supports your needs for building models, analyzing data, and presenting your analysis to others.

1. The DIAGRAM view gives you a way to create formulas; you can see the relationships among variables in a formula and the relationships among formulas in a model (see fig. 1.1).

2. The TABLE view organizes information into lists, giving you an easy way to enter and view data and calculate formulas (see fig. 1.2).

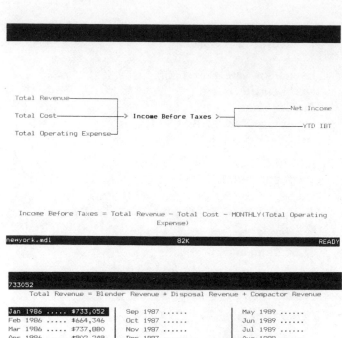

Income Before Taxes = Total Revenue - Total Cost - MONTHLY(Total Operating
Expense)

Fig. 1.1. The DIAGRAM view depicts the relationships between your variables.

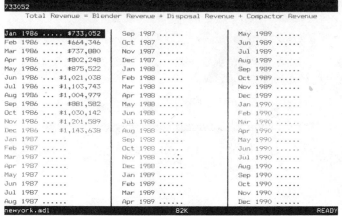

Fig. 1.2. The TABLE view organizes information into lists.

3. The FORMULAS view displays a list of formulas sorted either alphabetically or by the relationships among them (see fig. 1.3).

4. The CHART view allows you to view your data in bar-graph form and to view it alone or with data presented in another view, such as WORKSHEET, TABLE, or DIAGRAM (see fig. 1.4). For input data, the CHART view allows you to change existing data or enter new data by increasing or decreasing the size of the bars.

5. The QUICK GRAPH view displays a line graph of data entered for a variable and allows you to redraw the graph by changing data points on the graph itself (see fig. 1.5).

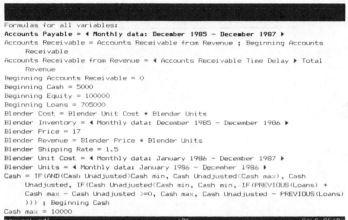

Fig. 1.3. The FORMULAS view displays a list of formulas.

```
Formulas for all variables:
Accounts Payable = ◄ Monthly data: December 1985 - December 1987 ►
Accounts Receivable = Accounts Receivable from Revenue ; Beginning Accounts
        Receivable
Accounts Receivable from Revenue = ◄ Accounts Receivable Time Delay ► Total
        Revenue
Beginning Accounts Receivable = 0
Beginning Cash = 5000
Beginning Equity = 100000
Beginning Loans = 705000
Blender Cost = Blender Unit Cost * Blender Units
Blender Inventory = ◄ Monthly data: December 1985 - December 1986 ►
Blender Price = 17
Blender Revenue = Blender Price * Blender Units
Blender Shipping Rate = 1.5
Blender Unit Cost = ◄ Monthly data: January 1986 - December 1987 ►
Blender Units = ◄ Monthly data: January 1986 - Decemher 1986 ►
Cash = IF(AND(Cash Unadjusted>Cash min, Cash Unadjusted<Cash max), Cash
        Unadjusted, IF(Cash Unadjusted<Cash min, Cash min, IF(PREVIOUS(Loans) +
        Cash max - Cash Unadjusted >=0, Cash max, Cash Unadjusted - PREVIOUS(Loans)
        ))) ; Beginning Cash
Cash max = 10000
newyork.mdl                                    69K                    CALC READY
```

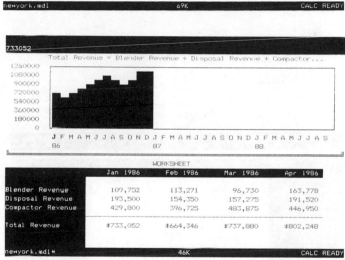

Fig. 1.4. The CHART view shows data presented in a bar graph and can appear with another Javelin view.

6. The WORKSHEET view displays your data in rows and columns, allowing you to enter data and formulas in much the same way you would with a spreadsheet program such as 1-2-3. However, a Javelin worksheet is far more flexible than a conventional spreadsheet. For example, you can use a Javelin worksheet with the other views (see fig. 1.6).

7. The NOTES view gives you a special window for entering your assumptions or explanations of data as you develop and check your model (see fig. 1.7.)

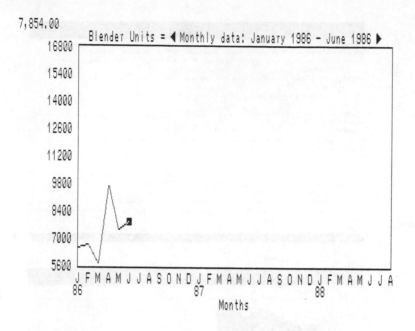

Fig. 1.5. You can play "What if" with the QUICK GRAPH view by simply moving the cursor.

WORKSHEET

	Jan 1986	Feb 1986	Mar 1986	Apr 1986
Blender Revenue	109,752	113,271	96,730	163,778
Disposal Revenue	193,500	154,350	157,275	191,520
Compactor Revenue	429,800	396,725	483,875	446,950
Total Revenue	$733,052	$664,346	$737,880	$802,248

newyork.mdl* 46K CALC READY

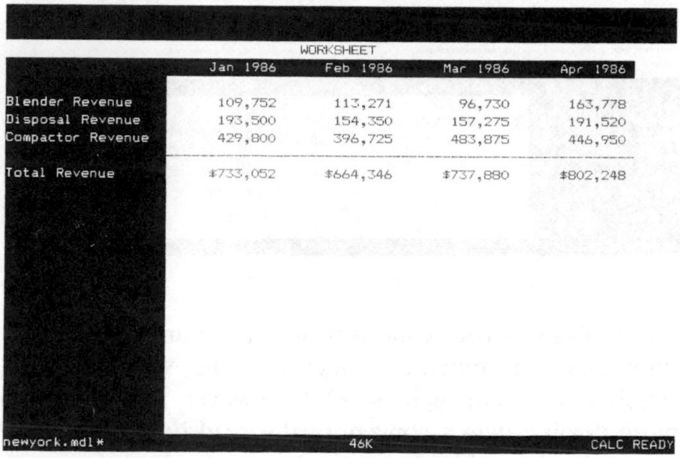

Fig. 1.6. Javelin's WORKSHEET is more than just a spreadsheet.

8. The ERRORS view tells you immediately whether a formula has an error, what the error is, and whether the variables have any problems (see fig. 1.8).

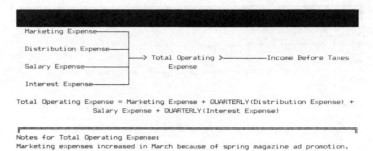

```
Marketing Expense─────┐
Distribution Expense──┤
                      ├─> Total Operating >──────────Income Before Taxes
Salary Expense────────┤      Expense
Interest Expense──────┘

Total Operating Expense = Marketing Expense + QUARTERLY(Distribution Expense) +
                Salary Expense + QUARTERLY(Interest Expense)

Notes for Total Operating Expense:
Marketing expenses increased in March because of spring magazine ad promotion.
```

```
newyork.mdl*                                    82K                         READY
```

Fig. 1.7. The NOTES view
encourages documentation as you
build your model.

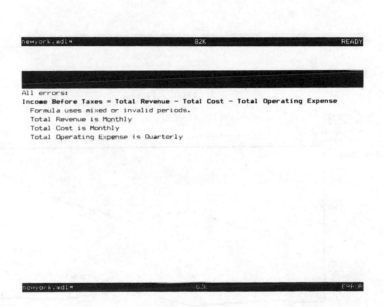

```
All errors:
Income Before Taxes = Total Revenue - Total Cost - Total Operating Expense
    Formula uses mixed or invalid periods.
    Total Revenue is Monthly
    Total Cost is Monthly
    Total Operating Expense is Quarterly
```

```
newyork.mdl*                                    83K                         ERROR
```

Fig. 1.8. The ERRORS view helps
you audit your model.

9. The MACRO view shows you the programs you've created to automate the sequences of keystrokes you use frequently with Javelin models (see fig. 1.9).

10. The GRAPH view displays a line, bar, percent-bar, stacked-bar, horizontal, or pie graph or XY scatter plot of the data in your model (see figs. 1.10 through 1.17).

```
Macro Build box:
@SLASH dbr
@PROMPT What is the name of this Rollup building block?
@READ @ENTER
@DOWN @ENTER
@PROMPT Create the organization chart here. Type F7 when ready to continue
@READ @ENTER
@PAUSE
@ESC @DOWN @DOWN @ENTER
@PROMPT Enter the variables you want to use here. Type F7 to continue.
@READ @ENTER
@PAUSE
@ESC @DOWN @DOWN @DOWN @ENTER
```

```
consol.mdl                          40K                          READY
```

Fig. 1.9. The MACRO view helps you view or modify macros.

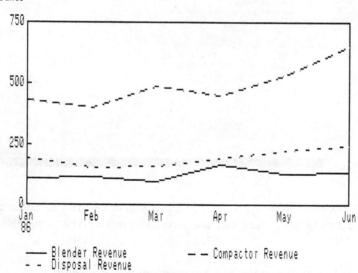

Fig. 1.10. A line graph in GRAPH view.

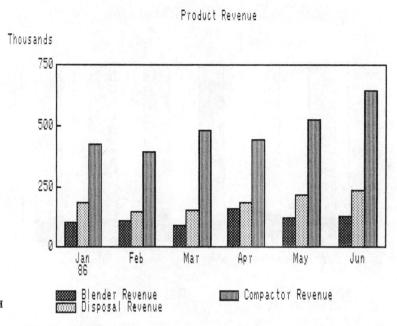

Fig. 1.11. A bar graph in GRAPH
view.

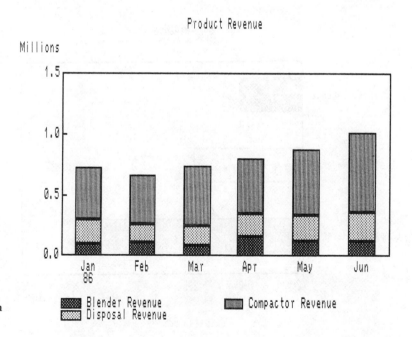

Fig. 1.12. A stacked-bar graph in
GRAPH view.

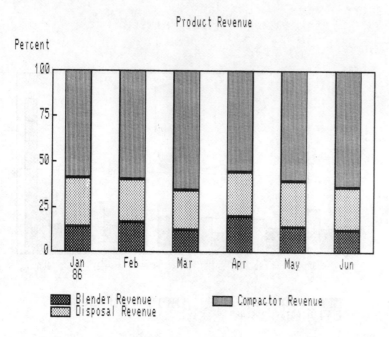

Fig. 1.13. A percent bar graph in GRAPH view.

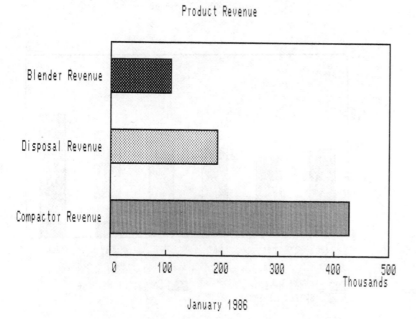

Fig. 1.14. A horizontal bar graph in GRAPH view.

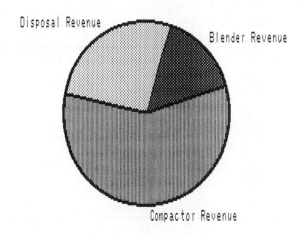

Fig. 1.15. A pie graph in GRAPH
view.

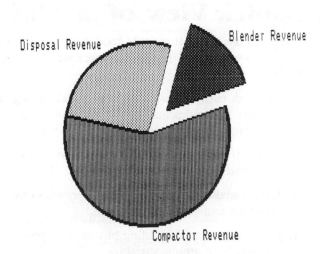

Fig. 1.16. An exploded pie graph
in GRAPH view.

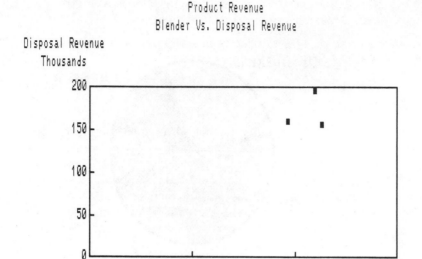

Fig. 1.17. An XY scatter plot graph in GRAPH view.

A Quick View of Javelin

Through discussion of the single model presented in the following sections, you'll get acquainted with seven features we've identified as Javelin's most powerful:

1. You can easily create complex models, using variables created in plain English—variables that Javelin remembers and which can be automatically retrieved with Javelin's SPELL key (Tab).

2. You can view data in a number of ways with one or two views displayed at one time.

3. Javelin makes creating complex formulas easy through the use of variables and range of functions.

4. Javelin's powerful building blocks help you understand complex relationships among variables.

5. Javelin worksheets display data in rows and columns like those of conventional spreadsheet programs, but you can create Javelin worksheets without inputting any data or labels manually.

6. Javelin can consolidate complete models or selected variables and distinguish original variables from consolidated ones.

7. Javelin is a powerful tool for presenting business models to others, electronically and in printed form.

A Javelin Model

To understand the power of Javelin, take a look at an Income Statement model for use by Future Home Appliances, Inc., a company distributing three household kitchen products (blenders, kitchen disposals, and trash compactors). The company has regional offices in New York and Los Angeles and must prepare Income Statements for each office. Both statements must be consolidated in a corporate Income Statement that will be used in analyzing the company's financial position—an important part of business planning. This task can be done with precision using Javelin.

Variables

Creating formulas is easy in Javelin because variables have descriptive names, as you can see from the FORMULAS view in figure 1.18. This makes checking your equations much less cumbersome than checking equations in conventional spreadsheet programs. *Total Operating Expense*, for example, is defined as the sum of *Marketing Expense, Distribution Expense, Salary Expense*, and *Interest Expense*. A variable defined in this way is certainly easier to understand than a variable defined as the sum of four spreadsheet cells.

Fig. 1.18. Variables written in English.

```
Formulas for all variables:
Loans = IF(PREVIOUS(Loans) + Cash - Cash Unadjusted <0, 0, PREVIOUS(Loans) +
     Cash - Cash Unadjusted) ; Beginning Loans
Marketing Expense - ◀ Quarterly data: 1 Quarter 1986 - 4 Quarter 1986 ▶
Month = ◀ Monthly data: January 1986 - January 1989 ▶
Net Income = Income Before Taxes - Taxes
Plant and Equipment = ◀ Monthly data: December 1985 - January 1988 ▶
Predicted Blender Sales = TREND(Blender Units,Jan 1987,Dec 1987)
Salary Expense = ◀ Quarterly data: 4 Quarter 1985 - 4 Quarter 1987 ▶
Taxes = IF(Month = 1, YTD Taxes, YTD Taxes - PREVIOUS(YTD Taxes))
Total Assets = Cash + Accounts Receivable + Total Inventory + Plant and
     Equipment
Total Cost = Blender Cost + Disposal Cost + Compactor Cost
Total Cost Per Unit = ◀ UNDEFINED ▶
Total Inventory = Blender Inventory + Compactor Inventory + Disposal Inventory
Total Liability and Equity = Accounts Payable + Loans + Equity
Total Operating Expense = Marketing Expense + QUARTERLY(Distribution Expense) +
     Salary Expense + QUARTERLY(Interest Expense)
Total Revenue = Blender Revenue + Disposal Revenue + Compactor Revenue
Total Units = Blender Units + Disposal Units + Compactor Units
YTD IBT = YTD(Income Before Taxes)
YTD Taxes = ◀ Taxes Lookup Table ▶ YTD IBT
newyork.mdl*                              48K                           READY
```

Ease of Using Variables: The SPELL Key

In addition to making formula creation easy, Javelin automates retrieval of a variable once you've created it. After you enter the first few characters of the variable name, Javelin's SPELL key (Tab) can fill in the untyped portion from the list of variables defined in your application. If you haven't typed enough characters for Javelin to select a single variable, you are given a list of variables whose names begin with the letters you have entered. You can then choose the variable from the list. Entering *To*, for example, brings up a list of variables beginning with *to*, as shown in figure 1.19.

As explained in Chapter 3, Javelin also "understands" that you may not remember whether you originally entered a variable name in all lowercase letters, all uppercase, or a combination of both. Javelin therefore retrieves the original variable even when you've entered the name in a different case. For example, if you enter *operating expense total* rather than *Total Operating Expense*, Javelin knows they are the same variable. The SPELL key, however, will not retrieve a variable consisting of multiple parts such as *Total Operating Expense* if you reverse parts (*Expense Total Operating*). See Chapters 2 and 3 for more information on the SPELL key.

Fig. 1.19. The SPELL key displays the variables you may be seeking.

Javelin's FORMULAS, ERRORS, and DIAGRAM Views

As you develop a Javelin model, the FORMULAS view can tell you how every variable is calculated. Asking Javelin to display the roots for *Net Income*, for example, results in the list of variables in figure 1.20. You can print the list or move the cursor through it. Viewing the branches of *Total Revenue*—those variables that *it* affects—produces the list of variables in figure 1.21.

Fig. 1.20. FORMULAS view showing variables that affect *Net Income* roots of *Net Income*).

Fig. 1.21. FORMULAS view showing variables affected by *Total Revenue* (branches of *Total Revenue*).

Javelin can also display only the variables and formulas that cause errors in your model. The ERRORS view instantly lists problem variables and formulas. Three keystrokes, */VE*, give you a listing of all errors. The slash (/) brings up the command menu, *V* requests a new view, and *E* asks for ERRORS. Note how figure 1.22 indicates the error that results from mixing time periods in a single formula.

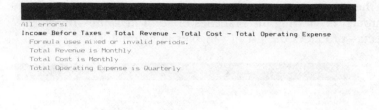

```
All errors:
Income Before Taxes = Total Revenue - Total Cost - Total Operating Expense
  Formula uses mixed or invalid periods.
  Total Revenue is Monthly
  Total Cost is Monthly
  Total Operating Expense is Quarterly
```

```
newyork.mdl*                        43K                      CALC ERROR
```

Fig. 1.22. ERRORS view reveals
the error caused by mixing time
periods in a formula.

As useful as the listing of formulas is, the DIAGRAM view can be an even better
tool. Figure 1.23, for example, shows the variables directly affecting and affected
by *Total Revenue*. Displaying this view is easy; it's a matter of selecting /View
Diagram and telling Javelin the variable for which you want a diagram.

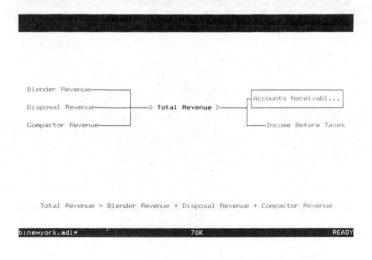

```
Blender Revenue
Disposal Revenue  ──> Total Revenue >──┌─ Accounts Receivabl...
Compactor Revenue                      └─ Income Before Taxes
```

```
      Total Revenue = Blender Revenue + Disposal Revenue + Compactor Revenue
b:newyork.mdl*                      70K                           READY
```

Fig. 1.23. DIAGRAM view
showing variables affecting and
affected by *Total Revenue*.

When you select a command, Javelin displays all menu choices at once; you
need not move the cursor through multiple levels of menu choices (see
fig. 1.24).

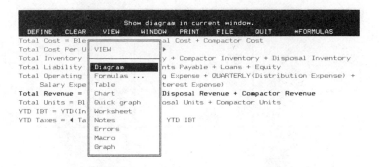

Fig. 1.24. Javelin displays all the menu choices for a command at once.

Javelin Windows

Javelin enables you to split the screen into two windows and combine any two of eight views: DIAGRAM, FORMULAS, TABLE, CHART, WORKSHEET, NOTES, ERRORS, and MACRO. You'll find this window capability quite different from that of programs like Symphony and Framework®. When you create multiple windows in Symphony or Framework, only one window is active, and changes made in one window are not immediately reflected in another. With Javelin, both windows are always active. And when you've synchronized windows, both windows display the same variable; changes made in one window are reflected in the other.

Figure 1.25, for example, shows two windows that present data for the number of blenders sold by the New York office between January, 1986, and June, 1986. The top window displays the TABLE view, the bottom window the CHART view. Data in the table can be entered or edited as usual. You use the arrow keys to enter or edit data in the chart if, for instance, you want to increase the number of units for June, 1986, from 7854 to 9554. The table and chart windows automatically reflect new data entered into either (see fig. 1.26).

You'll see how powerful Javelin is when you combine and synchronize various views—synchronizing the TABLE view with the DIAGRAM or FORMULAS views, for example. In one window, you can use the TABLE view as your "working view" to enter formulas and data; in the second window, use the DIAGRAM or FORMULAS view as your "conceptual view"—the view that, by enabling you to review the logic and relationships among variables, helps you think through your model as you build it.

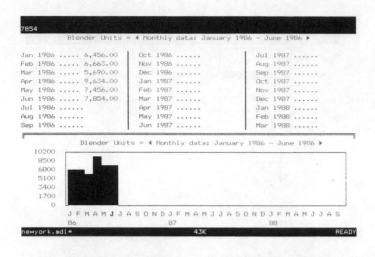

Fig. 1.25. Javelin's windowing feature showing synchronization between the TABLE and CHART views.

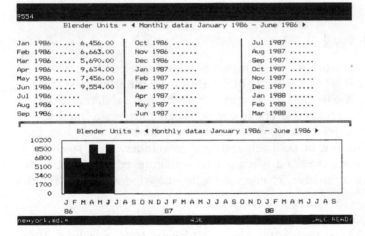

Fig. 1.26. TABLE and CHART windows automatically reflect new data entered into either view.

Complex Formulas

The FORMULAS view demonstrates Javelin's sophisticated handling of complex formulas. Consider, for example, the formula for *Cash* in our Income Statement model. By selecting /View Formula Roots for the variable *Cash*, you can have Javelin display the formula for *Cash* along with the variables that affect *Cash* (see fig. 1.27). Notice how the logic of our application is apparent in the formulas: borrowing requirements are a direct result of cash generation and cash use.

```
Formulas for all variables affected by Cash:
Cash = IF(AND(Cash Unadjusted>Cash min, Cash Unadjusted<Cash max), Cash
Unadjusted, IF(Cash Unadjusted<Cash min, Cash min, IF(PREVIOUS(Loans) + Cash
max - Cash Unadjusted >=0, Cash max, Cash Unadjusted - PREVIOUS(Loans)))) ;
Beginning Cash
• Cash Unadjusted=PREVIOUS(Cash)-CHANGE(Accounts Receivable)-CHANGE (Total
    Inventory)-CHANGE(Plant and Equipment)-CHANGE(Accounts Payable)+Net Income;
Beginning Cash
• • Loans = IF(PREVIOUS(Loans) + Cash - Cash Unadjusted <0, 0, PREVIOUS(Loans) +
    Cash - Cash Unadjusted) ; Beginning Loans
• • • Interest Expense = Loans * ((Interest Rate/100)/12)
• • • • Total Operating Expense = Marketing Expense + QUARTERLY(Distribution
    Expense) + Salary Expense + QUARTERLY(Interest Expense)
• • • • • Income Before Taxes = Total Revenue - Total Cost - MONTHLY(Total
    Operating Expense)
• • • • • • Net Income = Income Before Taxes - Taxes
• • • • • • • Cash Unadjusted = ◄ CIRCULAR DEFINITION ►
• • • • • • • Equity = PREVIOUS(Equity) + Net Income ; Beginning Equity
• • • • • • • • Equity = ◄ CIRCULAR DEFINITION ►
• • • • • • • • Total Liability and Equity = Accounts Payable + Loans + Equity
• • • • • • YTD IBT = YTD(Income Before Taxes)
• • • • • • • YTD Taxes = ◄ Taxes Lookup Table ► YTD IBT
newyork.mdl*                                     69K                                    READY
```

Fig. 1.27. FORMULAS view showing roots for variable *Cash*.

The *Cash* formula can be analyzed as follows:

If *Unadjusted Cash* is between $5,000 and $10,000, make no further adjustments. If *Unadjusted Cash* falls below $5,000, however, borrow enough to bring cash levels back to $5,000. If *Unadjusted Cash* is more than $10,000, reduce loans and retain only $10,000 cash. Finally, if loans are reduced to 0, begin accumulating cash.

The variable *Cash Unadjusted* is the starting point. *Cash Unadjusted* refers to the cash level without adjustments for new loan levels. To calculate *Cash Unadjusted*, cash from the last period is adjusted for the change in every account except loans. This includes the change in *Equity*, which is equal to current *Net Income*.

Cash Unadjusted = PREVIOUS(Cash) - CHANGE(Accounts Receivable) - CHANGE(Total Inventory) - CHANGE(Plant and Equipment) - CHANGE(Accounts Payable) + Net Income;Beginning Cash

Note the semicolon (;) before *Beginning Cash*. Javelin includes this special operator for "or else" operations. It gives Javelin the option of using the expression after the semicolon if the expression before the semicolon cannot be calculated. An example is the last part of the formula before *Cash* in figure 1.27. In simple form, the semicolon (;) operator tells Javelin, "If loans are reduced to 0, begin accumulating cash."

Settings Sheets

Whenever Javelin calculates a formula, it does so based on the time-period setting of the variable defined by the formula. And once they are calculated, formula values are displayed in a format determined by the format setting. Time-period and format settings can be entered and saved through Javelin's settings sheets.

The Model settings sheet has the default settings for the whole application. If, for example, most time-series variables in your model were linked to quarterly time periods, you would set *Quarter* as the period in the Model settings sheet.

You may find, however, that certain variables should have individual settings (see fig. 1.28). Javelin maintains a separate settings sheet for each variable. It is appropriate, for example, to sum all periods when combining months into quarters and years in Income Statements. But Balance Sheet variables need to be treated differently. The proper Balance Sheet value in any quarter or year uses the values in the last month of that quarter or year. You would use the *Combine Periods By* setting on the Variable settings sheet to take previous periods into account. By examining the settings sheet, you get a sense of how Javelin handles time.

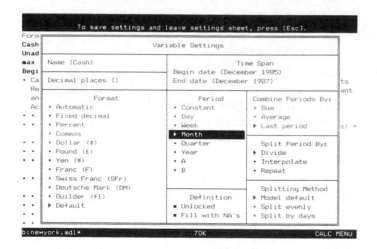

Fig. 1.28. The Variable settings sheet allows you to establish individualized settings for time and format.

Building Blocks

Notice that the highlighted variable Accounts Receivable from Revenue is defined as a Time Delay building block in the list of formulas in figure 1.29. Javelin's building blocks represent complex relationships among variables as a single graph or diagram. Building blocks can treat relationships in lookup tables, time-delay curves, or consolidated models, without requiring that you enter complicated formulas to do so.

Fig. 1.29. The Time Delay building block calculates *Accounts Receivable* based on the delay between earning revenue and collecting receivables.

```
Formulas for all variables:
Accounts Payable = ◀ Monthly data: December 1985 - December 1987 ▶
Accounts Receivable = Accounts Receivable from Revenue ; Beginning Accounts
    Receivable
Accounts Receivable from Revenue = ◀ Accounts Receivable Time Delay ▶ Total
    Revenue
Beginning Accounts Receivable = 0
Beginning Cash = 5000
Beginning Equity = 100000
Beginning Loans = 705000
Blender Cost = Blender Unit Cost * Blender Units
Blender Inventory = ◀ Monthly data: December 1985 - December 1986 ▶
Blender Price = 17
Blender Revenue = Blender Price * Blender Units
Blender Shipping Rate = 1.5
Blender Unit Cost = ◀ Monthly data: January 1986 - December 1987 ▶
Blender Units = ◀ Monthly data: January 1986 - December 1986 ▶
Cash = IF(AND(Cash Unadjusted>Cash min, Cash Unadjusted<Cash max), Cash
    Unadjusted, IF(Cash Unadjusted<Cash min, Cash min, IF(PREVIOUS(Loans) +
    Cash max - Cash Unadjusted >=0, Cash max, Cash Unadjusted - PREVIOUS(Loans)
    ))) ; Beginning Cash
Cash max = 10000
newyork.mdl *                                    69K                          READY
```

Five special applications are available through Javelin building blocks:

1. Defining the delayed effects of one variable on another graphically as a time delay curve

2. Consolidating data from other Javelin models

3. Importing data from other Javelin models

4. Creating a lookup table

5. Defining the current relationship between two variables by representing it graphically in a curve

Javelin's Time Delay building block is used in the sample model to create a visual summary of the relationship between the current *Accounts Receivable* and past *Total Revenue* amounts. The program prompts you for the input variable, *Total Revenue*, and the output variable, *Accounts Receivable* (see fig. 1.30). After you have indicated input and output variables and the time period (days, weeks, months, etc.) for the delay, Javelin displays the graph pictured in figure 1.31. Below the graph, Javelin displays the results of the curve as you build it. You can use the arrow keys to build the curve representing the delay in collecting receivables.

Notice how Javelin presents *Accounts Receivable* in the time-delay graph in figure 1.31. Eighty percent of current revenues are uncollected at the end of the first month, 30 percent uncollected at the end of the second month, and 10

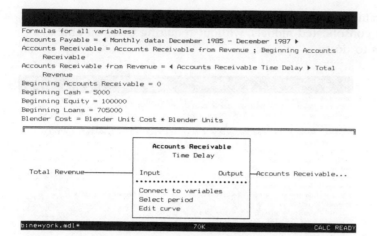

Fig. 1.30. DIAGRAM view of
Time Delay building block for
Accounts Receivable.

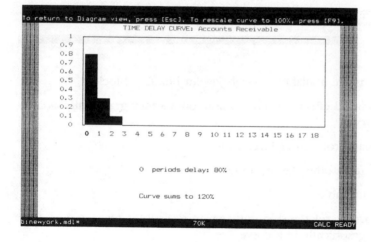

Fig. 1.31. CHART view of Time
Delay building block for
Accounts Receivable.

percent at the end of the third month. Javelin shows that the sum of the time-delay curve equals 120 percent, reflecting the delayed effect of the difference between sales and receivables. Here's just one example of the precision of Javelin's logic: Total collection from any one month's revenues cannot exceed 100 percent, but *Accounts Receivable*, which represents the uncollected portion of several months' revenues, can be more or less than one month's revenue. Total collections of a month's revenues don't have to equal 100 percent.

Worksheet Power

Javelin's WORKSHEET may seem similar to a spreadsheet, but don't be fooled by the similarity. (See fig. 1.32 for a worksheet view of our Income Statement.) Javelin is no spreadsheet clone. To understand the difference, you must note that Javelin stores all the information for an application in an Information Base, not in the worksheet's cells.

```
                                                    Income Statement
                                        1 Q 1986      2 Q 1986

Revenue
   Blender            319,753.00     424,048.00
   Compactor        1,310,400.00   1,621,900.00
   Disposal           505,125.00     652,860.00
   ---------        ------------   ------------
   Total            2,135,278.00   2,698,808.00

Cost
   Blender            282,499.30     305,663.38
   Compactor          588,360.00     633,773.38
   Disposal           267,712.15     326,366.66
   --------         ------------   ------------
   Total            1,138,571.45   1,265,803.42

Expense
   Distributi         202,288.50     254,715.00
   Interest            17,918.75      16,156.25
   Marketing            2,400.00       3,600.00
   Salary             240,000.00     240,000.00
newyork.mdl*                                       56K                          CALC READY
```

Fig. 1.32. The WORKSHEET draws its information from the Information Base.

The worksheet's power is best illustrated as it relates to other views. The Income Statement referred to throughout this section was developed through the FORMULAS, DIAGRAM, and CHART views in figures 1.18, 1.22, and 1.25. Basic data was entered by using the TABLE and CHART views pictured in figure 1.25. To bring variables and data together into one concise report, however, you need to use the WORKSHEET view. The printed report in figure 1.33 is one example of the reporting capabilities of the WORKSHEET view.

Although the WORKSHEET view can be an aid in creating relationships and equations and in entering data, its real strength is in analyzing and reporting information. Examine the Income Statement in figure 1.34. The equations to determine these values already exist, and the data is loaded, so the results are already stored in Javelin's Information Base. All you need to do is provide the worksheet with variable names and dates for the borders. Once you have provided this information, Javelin will fill the rest of the worksheet with data from its Information Base.

The speed and ease of entering variable names in the WORKSHEET view are unsurpassed by any spreadsheet program. Javelin can produce multiple

Future Home Appliances, Inc. 22 Jan 1986

	Dec 1985	Jan 1986	Feb 1986	Mar 1986	Apr 1986	May 1986	Jun 1986	Jul 1986	Aug 1986
Assets:									
Cash	5,000	5,000	5,000	10,000	10,000	10,000	10,000	10,000	10,000
Accounts Rec	0	586,442	751,392	862,913	929,597	1,014,880	1,182,832	1,285,841	1,194,236
Total Invent	0	19,500	19,500	19,500	21,700	22,400	25,000	25,200	27,400
Plant and Eq	800,000	800,000	800,000	800,000	800,000	800,000	800,000	800,000	800,000
Total Assets	805,000	1,410,942	1,575,892	1,692,413	1,761,297	1,847,280	2,017,832	2,121,041	2,031,636
Liability									
Accounts Pay	0	2,000	2,000	2,000	2,000	2,000	2,000	2,000	2,000
Loans	705,000	1,194,538	1,287,079	1,281,294	1,226,056	1,152,935	1,103,923	1,108,923	1,113,923
Equity	100,000	214,394	286,793	409,090	533,189	692,271	911,812	1,151,943	1,350,002
Total Liabil	805,000	1,410,932	1,575,872	1,692,383	1,761,245	1,847,206	2,017,735	2,262,866	2,465,926
Net Income		114,394	72,400	122,296	124,100	159,082	219,541	240,131	198,060

Future Home Appliances, Inc. 22 Jan 1986

	Sep 1986	Oct 1986	Nov 1986	Dec 1986	1986	1987
Assets:						
Cash	10,000	10,000	10,000	10,000	10,000	10,000
Accounts Rec	1,109,055	1,184,462	1,290,764	1,261,499	1,261,499	0
Total Invent	27,400	30,200	30,200	34,500	34,500	
Plant and Eq	800,000	800,000	800,000	800,000	800,000	800,000
Total Assets	1,946,455	2,024,662	2,130,964	2,105,999	2,105,999	
Liability						
Accounts Pay	2,000	2,000	2,000	2,000	2,000	3,000
Loans	1,118,923	1,123,923	1,128,923	1,133,923	1,133,923	1,193,923
Equity	1,538,003	1,761,198	2,019,655	2,253,924	2,253,924	100,000
Total Liabil	2,658,926	2,887,121	3,150,578	3,389,847	3,389,847	1,296,923
Net Income	188,001	223,195	258,457	234,268	2,153,924	

Fig. 1.33. A report showing the capabilities of the WORKSHEET view.

worksheets for a single model. And unlike a spreadsheet program, in which the entire model must reside in the worksheet, Javelin lets you define only what you want to see in a worksheet.

Javelin automates the process of entering nested variable names, as in figure 1.34, with a worksheet command. Notice that there is no variable named *Marketing* but there is one named *Marketing Expense*, which is equal to $2,400 in the first quarter. Javelin will combine *Expense* with the variable names *Marketing*, *Salary*, *Distribution*, *Interest* and *Total Operating* as it searches its Information Base for values. Javelin will try both *Marketing Expense* and *Expense Marketing* as it searches for information.

If you use the WORKSHEET as a standard spreadsheet and define the value of each cell, you do not realize Javelin's capability for understanding variables linked to time. In our model Income Statement, for example, most variables were originally linked to monthly periods; only *Marketing Expense* and *Salary Expense* were defined as quarterly variables. When the worksheet for the Income Statement was created, Javelin calculated values for quarter and year totals by identifying the periods in the worksheet's top border (see fig. 1.34). Javelin automatically provides first quarter 1986 values just as it understands the request for total 1986 values. In addition to the capability of handling time-series variables, Javelin's WORKSHEET view handles constants as well. See Chapter 5 for a complete description of the kinds of data the WORKSHEET view can display.

	Income Statement				
	1 Q 1986	2 Q 1986	3 Q 1986	4 Q 1986	1986
Revenue					
Blender	319,753.00	452,948.00	430,695.00	489,753.00	1,693,149.00
Compactor	1,310,400.00	1,621,900.00	1,803,200.00	1,928,850.00	6,664,350.00
Disposal	505,125.00	652,860.00	710,730.00	755,010.00	2,623,725.00
Total	2,135,278.00	2,727,708.00	2,944,625.00	3,173,613.00	10,981,224.00
Cost					
Blender	282,499.30	326,029.38	251,704.79	232,038.10	1,092,271.57
Compactor	588,360.00	633,773.38	677,308.58	715,927.81	2,615,369.77
Disposal	267,712.15	326,366.66	315,708.49	310,690.18	1,220,477.48
Total	1,138,571.45	1,286,169.42	1,244,721.86	1,258,656.09	4,928,118.82
Expense					
Distributi	202,288.50	257,265.00	278,584.50	300,210.00	1,038,348.00
Interest	31,855.31	26,632.71	25,989.46	25,873.24	110,350.71
Marketing	2,400.00	3,600.00	4,800.00	5,200.00	16,000.00
Salary	240,000.00	240,000.00	252,000.00	282,000.00	1,014,000.00

newyork.mdl*   82K   READY

Fig. 1.34. The WORKSHEET automatically calculates total values for quarter and year for the Income Statement model.

Consolidating Information with Javelin

The single Income Statement model we created for the New York distribution office may be duplicated with the DOS COPY command and sent to each office as a planning tool. Each office can rename the file, enter data pertinent to its own operations, and return the file to the corporate office for consolidation with other income statement files.

In that way you can combine two or more files. Through Javelin's consolidation tool, called the Rollup building block, you can create in minutes an organizational chart like the one displayed in figure 1.35. This chart tells Javelin how to combine single applications into larger ones and identifies the files that contain each application. You can identify the variables you want to pull from every application for inclusion in the consolidated application. You may decide, for example, to exclude some variables in the original model because you need only to consolidate revenues for individual products, not units sold or price for each product.

With one keystroke, Javelin will search each application and place the requested information in the consolidated file. When the consolidation is completed, you can ask Javelin for information for the total organization. As figure 1.34 shows, you can easily view data for individual distribution offices as well as the

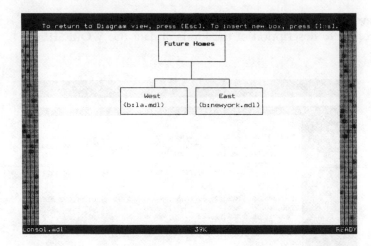

Fig. 1.35. The Rollup building block can combine complete models or selected variables.

consolidated total in the WORKSHEET view. Creating such a worksheet is simply a matter of entering variable names for individual offices in the top border, entering Income Statement variables in the left border, and indicating the date in the upper left corner. Javelin does the rest, dropping data into the worksheet.

Presenting Your Analysis

If you think Javelin is a sophisticated tool for creating models and entering the data on which your analysis depends, wait until you see Javelin's presentation capabilities. First, you can print your model, including its logic, from the FORMULAS, TABLE, WORKSHEET and DIAGRAM views (although only one screen of the DIAGRAM view will print at a time). Second, you can present your model in graphic form with the CHART, QUICK GRAPH, and GRAPH views.

The CHART view displays a bar graph of a variable's data and enables you to change the graph instantly simply by moving the cursor. A CHART view of total operating expenses for the Los Angeles office, for example, shows that expenses increased dramatically within a three-month period (see fig. 1.36).

The QUICK GRAPH view gives a line graph that, depending on the variable, can be changed like the graph in the CHART view by simply moving the cursor. You can graphically represent a steady growth in compactor sales for your New York office over the next six months by displaying a QUICK GRAPH view of *Compactor Units*, then extending the graph line freehand over the period from July to December, 1986 (see figs. 1.37 and 1.38).

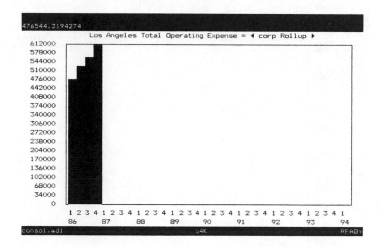

Fig. 1.36. The CHART view of
Los Angeles Office Expenses.

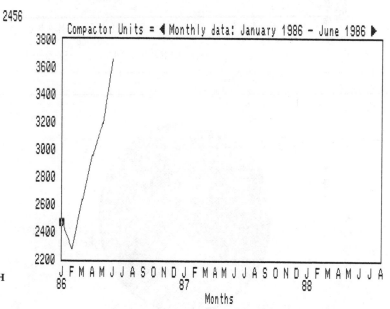

Fig. 1.37. The QUICK GRAPH
view before altering data.

Javelin's GRAPH view produces high-quality line, pie, and XY plot graphs, and
four types of bar graphs. Unlike CHART and QUICK GRAPH, the GRAPH view
gives you options for defining labels and legends. A pie graph of total corporate
revenue from blenders, compactors, and disposals is shown in figure 1.39. The
GRAPH view frees you from working through multiple levels of graph
commands as in 1-2-3; the job of creating a graph is simplified by a single
setting sheet for each graph you want to create (see fig. 1.40).

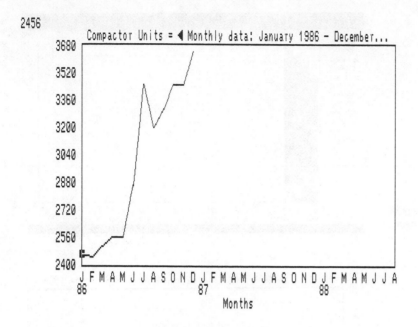

Fig. 1.38. The QUICK GRAPH view after using the cursor to alter data.

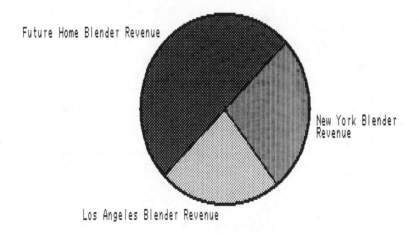

Fig. 1.39. GRAPH view showing pie-graph option.

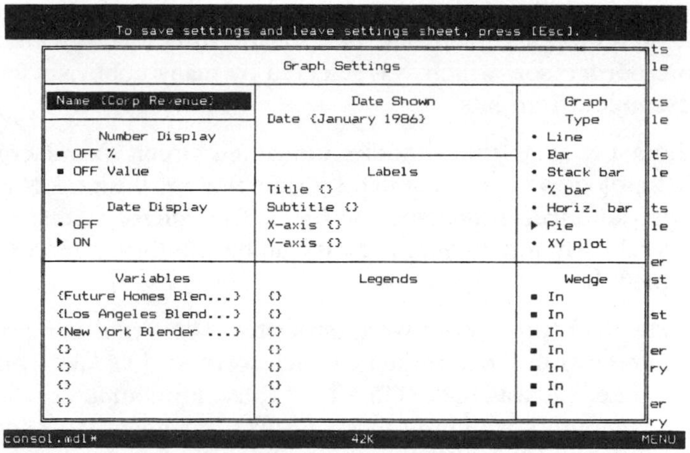

```
              To save settings and leave settings sheet, press [Esc].
                                                                          ts
                              Graph Settings                              le
  Name (Corp Revenue)              Date Shown                 Graph       ts
                           Date (January 1986)                Type       le
       Number Display                                       • Line
  ▪ OFF %                                                   • Bar         ts
  ▪ OFF Value                        Labels                 • Stack bar   le
                           Title ()                          • % bar
       Date Display        Subtitle ()                       • Horiz. bar ts
  • OFF                    X-axis ()                          ▶ Pie       le
  ▶ ON                     Y-axis ()                         • XY plot
                                                                          er
       Variables                    Legends                  Wedge       st
  (Future Homes Blen...)  ()                                ▪ In
  (Los Angeles Blend...)  ()                                ▪ In          st
  (New York Blender ...)  ()                                ▪ In
  ()                      ()                                ▪ In          er
  ()                      ()                                ▪ In          ry
  ()                      ()                                ▪ In          er
                                                                          ry
 consol.mdl*                         42K                            MENU
```

Fig. 1.40. The Graph settings sheet simplifies the task of creating the graph you want.

The History of Javelin

The story of Javelin begins with the history of business applications software. Javelin evolved from the development of microcomputer software designed to help businesses make accurate decisions and increase their productivity. With hardware and software to assist with record keeping and do the numerical analysis necessary for financial planning, managers had access to the tools that for years had been restricted to data-processing departments and their mainframe computers.

As could be expected, the first business applications programs for microcomputers were primitive, taking care of some but not all financial and business analysis needs. Early spreadsheet software tremendously speeded up the calculation of spreadsheets. And when integrated programs such as 1-2-3, Symphony, and Framework came along, they offered expanded capabilities for viewing and presenting data. But before Javelin, no single program had been sophisticated enough to meet model building, error checking, analysis, and presentation needs all in one. Javelin, 10 years after the introduction of the microcomputer to business, opens a new generation in business applications software.

Introduction of Microcomputers to Business

In 1974 Intel Corporation developed the first microprocessor, the 8008. It contained thousands of electronic circuits on a single silicon chip. The processing power of the room-sized computers of a few years earlier could now fit on a chip less than one inch square. Intel followed the 8008 with the 8080 microprocessor, which was selected by many hobbyists for their computers assembled from kits.

About the same time, another integrated circuit manufacturer, MOS Technologies (later acquired by Commodore Business Machines), developed a more advanced processor, the 6502. This microprocessor was selected for several early microcomputers, including the Commodore® PET and the Apple® II.

These microprocessors were integrated with other components to make the first commercial microcomputers, which were sold as kits. The most famous computer kit was the MITS Altair. These kit computers did not look much like the computers we know today. Instead of familiar video displays and keyboards, the front panels had lights and switches that were used to program the machines. Programming was done in machine language, and printers and disk drives were not available. Needless to say, the first micros were as inaccessible and impractical for the average businessperson as mainframe computers.

Appliance Computers

In 1977 Steve Wozniak and Steve Jobs introduced a microcomputer kit called the Apple® I, which eventually sold 500 units. They soon offered the Apple II, which, unlike all the computers that had gone before, was sold preassembled. It also had a disk drive and a disk operating system.

Around that time, Tandy®/Radio Shack® also developed a microcomputer, the TRS-80™ Model I, around an advanced derivative of the 8080 chip, the Z80® (manufactured by Zilog).

These appliance computers opened the doors of microcomputing for nontechnical users. The Apple II and the TRS-80 were shipped fully assembled and factory tested and were sold through a new kind of store, the computer store. Both computers had several expansion slots that could be used to attach devices such as printers, disk drives, and modems.

The BASIC programming language was provided on chips inside the computers or on a floppy disk packaged with the machine. Because BASIC is easier to learn and use than machine language or assembly language, users of these computers found it practical to write their own programs in BASIC.

In the early days of microcomputers, little "canned" software (written for a specific purpose and sold by a software publisher) was available. Business users of microcomputers therefore were left with three choices: become experts in programming, pay a programmer, or accomplish little with their expensive equipment. Because most businesspeople were too busy (or too intimidated) to learn BASIC, many of those who bought micros during this period found themselves unable to use the power of their new machines. Countless others avoided microcomputers altogether.

Spreadsheets—the First Generation of Business Applications Programs

The first truly successful business applications tool for microcomputers, VisiCalc®, was introduced to the public in 1978. From then until 1983, it was the most popular computer program of all time, selling more than 400,000 copies. Some observers contend that VisiCalc launched the entire personal computer industry. Whether or not that is true, VisiCalc did introduce the electronic replacement for the accountant's traditional tools: columnar pad, pencil, and calculator. And there is no question that VisiCalc "wrote the rules" for all the spreadsheet programs that have followed.

Even as early as VisiCalc, however, software developers realized the need to provide more than a sophisticated calculator. Later versions of VisiCalc included data management functions and the capability to transfer spreadsheet data for producing graphs. The need to make spreadsheet programs more than sophisticated calculators drove the development of new "integrated" spreadsheet products.

VisiCalc was created in 1978 by Robert Frankston and Dan Bricklin in Cambridge, Massachusetts. Bricklin, a student at Harvard Business School, was frustrated with the tedium of analyzing three business cases a night, five days a week. Many of these cases required the preparation of intricate financial analyses. He decided that there had to be some way of reducing the time required for completing the analyses. Teaming up with his programmer friend Frankston, Bricklin discovered a way to make use of Apple's new microcomputer in order to reduce the tedium of creating and editing the spreadsheets Bricklin had to complete for his analyses. Bricklin and Frankston developed VisiCalc to replace the ledger pad, pencil, and calculator. And the electronic spreadsheet for microcomputers was born!

VisiCalc met a clear need in the business world for a personal analysis tool. Like the electronic spreadsheets that followed it, VisiCalc was a tremendously valuable tool for entering, saving, and displaying a model on-screen or on paper. One would be hard pressed to call VisiCalc and related spreadsheet programs comprehensive business analysis tools, however, particularly in comparison with the financial modeling systems available on time-sharing systems. VisiCalc and other spreadsheet programs did not actually help the user define business problems, and they were limited in their ability to help with analysis and error checking.

Although VisiCalc did not have the capabilities of mainframe financial analysis packages, it offered business managers several major improvements. First, the program ran on personal computers. The combination of VisiCalc and the Apple microcomputer, for example, created a legitimate business and professional application for desktop computers. For the first time, a financial, sales, or production manager had a personal tool for numerical analysis. Computer time didn't have to be shared with every other manager in the firm. Analyses could be adjusted until they were correct with no worry about computer-user budgets or EDP procedures. Second, VisiCalc provided a true electronic representation of the accountant's pad. Creating, editing, and using financial models were dramatically easier with VisiCalc.

VisiCalc and Apple II were not alone for long in the business applications game. VisiCalc versions soon were produced to run on other microcomputers besides the Apple II, including the IBM Personal Computer, IBM compatibles, and Tandy/Radio Shack's TRS-80. In 1980 Sorcim Corporation introduced SuperCalc®, a spreadsheet program for personal computers using the CP/M® operating system. Like VisiCalc, SuperCalc provided sophisticated spreadsheet capabilities. Other programs soon entered the competition, including CalcStar®, PerfectCalc, and Multiplan®.

Data Management

Along with capabilities for creating, editing, and using financial models, some spreadsheet programs provided limited data management features. In spreadsheet programs, data management functions operate within the column-row structure. VisiCalc, for example, has a lookup function that allows users to retrieve numerical items from an indexed row or column. Multiplan has a lookup function that uses true tables rather than single rows or columns. With Multiplan, you can create a multicolumn table and use one index column to retrieve data from a number of columns.

Another data management feature included in some early spreadsheet programs was the capability for sorting columns and tables of data. Multiplan and SuperCalc[2], for example, enable users to specify the range to be sorted (one or more columns of data), the column by which the sort is to be performed, and the type of sort (ascending or descending order in either numerical or alphabetical order). Early spreadsheet programs containing lookup and sort capabilities could be used as simple list-management programs.

Graphics Capabilities

First-generation spreadsheet packages also enabled users to create graphics from data in the spreadsheet, but most required that the data be transferred to a different program before the information could be graphed. VisiCalc had to be transferred to VisiPlot™, for example. One limitation to these graphics programs was that they were not truly integrated.

Integrated Programs— The Second Generation

The next generation in business applications software began with the development of integrated software packages. These provided all the electronic spreadsheet capability—and more—of early packages like VisiCalc and SuperCalc, plus sophisticated graphics; data management; and, in some, word processing and communications. 1983 marked the arrival of such integrated programs and of the most successful business applications programs ever: Lotus 1-2-3.

1-2-3 was in fact conceived because of the need to simplify the creation of graphs from early spreadsheet programs. Mitch Kapor, who developed the original concept for 1-2-3, stated in an interview in November 1983:

> . . . the notion of integrated software originally came out of frustration I had as a user about the inconvenience of going from one thing to another, in this case a spreadsheet to a graph. (*Absolute Reference, The Journal for 1-2-3 and Symphony Users*, November, 1983.)

Kapor, along with Jonathan Sachs, decided to provide a spreadsheet with integrated graphics and more sophisticated data management capabilities than were contained in any other spreadsheet program. This decision was based upon looking at Context MBA®, the first integrated program for business microcomputer users. Context MBA incorporated five applications: spreadsheet, graphics, data management, text processor, and data communications. Although Context MBA was a powerful program, it suffered from criticism about its speed and jack-of-all-trades orientation.

Lotus 1-2-3

Evolving directly from programs like VisiCalc, 1-2-3 was designed to beat VisiCalc at its own game. First, 1-2-3 integrated the spreadsheet with graphics and data management capabilities. Second, 1-2-3's overall design, command syntax, and built-in functions were based on the conventions used by VisiCalc.

1-2-3 utilized the power of the 16-bit IBM PC better than did spreadsheet programs designed to run on 8-bit Apple and CP/M computers. By the end of 1983, 1-2-3 had become one of the most successful software programs ever produced. It was an industry standard.

By mid-1985, three different releases of Lotus 1-2-3 had entered the market. Six months after 1-2-3's initial release, Lotus upgraded 1-2-3 to Release 1A. Release 1A, prompted in part by the proliferation of new personal computer models and the need to support hardware other than the standard IBM PC, included new features such as upgraded 1-2-3 keyboard macros.

Beyond the Spreadsheet

Since the introduction of 1-2-3, business software has moved along a road paved by Context MBA. In 1984, Lotus introduced Symphony, and several other software developers introduced similar packages. These programs integrated spreadsheet, data management, and graphics capabilities resembling those of 1-2-3, and also had word-processing and communications functions.

Symphony is a multifunctional program that enables users to shift from one application to another and to display data in various forms—spreadsheet, word-processing text, and graphs—on the screen at the same time. However, the spreadsheet remains Symphony's most powerful capability, maintaining the conventional column-row structure for entering and displaying formulas and data. And all environments exist within Symphony's 256-column by 8,192-row worksheet.

Other integrated programs like Framework and Enable also provide the five applications that Symphony provides. The programs all differ in their capabilities, however. Symphony, as was previously mentioned, is a strong spreadsheet package; Framework provides powerful capabilities for organizing data within windows that can be linked. Enable has a sophisticated word processor but lacks the worksheet size and power of Symphony.

Javelin: The New Generation

Through its ability to store information in one information base, Javelin gives new meaning to the concept of integrated software. Unlike programs that claim to be integrated (for example, Symphony, Enable, and Framework) because they easily transfer data among environments—spreadsheet, graphics, word processing, and data base—Javelin is the first truly integrated program because it makes natural the integration of data among all its views. The purpose of integration in Symphony, Framework, and Enable is presentation. You can combine spreadsheet data into text, move records and fields into the spreadsheet, and so on. But integrating the data is an involved, multistep process.

Integration in Javelin is automatic, natural, and effortless. Data can be viewed in various ways when you need it, when you want it, and when others need to see it. In fact, the power in Javelin comes from its synergy—the flexibility to combine so many operations quickly. You'll appreciate this when you begin using Javelin's 10 views.

The concept for Javelin was developed by Robert Firmin and Stanley Kugell, who founded Javelin Software Corporation in January, 1983. They conceived Javelin in response to businesspeople's need for a tool that does more than calculate numbers. They wanted Javelin to be a superior, much more powerful program than integrated spreadsheets.

To develop Javelin, the two designers combined Kugell's programming knowledge with Firmin's business and financial analysis experience. Kugell had worked at MIT's artificial intelligence lab, at Stanford University, and at the XEROX Palo Alto Research Center, where he contributed to pioneering work on a better user interface. Firmin's business background included an M.B.A. degree from Columbia University, a Ph.D. from the University of Chicago, and experience as a market analyst and financial planning and analysis manager at Prime Computer. He was chief financial officer at Computer Pictures Corporation of Boston when he met Kugell, who worked there as a software designer and programmer.

Firmin conceived the idea for Javelin because of his frustration with the inability of other software to perform business analysis. Javelin therefore grew out of Firmin's frustration and his knowledge of modeling and analysis, and of Kugell's ability to turn sophisticated computer technology into programs that are easy to use and understand. After two years of development and testing, including testing with 25 of the largest companies in the United States, Javelin entered the business applications software market in the fall of 1985.

Javelin versus 1-2-3

If you have used 1-2-3, making the transition to Javelin will be easy once you understand the differences in how the two programs store and handle data. Javelin won't be foreign ground because some of its worksheet operations, such as formatting values and setting column width, are similar to those of 1-2-3. And you will find that Javelin has more power than 1-2-3 in its number of functions and in its capabilities for importing and consolidating data.

How Javelin and 1-2-3 Store and Handle Data

If you're making the transition from using 1-2-3 for your business analysis tasks to using Javelin, you'll need to understand, first, the difference in the way the two programs store data. In 1-2-3 (and Symphony), formulas, data, and labels are entered in spreadsheet cells which define program operations. In Javelin, however, information is stored in the central information base. The same data can be used in different reports without your having to copy or rearrange it, and all data and formulas are available in one place for debugging, verifying, or changing your model. Although Javelin's worksheet may appear similar to 1-2-3's worksheet, keep in mind the fact that Javelin's worksheet is only one of many views in which the same data can be displayed.

Another important difference between 1-2-3 and Javelin is the way the two programs handle time. Javelin is programmed to think in time, and data may be defined with respect to time periods—days, weeks, months, quarters, and years. Whenever a variable has the same value for every period, you can easily tell Javelin that this variable is a constant. 1-2-3 requires that you enter time-series labels and replicate data and formulas across spreadsheet rows or columns in order to define time-series variables.

Javelin's WORKSHEET and 1-2-3

When you use Javelin's WORKSHEET view, you will find many operations that are the same as in 1-2-3 and a few that are welcome additions. Formatting values in the Javelin worksheet, for example, is much as it is with 1-2-3: Javelin provides both a global worksheet format command and a format command for a range of values. Commands for changing column width, copying, and erasing data are much like the column width, copy, and erase commands in 1-2-3. Deleting and inserting columns and rows in Javelin are, however, much easier than they are with 1-2-3. You simply move the cursor to a variable in the top or left border of the worksheet and press the Del key to delete a row or column. But this does not delete data from the information base. Pressing the Ins key inserts a row or column. Javelin also allows you to create multiple worksheets on the same screen (see fig. 1.41).

A significant convenience is Javelin's capability to fill the worksheet with values from Javelin's information base once you have defined the variables you want to display. And when data is added to the variables defined in the worksheet, the change is reflected in Javelin's other views (see fig. 1.42).

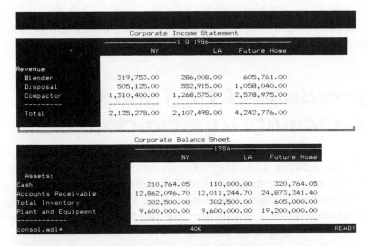

Fig. 1.41. You can display multiple worksheets in the WORKSHEET view.

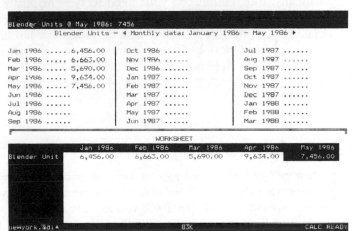

Fig. 1.42. Data entered into the WORKSHEET view is reflected in the TABLE view.

Importing and Consolidating with Javelin versus 1-2-3

Javelin goes far beyond 1-2-3 in capabilities to import and consolidate data. Unless you're consolidating one file exactly with another in 1-2-3, the process can be quite involved. 1-2-3 consolidates according to position; consolidation ranges must match exactly, or you'll have erroneous consolidated data. Javelin consolidates according to name, freeing you from having to keep consolidation ranges straight. Javelin provides a number of options for importing and consolidating, including consolidating all variables and data from one file to another, consolidating only selected variables and data, and importing without consolidating. (Chapter 6 provides more information on importing and consolidating.)

Javelin and 1-2-3 Macro Capability and Functions

Other features that will help you make the transition from 1-2-3 to Javelin include macros and many formula functions. Although not as powerful as the macro capability available in 1-2-3, Release 2, Javelin's macro capability includes a set of basic macro commands, such as those for branching, creating subroutine calls, creating user menus, and allowing user input. Unlike 1-2-3 Releases 1A and 2, Javelin does have a "learn mode" for recording keystrokes automatically, thus eliminating your need to type manually every macro line. Javelin's function list compares respectably with 1-2-3's, containing comparable financial, logical, statistical, and arithmetic functions. Javelin goes beyond 1-2-3 by also supplying functions for trend and regression analysis and functions for handling time (see Appendix B for a complete list of Javelin functions, and Appendix C for a detailed comparison of 1-2-3 and Javelin functions.)

Conclusion

This chapter has introduced you to the power of Javelin by describing its capabilities, its origin in a brief history of spreadsheet software, and Javelin's similarities to 1-2-3. With this background in hand, you're ready to begin getting your feet wet by experimenting, and then by using Javelin for one of your applications.

2

Getting Started
with Javelin

Before using Javelin, you need to know the basics of setting up the program and tailoring it to your particular system to ensure smooth running. In addition, an understanding of basic file operations is essential before you can begin to create and save files. This chapter shows you:

- How to make backup of copies of those Javelin disks that are not copy-protected

- How to install and begin using Javelin on your system

- How to understand what you see on the Javelin screen

- How to use the keyboard with Javelin

- How to load, name, save, and delete files

The Javelin Disks

The complete Javelin system consists of the following disks:

1. Startup (two copies)

2. Program

3. Help

4. Drivers

5. Demonstration

6. Case Studies 1

7. Case Studies 2

8. Case Studies 3

Like the ignition key in your car, the Startup disk starts the program. The Program disk holds the elements necessary for Javelin's operation on your PC. The Help disk provides you with instant access to the complete help library for Javelin when you press the HELP key (F1). The Drivers disk contains files that furnish the program with information about your monitor and printer.

An excellent introduction to Javelin, the Demonstration disk presents an example of Javelin's distinctive approach to business analysis and reporting, showing you all the Javelin views. The Case Studies disks present actual uses of Javelin in the real world.

Original Disks and Backup Disks

Your first step should be to make backup copies of all *original* Javelin disks except the Startup disks, which are copy-protected. These disks should then be stored in a safe place away from your operating area. For example, if you should lose or damage your copy of the Program disk, you will still have the original disk to create another backup copy.

You should always use *backup* disks when running Javelin. You make backup disks by copying the original disks, following the steps outlined in this chapter and in your Javelin manual.

Making Backups of Your Original Disks

Note: Have at least six (6) disks handy before starting to copy the original disks.

All disks, whether new or used, should be formatted with DOS prior to making backup copies of the Javelin disks. Make sure that each backup disk is labeled correctly with its corresponding original disk name and the words *backup copy* underneath. Careful labeling will prevent confusion when your work space is strewn with several disks. To format a disk, use the DOS FORMAT command.

If you have a two-drive system:

1. Boot DOS from drive A, if necessary.

2. Place the original DOS disk in drive A. (The FORMAT command is not on the main DOS command file that you copy to applications disks, so the original DOS disk, or an exact copy of it, is necessary.)

3. Place a blank disk in drive B.

4. Now enter *format b:* and follow the instructions on the screen.

If you have a hard drive system:

1. Boot DOS from drive C, if necessary.

2. Place a blank disk in drive A.

3. Enter *format a:* and follow the instructions on the screen.

Warning: Do not omit the *a:* in *format a:* because you could erase everything on the hard disk.

To ensure a clean disk surface for new information, you should reformat used disks before you install the program. Merely erasing or deleting files is not enough to ensure this clean surface. Reformatting a used disk reveals any "bad sectors" or unusable space on the disk.

The actual copying procedure involves the DOS DISKCOPY program and several blank, formatted disks.

> **Note:** You cannot make a backup copy of the original Startup disk or the factory-supplied backup copy of the Startup disk. Attempting to use the DOS DISKCOPY procedure on either Startup disks may damage them beyond repair.

Copying Disks with a Floppy System

To copy your original disks on a floppy disk system, place the DOS system disk in drive A, turn the computer on, respond to the prompts for date and time, then type the following at the A> prompt:

    diskcopy a: b:

DOS then directs you to insert the source disk in drive A, the target disk in drive B, and to press any key to begin copying.

```
Insert SOURCE diskette in drive A:
Insert TARGET diskette in drive B:
Press any key when ready . . .
```

Place the Javelin Program disk in drive A, insert a formatted blank disk in drive B, and press Enter. When the disk is copied, DOS responds with the following message:

```
Copy complete
Copy another (Y/N)?
```

Press *Y*, remove the Program disk from drive A and the backup copy from drive B, and repeat the copy procedure for the remaining original disks. Remember that, except for the two Startup disks, all the original disks should be backed up. If you have any further questions, consult your DOS manual or contact your dealer for help.

Copying Disks with a Hard Disk System

You can follow the procedure outlined for floppy systems if your PC has both a hard disk and two floppy disk drives. If you have a hard disk with only one floppy disk drive, use the following procedure.

If your hard disk has DOS files in either the root directory or another directory (sometimes called BIN or UTILITY), go to the directory with the DISKCOPY.COM file. If the DISKCOPY.COM file is not on your hard disk, you can copy this file from your DOS disk to the hard disk, or simply run the copy procedure from the DOS disk.

In any case, go to the drive and directory that contains the DISKCOPY command. At the DOS prompt, type

    diskcopy

The DISKCOPY program responds with the following prompt:

    Insert SOURCE diskette in drive A:
    Press any key when ready . . .

Press Enter. After making one pass of your original disk, DISKCOPY prompts:

    Insert TARGET diskette in drive A:
    Press any key when ready . . .

Because the PC treats your one floppy drive as both drives A and B, just swap floppy disks as prompted. (To keep from using the same disk twice, remember to label the empty disks before copying with the corresponding Javelin original disks.)

As each disk is copied, DOS responds with the following message:

    Copy complete
    Copy another? (Y/N)?

Press *Y* in response to this prompt each time it appears until you have copied all the Javelin disks. After you have copied the last of the original Javelin disks, press *N* to end the DISKCOPY procedure. Remember that, except for the two Startup disks, all of the original disks should be backed up. If you have further questions, consult your DOS manual or contact your dealer.

Installing Javelin

Like any software straight from the box, Javelin must be installed before it can be used. Although you can run Javelin directly from the original disks, you could be taking an unnecessary risk. Making backup copies of the disks should be your first priority.

Note: Do take the extra time necessary to back up your original disks.

To begin, you must install the program on either floppy or hard disks, remembering that the Startup disks are copy-protected and cannot be transferred to backup disks. First, make sure that you have the four primary disks handy: Startup, Program, Help, and Drivers. The next section covers floppy installation, followed by suggestions for hard disk installation.

Installing Javelin on a Floppy Disk System

To install Javelin on a floppy disk system, you must place the proper Drivers disk files on your backup Program disk. The Driver files are necessary for displaying or printing graphs.

Place the Javelin backup Program disk in drive A of your computer, and the Javelin backup Drivers disk in drive B. At the prompt, type *a:* and press Enter to make sure that you are using drive A.

Next, type

   jconfig b: a:

Press Enter. Javelin should reply with the screen in figure 2.1. Press *Y* if you have a color monitor; otherwise, press *N*. Respond in the same way for the next screen, shown in figure 2.2.

You then need to put the appropriate screen and printer drivers on the Program disk. Following the program's prompts (see fig. 2.3), replace the Javelin backup Program disk with the backup Drivers disk.

The next screen you see lists various monitors available (see fig. 2.4). Enter the name of the type of driver that corresponds to your type of monitor. For example, if you have an IBM Enhanced Graphics adapter and any monitor, you would type *IBMEGA*, then press Enter. If you do not have a graphics monitor, simply press Enter.

```
              Screen configuration


Does your screen show red, blue, and green squares below (Y/N) ?
```

Fig. 2.1. Determining monitor type.

```
              Screen configuration


Does your screen show the two squares below in different colors (Y/N) ?
```

Fig. 2.2. The second configuration screen.

```
        Screen configuration




    Configuring for color screen.

Insert Drivers Diskette in drive B:

      Press ◄┘ when ready.
```

Fig. 2.3. Javelin prompts for Drivers disk.

```
                    Driver configuration

        Select name of screen driver and press ◄┘ : IBMGRAPH


Driver      Graphics adapter for screen
======      ===========================

IBMGRAPH    - IBM Color/Graphics adapter
            - Compaq adapter
            - Hercules Color/Graphics adapter
            - Any adapter that emulates IBM Graphics

IBMEGA      - IBM Enhanced Graphics adapter and any monitor

HERCMONO    - Hercules Graphics Card for monochrome monitor


    If you do not have a graphics monitor, just press ◄┘.
```

Fig. 2.4. Selecting your monitor.

The program then presents you with a list of printers and asks you to make a selection that best matches the type of printer you have (see fig. 2.5). Choose a printer by typing the name as shown on the screen and press Enter. If your printer is not listed, just press Enter. You can then follow the screen prompts through the rest of the procedure, and in a few minutes, you will have the correct drivers installed on your original Javelin Program disk.

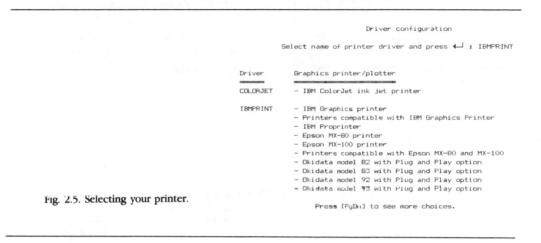

```
                                           Driver configuration

                        Select name of printer driver and press ◄┘ : IBMPRINT


            Driver        Graphics printer/plotter
            ======        ========================
            COLORJET      - IBM ColorJet ink jet printer

            IBMPRINT      - IBM Graphics printer
                          - Printers compatible with IBM Graphics Printer
                          - IBM Proprinter
                          - Epson MX-80 printer
                          - Epson MX-100 printer
                          - Printers compatible with Epson MX-80 and MX-100
                          - Okidata model 82 with Plug and Play option
                          - Okidata model 83 with Plug and Play option
                          - Okidata model 92 with Plug and Play option
                          - Okidata model 93 with Plug and Play option

                               Press [PgDn] to see more choices.
```

Fig. 2.5. Selecting your printer.

Installing the DOS system on the Startup disk is the final step in setting up Javelin for a floppy system. To do this, place the DOS system disk in drive A, the Javelin Startup disk in drive B, and type the following:

a:sys b:

Press Enter. Next, type

copy a:command.com b:

and press Enter once more. Your Startup disk is now a "boot" disk, which means that when you load this disk it will load DOS as well. (Consult your DOS User's Manual if you have any questions regarding this procedure).

Installing Javelin on a Hard Disk System

Note: The Javelin hard disk installation procedure will look for a directory called "JAV" on the hard disk. If a JAV directory already exists, the installation procedure will write the Javelin files to that directory, overwriting any existing files of the same name.

The Javelin system requires about 800K of free disk space on your hard disk. This does not include the space needed for your models. Before you start installing Javelin, make sure that you have enough space on your hard disk to support the system.

Place the original Javelin Startup disk in the floppy disk drive. (The original or "factory" disk must be used for the hard disk installation procedure, because when Javelin is installed, this disk write protects the program.) Type *a:*, press Enter, type *install*, and press Enter once more. The resulting installation screen asks that you identify your drives (see fig. 2.6). If your system is like most PC systems, just press Enter twice to accept the defaults. If not, enter the drive letters for your particular system. Wait until the drive action stops before proceeding.

```
Enter the drive you are installing from (A):

  Enter the drive you are installing to (C):
```

Fig. 2.6. Javelin asks you to
identify your drives before it
```
           (Press [Ctrl]-C to abort.)
```
begins the installation procedure.

In response to the next screen prompt (see fig. 2.7), you remove the original Startup disk from drive A, replace it with the Program disk, and press Enter. Javelin then asks you to insert the Help disk in drive A (see fig. 2.8). Replace the Program disk with the Help disk.

```
     JAVELIN Installation Program



Insert Javelin Program Diskette in Drive A:

      Press ◄┘ when ready.
```

Fig. 2.7. Javelin prompts you to
```
           (Press [Ctrl]-C to abort.)
```
insert the Program disk.

```
Insert Javelin Help Diskette in drive A:
      Press ◄┘ when ready.
```

Fig. 2.8. Javelin prompts you to
insert the Help disk.

At this stage, Javelin begins installing the driver files. You are prompted to show the type of monitor you have (see fig. 2.1). If you have a color monitor, press Y for yes; otherwise, press N for no. The next screen also deals with composite video and color monitors. If the two squares shown on the screen appear in different colors, answer Y; otherwise, press N (see fig. 2.2).

The installation program then moves on to the task of installing the proper screen and printer drivers. You will see a screen asking that you insert the Drivers disk (see fig. 2.3). Replace the Javelin Program disk with the Drivers disk. When the Drivers disk is in place, the program asks that you indicate your driver configuration (see fig. 2.4). You enter the name of the screen driver that corresponds to your type of graphics adapter. The next screen asks for the name of your printer (see fig. 2.5). Type the printer driver that corresponds to your printer and press Enter.

The screen should then tell you that Javelin has been installed successfully.

Handling Problems with Installation

You should have no problems installing your Javelin disks to working copies, but if you do, you can stop the installation procedure by rebooting the computer (press and hold down the Ctrl and Alt keys and then press also the Del key, then release them). If you are installing Javelin on a hard disk, be sure that the red light on the disk is off before you reboot the computer. Start the installation procedure from the beginning. If you continue to get error messages, return your Javelin package for a new product or call Javelin's technical support center (see the Javelin documentation for this number).

If you receive an Abort, Retry, Ignore message during floppy disk installation, remove the disk, reinsert it, and press R to Retry. Often, this will solve the problem. If the error is repeated, press A to abort the procedure. If the error occurs on the hard disk, go ahead and abort the process. Do not select I for Ignore or you may cause part of the Javelin system to be improperly transferred to your backup disks, which can only result in eventual problems.

Preparing Data Disks

Javelin uses the standard DOS formatted disk. You should have several of these disks set aside just for your Javelin models. If you have a hard disk, you can copy your models from the hard disk to formatted floppy disks to protect those models from being lost should your hard disk become damaged.

You can create blank disks for your models by formatting new disks or reformatting used disks. The DOS FORMAT program is used to create these blank disks. Either place the DOS System disk in drive A or, if you have a hard disk, find the directory showing the FORMAT.COM program and, at the appropriate DOS prompt, type

format a:

If your system is a two floppy disk system, DOS responds by asking you to place a disk in drive B. After formatting one disk, the program asks if you want to format another or exit to DOS. Format two or three extra data disks because you will probably need them eventually. To avoid confusion, remember to label these disks as you create and save models.

Starting Javelin

You can start Javelin several ways. The best way for you will depend on whether you have a floppy or hard disk system, whether you wish to load an already existing model along with Javelin, and so on.

Starting Javelin on a Floppy Disk System

You can start Javelin from floppy disks two different ways. Both methods will successfully boot the Javelin system, and there is no functional difference.

Method 1: Place the backup Program disk in drive A and the original Startup disk in drive B. Type *b:*, press Enter, type *jav*, and press Enter once more.

When the Javelin Startup screen appears (see fig. 2.9), take out of drive B the Startup disk and replace it with the disk you will use to store your models.

Method 2: Place the Startup disk in drive A and the models disk in drive B. Type *a:*, press Enter, type *jav*, and then press Enter again. A screen prompt then asks you to insert the Program disk in drive A. After inserting the backup Program disk in drive A, press Enter.

Starting Javelin on a Hard Disk System

As Javelin is installed on your hard disk, a batch file is created in the root directory (the root directory is the location of the CONFIG.SYS, COMMAND.COM, and AUTOEXEC.BAT files on the hard disk).

To run Javelin from the root directory, you must first type *cd* and then press Enter to get into the root directory. You then type *jav* and press Enter to start the JAV.BAT file processing. If you are in the JAV directory, all you have to do is type *jav* and then press Enter to get Javelin up and running.

An alternative method involves modifying slightly the Javelin JAV.BAT file. To do this, you would type the following:

```
copy con:jav.bat
cd\jav
jav %1
cd\
```

After typing these lines, press the F6 function key and then the Enter key.

This procedure uses the DOS COPY command to create a new JAV.BAT file. By typing *jav* from the root directory, the JAV.BAT file transfers you to the Javelin directory and starts Javelin. You can also have Javelin load a model while starting up. For instance, to load a model called BLDGCOST, you would type *jav bldgcost* and press Enter. (See the "Loading Files" section near the end of this chapter for instructions on loading a model after Javelin has been started.)

The Startup Screen

The Javelin startup screen is the first screen you see when actually beginning to use the program. This screen is similar to most of the screens you see in the system, so take a minute to become familiar with the screen.

Figure 2.9 shows the startup screen split characteristically in half. Each half screen constitutes a Javelin window. These special windows show different perspectives of data, called *views* (see Chapter 1 for a thorough discussion of views). At startup, the top window holds the DIAGRAM view, which displays a flowchart of the formulas you create for your models. The bottom window holds the TABLE view, which displays the actual calculated or input values associated with a variable.

Notice that Table view is highlighted on your screen. The ends of the line in the middle of the screen separating the two views point down toward the TABLE view to indicate that the latter view contains the cursor. When the ends, or hooks, of this dividing line point up, the view above the line contains the cursor.

The top line of the startup screen contains Javelin's copyright notice. This line is called the *edit line* because you can use it to edit or enter information when you are working with Javelin. The second line displays on the left the serial

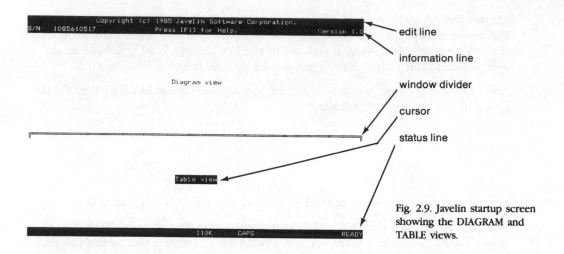

edit line

information line

window divider

cursor

status line

Fig. 2.9. Javelin startup screen showing the DIAGRAM and TABLE views.

number of your copy of the program, a message in the center to remind you to press the F1 function key for on-line Help, and on the right the version of Javelin you are using. This line, known as the *information line,* often shows prompts based on what you are doing.

The *status line* at the bottom of the screen indicates the name of the model currently in memory, the amount of free memory (also referred to as random-access memory, or RAM) left in your system, whether your CAPS or NUM keys are active, and the program's status. The left end of the status line is blank when you start Javelin. Once you begin to construct a model, an asterisk (∗) appears on the left end of the status line to indicate that an unsaved model is in machine memory. When you name a new model or load a preexisting model, the name of the model appears with the asterisk at the left edge of the status line.

The middle of the status line shows the current amount of free memory in your computer. As you develop your model, this number will become smaller. If memory becomes low and you attempt to load in some graphics or create too large a model, Javelin tells you that some memory should be cleared or that an error has occurred in loading the graphics or printer driver.

The CAPS and NUM indicators appear near the right end of the status line and indicate whether these keys have been activated or "locked on." This area also shows the MACRO indicator when a Javelin MACRO is running.

The program status indicator, which tells you what you are doing with the program at that moment, appears at the far right end of the status line. When you first start Javelin, the indicator reads READY. As you work on a model, the indicator reads CALC, MENU, ERROR, and so on.

Javelin's Windows

As mentioned previously, the Javelin startup screen appears with two windows. Each window holds a *view*. The two windows provide a means of looking at two different views of the same variable in a model, two different parts of a model, or two or more different variables in a model. To move between windows, use the SWITCH key (F6). This is the F6 function key located on your PC's function keypad. You'll notice that the hooks and cursor change windows when you press F6.

These windows can be altered with the /Window command on the Javelin main menu (see fig. 2.10).

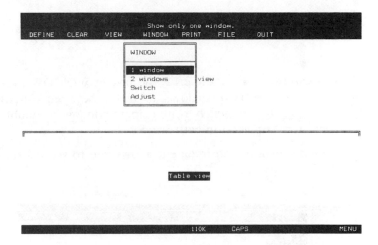

Fig. 2.10. Javelin main menu showing cursor on the /Window command.

Javelin's windows are a means of getting information from the Javelin system to you. The screen consists of two windows at startup; the TABLE VIEW window on top and the DIAGRAM VIEW window on the bottom. The windows can hold any of the Javelin views, except the GRAPH and QUICK GRAPH views. These two views momentarily override the Window settings and create a single window view.

Remember, you can tell which of the two windows is active in two different ways. First, simply locate the cursor, which is always in the active view. You can also determine which view is active by the way the hooks on the center line are pointing. The center double line on the Javelin screen separates the top window from the bottom. This double line ends with hooks on either side. These hooks point towards the active window.

The other method of controlling Javelin's window settings comes from the WINDOW main menu options (see fig. 2.11).

Fig. 2.11. The WINDOW
submenu.

As you can see from figure 2.11, the Javelin WINDOW main menu options allow
you to see one or two windows, to switch between windows, and to adjust the
window size. If you switch from a single window to double windows, the
current view is placed in both windows.

The double window environment allows you to see information in two different
formats (see fig. 2.12).

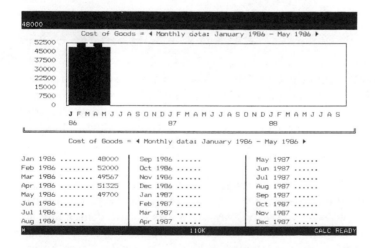

Fig. 2.12. CHART VIEW and
TABLE VIEW.

Figure 2.13 shows that a single window CHART VIEW provides much more
detail with the same information because the CHART VIEW can use the entire
screen to create the view, instead of using only half the screen.

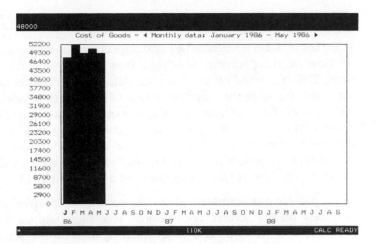

Fig. 2.13. A single CHART VIEW.

The other two commands on the WINDOW submenu have to do with switching windows and adjusting the size of the windows. The /Window Switch command produces the same result as pressing the SWITCH key. The /Window Adjust command allows you to change the amount of screen space for each window. Normally, the Javelin screen is divided into two windows with a 60/40 split. You can adjust the windows, however, to any size from 80/20 to 20/80 by using the /Window Adjust command. After you select the command, Javelin prompts you to adjust the windows with the cursor keys.

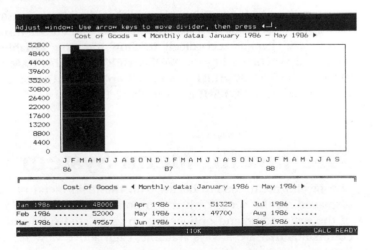

Fig. 2.14. Using the /Window
Adjust command.

Keep in mind that window adjustment is temporary. If you move from an adjusted two-window mode to a one-window mode, the window adjustment will not remain should you return to your original two windows.

Using Two Windows Rather than One

Most Lotus 1-2-3 (Release 1A) and SuperCalc³ users are accustomed to a single window on their screen, allowing a view of only one area of the worksheet at a time. This one-window view of your data has its obvious limitations. Javelin provides you with the valuable option of using a two-window view to look at your model. For example, you might want to look at both the CHART and WORKSHEET views of a particular variable in your model. As you edit the variable in the CHART view, the change would be immediately reflected in the WORKSHEET view. You could also use two separate DIAGRAM views to compare the "roots" and "branches" of a certain part of a model.

Once you have determined what you want from the two windows, you can have one view fill the screen. For example, you might use the FORMULAS and WORKSHEET views to analyze a situation, then fill the screen with the WORKSHEET view to correct any problems.

Synchronizing Two Windows

Sometimes, when two windows are on screen, you may want to move through one view and find related information in the other view. You can do this "blocking" or "tracking" with Javelin's SYNC function. This is done by pressing the SYNC key (F3).

You use the SYNC function to establish a direct relationship between the two views (or two windows). When you move the cursor through one view, the other view changes accordingly to show the same variable. A good example would be synchronizing the WORKSHEET and DIAGRAM views so that moving through the WORKSHEET would call up the DIAGRAM associated with each variable in the WORKSHEET (see fig. 2.15).

The Javelin Menu System

The Javelin menu system begins with the main menu of commands that is displayed on the screen when you press the slash key (/) (see fig. 2.16). Each of the main command options has an associated submenu. In addition to the commands that are always available, each active view has additional commands known as *view-sensitive commands*.

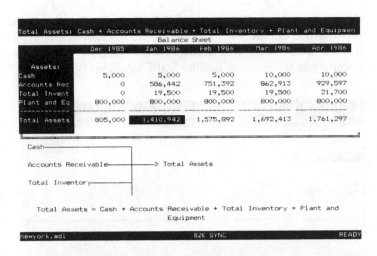

Fig. 2.15. Synchronized windows
with synchronized variables
highlighted.

Fig. 2.16. The Javelin main menu.

The Javelin Main Command Menu

Once you have Javelin running, you use the main menu selections to begin
working on a model. After you press the slash key (/), Javelin's command
options appear across the top of the screen:

    DEFINE CLEAR VIEW WINDOW PRINT FILE QUIT

If you are familiar with Lotus 1-2-3's main menu, you will notice Javelin's
similarity.

The various Javelin submenus (see fig. 2.17) become active when a main
selection has been chosen. You access the separate submenus either by typing

the first letter of the command (**D**, **C**, **V**, **W**, **P**, **F**, or **Q**, respectively) or by moving the cursor with one of the cursor-movement keys to the command. The novice Javelin user will probably want to move the cursor through the different commands to become familiar with submenu options.

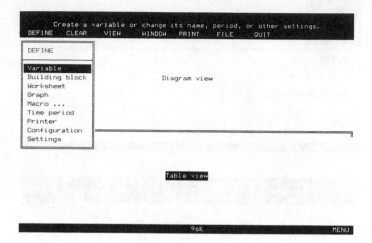

Fig. 2.17. /**D**efine command submenu.

As an example of submenus, let's look at the Model settings sheet (the part of the Javelin model where you set model parameters) two different ways. The first, and simplest, method is to type */DS* to select the /**D**efine **S**ettings command. The second method is to press the slash key (/), move the cursor to the **D**efine command, press Enter, move the cursor to the **S**ettings option, and press Enter again. Both methods will take you to the Model settings sheet. You exit from the settings sheet by pressing Esc.

Submenus for View-Sensitive Commands

In addition to the seven main menu commands listed in the previous section, Javelin has other commands that operate within specific views, with submenus that can be activated by simply typing an asterisk (*). These view-sensitive commands are the /*Worksheet, /*Errors, /*Roots, /*Branches, and /*Formulas commands.

Although spreadsheet users will appreciate Javelin's WORKSHEET view, they will notice that most of the program's spreadsheet functions are not found on the main menu but instead appear in the /*Worksheet menu. Likewise, certain FORMULAS view commands can be accessed only from the /*Formulas main menu.

To use any of the view-sensitive commands, the view must be active with the cursor in the view. For example, to use the /*Worksheet menu options, you must have the cursor in the WORKSHEET view (see fig. 2.18).

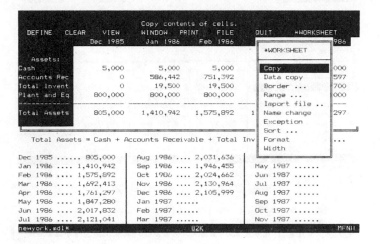

Fig. 2.18. /*Worksheet main menu options.

Using the Settings Sheets

If you're a spreadsheet user, you'll find a powerful feature in Javelin's capability to define different aspects of both the Javelin system and the model you are developing. Javelin's settings sheets let you define the unique characteristics of a variable, the precision and currency format of separate worksheets in the same model, the location on disk of the entire model, and other settings.

Javelin has a number of built-in settings that you can adjust. These built-in settings or *defaults* represent settings that the designers thought would be used most often. For example, wherever you define a time-series variable, the default time period is monthly.

You can determine all the defaults and settings by using the /Define command and its submenu (see fig. 2.19). Some of the /Define command options are established at the time of installation and can be changed with the configuration and printer options. Examples of defaults set during installation are the drivers Javelin uses to display and print graphs. You can always change these settings with the /Define command.

The /Define command also lets you create or change variables, building blocks, worksheets, graphs, time periods, and the entire model.

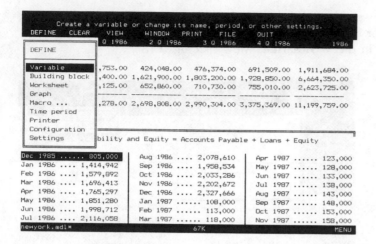

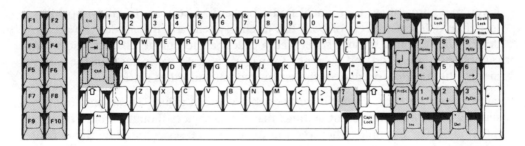

Fig. 2.19. /Define menu options.

Using the Keyboard with Javelin

Javelin has several keys designated for its own special ways of handling data. These special keys include keys on the typewriter part of the keyboard as well as the various function and cursor keys on the standard IBM PC keyboard (see fig. 2.20).

Fig. 2.20. IBM PC keyboard showing special Javelin keys highlighted.

On the standard PC keyboard, the main or typewriter-like area is called the *alphanumeric* keyboard. Your fingers rest over the letter keys and can reach the top row of numbers, like a typewriter keyboard.

The calculator-style keyboard to the right of the alphanumeric keyboard is the numeric/cursor keypad, which serves two functions. In one mode, the numeric/

cursor keyboard moves the cursor, with the 8, 6, 2, and 4 keys representing Up, Right, Down, and Left arrows respectively, and the 7, 9, 3, and 1 keys are the Home, PgUp, PgDn, and End keys. These keys are described later in more detail in the section "The Function Keys." In addition to the numeric/cursor keys, this keypad also contains the Insert and Delete keys. Finally, located above this keypad is the Break or Scroll Lock key.

The ten function keys are located to the left of the alphanumeric keyboard. Javelin's use of these keys is discussed under "The Function Keys."

The Locking Keys

Several keys on the PC keyboard, such as the Caps Lock and Num Lock keys, are called *lock* keys because they function as toggle switches (see fig. 2.21). When the Caps Lock key is off, the alphanumeric keyboard transmits letters in lowercase, unless you use the Shift key. When the Caps Lock key is turned on, the keyboard transmits letters in uppercase. The Num Lock key determines whether the Numeric/Cursor keypad is in number or cursor mode. In number mode, the keypad acts like a calculator keypad, and cursor mode causes the keypad to activate cursor movement.

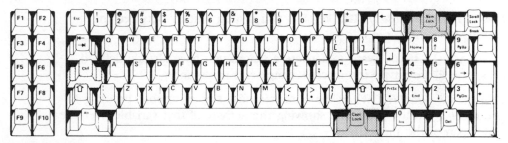

Fig. 2.21. Keyboard with Caps
Lock and Num Lock keys
highlighted.

The Function Keys

The way Javelin uses the function keys will be discussed throughout the book, but brief explanations follow.

F1 (HELP): This key activates context-sensitive, on-line help. This means that what you see when you press F1 depends on what you are doing in Javelin at that moment.

F2 (EDIT): When the cursor is on a name or formula, pressing the F2 key copies that item in the top line of the screen, where normal editing occurs. Pressing Esc before Enter cancels editing and returns the original formula. See Chapter 3 for more information on editing formulas.

F3 (SYNC): This key synchronizes two windows. For example, suppose that the FORMULAS view is in the bottom window and the WORKSHEET view is in the top window. By moving the cursor through the variable names in the WORKSHEET, you can see a specific formula highlighted in the WORKSHEET and FORMULAS views at the same time.

F4 (POINT): Pressing the POINT key copies the name of the highlighted variable to the edit line, saving you the trouble of typing the variable name. For instance, if the cursor were on the variable *Beginning Inventory*, pressing the POINT key would place only the name "Beginning Inventory" on the edit line. If you want a different variable, move the cursor to that variable, and it will appear on the edit line. To end the POINT function and select your variable, press Enter.

F5 (GO TO): This key is used to make Javelin "jump" to a named variable. If the cursor were on *Gross Sales* and you want to look at *Net Profits*, you could press F5, type *Net Profits*, and then press Enter. Javelin would bring the variable *Net Profits* into the current view.

F6 SWITCH(Windows): This key lets you switch quickly between the windows on the screen.

F7 (MACRO): If you want to activate a macro you have already defined, press the F7 key, type the macro's name, and press Enter.

F8 (QUICK GRAPH): When the cursor is on a single variable, pressing F8 produces a Javelin line graph showing the activity of that variable over the time span of the model.

F9 (CALC): Pressing the CALC key causes Javelin to perform all calculations throughout the model. The program is aware of any new information you add to your model, and indicates the need for recalculation by displaying the CALC message at the right end of the status line.

F10 (GRAPH): Pressing F10 shows the graph you changed most recently. However, before meaningful graphs can be generated on the screen or sent to the printer, they must first be defined with the /Define Graph command.

Cursor Movement and Editing Keys

Some basic key combinations used in general editing are described in this section. Detailed discussions of those Javelin keys that are view-dependent can be found in subsequent chapters.

→ *(Right arrow):* Moves the cursor one character to the right on the edit line. If the cursor is at the rightmost end of the edit line, pressing → enters what is on the edit line and moves the cursor in the view.

← *(Left arrow):* Moves the cursor one character to the left on the edit line. If the cursor is at the leftmost end of the edit line, pressing the Left-arrow key causes Javelin to beep.

↑ *(Up arrow):* Enters the information on the edit line into Javelin's information base and causes the cursor to move up one line in the current view

↓ *(Down arrow):* Enters the information on the edit line into Javelin's information base and causes the cursor to move down one line in the current view.

Home: Moves the cursor to the beginning of the edit line

PgUp: Moves the cursor one screen line, or roughly 65 characters, to the left. For example, if you find that your formula is too long to fit on the edit line, pressing PgUp will move you one screen line of text to the left.

PgDn: Moves the cursor one screen line, or roughly 65 characters, to the right. If you are editing a formula that is too long to fit on the edit line, pressing PgDn will move you one screen line of text to the right.

End: Moves the cursor to the end of the formula in the edit line

Esc: Clears the edit line

Enter: Enters the formula, name, setting, etc., into the model

Del: Deletes the character at the cursor position

Bksp: Deletes the character to the left of the cursor position

Ctrl– ← *(Left arrow):* Moves the cursor one word or expression to the left

Ctrl– → *(Right arrow):* Moves the cursor one word or expression to the right

Ctrl–Bksp: Deletes one word or expression to the left of the cursor

Ctrl–C: Same as Esc. Clears the edit line

Ctrl–K: Clears all text to the right of the cursor

Ctrl–Y: "Yanks" back all information cleared by Ctrl-K. Using this combination, you can restructure formulas without having to retype.

The SPELL Key

The SPELL key is a unique Javelin feature that saves you many keystrokes and prevents typing errors. When you press the SPELL key, identified on the PC keyboard as the Tab key, Javelin either completes the name or shows a list of possibilities. For example, if you were to call up a worksheet with the /View Window command, Javelin would ask you for the worksheet name. By pressing the SPELL key, you would quickly see a list of all the worksheet names in that model. You could then use the cursor to highlight the name of the worksheet you wanted, rather than typing it, or you could enter a new name.

As another example, suppose that you are defining a new equation, using existing variable names. You type the name of the new variable and then use the SPELL key to see a list of other variables and functions available for building the equation. When you type a formula and use the SPELL key, you also see a list of Javelin's own functions.

The following sections illustrate the use of the SPELL key in a typical Javelin work session.

Editing Formulas with the SPELL Key

Assume for this example that you would like to edit the variable *Printing Reports*.

With the cursor on the edit line, but before typing any characters, press the SPELL key (Tab). Javelin responds with a complete list of all available names, as in figure 2.22. The word MORE followed by a Down arrow in the lower right corner of the window indicates that the list is longer than the window. You can use the cursor keys to move through the choices, or, if the cursor is on the correct choice, press Enter to select that choice. Press PgDn to see the rest of the list.

To display the *Printing Reports* variable in the edit line, press *p*, then press the SPELL key (Tab) again. You would see the display of a smaller POSSIBILITIES list, this time displaying only the possible variable names that begin with the letter P. Move the cursor to Printing Reports and press Enter.

Another option would be to type *Pr*, *PR*, or *pr*, and then press the SPELL key (Tab). Javelin will display an even smaller list containing only possibilities that

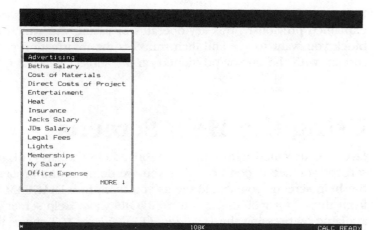

Fig. 2.22. The Javelin SPELL
window.

contain any variable names beginning with *pr*. When you type enough letters to
identify a particular variable, Javelin fills in the rest of the variable name when
you press the SPELL key (Tab). For example, if you type *p*, *r*, and *i*, in any
combination of uppercase and lowercase, and press the SPELL key (Tab, Javelin
will spell out *Printing Reports*.

Using the SPELL Key with the GO TO Key

The GO TO key (F5) "jumps" from one variable to another variable in your
model. When you press F5, Javelin prompts:

Goto variable or building block:

You can respond either by typing the name of the variable you want to go to or
by pressing the SPELL key (Tab). This combination of the GO TO and SPELL
keys lets you place the cursor on the intended formula.

Moving the Cursor on
the Javelin Screen

The way you move the cursor depends on the current view. For example, in the
WORKSHEET view, you can move the cursor from cell to cell. Movement in a
current QUICK GRAPH view can proceed only along the graph line.

Using the GO TO key (F5) is one way of moving the cursor quickly. As explained previously, this key operates by asking you which variable or building block you want to see and then transfers the information you requested to the screen, with the cursor positioned on the subject you want.

Using the Help Screens

Javelin is designed with context-sensitive help screens. This means that the help screens you see depend on what you are doing in the program. For example, the help screens you would see as you work in a DIAGRAM view are different from those you would see in the ERRORS view. Help screens are always available by pressing the HELP key (F1). Figure 2.23 shows the help screen you would see in the TABLE view.

Javelin's help screens provide immediate information on what you are doing in the program at a given moment.

Using the Tutorials and Case Studies

To help you begin learning Javelin, the Javelin disk package includes a text tutorial and three disks containing case study files, each illustrating a specific Javelin feature or application. The *Guide to Learning Javelin*, a hands-on tutorial, teaches you the mechanics of getting started and introduces you to Javelin's basic operations. By completing each section of the *Guide to Learning Javelin* in the order presented, you develop a simple Javelin model that quickly teaches you how to create Javelin formulas, use function keys, enter data, use Javelin views, create worksheets, and create graphs.

Unlike the series of related lessons in the *Guide to Learning Javelin*, Javelin's 3 case study disks, containing 17 files, can be used in whatever order fits your needs. Four files are specially developed for the needs of particular types of Javelin users: two files that introduce spreadsheet users to Javelin, and two that introduce nonspreadsheet users to Javelin. The remaining 13 files focus on a single Javelin feature or application, with keystroke-by-keystroke instructions. In addition to the four files addressed to spreadsheet and nonspreadsheet users, the topics covered on the three case study disks include:

Solving a Problem with Javelin
Constants and Time-Series Variables
Entering Data and Formatting Numbers
Graphing with Javelin

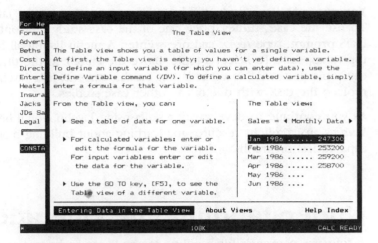

Fig. 2.23. Press F1 to see the
Help screen for a particular view
(TABLE view shown).

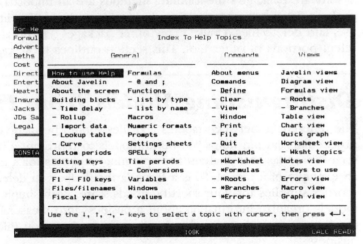

Fig. 2.24. The Help Index.

The Javelin Worksheet
More on the Javelin Worksheet
Importing Data into a Javelin Model

The Javelin Sum Function
Time-Series Functions
Time Periods and Conversions

The Time Delay Building Block
The Lookup Table Building Block
The Rollup Building Block

You use each case study disk by itself, independent of the Javelin program disk. To use the case studies, place one of the case study disks into drive A. At the DOS prompt, type *learn* and press Enter. A menu listing all of the case study topics appears. To select a topic, move the cursor to the title and press Enter. If the topic you want to cover is not on the current disk, Javelin prompts you to replace the disk with one of the other case studies.

As you continue to develop your skills using Javelin, you'll find the *Javelin Case Studies* an excellent resource for learning about building blocks, importing capabilities, or graphs.

Understanding File Operations

A software package's file-handling methods are an important part of using that package. Javelin is no exception. Like most packages, Javelin allows you to load, use, and delete files. Unlike many other packages, Javelin also allows you to read select portions of other files. This section outlines these capabilities.

Distinguishing Models from Files

The differences between models and files should be made clear before proceeding. Javelin helps you build models to represent a business situation. A set of formulas that analyzes the operating expenses for a multinational firm is an example of a model. So is a formula that helps you determine when to reorder supplies for your sporting goods store. Both simple and complex models organize information about a business into measurable data in equation form, creating a structure that Javelin uses to show you things about your business.

If you use the models you develop repeatedly, you will want to save them to disk. When you save a Javelin model to disk, you are saving everything that you have worked on since you loaded the model or last cleared all aspects of the model. When you save a model to a disk, the model then becomes a file. One model, one file.

A model you save becomes a file, but files don't always contain models. You may, for example, want to create library files in Javelin (a MACRO Library, for example). A library file does not generally contain relationships, but may contain items like worksheet formats (a WORKSHEET Library), listings of variable values (a DATA library), building block templates (a BUILDING BLOCK Library), or custom time periods (a TIME PERIOD library).

When you save a Javelin model, you save the whole model, but that does not mean you must retrieve the model as a whole. Javelin allows you to create a model, using pieces from other models.

A key concept here is understanding that several things go into making a whole model (graphs, worksheets, etc.). Each model can be made up of its own parts or can use parts from other models. The Javelin system allows you to access one model's parts from another model. Thus, you can create new models from bits and pieces of other models. See Chapter 7 on importing and consolidating data.

Naming Files

You should give each model you create a different, preferably descriptive, name. The computer recognizes a name consisting of an eight-character file name followed by a period and a three-character extension, as follows:

> filename.ext

Javelin's requirements for the first part of the file name are few. The name must be unique and contain eight characters or fewer, but you may be as inventive as you want. Usually you name a file according to its purpose. Table 2.1 shows the most common file name extensions and their meanings.

Saving Files

Files may be saved to disk with either of two commands. One is the /Quit Save command, which you use when you are ready to end a Javelin work session. To quit Javelin and save your model to disk, type

> /QSfilename

Press Enter. If you have been working previously on that file, Javelin will ask whether you want to save the modified file by writing over the old one (see fig. 2.25). You can rename the file at this time, if you want, by typing *n* for "no" and starting over.

If you make changes and try to Quit without saving the file, Javelin displays the message Model not saved. Quit anyway? (see fig. 2.26). Press *N* for "no" to start over and save the file, or press *Y* to quit Javelin without saving the file.

You can also save a file to disk without quitting Javelin. Press the slash key (/) to display the main command menu, select File, then choose Save from the submenu. When Javelin asks for the name of the file (see fig. 2.27), you type

Table 2.1
Common File Name Extensions

Extension	Description
.TXT	Contains numbers and letters that can be read without need for interpretation by special programs
.PRN	Contains codes necessary to achieve certain printing effects: boldface, super- and subscripts, for example. This type of file is usually created when printer output is directed to a disk file for later printing.
.MDL	A Javelin model that has been saved as a file
.CFG	Configuration files are produced by Javelin at setup or when you save information settings from the Configuration settings sheet. They contain settings for drivers, printers, and so on.
.OVL	Files needed to start and run the Javelin program.
.COM	A command (program) file
.EXE	An executable program file

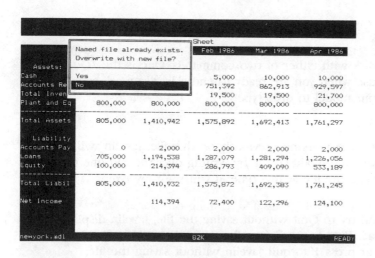

Fig. 2.25. Saving a file.

the file name and press Enter. If there is another file with a similar name, Javelin asks whether you want to write over the existing file or choose another file name.

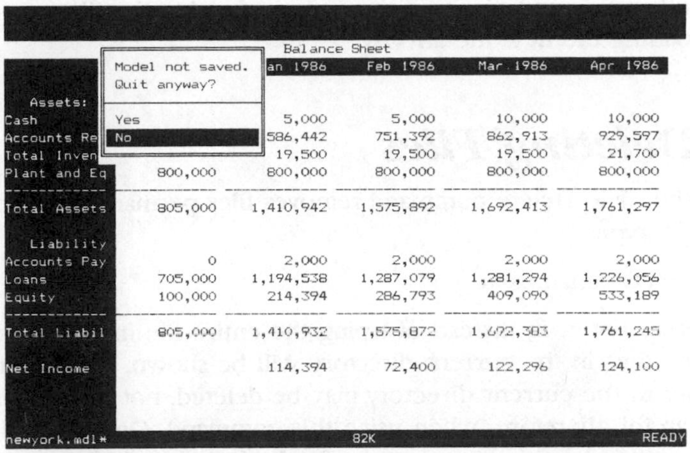

Fig. 2.26. Quitting Javelin before saving a file.

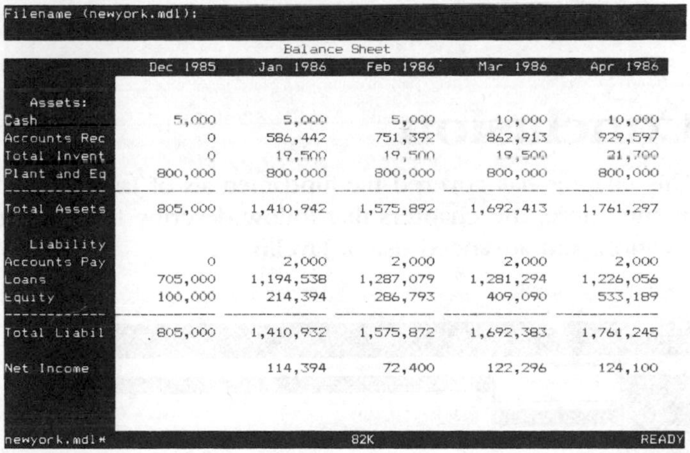

Fig. 2.27. Saving a file with a file command option.

Loading Files

In the section on starting Javelin, you saw how to start the program and load a file at the same time. Once Javelin is up and running on your computer, you use a different command.

To use the file load command, type

/FLfilename

This command tells the computer to load the file with file name *filename.ext*. If another file is currently in Javelin's memory and has not been saved, Javelin will tell you so and give you the option of saving the file in memory to disk or loading the new file anyway.

Deleting Files

The /File Delete command removes files permanently from disks. To remove a file, type

   /FDfilename.ext

Press Enter. If, instead of typing the entire file name, you use the SPELL key, all the files in the current directory will be shown, as in figure 2.28. Note that *any* file in the current directory may be deleted, not just a data file. Be extremely careful, therefore, when using this command. Once a file is deleted using this command, you cannot get the file back. Javelin helps you by asking you to make sure that you chose the right file and do want to delete it (see fig. 2.29).

Conclusion

This chapter has covered the fundamentals of Javelin. Building on what you've learned here, the chapters that follow describe file manipulation, model creation, and advanced use of Javelin.

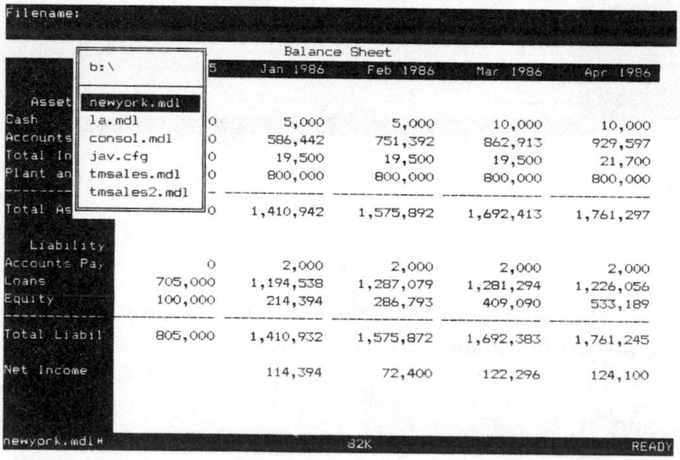

Fig. 2.28. Deleting a file.

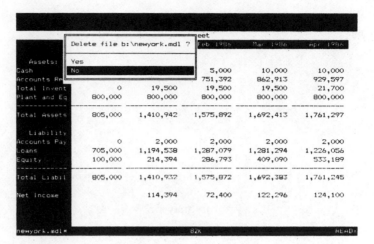

Fig. 2.29. Javelin prompts to confirm deletion.

## Part II

Building a Javelin Model

3

Using the DIAGRAM, FORMULAS, TABLE, and NOTES Views

Chapter 1 introduced all 10 Javelin views. This chapter describes how you can use Javelin's DIAGRAM, FORMULAS, TABLE, and NOTES views to begin creating your business models. These four views can help you create formulas, enter data, and document assumptions about the formulas you've entered. This chapter describes

- How to enter formulas, variables, and data in various views and the way Javelin's "Information Base" stores information

- How to use the DIAGRAM view to show the logic behind your model by displaying the relationships between variables

- How to use the FORMULAS view to display every formula and the variables on which these formulas are built

- How to use the TABLE view to see instantly a data table for a variable using whatever time period applies

- How to use the NOTES view to create notes linked to a specific variable so that your assumptions and model logic can be documented for any variable

In addition to describing each view, this chapter also introduces you to the commands and special keys that you will need to understand to use the four views emphasized in the following sections:

81

Developing Business Models with Javelin

As one of the most powerful business analysis tools available today, Javelin lets you enter formulas in plain English and automatically helps you keep track of relationships as you build a model. This chapter shows you exactly how to use Javelin to develop business models with the DIAGRAM, FORMULAS, TABLE, and NOTES views.

By learning about these four views, you'll see the tremendous advantage Javelin has over popular spreadsheet programs. Javelin offers multiple views compared with the one worksheet view spreadsheets provide for entering data and displaying formulas. You no longer need an additional utility program or special format commands to view formulas as 1-2-3 or Symphony worksheets require.

Nor do you have to settle for viewing a single formula (or part of a formula if it is longer than 80 characters) at one time (see fig. 3.1). The only method of deriving a complete or even partial listing of 1-2-3 formulas is to use a special command for printing cell formulas. And to get a final printed copy, you must enter at least four separate commands. But even then, neither 1-2-3 nor Symphony provides a way of instantly seeing the logic of your model or quickly getting a summary of your formulas as you develop the model.

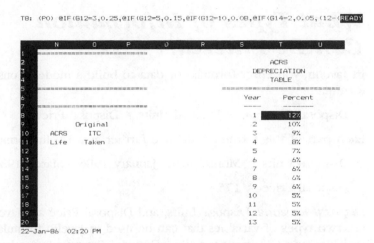

Fig. 3.1. 1-2-3 worksheet with
formula in control panel.

Javelin's DIAGRAM, FORMULAS, TABLE, and NOTES views keep track of all
formulas, variables, and logic as you build a model. And if you're analyzing a
model built by someone else, Javelin's DIAGRAM, FORMULAS, TABLE, and
NOTES views give you a detailed road map of the model's logic. You need not
waste time querying the creator of a model about its formulas and assumptions.

Using Formulas, Variables, and Data

Before we begin to look at building a Javelin model, using the DIAGRAM,
FORMULAS, and TABLE views, four concepts are essential to understanding how
Javelin works and how it is different from popular spreadsheet programs. These
concepts are

1. The types of information that can be entered into the various Javelin
   views

2. How Javelin stores information and displays it in different views

3. What constitutes a Javelin formula (operators, rules of syntax, etc.)

4. How Javelin handles variables (guidelines for using variables)

What Types of Information Can Be Entered?

In Javelin, you enter formulas or data to build a model. Consider the following formula:

Disposal Revenue = Disposal Units * Disposal Price

Each part of this formula is defined further as a Javelin formula:

Disposal Units = Monthly data: January 1986 – March 1986

Disposal Price = 175

Disposal Revenue, Disposal Units, and Disposal Price are Javelin variables. There are two types of variables that can be used in Javelin formulas: (1) calculated variables and (2) input variables. *Disposal Revenue* is a calculated variable because it is the result of two other formulas. *Disposal Units* and *Disposal Price* are input variables. Input variables hold data entered over time or as a constant. If, for example *Disposal Price* remains constant at 175 no matter how many units are sold, you would instruct Javelin to handle this variable as a constant by entering:

Disposal Price = 175

How Does Javelin Store Information?

Formulas, variables, and data that you enter are stored in Javelin's central Information Base. The Information Base consists of two parts—a logic base and a database. The logic base holds formulas; the database holds constants or time-series data. The Javelin views all have access to the formulas and data in your model.

Because of the way Javelin handles information, you can instantly see the same data in database or worksheet form. In contrast, if you want to display the same data in both a spreadsheet and a database in 1-2-3, you must copy the data to two locations on the worksheet. To create a balance sheet listing total assets for a single month and also a database that will store monthly total assets for the year, you need to copy total assets data to two areas of the worksheet (see fig. 3.2). Javelin lets you see data from the Information Base in different ways without requiring that you copy any information.

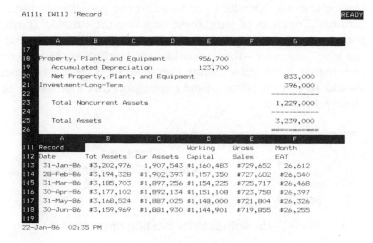

A111: [W11] 'Record   READY

	A	B	C	D	E	F	G
17							
18	Property, Plant, and Equipment				956,700		
19	Accumulated Depreciation				123,700		
20	Net Property, Plant, and Equipment						833,000
21	Investment-Long-Term						396,000
22							
23	Total Noncurrent Assets						1,229,000
24							
25	Total Assets						3,239,000
26							

	A	B	C	D	E	F
111	Record					
112	Date	Tot Assets	Cur Assets	Working Capital	Gross Sales	Month EAT
113	31-Jan-86	$3,202,976	1,907,543	$1,160,483	$729,652	26,612
114	28-Feb-86	$3,194,328	$1,902,393	$1,157,350	$727,602	$26,540
115	31-Mar-86	$3,185,703	$1,897,256	$1,154,225	$725,717	$26,468
116	30-Apr-86	$3,177,102	$1,892,134	$1,151,108	$723,758	$26,397
117	31-May-86	$3,168,524	$1,887,025	$1,148,000	$721,804	$26,326
118	30-Jun-86	$3,159,969	$1,881,930	$1,144,901	$719,855	$26,255
119						

22-Jan-86 02:35 PM

Fig. 3.2. Data displayed in spreadsheet and database format in 1-2-3.

What Is a Javelin Formula?

Javelin formulas are created with variables you choose and enter following some basic syntactic rules:

> variable = (expression involving other variables)

The spacing you use does not affect the meaning of the formula. Look, for example, at the following formulas:

> Total Revenue=Blender Revenue+Disposal Revenue+Compactor Revenue

> Loans = IF(PREVIOUS(Loans) + Cash, – Cash Unadjusted < 0, 0,
> PREVIOUS(Loans), + Cash – Cash Unadjusted) ; Beginning Loans

Both are acceptable Javelin formulas even though they differ in spacing. Notice that the first formula contains no spaces between variables and the equal sign and between variables and the operators (+), but the second formula does have spaces.

Complex Javelin formulas can consist of variables, operators, functions, and values.

> variable = (expression involving variables, operators, functions, etc.)

In addition to containing the variables *Loans, Cash, Cash Unadjusted*, and *Beginning Loans*, the formula for *Loans* contains two Javelin functions: IF and PREVIOUS. IF is one of Javelin's logical functions; PREVIOUS is a time function. PREVIOUS returns the values from the previous time period for the variable specified (*Loans* in this case). (See Appendix A for a complete description of all Javelin functions.)

Notice also the specific operators and the parentheses used in the *Loans* formula. Two sets of parentheses enclose the variable *Loans*, and the formula uses four operators: plus (+), minus (−), less than (<), and "or else" (;). The "or else" operator—the semicolon—is Javelin's special operator. The semicolon means that if the value before the semicolon cannot be calculated, Javelin should return the value of the expression that follows the semicolon (see table 3.1).

Table 3.1
Mathematical Operators

Operator	Description
( )	Parentheses for nesting operations
+ and −	Plus and minus used to indicate positive or negative expressions
^	Exponents
* and /	Multiplication and division
+ and −	Addition and subtraction
;	Or else

Like spreadsheet programs, Javelin is finicky about parentheses and will alert you when an incorrect number of parentheses encloses an argument. Unlike spreadsheet programs, Javelin helps you avoid problems with parentheses by displaying the syntax required to complete a function as soon as you begin entering the function. In the preceding *Loans* formula, for example, as soon as you type PREVIOUS, Javelin displays in the information line the syntax required to complete the function (see fig. 3.3).

Mathematical and Logical Operators

In Javelin, you can use the mathematical operators shown in table 3.1. Keep in mind that the semicolon (;) instructs Javelin to use what follows the semicolon if what precedes it is not available. Consider the *Loans* formula, for example:

```
Loans = IF(PREVIOUS(Loans) + Cash − Cash Unadjusted < 0, 0,
            PREVIOUS(Loans), + Cash − Cash Unadjusted) ; Beginning Loans
```

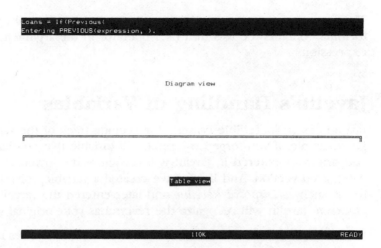

Fig. 3.3. PREVIOUS displayed in
information line.

The semicolon in this formula tells Javelin to return the value for *Beginning Loans* if what precedes the semicolon is not available.

To use operators, you must know their order of precedence—the order in which operations are performed. The list in table 3.1 is arranged in descending order of precedence. Operators with equal precedence (listed on the same line in table 3.1) are evaluated from left to right. You can always use parentheses, though, to override the order of precedence.

In addition to the mathematical operators listed in table 3.1, Javelin recognizes the logical operators in table 3.2.

Table 3.2
Logical Operators

Operator	Description
=	Equal to
>	Greater than
<	Less than
> =	Greater than or equal to
< =	Less than or equal to
< >	Not equal to

The formula for *Loans* uses both mathematical and logical operators. The formula contains the less than (<) operator in the argument for the IF expression.

Javelin's Handling of Variables

Javelin has an incredible capacity for keeping track of the variables you enter. For example, if you forget to capitalize a variable that you had capitalized when you originally entered it, Javelin will recognize the lowercase version as the capitalized version. And if you have created a variable consisting of two or more terms such as *Disposal Revenue* and later entered the variable as *Revenue Disposal*, Javelin will recognize the reversal as your original variable.

Javelin is programmed to catch some variations, but it does have its limitations. It will *not* catch, for example, a misspelling or typographical error when you reenter an existing variable. Suppose that you entered the following formula:

Disposal Revenue = Disposal Units * Disposal Price

If you try to enter a constant for *Disposal Price* by typing

Dipsosal Price = 175

Javelin would interpret this as a new variable because of the difference in spelling between the original—*Disposal*—and the second version—*Dipsosal*. The list shown in the POSSIBILITIES menu on the screen indicates that you now have both *Disposal Price* and *Dipsosal Price* as variables (see fig. 3.4). If you don't first notice that Javelin has created a new variable, look closely at the views displayed on screen. *Disposal Price* is still UNDEFINED.

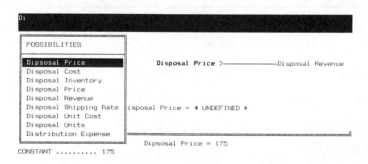

Fig. 3.4. Javelin interprets a misspelling as a new variable.

Using the SPELL key To Enter Variables

Javelin's SPELL key (Tab) helps you avoid problems entering variables. It provides a list of names of variables, functions, files, etc. so that you don't need to enter a name manually. (See list in shaded block.) Suppose, for example, that you had entered the variables *Blender Revenue, Disposal Revenue,* and *Compactor Revenue* and wanted to enter the formula:

Total Revenue = Blender Revenue + Disposal Revenue +
                     Compactor Revenue

Instead of typing the formula, you can enter it by using Javelin's SPELL key (Tab) to enter automatically those variables that already exist. Begin by typing the variable *Total Revenue* and the equal sign:

Total Revenue =

With the cursor positioned after the equal sign, press the SPELL key (Tab) and Javelin will display a list of variables that you created previously (see fig. 3.5). This POSSIBILITIES menu also displays functions you can use in the formula.

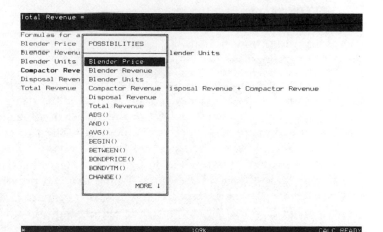

Fig. 3.5. Complete list of model variables.

To continue creating your formula, move the cursor to the variable you want entered as the next part and press Enter. To create the formula for *Total Revenue*, for example, you would select the variable *Blender Revenue* and press Enter. If the list of variables is long, you can reduce the number of choices by typing the first few characters of the variable before pressing the SPELL key (Tab). If you were to type *Total Revenue = Bl* before pressing the SPELL key (Tab), Javelin would fill in as much of the variable as is uniquely defined by *Bl* and then show a list of only those variables that begin with *Bl*, as in figure 3.6.

If you were to type *Total Revenue = Blender Re* and press the SPELL key (Tab), Javelin would enter the variable *Blender Revenue* because no other variable begins with these letters.

Once Javelin enters the variable *Blender Revenue*, you can complete the formula by typing the appropriate operators (+) and entering the last two variables (*Compactor Revenue* and *Disposal Revenue*), using the SPELL key (Tab).

The SPELL Key (Tab)

Javelin's SPELL key will retrieve other types of lists in addition to variables. The SPELL key makes it particularly easy to respond to prompts when completing command operations. It can be used to access lists of:

- Variables and functions
- Files and directories
- Javelin worksheets
- Building blocks
- Functions
- Macros
- Custom time periods
- Graph names

Whenever Javelin asks you for a name to complete a command operation, you can press the SPELL key. Javelin will enter the name if no other name matches those characters or will provide a list of all names containing those initial characters. If, for example, you wanted to retrieve a variable named *Chicago Sales* and typed *ch*, Javelin would provide a list of all variables beginning with *ch* as in figure 3.7. The SPELL key will not find a variable name if you reverse parts. Typing *Rev* and pressing SPELL will not find *Blender Revenue, Disposal Revenue*, or *Compactor Revenue*. Remember also that when you enter, select, and use variable names, file names, macro names, worksheet names, etc., Javelin reads upper- and lowercase letters interchangeably. For more information on the SPELL key, see Chapter 2 and Appendix B, Javelin Command Summary.

Guidelines for Entering Variables

Javelin can't second guess you on misspellings and typographical errors. But it can eliminate the need to reenter manually already existing variables, thus reducing the possibility of error. Using the SPELL key (Tab), therefore, is a good habit to form. You would be wise, also, to follow the conventions for creating and using variables in Javelin, described in the sections that follow.

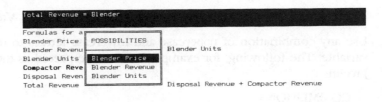

Fig. 3.6. Selective list of variables.

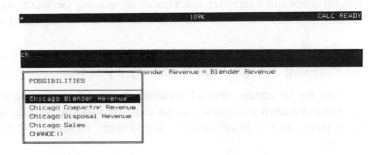

Fig. 3.7. Using the SPELL key
(Tab) to list variable names
beginning with *ch*.

Using Accepted Characters in Javelin Variables

Use any combination of letters, numbers, blank spaces, and the characters ., —,
%, and & to create Javelin variables. Javelin will accept, for example, any of the
following as variables:

Commission	12% Market Share
Jones Salary	SP__TOTALS
Warehouse 23	Jones & Son

Be careful that you don't use mathematical and logical operators in variable
names. Javelin will not accept the variable or will misinterpret a single variable
like *Spring-Summer Sales*.

Mixing Uppercase and Lowercase Letters in Variables

Use any combination of uppercase and lowercase letters to represent the same variable. The following, for example, are all interpreted as the same variable in Javelin:

COMMISSIONS
Commissions
commissions
coMMiSSions

Using Blank Spaces in Variables

Javelin does not interpret differences in spacing between words as different variables. *Jones   &   Son* and *Jones & Son* are interpreted as the same variable.

Reversing Items Separated by Spaces

Do not try to create distinct variables by merely reversing the order of items (items separated by spaces) in an existing variable. Javelin accepts reversals of such items as the same variable. If you were to enter the following formula, for example,

Total Revenue National = Chicago Revenue +
                    Atlanta Revenue + NY Revenue

And then later were to type

Revenue Chicago = 456723

Javelin would interpret *Revenue Chicago* as the original *Chicago Revenue*.

Be particularly careful about using spaces in variables. Suppose that you entered the following formula,

Office Expenses = Region 1 Office 1 +
                    Region 1 Office 2

Javelin interprets all of the following variations of *Region 1 Office 2* as the same variable:

1 Region Office 2
1 Region 2 Office
Region 2 Office 1 = Region 1 Office 2
1 2 Region Office
Region Office 1 2
Region 1 2 Office

Reversing Items Not *Separated by Spaces*

If you reverse items in a variable not separated by spaces, Javelin interprets the reversal as a new variable. If, for example, you enter the variable *Bin4Part3* and later enter *Part3Bin4*, Javelin interprets the second as a new variable.

Be careful about reversing items not separated by spaces.

In general, when you create and use Javelin variables, keep the preceding conventions and guidelines in mind. Try also to maintain a system that will work for you and for others using the same model. Maintaining conventions for using Javelin variables is particularly important when the same model is used by other offices within the same company. When you choose variable names, you'll also need to consider whether the names will be used in Javelin's WORKSHEET view. The variable names you choose will affect the options for producing reports. (See Chapter 5 for more information on variables names in worksheets.)

When creating variables, pick simple descriptive terms that are easily remembered. Try to maintain a list of "accepted variables" and stick to using them. Don't depend too much on your memory; instead, use Javelin's SPELL key (Tab) to remind you of variables you've created. And occasionally, print out a list of your variables by using Javelin's FORMULAS view, keep the list handy, and use it as you continue to work on the model. (See Chapter 11 for directions on printing a Javelin view.)

Procedure and Keys for Editing Formulas

Before discussing specific views, one more general note is in order. You will be learning shortly to enter formulas into Javelin and soon thereafter you will want to know about editing them. Because the procedure is the same for the DIAGRAM, FORMULAS, TABLE, CHART, WORKSHEET, and ERRORS views, we discuss it here.

Suppose, for example, that you want to edit a formula in the FORMULAS view (see fig. 3.8). To edit a formula or variable, move the cursor to the item you want to edit, then press the Edit key (F2). Javelin displays the formula on the edit line (see fig. 3.9). To perform the edit, use the keys listed in table 3.3.

Suppose, for example, that you entered the wrong price for *Disposal Price*. Instead of 175, the price should have been entered as 180. How would you correct it?

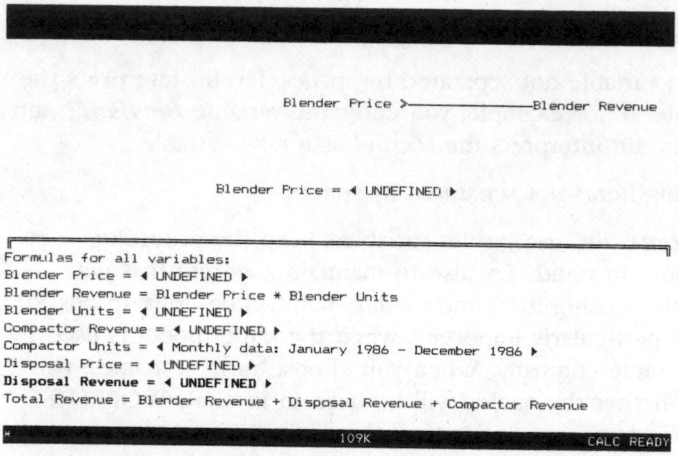

```
                                   Blender Price >————————————Blender Revenue



                              Blender Price = ◄ UNDEFINED ►


Formulas for all variables:
Blender Price = ◄ UNDEFINED ►
Blender Revenue = Blender Price * Blender Units
Blender Units = ◄ UNDEFINED ►
Compactor Revenue = ◄ UNDEFINED ►
Compactor Units = ◄ Monthly data: January 1986 - December 1986 ►
Disposal Price = ◄ UNDEFINED ►
Disposal Revenue = ◄ UNDEFINED ►
Total Revenue = Blender Revenue + Disposal Revenue + Compactor Revenue
                                       109K                                    CALC READY
```

Fig. 3.8. The FORMULAS view for the Revenue model.

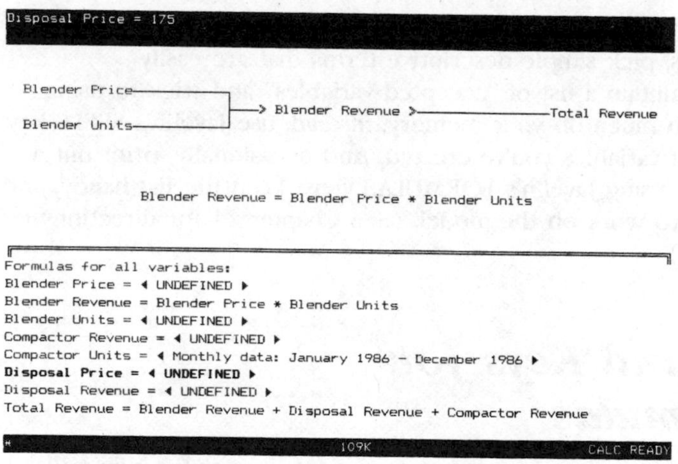

```
Disposal Price = 175


    Blender Price————————┐
                         ├——> Blender Revenue >————————————Total Revenue
    Blender Units————————┘


            Blender Revenue = Blender Price * Blender Units


Formulas for all variables:
Blender Price = ◄ UNDEFINED ►
Blender Revenue = Blender Price * Blender Units
Blender Units = ◄ UNDEFINED ►
Compactor Revenue = ◄ UNDEFINED ►
Compactor Units = ◄ Monthly data: January 1986 - December 1986 ►
Disposal Price = ◄ UNDEFINED ►
Disposal Revenue = ◄ UNDEFINED ►
Total Revenue = Blender Revenue + Disposal Revenue + Compactor Revenue
                                       109K                                    CALC READY
```

Fig. 3.9. *Disposal Price* on edit line.

1. Move the cursor to the formula you want to edit (see fig. 3.9).

2. Press the Edit key (F2).

3. When the variable appears in Javelin's edit line, press the End key to move the cursor to the the last digit in 175.

4. Press the Bksp key twice to delete 75.

5. Type *80* to change the value to 180.

6. Press Enter to complete the edit. The changed variable will be entered in the FORMULAS view, as in figure 3.10. To see the changed results, press the CALC key (F9).

Table 3.3
Cursor Keys for Editing Formulas

Key	Operation
←	Moves cursor one character to left
→	Moves cursor one character to right. If cursor is at end of the line, the right arrow will end the edit, save your changes, and move the cursor in the current view.
↑	Enters your change, moves cursor up one line
↓	Enters your change, moves cursor down one line
Home	Moves cursor to beginning of edit line
End	Moves cursor to end of Edit line
Ctrl- →	Moves cursor one word to right
Ctrl- ←	Moves cursor one word to left
Del	Deletes character where cursor is positioned
Bksp	Deletes character to left of cursor
Ctrl-Bksp	Deletes word to left of cursor
Ctrl-K	Deletes to end of line
Ctrl-Y	Recovers text deleted by last Ctrl-K operation
SPELL (Tab)	Provides a list of variables or functions to insert in edit line at cursor position
POINT (F4)	Enters variable at cursor (POINT mode is ended when you press Enter or Esc.)
Enter	Ends the edit and saves your changes
Esc	Clears edit line; restores formula to version existing before you began editing

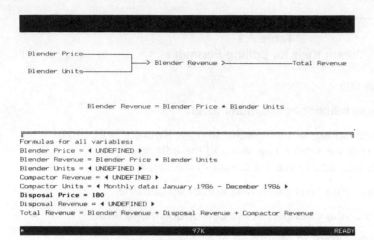

```
Blender Price
                          ──> Blender Revenue >──────────Total Revenue
Blender Units


         Blender Revenue = Blender Price * Blender Units


Formulas for all variables:
Blender Price = ◀ UNDEFINED ▶
Blender Revenue = Blender Price * Blender Units
Blender Units = ◀ UNDEFINED ▶
Compactor Revenue = ◀ UNDEFINED ▶
Compactor Units = ◀ Monthly data: January 1986 - December 1986 ▶
Disposal Price = 180
Disposal Revenue = ◀ UNDEFINED ▶
Total Revenue = Blender Revenue + Disposal Revenue + Compactor Revenue
                                97K                              READY
```

Fig. 3.10. Changed variable in FORMULAS View.

Using the DIAGRAM View

To understand how Javelin works, let's begin by examining one way of using Javelin's DIAGRAM, FORMULAS, TABLE, and NOTES views for creating a sales-revenue model for the company introduced in Chapter 1. Imagine that you have the task of calculating total sales revenues for your company's New York division. Specifically, you want to track the total revenue for three products—blenders, compactors, and disposals.

You need to enter four formulas:

1. A formula to calculate blender revenue

2. A formula to calculate compactor revenue

3. A formula to calculate disposal revenue

4. A formula to calculate total revenue

You can enter the formulas in whatever order you want. As soon as you enter one formula, Javelin takes note of the variable names. It keeps track of all relationships whenever the variables are used in other formulas.

The initial Javelin screen displays two views: DIAGRAM view in the top half and TABLE view in the bottom half (see fig. 3.11). You can begin entering formulas from either view. The highlighted cursor indicates the current view. If you want to begin entering formulas with the cursor highlighted in the DIAGRAM view, press the WINDOW key (F6) to switch windows. You can also enter formulas from other views: FORMULAS, CHART, WORKSHEET, or ERRORS.

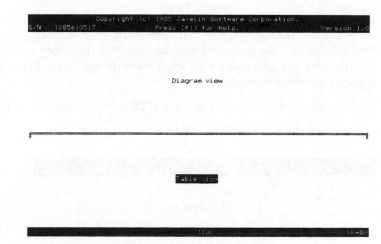

Fig. 3.11. Javelin start-up screen.

Entering Formulas and Variables in the DIAGRAM View

Entering a formula in a Javelin view involves simply typing the formula and pressing the Enter key. With the cursor in the DIAGRAM view, for example, you can enter the formula for blender revenue by typing the following formula and pressing Enter (see fig. 3.12).

Blender Revenue = Blender Units * Blender Price

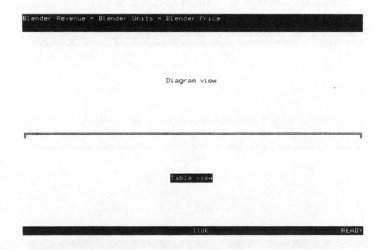

Fig. 3.12. *Blender Revenue* on edit line.

After the formula is entered, it is displayed in two forms: (1) in a diagram showing the relationships of variables and (2) as originally entered in the edit line (fig. 3.13). To complete the formulas for the other two products, compactors and disposals, type each formula and press Enter as you did for the blender revenue formula.

Compactor Revenue = Compactor Units * Compactor Price

Disposal Revenue = Disposal Units * Disposal Price

```
Blender Units
                            > Blender Revenue
Blender Price


        Blender Revenue = Blender Units * Blender Price


        Blender Revenue = Blender Units * Blender Price
NOT YET CALCULATED
```

Fig. 3.13. *Blender Revenue* entered in the DIAGRAM view.

```
                    109K                              CALC READY
```

Notice how the current view, the DIAGRAM view, changes as formulas are entered to show the variable most recently entered. The DIAGRAM view also shows how variables are linked, which variables affect others, and which variables are affected by others (see fig. 3.14).

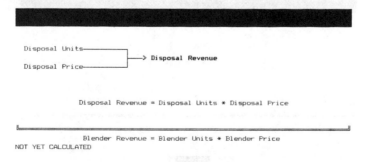

```
Disposal Units
                            > Disposal Revenue
Disposal Price


        Disposal Revenue = Disposal Units * Disposal Price


        Blender Revenue = Blender Units * Blender Price
NOT YET CALCULATED
```

Fig. 3.14. *Disposal Revenue* entered in the DIAGRAM view.

```
                    109K                              CALC READY
```

Moving the Cursor in the DIAGRAM view

You can use the cursor keys to move through the DIAGRAM view of the model you've created up to this point. With the cursor highlighting *Disposal Revenue*, as shown in figure 3.14, you can highlight other parts of the formula by pressing the Left-arrow key. If other variables were linked to *Disposal Units* or *Disposal Price*, pressing the Left-arrow key a second time would highlight them.

If you want to move quickly from one part of the DIAGRAM view to another, type or enter the variable through the SPELL key (Tab). Press Enter and the DIAGRAM view will display the desired variable.

Using the FORMULAS View

The FORMULAS view allows you to see a full-screen listing of the formulas and variables that you have entered in a model and indicates whether variables have been defined (see fig. 3.16). You'll find it very useful to combine the FORMULAS view with another view as you build your model.

You may want, for example, to combine the DIAGRAM and FORMULAS views. Let's change the TABLE view in figure 3.15 to a FORMULAS view. Be sure your cursor is in the bottom window. If the cursor is in the top window, move it to the bottom window by pressing the WINDOW key (F6). Next, select the /View Formulas All command and press Enter. Javelin will show the FORMULAS view in the bottom window (see fig. 3.16). (To see a full screen view of your formulas, enter the /Window 1 window command with the cursor in the FORMULAS view.)

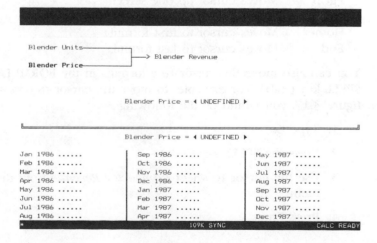

Fig. 3.15. Screen with DIAGRAM and TABLE views.

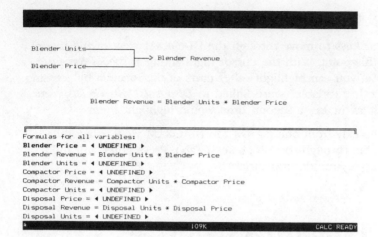

Fig. 3.16. Screen with DIAGRAM and FORMULAS views.

Moving the Cursor in the FORMULAS view

As your list of formulas and variables grows, you will want to move as quickly as possible within the view. Use the following keys to move the cursor through formula lists displayed in the FORMULAS view:

Key	Function
↑	Moves cursor up one formula
↓	Moves cursor down one formula
PgUp	Moves cursor up one screen
PgDn	Moves cursor down one screen
Home	Moves cursor to first formula
End	Moves cursor to last formula

You can also move the cursor to a formula in the FORMULAS view by using the SPELL key (Tab). For example, to move the cursor to Compactor Revenue in figure 3.17, you would do the following:

1. Type *Co*.

2. Press the SPELL key (Tab).

3. Use the cursor to select *Compactor Revenue* from the POSSIBILITIES menu.

4. Press Enter.

Options for Viewing Types and Parts of Formulas

Javelin provides two options for viewing formulas. First, options for viewing formulas are provided by the /View Formulas command. Second, options for viewing formulas are provided by the /*Formulas command. The first command (/View Formulas) can be accessed from any Javelin view; the second command (/*Formulas) is a "view-sensitive" command that can only be accessed when the FORMULAS view is active.

Javelin's /View Formulas command provides three options for viewing formulas:

Option	*Command*
View all formulas	/View Formulas All
View only the branches of a specific variable	/View Formulas Branches
View only the roots of a specific variable	/View Formulas Roots

Branches are those variables that are affected by another variable; roots are those variables that affect another variable.

Figure 3.16 shows the result of using the View Formulas All command to get a complete list of formulas in your model. To see the roots of the formula *Disposal Revenue*, you would move the cursor to the formula, select the View Formulas Roots command and press Enter when prompted for a variable name. Javelin would display the formulas for all variables that affect *Disposal Revenue* (see fig. 3.17).

When you select /View Formulas Roots or Branches, Javelin indicates the relationship of variables through indentation. In figure 3.17, a single indentation indicates the variables that make up the formula for *Disposal Revenue*. If *Disposal Units* was a calculated variable, the Formulas Roots View would show the variables of this formula at a second level of indentation. After moving the cursor to *Disposal Price*, you could display all branches for this variable by selecting View Formulas Branches.

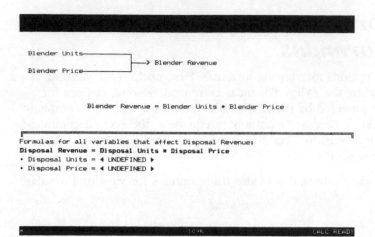

Fig. 3.17. *Disposal Revenue*
formula roots.

With the FORMULAS view as the active view, the /*Formulas command provides seven options for viewing types and parts of formulas:

Option	Command
View all formulas	/*Formulas **All**
View input variables	/*Formulas **Inputs**
View model results	/*Formulas **Results**
View undefined variables	/*Formulas **Undefined**
View circular references	/*Formulas **Circular**
View variables with notes	/*Formulas **Notes**
View time spans of variables	/*Formulas **Time spans**

To see the six input variables for the revenue model, you would select /*Formulas Inputs (see fig. 3.18). If you had assigned values to all price variables, but had not given any values to units variables, the /*Formulas Undefined command would list those variables shown in Figure 3.19. If you entered values for *Blender Units* sold between January, 1986, and March, 1986, the /*Formulas Time-spans command would show that values had been entered for those months (see fig. 3.20).

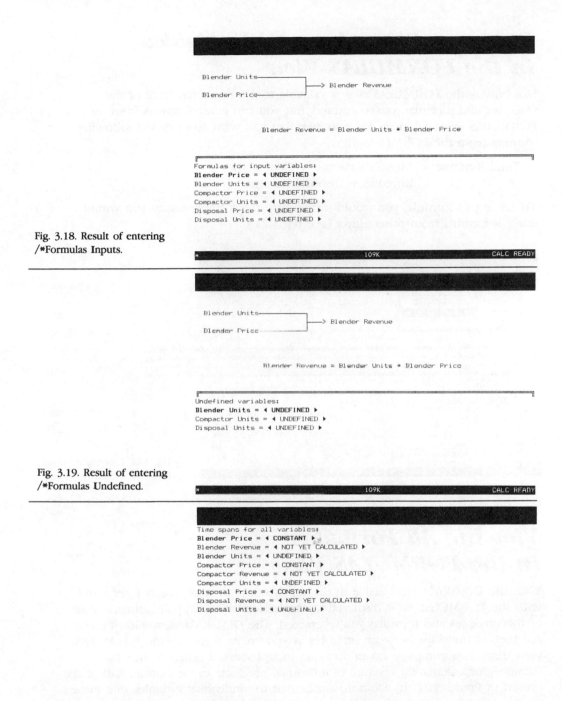

Fig. 3.18. Result of entering
/*Formulas Inputs.

Fig. 3.19. Result of entering
/*Formulas Undefined.

Fig. 3.20. Result of entering
/*Formulas Time-spans.

Entering Formulas and Variables in the FORMULAS View

Not only is the FORMULAS view a valuable tool for keeping track of the variables and formulas you've entered, but you can enter formulas from the FORMULAS view. Suppose, for example, that you want to enter the following formula from the FORMULAS view:

> Total Revenue = Blender Revenue + Compactor
> Revenue + Disposal Revenue

To enter this formula, you would simply type the formula just as you would enter a formula from other views (see fig. 3.21).

Fig. 3.21. Entering a formula from the FORMULAS view.

Viewing All Formulas in the FORMULAS View

With the DIAGRAM view active in the top window of your Javelin screen and with the FORMULAS view displayed in the bottom window, you can review all of the variables and formulas you've created. The DIAGRAM view allows you to see the relationships between variables as you create formulas; the FORMULAS view displays a complete list of formulas in alphabetical order. Notice the formulas for calculating revenue of individual products in the bottom half of the screen in figure 3.22. In addition, notice that the individual variables that make up the formulas are also listed. Use the keys listed in the "Moving Around the FORMULAS View" section to move the cursor through your formula list.

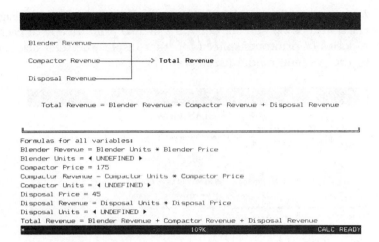

Fig. 3.22. Complete formula list.

Synchronizing the TABLE View with the DIAGRAM View

If you begin creating a Javelin model using the start-up views (DIAGRAM and TABLE) and move the cursor to the DIAGRAM view, you'll find as you enter formulas that the DIAGRAM view changes with each formula you enter. The TABLE view, however, continues to display the first formula entered even after you have entered two or more formulas.

The TABLES view will change along with the DIAGRAM view if you synchronize the two views by using Javelin's SYNC key (F3). A more dynamic way of combining Javelin views while you build a model is to combine the FORMULAS and the DIAGRAM views.

Viewing Formula Relationships through the DIAGRAM View

As you enter formulas and continue to build your model, the DIAGRAM view reminds you of the relationships among variables. For example, after you have entered the formula for *Total Revenue* on the edit line and pressed Enter, the DIAGRAM view displays the formula as in figure 3.22. If you were to scroll the cursor highlighting *Total Revenue* to the left two times, Javelin would display those variables making up the formula for *Blender Revenue* (see fig. 3.23). Then, by moving the cursor back to the right a few times, you can return to *Total Revenue*. From this position, you can access the diagrams for *Compactor*

Revenue and *Disposal Revenue*. Not only can you view a diagram of variable relationships on screen, but you can also print a copy of each screen's diagram. A series of printouts spliced together display the total diagram for all variables in the revenue model (see fig. 3.24).

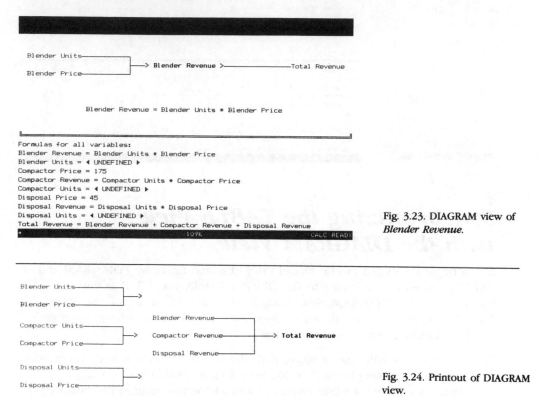

Fig. 3.23. DIAGRAM view of *Blender Revenue*.

Fig. 3.24. Printout of DIAGRAM view.

Using the TABLE View

Previous sections of this chapter emphasized using Javelin's DIAGRAM and FORMULAS views for entering formulas and variables. The TABLE view can also be used for this purpose. If, for example, the TABLE view is the current view and you want to enter a formula into your model, you do not need to return to another view. The formula for *Total Revenue* can be entered from the TABLE view in exactly the same way as in the FORMULA view (see fig. 3.25). A much more usual function of the TABLE view is entering time-series data for input variables.

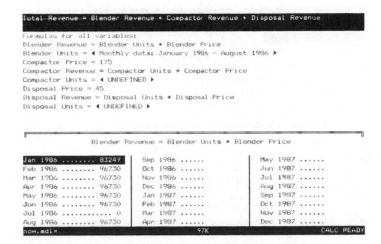

Fig. 3.25. Entering a formula from the TABLE view.

Synchronizing the TABLE View with the FORMULAS View

You'll see how powerful Javelin is when you synchronize the TABLE view with other views on a two-window screen. In one window, for example, you can use the TABLE view as your "working view" to enter formulas and data; in the second window, you can use the DIAGRAM view or FORMULAS view as your "conceptual view," helping you think through your model as you build it, by letting you review the logic of your model and relationships among variables.

The power of synchronizing the TABLE view with either the DIAGRAM or the FORMULAS view is particularly evident when contrasted with traditional spreadsheeting tools. With 1-2-3 or Symphony, you obviously have tools for entering formulas and data. But how do they help you conceptualize and check your model as you build it? They don't. That is left to you—your memory and maybe a few scratch notes.

If you synchronize (SYNC key, F3) the TABLE view with another active view such as DIAGRAM or FORMULA, the TABLE view will tell you

- whether a formula has been CALCULATED (see fig. 3.26)

- whether a variable has been assigned a CONSTANT value and will indicate that value if assigned (see fig. 3.27)

- whether a variable is undefined or what values have been entered for that variable (see fig. 3.28)

```
     Total Revenue = Blender Revenue + Compactor Revenue + Disposal Revenue
NOT YET CALCULATED
```

```
Formulas for all variables:
Blender Price = ◄ UNDEFINED ►
Blender Revenue = Blender Units * Blender Price
Blender Units = ◄ Monthly data ►
Compactor Price = ◄ UNDEFINED ►
Compactor Revenue = Compactor Units * Compactor Price
Compactor Units = ◄ UNDEFINED ►
Disposal Price = ◄ UNDEFINED ►
Disposal Revenue = Disposal Units * Disposal Price
Disposal Units = ◄ UNDEFINED ►
now.mdl*                            109K                          CALC READY
```

Fig. 3.26. TABLE view displaying
NOT YET CALCULATED message.

```
180
                              Disposal Price = 180
CONSTANT ......... 180
```

```
Formulas for all variables:
Blender Price = ◄ UNDEFINED ►
Blender Revenue = Blender Units * Blender Price
Blender Units = ◄ Monthly data ►
Compactor Price = ◄ UNDEFINED ►
Compactor Revenue = Compactor Units * Compactor Price
Compactor Units = ◄ UNDEFINED ►
Disposal Price = 180
Disposal Revenue = Disposal Units * Disposal Price
Disposal Units = ◄ UNDEFINED ►
now.mdl*                            109K                          CALC READY
```

Fig. 3.27. TABLE view displaying
a constant.

```
                       Compactor Units = ◄ UNDEFINED ►

Jan 1986 ......        Oct 1986 ......        Jul 1987 ......
Feb 1986 ......        Nov 1986 ......        Aug 1987 ......
Mar 1986 ......        Dec 1986 ......        Sep 1987 ......
Apr 1986 ......        Jan 1987 ......        Oct 1987 ......
May 1986 ......        Feb 1987 ......        Nov 1987 ......
Jun 1986 ......        Mar 1987 ......        Dec 1987 ......
Jul 1986 ......        Apr 1987 ......        Jan 1988 ......
Aug 1986 ......        May 1987 ......        Feb 1988 ......
Sep 1986 ......        Jun 1987 ......        Mar 1988 ......
```

```
Formulas for all variables:
Blender Price = ◄ UNDEFINED ►
Blender Revenue = Blender Units * Blender Price
Blender Units = ◄ Monthly data ►
Compactor Price = ◄ UNDEFINED ►
Compactor Revenue = Compactor Units * Compactor Price
Compactor Units = ◄ UNDEFINED ►
Disposal Price = 180
Disposal Revenue = Disposal Units * Disposal Price
Disposal Units = ◄ UNDEFINED ►
now.mdl*                            109K SYNC                     CALC READY
```

Fig. 3.28. TABLE view displaying
UNDEFINED message.

Entering Data in the TABLE View

How do you use the TABLE view to enter data? Let's look again at our revenue model. Figure 3.29 indicates that four formulas have been entered and six variables (price and units sold for each appliance) are undefined. You need to define the variables as calculated (total revenue), constants (price), or time-series variables (units sold over time).

Defining Constants

Constants can be entered in any of the three views discussed in this chapter—the DIAGRAM, FORMULAS, or TABLE view. And the process is identical in all three. Suppose, for example, that you need to enter constant values for the following three variables displayed in figure 3.29 in the FORMULAS view:

Blender Price
Compactor Price
Disposal Price

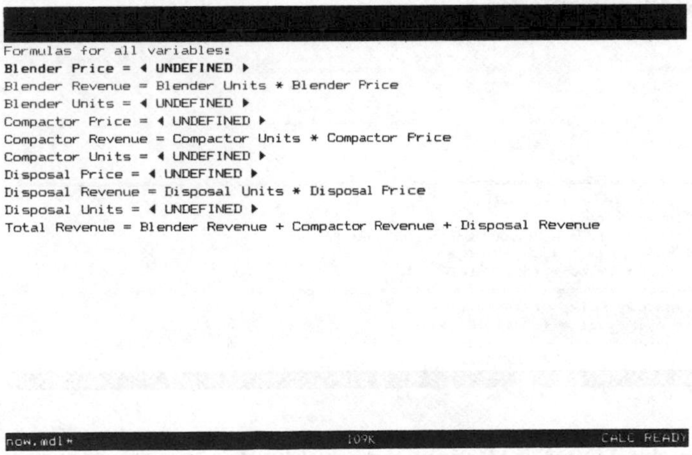

```
Formulas for all variables:
Blender Price = ◀ UNDEFINED ▶
Blender Revenue = Blender Units * Blender Price
Blender Units = ◀ UNDEFINED ▶
Compactor Price = ◀ UNDEFINED ▶
Compactor Revenue = Compactor Units * Compactor Price
Compactor Units = ◀ UNDEFINED ▶
Disposal Price = ◀ UNDEFINED ▶
Disposal Revenue = Disposal Units * Disposal Price
Disposal Units = ◀ UNDEFINED ▶
Total Revenue = Blender Revenue + Compactor Revenue + Disposal Revenue
```

Fig. 3.29. Blender, compactor, and disposal prices undefined.

In the FORMULAS view, Javelin gives you three ways to enter constant values for each of these variables:

1. Move the cursor to a variable, press the EDIT key (F2), type the equal sign, type the value of the constant, and then press Enter.

2. Use the SPELL key (Tab) to select a variable from the POSSIBILITIES list, type the value of the constant and press Enter.

3. Move the cursor to a variable, press the POINT key (F4), the value of the constant, and press Enter.

The POINT Key (F4)

The POINT key automatically enters a variable on the edit line to complete a formula, enter data, or complete a command operation. The POINT key enters the variable highlighted by the cursor in the current active view. To use the POINT key, press F4, move the cursor to the variable you want entered, and press Enter when the edit line contains the variable.

In the DIAGRAM view you could enter the constant for *Blender Price* by moving the cursor to that variable, pressing the EDIT key (F2), and typing = *17*. (Instead of moving the cursor to Blender Price, you could use the SPELL key to select the variable.) Press Enter and Javelin indicates the value you have assigned to *Blender Price* (see fig. 3.30).

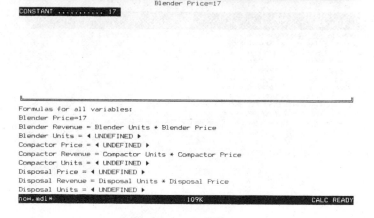

Fig. 3.30. DIAGRAM view showing a constant value for *Blender Price*.

In the FORMULAS view, you could enter the constant for *Compactor Price* by moving the cursor to that variable and pressing the POINT key (F4). When Compactor Price appears in the edit line, type = *175* and press Enter. Notice that the value for this variable is now shown as 175 (see fig. 3.31).

Finally, in the TABLE view you could enter the constant for *Disposal Price*. With the cursor in the TABLE view, enter *Disposal Price* on the edit line by using the SPELL key (Tab). You would complete the operation by typing = *44* and pressing Enter. The TABLE view will display the variable name and the constant value you have assigned to it (see fig. 3.32).

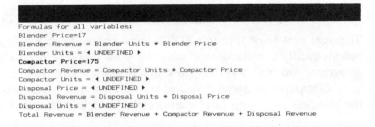

Fig. 3.31. FORMULAS view
showing a constant value for
Compactor Price.

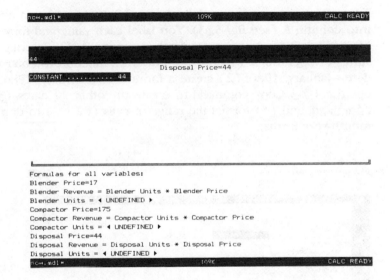

Fig. 3.32. TABLE view showing a
constant value for *Disposal Price*.

Once you've entered a constant value for each variable, Javelin will use that
value to calculate *Blender Revenue, Compactor Revenue,* and *Disposal Revenue.*
If you want to change a constant to a different value, use the EDIT key (F2).

If you want to change a variable defined as a constant to a time-series variable,
use the /Clear Variable command. Remember, however, that changing the
variable will, in turn, change any formulas affected by the variable. In other
words, clearing a variable does not clear a formula in which the variable is used,
but it does clear the original data necessary to calculate the formula.

Entering Data: Javelin versus 1-2-3

The real power of Javelin's TABLE view comes from the capability to create automatically a "time-series" table for you. If you've used a popular spreadsheet program, you will soon see how much work and time the TABLE view saves you. Compare the steps required to set up a time-series worksheet in 1-2-3 with the process of having Javelin automatically define the time series for you.

Consider the steps required to assign a series of dates to a 1-2-3 worksheet containing the Revenue model described in preceding sections. Suppose that you want to create a model that will hold 12 months of data (January, 1986–December, 1986) for the revenue from the three products—blenders, compactors, and disposals—plus the total revenue from all three.

To set up a time-series worksheet in 1-2-3, you first begin by entering labels into column A (see fig. 3.33). You label each value and formula entered in the worksheet. Second, you enter dates in range B2..N2. Entering dates requires a series of operations: (1) use 1-2-3 @DATE function to enter the beginning date—January, 1986; (2) create a formula for February, 1986, so that you can use the 1-2-3 Copy command to create the other 22 dates; (3) use the Copy command; and (4) format the range of cells (B2..N2) to display each date in a month-year format.

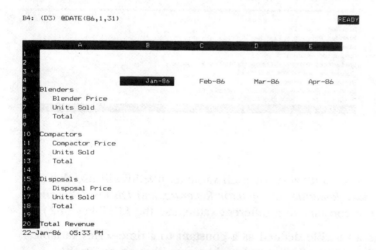

Fig. 3.33. Setting up a time-series worksheet in 1-2-3.

The time required to create a time-series worksheet in 1-2-3 is not the only disadvantage in comparison with Javelin. 1-2-3's inability to link data to a specific time period is a disadvantage also. In a 1-2-3 worksheet for blender, compactor, disposal, and total revenue, for example, the dates (January, 1986–December, 1987) act merely as labels.

Entering Data for Time-Series Variables

In our model *Blender Units*, *Compactor Units*, and *Disposal Units*, are time-series variables linked to a table of time periods. Because Javelin automatically links variables with a time span and period, the program will, in the TABLE view, automatically assign a time-period table to your undefined variables (see fig. 3.28).

If you were to synchronize the FORMULAS view with the TABLE view, using the SYNC key (F3), and then moving the cursor through each undefined variable, Javelin would display a time-period table for each. If you move the cursor to highlight Compactor Units, for example, Javelin displays a table with monthly intervals (the default period) that runs from January, 1986, to January, 1987, (the default time span) as shown in figure 3.28. You can change the period for the TABLE from monthly to daily, weekly, quarterly, yearly, using the /Define Variable command (see Chapter 4).

If you move the cursor back to the TABLE view in figure 3.28 and locate it at Jan 1986, you can change the table to display months prior to January, 1986, by pressing the Up-arrow key (↑). Similarly, moving the cursor to the last month displayed (Jan 1987) and pressing the Down-arrow key (↓) displays months after January, 1987. Javelin is capable of beginning a time-period table with January, 1904, and extending that table to December, 2082.

Entering Data into the TABLE View: Procedures and Keys

If you don't need to change any of the settings that affect the period and time span for model variables, you're ready to begin entering values in the TABLE view. To enter values for the number of blender units sold in January, February, and March, 1986, for example, complete the following steps:

1. If the TABLE view is not on screen, select /View Table to access the view. If the TABLE view is displayed but the cursor is presently in another view, press the WINDOW key (F6) to move the cursor to the TABLE view.

2. Select the variable for which you want to enter values. To select *Blender Units*, for example, use the SPELL key (Tab) to choose the variable and press Enter.

3. When the table for the variable you want is displayed, move the cursor to the time period where you want to begin entering values.

4. Type the value.

5. *To enter the same value in consecutive periods,* type the value in the first period and press Enter twice. If, for example, the blender units for February and March are both 5690, move the cursor to Feb 1986, type *5690*, and press Enter twice. The value 5690 will appear in both periods, as in figure 3.34.

```
          Blender Units = ◀ Monthly data: January 1986 - March 1986 ▶

Jan 1986 ......... 4897     Sep 1987 ......        May 1989 ......
Feb 1986 ......... 5690     Oct 1987 ......        Jun 1989 ......
Mar 1986 ......... 5690     Nov 1987 ......        Jul 1989 ......
Apr 1986 ......            Dec 1987 ......        Aug 1989 ......
May 1986 ......            Jan 1988 ......        Sep 1989 ......
Jun 1986 ......            Feb 1988 ......        Oct 1989 ......
Jul 1986 ......            Mar 1988 ......        Nov 1989 ......
Aug 1986 ......            Apr 1988 ......        Dec 1989 ......
Sep 1986 ......            May 1988 ......        Jan 1990 ......
Oct 1986 ......            Jun 1988 ......        Feb 1990 ......
Nov 1986 ......            Jul 1988 ......        Mar 1990 ......
Dec 1986 ......            Aug 1988 ......        Apr 1990 ......
Jan 1987 ......            Sep 1988 ......        May 1990 ......
Feb 1987 ......            Oct 1988 ......        Jun 1990 ......
Mar 1987 ......            Nov 1988 ......        Jul 1990 ......
Apr 1987 ......            Dec 1988 ......        Aug 1990 ......
May 1987 ......            Jan 1989 ......        Sep 1990 ......
Jun 1987 ......            Feb 1989 ......        Oct 1990 ......
Jul 1987 ......            Mar 1989 ......        Nov 1990 ......
Aug 1987 ......            Apr 1989 ......        Dec 1990 ......
now.mdl*                        109K          NUM          CALC READY
```

Fig. 3.34. Entering the same values in the TABLE view.

6. *To repeat an existing value in periods that follow,* move the cursor to the existing value and press the Insert key (Ins). Continuing to press Ins will continue to insert values in the period below the cursor and move other values forward.

7. *To delete a value,* move the cursor to the value and press the Delete key (Del). Continuing to press Del will delete consecutive values as well as the original value where the cursor is positioned.

Whenever you skip a value in the table, Javelin will automatically enter #NA or 0, depending on a setting you can change for each variable. The default setting is #NA. To change from the #NA setting to 0, select /Define Variable and move the cursor to the Definition box. Next, move the cursor to the Fill with 0's setting, and press Enter (see fig. 3.35).

Using /Define Settings and /Define Variable

In Javelin you control how the variables and data you enter are calculated and displayed using the /Define Settings and /Define Variable commands. If you don't use these commands, Javelin assumes all variables are controlled by default settings.

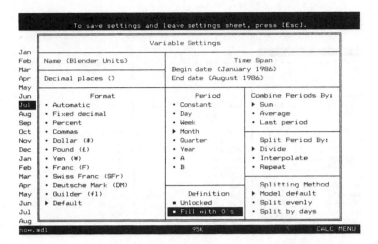

Fig. 3.35. Using the Variable settings sheet to change the #NA setting to 0.

To make full use of Javelin's powerful capabilities, however, you'll need to understand these commands and the settings sheets they affect. The Model settings sheet (accessed by the /Define Settings command) contains settings for the whole model. All variables you enter take on these settings unless you define a specific setting for an individual variable. By comparison, the Variable settings sheet (accessed with the /Define Variable command) affects specific variables. When you use the /Define Variable command, you override the Model Settings for a specific variable.

Setting Formats with /Define Settings and /Define Variable

In what form do you want the results of your Javelin calculations to appear? Do you want *Total Revenue* expressed in Yen? How many decimal places do you want displayed? Javelin lets you choose from a variety of formats for displaying numeric values. Note that you can also set formats that apply only to your worksheets.

The format options available with /Define Settings and /Define Variable are the same:

Automatic: This format is the default format setting displaying values with as many decimals places as needed (see fig. 3.36).

Fixed Decimal: This format lets you control the number of places to the right of the decimal point. You can change the number of places in

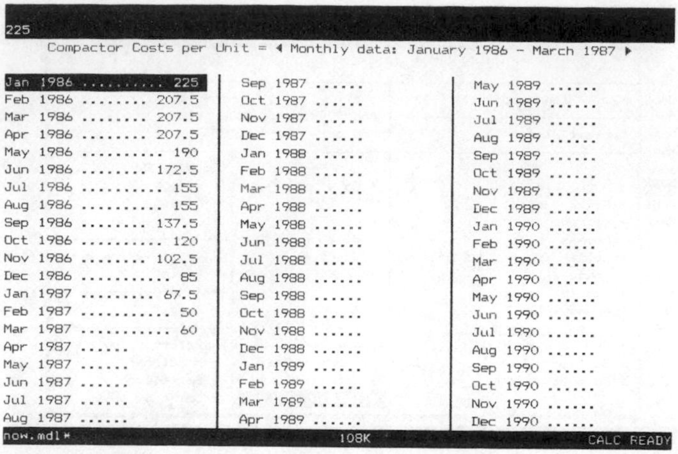

```
225
     Compactor Costs per Unit = ◄ Monthly data: January 1986 - March 1987 ►

Jan 1986 .......... 225     Sep 1987 ......        May 1989 ......
Feb 1986 ........ 207.5     Oct 1987 ......        Jun 1989 ......
Mar 1986 ........ 207.5     Nov 1987 ......        Jul 1989 ......
Apr 1986 ........ 207.5     Dec 1987 ......        Aug 1989 ......
May 1986 .......... 190     Jan 1988 ......        Sep 1989 ......
Jun 1986 ........ 172.5     Feb 1988 ......        Oct 1989 ......
Jul 1986 .......... 155     Mar 1988 ......        Nov 1989 ......
Aug 1986 .......... 155     Apr 1988 ......        Dec 1989 ......
Sep 1986 ........ 137.5     May 1988 ......        Jan 1990 ......
Oct 1986 .......... 120     Jun 1988 ......        Feb 1990 ......
Nov 1986 ........ 102.5     Jul 1988 ......        Mar 1990 ......
Dec 1986 ........... 85     Aug 1988 ......        Apr 1990 ......
Jan 1987 ......... 67.5     Sep 1988 ......        May 1990 ......
Feb 1987 ........... 50     Oct 1988 ......        Jun 1990 ......
Mar 1987 ........... 60     Nov 1988 ......        Jul 1990 ......
Apr 1987 ......            Dec 1988 ......        Aug 1990 ......
May 1987 ......            Jan 1989 ......        Sep 1990 ......
Jun 1987 ......            Feb 1989 ......        Oct 1990 ......
Jul 1987 ......            Mar 1989 ......        Nov 1990 ......
Aug 1987 ......            Apr 1989 ......        Dec 1990 ......
now.mdl *                        108K                       CALC READY
```

Fig. 3.36. Values displayed in Automatic format.

the Decimal places setting by selecting Format, highlighting the setting, and pressing Enter.

Percent: This format is used to display percentages with the number of decimal places controlled by you. The values displayed are the result of what you enter, multiplied by 100 and followed by a percent sign (see fig. 3.37).

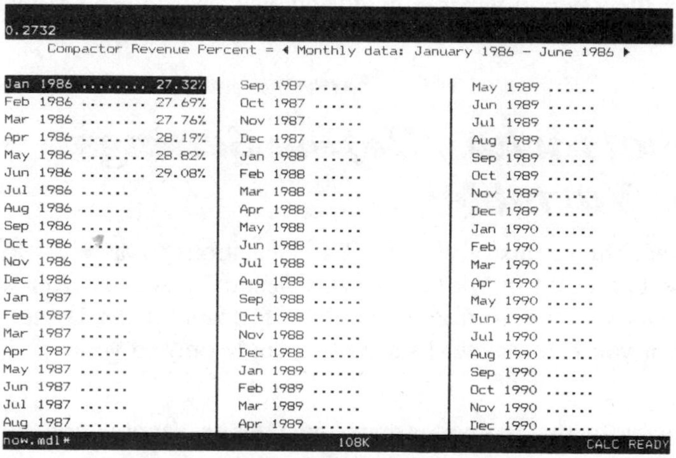

```
0.2732
     Compactor Revenue Percent = ◄ Monthly data: January 1986 - June 1986 ►

Jan 1986 ........ 27.32%     Sep 1987 ......       May 1989 ......
Feb 1986 ........ 27.69%     Oct 1987 ......       Jun 1989 ......
Mar 1986 ........ 27.76%     Nov 1987 ......       Jul 1989 ......
Apr 1986 ........ 28.19%     Dec 1987 ......       Aug 1989 ......
May 1986 ........ 28.82%     Jan 1988 ......       Sep 1989 ......
Jun 1986 ........ 29.08%     Feb 1988 ......       Oct 1989 ......
Jul 1986 ......             Mar 1988 ......       Nov 1989 ......
Aug 1986 ......             Apr 1988 ......       Dec 1989 ......
Sep 1986 ......             May 1988 ......       Jan 1990 ......
Oct 1986 ......            Jun 1988 ......       Feb 1990 ......
Nov 1986 ......             Jul 1988 ......       Mar 1990 ......
Dec 1986 ......             Aug 1988 ......       Apr 1990 ......
Jan 1987 ......             Sep 1988 ......       May 1990 ......
Feb 1987 ......             Oct 1988 ......       Jun 1990 ......
Mar 1987 ......             Nov 1988 ......       Jul 1990 ......
Apr 1987 ......             Dec 1988 ......       Aug 1990 ......
May 1987 ......             Jan 1989 ......       Sep 1990 ......
Jun 1987 ......             Feb 1989 ......       Oct 1990 ......
Jul 1987 ......             Mar 1989 ......       Nov 1990 ......
Aug 1987 ......             Apr 1989 ......       Dec 1990 ......
now.mdl *                        108K                       CALC READY
```

Fig. 3.37. Values displayed in Percent format.

Commas: The commas format displays commas separating hundreds from thousands, hundreds of thousands from millions, etc.

Currency formats: Javelin makes seven international currency formats available: Dollar, Pound, Yen, Franc, Swiss Franc, Deutsche Mark, and Guilder (see fig. 3.38).

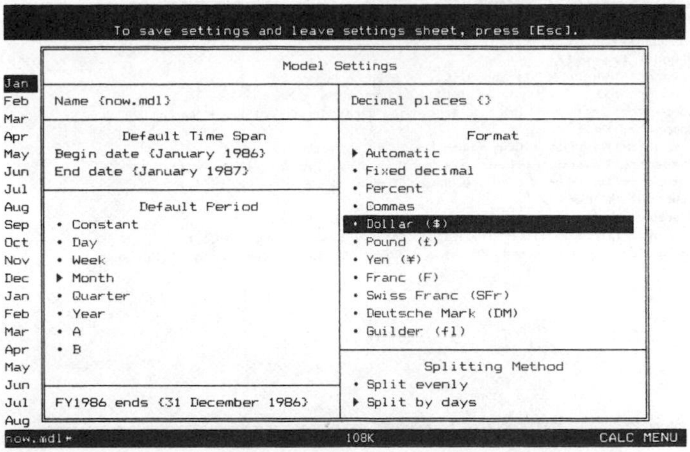

Fig. 3.38. Currency format options.

To change the format setting with either /Define Settings or /Define Variable, move the cursor to the desired setting and press Enter. Javelin automatically assigns two decimal places whenever you select *Fixed Decimal*, *Percent*, *Commas*, or the currency formats, but you can change that by moving the cursor to the Decimal places box in /Define Settings or /Define Variable, typing the number of decimal places you want displayed, and pressing Enter.

Setting a Format for the Revenue Model

The list of variables in figure 3.39 indicates that all revenue and price variables require currency formats, while unit variables can use either the Automatic or Fixed options. At this point in your model building, therefore, Dollar format would be appropriate for the model. To enter Dollar as the model format, select /Define Settings, move the cursor to Dollar, and press Enter. If you want to keep the default decimal place setting (2), press Esc to enter your new format; if you want to change the number of decimal places (to 0, for example), move the cursor to Decimal places, type *0*, press Enter, and then press Esc.

Using the NOTES View

Javelin's NOTES view lets you attach text to any variable in your model. When you use the NOTES view, the text you enter remains linked with a specific variable so that you can display the note with other views of the variable. The NOTES view is an extremely useful tool for:

```
Formulas for all variables:
Blender Price=17
Blender Revenue = Blender Units * Blender Price
Blender Units = ◀ Monthly data: January 1986 - March 1986 ▶
Compactor Costs per Unit = ◀ Monthly data: January 1986 - March 1987 ▶
Compactor Price=175
Compactor Revenue = Compactor Units * Compactor Price
Compactor Revenue Percent = ◀ Monthly data: January 1986 - June 1986 ▶
Compactor Units = ◀ Monthly data: January 1986 - March 1986 ▶
Disposal Price=44
Disposal Revenue = Disposal Units * Disposal Price
Disposal Units = ◀ Monthly data: January 1986 - March 1986 ▶
Total Revenue = Blender Revenue + Compactor Revenue + Disposal Revenue
```

```
now.mdl*                          108K                    CALC READY
```

Fig. 3.39. Formulas list for Revenue model.

- Documenting the logic and assumptions of your Javelin model and individual variables

- Documenting the source for data in your model

- Documenting the macros you create in your model

- Providing special instructions to others using the model

- Entering text that you will want to transfer to another word-processing program and use in a report

The following examples illustrate some of these uses.

Documenting model logic and assumptions is the most important function of the NOTES view. Suppose, for example, that in the product revenue model used in this chapter, product prices are the average of several different prices: those calculated from a discount schedule to distributors, those calculated from a discount schedule to retailers, and those that are direct mail prices to customers. Suppose further that the average price per product is calculated in another Javelin model. Given these circumstances, you can use Javelin's NOTES view to document the price figure for each product (see fig. 3.40).

To attach a NOTES view to *Blender Price*, for example, you begin by selecting the /View Notes command. Javelin then displays a prompt asking for the variable name for the NOTES view. Depending on the view that is current, you can select the variable for your note in one of three ways:

1. If you are in the TABLE or CHART view of the variable to which you want to attach a note, press Enter.

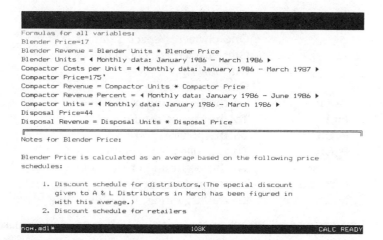

```
Formulas for all variables:
Blender Price=17
Blender Revenue = Blender Units * Blender Price
Blender Units = ◄ Monthly data: January 1986 - March 1986 ►
Compactor Costs per Unit = ◄ Monthly data: January 1986 - March 1987 ►
Compactor Price=175'
Compactor Revenue = Compactor Units * Compactor Price
Compactor Revenue Percent = ◄ Monthly data: January 1986 - June 1986 ►
Compactor Units = ◄ Monthly data: January 1986 - March 1986 ►
Disposal Price=44
Disposal Revenue = Disposal Units * Disposal Price

Notes for Blender Price:

Blender Price is calculated as an average based on the following price
schedules:

        1. Discount schedule for distributors.(The special discount
           given to A & L Distributors in March has been figured in
           with this average.)
        2. Discount schedule for retailers
```

Fig. 3.40. NOTES view for
Blender Price.

`now.mdl *`   `103K`   `CALC READY`

2. If you are in the FORMULAS, DIAGRAM, or WORKSHEET view, and the cursor is highlighting the variable to which you want to attach a note, press Enter at the prompt.

3. Use the SPELL key (Tab) to select the variable.

After you've made the NOTES view the current view, you can use the GO TO key (F5) to access NOTES views of other variables.

The GO TO Key (F5)

Use the GO TO key to move the cursor quickly to a variable or to a building block (See Chapters 6 and 7 for discussions of building blocks.) To move quickly to a note in the NOTES view, for example, press the GO TO key, enter the variable, and press Enter.

After you have selected the NOTES view for the variable, you can type the text you want to enter. Javelin's NOTES view is limited in cursor movement and editing capabilities, but a "survival" set of functions is available. First, the NOTES view automatically wraps text when the cursor reaches the 80-character limit of your screen. Second, you can delete single characters with the Del or Bksp key, but editing capabilities are limited to these functions only. Third, you can move the cursor in a NOTES view by using the following keys:

Key	Cursor Movement
→	One character/space right
←	One character/space left
↑	One line up
↓	One line down
Home	To the beginning of the line
End	To the end of the line
PgUp	To the previous screen
PgDn	To the following screen
Ctrl-Home	To the beginning of the note
Ctrl-End	To the end of the note
Enter	To the beginning of the next line

You can use all the characters on the alphanumeric keyboard, with the exception of the slash key (/), the same way you use the keys with a word-processing program. When you press the slash key (/), the Javelin main menu is displayed. If you need to use the slash in text in the NOTES view, press Ctrl-Q and then press the slash key (/).

Using the NOTES View for Special Purposes

As indicated in the list at the beginning of the discussion of the NOTES view, this view is not only a valuable tool for documenting models, variables, or macros, but also a valuable tool for providing instructions to other users of your Javelin models. By using a macro or a series of macros, you can develop special instruction screens with the NOTES view to help inexperienced users enter data into your model, calculate values, or produce reports.

You can also use the NOTES view to gather important information that you may want to include in a text report. You can, for example, use the NOTES view to record summaries of your analyses and conclusions from model data. Rather than attach the notes to one of the variables of your model, you can create a "dummy" variable used solely for holding such text.

Transferring NOTES Text to Other Programs

You can transfer text you have entered through the NOTES view to another word-processing program by saving the text to a print file.

To create a print file of data in any Javelin view, follow these steps:

1. Select the /Define Printer command.

2. When the /Define Printer settings sheet appears, move the cursor to New file in the *Output Device* box and press Enter.

3. Press Esc to save the setting.

4. Select the /Print Current view command and press Enter.

5. Type a file name when the Filename prompt appears.

(Do not enter an extension; Javelin automatically attaches a .PRN extension.)

6. Press Enter to save the print file.

Once saved as a print file, the text from your NOTES view can be read by any word-processing program or text editor capable of reading ASCII text files. Your word-processing program may require that you use a translation utility before the word processor can read the file as a document file.

No matter how you use Javelin's NOTES view, remember that it is limited in its capabilities. You'll find that a great amount of text entered through the NOTES view will use memory that would be better reserved for model formulas and data. If you try to use the NOTES view as a word processor, you'll quickly learn how cumbersome this view can be. If you limit the applications to those recommended in this section, however, you'll find the NOTES view a valuable tool.

Conclusion

Javelin is one of the most sophisticated tools available for creating models for business analysis. Unlike popular spreadsheet programs, Javelin's DIAGRAM, FORMULAS, TABLE, and NOTES views enable you to check the logic of your model and to see relationships between formulas and variables. But not only does Javelin help you check your model as you build it, Javelin makes entering formulas and data easier than any spreadsheet program available. In addition, Javelin's ability to keep track of the variables you enter for your model and create time-period tables for every time-series variable is unsurpassed by any business analysis program.

4

How Javelin
Handles Time

Time in Javelin, although one of its more powerful features, is also one of its more complex. Because Javelin understands the time-series nature of your data, the program can both display data connected to time and keep track of the relationship between data and time. You can, for example, enter sales information monthly and product costs biweekly, and then easily create formulas that mix the two. Or you can create worksheets that display data in the original time period—months, for example—ask for year-end totals, and mix quarterly totals with monthly and year-end values.

The following general introduction to the ways Javelin handles time will help you learn to use the program effectively. Specific examples illustrating Javelin's capabilities for handling time can be found in Chapters 5, 8, and 9.

Commands Emphasized in this Chapter

/Define Settings
/Define Variable
/Define Time period

Time Period and Time Span

Unless you define a variable as a constant, Javelin attaches a *time period* and *time span* to the variables you define. Time period is the particular unit of time assigned to your model and variable: daily, weekly, monthly, quarterly, yearly, or one of two custom periods. Time span is the range of time for which the variable has values. What time period and time span are assigned depend on the

123

settings in Javelin's Model and Variable settings sheets, discussed subsequently in this chapter. Data entered, for example, for the variable *Blender Units* in figure 4.1 is defined in terms of:

- time period (monthly)

- time span (January, 1986, through December, 1986)

```
6456
                Blender Units = ◀ Monthly data: January 1986 - December 1986 ▶

Jan 1986 ..... 6,456.00     Sep 1987 ......        May 1989 ......
Feb 1986 ..... 6,663.00     Oct 1987 ......        Jun 1989 ......
Mar 1986 ..... 5,690.00     Nov 1987 ......        Jul 1989 ......
Apr 1986 ..... 9,634.00     Dec 1987 ......        Aug 1989 ......
May 1986 ..... 7,456.00     Jan 1988 ......        Sep 1989 ......
Jun 1986 ..... 9,554.00     Feb 1988 ......        Oct 1989 ......
Jul 1986 ..... 9,457.00     Mar 1988 ......        Nov 1989 ......
Aug 1986 ..... 7,451.00     Apr 1988 ......        Dec 1989 ......
Sep 1986 ..... 8,427.00     May 1988 ......        Jan 1990 ......
Oct 1986 ..... 9,152.00     Jun 1988 ......        Feb 1990 ......
Nov 1986 ..... 9,568.00     Jul 1988 ......        Mar 1990 ......
Dec 1986 .... 10,089.00     Aug 1988 ......        Apr 1990 ......
Jan 1987 ......             Sep 1988 ......        May 1990 ......
Feb 1987 ......             Oct 1988 ......        Jun 1990 ......
Mar 1987 ......             Nov 1988 ......        Jul 1990 ......
Apr 1987 ......             Dec 1988 ......        Aug 1990 ......
May 1987 ......             Jan 1989 ......        Sep 1990 ......
Jun 1987 ......             Feb 1989 ......        Oct 1990 ......
Jul 1987 ......             Mar 1989 ......        Nov 1990 ......
Aug 1987 ......             Apr 1989 ......        Dec 1990 ......
newyork.mdl                          82K                          READY
```

Fig. 4.1. A time-series input variable displayed in the TABLE view.

Javelin lets you set the time period and time span for an entire model or for each variable. For example, if you change the model's time period from *Month* to *Quarter*, Javelin assumes that undefined variables will have a quarterly period. You can also change your model's time span. Javelin is capable of understanding time spans from January, 1904, to December, 2082. If you look at a TABLE view for any time-series variable set to the period *Month*, you can scroll back to January, 1904, or forward to December, 2082 (see fig. 4.2).

Let's look at a few examples illustrating the capabilities provided through settings and functions related to time. In Chapter 3, you were introduced to two of the commands; now we introduce one more, exploring specific options available through all three commands. In Javelin, the following commands affect time:

/Define Settings
(Settings controlling the whole model)

/Define Variable
(Settings controlling individual variables)

/Define Time period
(Used for creating customized time periods)

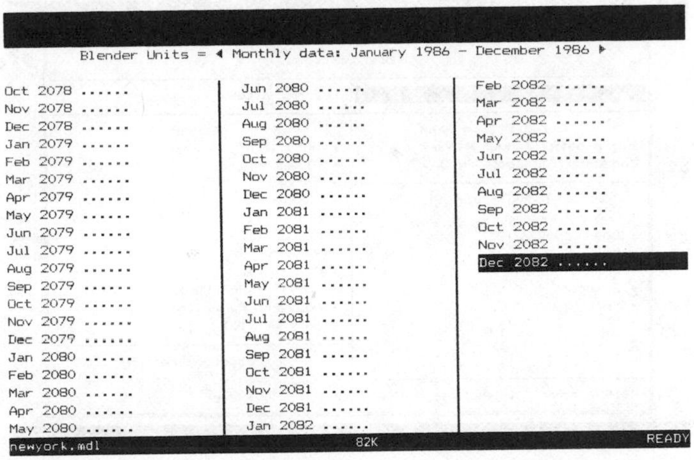

Fig. 4.2. Javelin's TABLE view can display time periods extending to December, 2082.

In addition, we will look at Javelin time functions—BEGIN, END, RANGE, and PREVIOUS—that enable you to control how Javelin uses time to calculate a formula.

Changing Time in the Whole Model (/Define Settings)

Three Model settings available through the /Define Settings command (see fig. 4.3) affect time for the whole model:

1. the Default Time Span

2. the Default Period

3. the Fiscal Year (FY)

Javelin supplies a default time span for the whole model based on the date in the computer's operating system. The default time span begins with the current month and ends exactly 12 months later. In our example, Javelin determined the begin date from the current month and year in DOS. The Model settings sheet in figure 4.3 shows January, 1986, as the *begin date* and January, 1987, as the *end date*, based on the DOS date January 22, 1986. (All examples in this chapter are based on the DOS date of January 22, 1986.)

As with the *Default Time Span* setting, Javelin provides a default period—the month. This default setting determines the period used for undefined time-series variables. Notice, for example, that the table in figure 4.4 is based on the

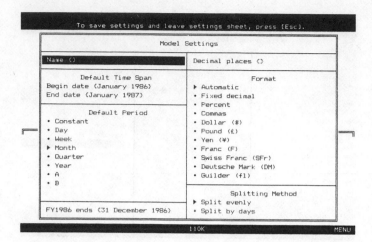

Fig. 4.3. Model settings sheet.

Default Time Span and *Default Period* settings in figure 4.3; the table, therefore, is incremented in months beginning with January, 1986. You can change the *Default Period* by using one of the formats for defining time periods listed in table 4.1

```
                      Blender Units = ◄ UNDEFINED ►

Jan 1986 ......      Sep 1987 ......      May 1989 ......
Feb 1986 ......      Oct 1987 ......      Jun 1989 ......
Mar 1986 ......      Nov 1987 ......      Jul 1989 ......
Apr 1986 ......      Dec 1987 ......      Aug 1989 ......
May 1986 ......      Jan 1988 ......      Sep 1989 ......
Jun 1986 ......      Feb 1988 ......      Oct 1989 ......
Jul 1986 ......      Mar 1988 ......      Nov 1989 ......
Aug 1986 ......      Apr 1988 ......      Dec 1989 ......
Sep 1986 ......      May 1988 ......      Jan 1990 ......
Oct 1986 ......      Jun 1988 ......      Feb 1990 ......
Nov 1986 ......      Jul 1988 ......      Mar 1990 ......
Dec 1986 ......      Aug 1988 ......      Apr 1990 ......
Jan 1987 ......      Sep 1988 ......      May 1990 ......
Feb 1987 ......      Oct 1988 ......      Jun 1990 ......
Mar 1987 ......      Nov 1988 ......      Jul 1990 ......
Apr 1987 ......      Dec 1988 ......      Aug 1990 ......
May 1987 ......      Jan 1989 ......      Sep 1990 ......
Jun 1987 ......      Feb 1989 ......      Oct 1990 ......
Jul 1987 ......      Mar 1989 ......      Nov 1990 ......
Aug 1987 ......      Apr 1989 ......      Dec 1990 ......
#                          110K                        READY
```

Fig. 4.4. TABLE view showing defaults for time span and period.

One other setting important to mention here is the *fiscal year* (FY1986) setting in the lower left box in the settings sheet (see fig. 4.3). Javelin's default setting is December for the current year (the year indicated by the *Begin date* setting and based on the current date in DOS).

Unless you change the fiscal year setting, all calculations and time periods are based on the calendar year. Suppose, for example, that you directed Javelin to

---

Table 4.1
Formats for Defining Time Periods

Note: When you enter time periods, use one of the following formats. You can mix uppercase and lowercase letters when entering time periods. Javelin will read both.

Time period	*Format*
For Days:	1 January 1986
	1 Jan 1986
	1ja86 (for dates between 1950 and 2049)
For Weeks:	1 week 1986
	1 w 1986
	1w86 (for dates between 1950 and 2049)
For Months:	January 1986
	Jan 1986
	ja86 (for dates between 1950-2049)
For Quarters:	1 quarter 1986
	1 Q 1986
	1 Q86 (for 1950-2049)
For Years:	1986
	86 (for dates between 1950 and 2049)
For custom time periods:	1 A Jan 1986 (when A is defined in terms of months)
	1 AJa86 (for 1950-2049)
	1 A (when A is not based on standard periods)

---

create a table for *Disposal Units* divided into quarters rather than months (see fig. 4.5). Based on the default setting for the fiscal year, Javelin interprets Quarter 1 as January, February, March, 1986; Quarter 2 as April, May, June, 1986, and so on.

You could direct Javelin to base quarters on a fiscal year beginning in July and ending in June of the following year. If, for example, you were to change the FY1986 setting in figure 4.3 from 31 December 1986 to 30 June 1986, Javelin would display a table divided into quarters for *Disposal Units* beginning with 3 Q 1986, the current quarter based on the DOS date January 22, 1986 (see fig. 4.6). Changing fiscal year end to June 30, 1986, tells Javelin that January, February, and March are the third quarter of the fiscal year, that April, May, and June are the fourth quarter, and so on.

```
                    Disposal Units = ◀ Quarterly data ▶
  1 Q 1986 ......        1 Q 1991 ......        1 Q 1996 ......
  2 Q 1986 ......        2 Q 1991 ......        2 Q 1996 ......
  3 Q 1986 ......        3 Q 1991 ......        3 Q 1996 ......
  4 Q 1986 ......        4 Q 1991 ......        4 Q 1996 ......
  1 Q 1987 ......        1 Q 1992 ......        1 Q 1997 ......
  2 Q 1987 ......        2 Q 1992 ......        2 Q 1997 ......
  3 Q 1987 ......        3 Q 1992 ......        3 Q 1997 ......
  4 Q 1987 ......        4 Q 1992 ......        4 Q 1997 ......
  1 Q 1988 ......        1 Q 1993 ......        1 Q 1998 ......
  2 Q 1988 ......        2 Q 1993 ......        2 Q 1998 ......
  3 Q 1988 ......        3 Q 1993 ......        3 Q 1998 ......
  4 Q 1988 ......        4 Q 1993 ......        4 Q 1998 ......
  1 Q 1989 ......        1 Q 1994 ......        1 Q 1999 ......
  2 Q 1989 ......        2 Q 1994 ......        2 Q 1999 ......
  3 Q 1989 ......        3 Q 1994 ......        3 Q 1999 ......
  4 Q 1989 ......        4 Q 1994 ......        4 Q 1999 ......
  1 Q 1990 ......        1 Q 1995 ......        1 Q 2000 ......
  2 Q 1990 ......        2 Q 1995 ......        2 Q 2000 ......
  3 Q 1990 ......        3 Q 1995 ......        3 Q 2000 ......
  4 Q 1990 ......        4 Q 1995 ......        4 Q 2000 ......
  *                              110K                      CALC READY
```

Fig. 4.5. TABLE view of *Disposal Units* showing quarterly time periods and the default fiscal year.

```
                    Disposal Units = ◀ Quarterly data ▶
  3 Q 1986 ......        3 Q 1991 ......        3 Q 1996 ......
  4 Q 1986 ......        4 Q 1991 ......        4 Q 1996 ......
  1 Q 1987 ......        1 Q 1992 ......        1 Q 1997 ......
  2 Q 1987 ......        2 Q 1992 ......        2 Q 1997 ......
  3 Q 1987 ......        3 Q 1992 ......        3 Q 1997 ......
  4 Q 1987 ......        4 Q 1992 ......        4 Q 1997 ......
  1 Q 1988 ......        1 Q 1993 ......        1 Q 1998 ......
  2 Q 1988 ......        2 Q 1993 ......        2 Q 1998 ......
  3 Q 1988 ......        3 Q 1993 ......        3 Q 1998 ......
  4 Q 1988 ......        4 Q 1993 ......        4 Q 1998 ......
  1 Q 1989 ......        1 Q 1994 ......        1 Q 1999 ......
  2 Q 1989 ......        2 Q 1994 ......        2 Q 1999 ......
  3 Q 1989 ......        3 Q 1994 ......        3 Q 1999 ......
  4 Q 1989 ......        4 Q 1994 ......        4 Q 1999 ......
  1 Q 1990 ......        1 Q 1995 ......        1 Q 2000 ......
  2 Q 1990 ......        2 Q 1995 ......        2 Q 2000 ......
  3 Q 1990 ......        3 Q 1995 ......        3 Q 2000 ......
  4 Q 1990 ......        4 Q 1995 ......        4 Q 2000 ......
  1 Q 1991 ......        1 Q 1996 ......        1 Q 2001 ......
  2 Q 1991 ......        2 Q 1996 ......        2 Q 2001 ......
  *                              110K                      CALC READY
```

Fig. 4.6. TABLE view of *Disposal Units* showing start of fiscal year in July.

Changing Time for Individual Variables (/Define Variable)

Unlike the Model settings sheet, the Variable settings sheet, accessed with the /**Define** Variable command, affects only a specific variable. Changes to a particular variable made with the Variable settings sheet take precedence over the settings from the Model settings sheet.

If a variable in your model uses a time period different from the default period, use /**Define** Variable to make the change on the Variable settings sheet. Suppose, for example, that instead of tracking revenue by the month for blenders, you want to track revenue by the week to analyze the effects on weekly sales of a special marketing promotion. How can you create a table with weeks as the period rather than months?

To assign the period *Week* to *Blender Units*, select the /**D**efine Variable command, move the cursor to Week in the Period box, press Enter, then press Esc to complete the setting (see fig. 4.7). To see how Javelin has changed the setting, look at *Blender Units* through the TABLE view (/**V**iew **T**able). The table for *Blender Units* data is tabulated weekly (see fig. 4.8). Notice that the formula for *Blender Revenue* containing the variable *Blender Units*, now calculates in weeks (see fig. 4.9). Calculated variables take the period of the time-series variables that make up the formula. If you need to combine variables with different time periods, use Javelin's time functions, described later in the "Converting Time Periods" section.

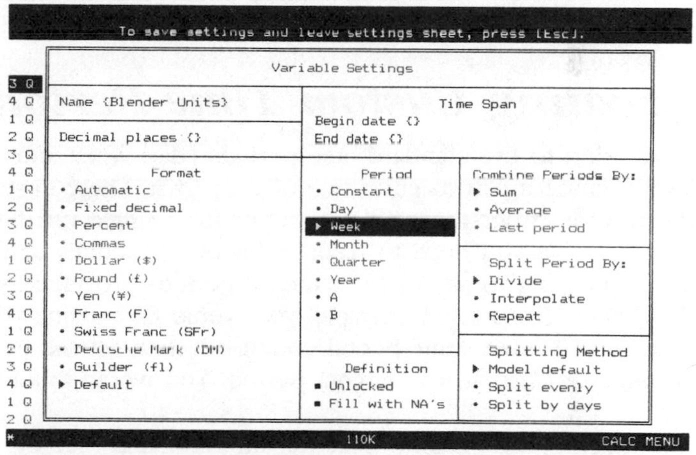

Fig. 4.7. Assigning a weekly time period to the *Blender Units* variable.

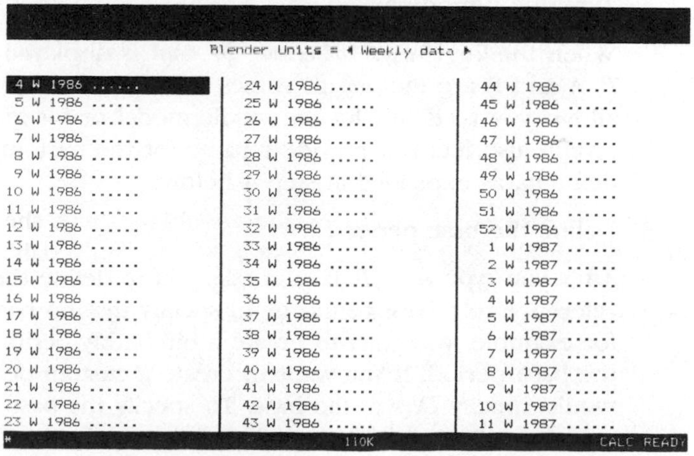

Fig. 4.8. TABLE view now showing weekly time period for *Blender Units*.

```
                    Blender Revenue = Blender Units * Blender Price

  4 W 1986 ......      24 W 1986 ......      44 W 1986 ......
  5 W 1986 ......      25 W 1986 ......      45 W 1986 ......
  6 W 1986 ......      26 W 1986 ......      46 W 1986 ......
  7 W 1986 ......      27 W 1986 ......      47 W 1986 ......
  8 W 1986 ......      28 W 1986 ......      48 W 1986 ......
  9 W 1986 ......      29 W 1986 ......      49 W 1986 ......
 10 W 1986 ......      30 W 1986 ......      50 W 1986 ......
 11 W 1986 ......      31 W 1986 ......      51 W 1986 ......
 12 W 1986 ......      32 W 1986 ......      52 W 1986 ......
 13 W 1986 ......      33 W 1986 ......       1 W 1987 ......
 14 W 1986 ......      34 W 1986 ......       2 W 1987 ......
 15 W 1986 ......      35 W 1986 ......       3 W 1987 ......
 16 W 1986 ......      36 W 1986 ......       4 W 1987 ......
 17 W 1986 ......      37 W 1986 ......       5 W 1987 ......
 18 W 1986 ......      38 W 1986 ......       6 W 1987 ......
 19 W 1986 ......      39 W 1986 ......       7 W 1987 ......
 20 W 1986 ......      40 W 1986 ......       8 W 1987 ......
 21 W 1986 ......      41 W 1986 ......       9 W 1987 ......
 22 W 1986 ......      42 W 1986 ......      10 W 1987 ......
 23 W 1986 ......      43 W 1986 ......      11 W 1987 ......
                                109K                           READY
```

Fig. 4.9. *Blender Revenue* shows effect of changing *Blender Units* to a weekly time period.

Creating Custom Time Periods

In addition to five standard time periods (day, week, month, quarter, and year), Javelin enables you to enter two of your own. These custom periods can be entered for either the whole model or for a single variable. Suppose, for example, that you need to report sales of a product's units bimonthly rather than according to any of the standard periods provided by Javelin. Using *Compactor Units* as an example, you would first define your custom period using the /**D**efine **T**ime period command, then set the period setting for *Compactor Units* to the custom period. You would follow these steps:

1. Select the /**D**efine **T**ime period command (see fig. 4.10).

2. Type the period name.

   When the `Custom period name:` prompt is displayed, enter either *A* or *B*. A and B are the default names for the two custom periods Javelin allows you to define for the whole model or for individual variables. Javelin also lets you provide a name for the custom period you're defining, as explained in step 4 below.

3. Define the base period.

   After you type *A* or *B*, Javelin asks you to define the period in reference to a base period or to specify that no base period applies. If, for example, you want to create a bimonthly period, specify *Month* as the base period. If you want to create a custom period of hours, you would specify *Day* as the base. To specify the base period, move the cursor to the appropriate period and press Enter.

4. Name your custom period, if you don't want to use the A or B default names.

   To assign a name, move the cursor to the Name setting as shown in figure 4.11, type the name, and press Enter. Once you have assigned a name to the custom period, the name is displayed in the Model and Variable settings sheets (see figs. 4.12 and 4.13). When you have entered both name and base period, press Esc.

5. Specify how many custom periods make up each base period.

   As soon as you name the custom time period and press Enter, Javelin displays a table where you can define the relationship between the custom period and base period, as in figure 4.14. You define the relationship by entering the number of custom periods making up each base period. To define bimonthly periods, for example, you would simply enter 2 for each month. (Type 2 and press Enter repeatedly to enter 2 for each month.)

6. Use the custom period as the model default or with individual variables.

   If you create a custom period and want to use it for the whole model, select /Define Settings, move the cursor to the custom period indicator (A, B, or the name you've defined), press Enter, and press Esc. If you want to use a custom time period with a variable, select /Define Variable, enter the variable name, move the cursor to the custom period indicator, press Enter, and press Esc.

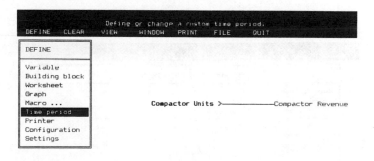

Fig. 4.10. Using the /Define Time period command to create a custom time period for *Compactor Units*.

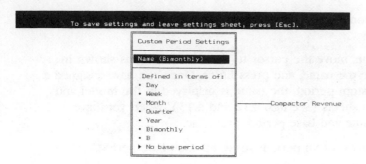

```
To save settings and leave settings sheet, press [Esc].

        Custom Period Settings

    Name (Bimonthly)

      Defined in terms of:
      • Day
      • Week
      • Month                              ─────Compactor Revenue
      • Quarter
      • Year
      • Bimonthly
      • B
    ► No base period


Compactor Units = ◄ Monthly data: January 1986 - June 1986 ►

█      109K                        CALC READY
```

Fig. 4.11. Naming the new time period *Bimonthly*.

```
To save settings and leave settings sheet, press [Esc].

                Model Settings

 Name ()                    Decimal places ()

      Default Time Span                  Format
 Begin date (January 1986)   ► Automatic
 End date (January 1987)     • Fixed decimal
                             • Percent                       ue
        Default Period       • Commas
 • Constant                  • Dollar ($)
 • Day                       • Pound (£)
 • Week                      • Yen (¥)
 ► Month                     • Franc (F)
 • Quarter                   • Swiss Franc (SFr)
 • Year                      • Deutsche Mark (DM)
 • Bimonthly                 • Guilder (fl)
 • B
                                  Splitting Method
                             ► Split evenly
 FY1986 ends (31 December 1986)  • Split by days

█      109K                        CALC MENU
```

Fig. 4.12. Custom time period *Bimonthly* shown on the Model settings sheet.

```
To save settings and leave settings sheet, press [Esc].

                Variable Settings

 Name (Compactor Units)              Time Span
                           Begin date (January 1986)
 Decimal places ()         End date (June 1986)

      Format              Period          Combine Periods By:
 • Automatic          • Constant          ► Sum            ue
 • Fixed decimal      • Day               • Average
 • Percent            • Week              • Last period
 • Commas             ► Month
 • Dollar ($)         • Quarter           Split Period By:
 • Pound (£)          • Year              ► Divide
 • Yen (¥)            • Bimonthly         • Interpolate
 • Franc (F)          • B                 • Repeat
 • Swiss Franc (SFr)
 • Deutsche Mark (DM)                     Splitting Method
 • Guilder (fl)        Definition         ► Model default
 ► Default           ▪ Unlocked           • Split evenly
                     ▪ Fill with NA's     • Split by days

█      109K                        CALC MENU
```

Fig. 4.13. Custom time period *Bimonthly* shown on the Variable settings sheet.

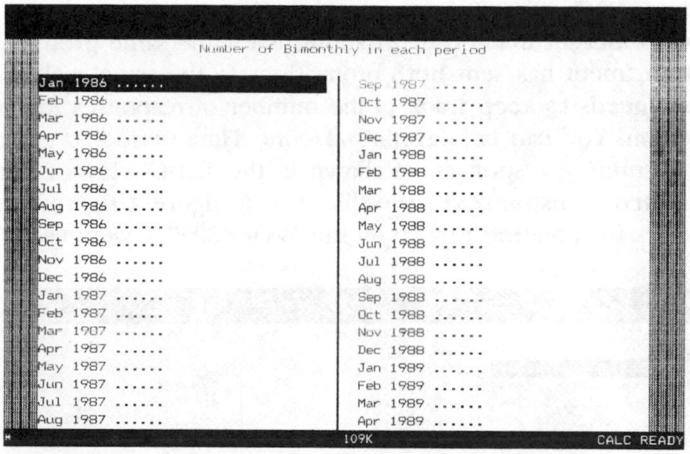

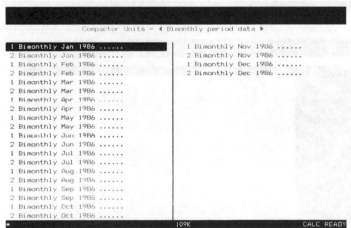

Fig. 4.14. TABLE view showing
list of base periods.

To assign the bimonthly custom period to *Compactor Units*, for example, you
would select /**Define Variable**, enter *Compactor Units*, move the cursor to
Bimonthly—the name we assigned to our custom period—press Enter, and press
Esc. If you view *Compactor Units* in the TABLE view, a table of custom periods
will be displayed (see fig. 4.15). You can then enter data for each bimonthly
period.

Fig. 4.15. Table of bimonthly
custom periods displayed for
Compactor Units.

You can also use the /**Define Time** period command to create a table that is
independent of time, based on a series that you define. Attaching a variable to a
table independent of time is particularly useful when you want to create
worksheets that display values for variables related not to time, but age,
geographical areas, etc. Consider the following example.

Suppose that your company's marketing department is testing the response to two different mail-order promotions for the same product. The marketing department has sent both promotions to the same regions across the country and needs to keep track of the number of responses for each promotion in each region. You can use Javelin's /Define Time period to create a series of regions for entering responses, as shown in the TABLE views in figure 4.16. Having created a customized series like that in figure 4.16, you can also use the custom series for creating reports in the WORKSHEET view (see fig. 4.17).

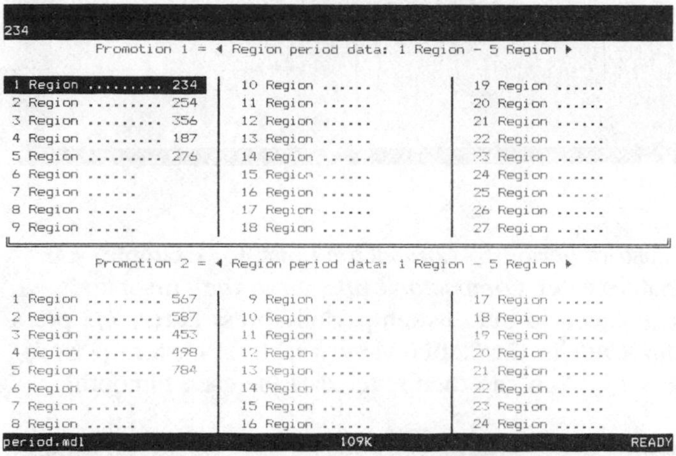

Fig. 4.16. TABLE view with custom series independent of time.

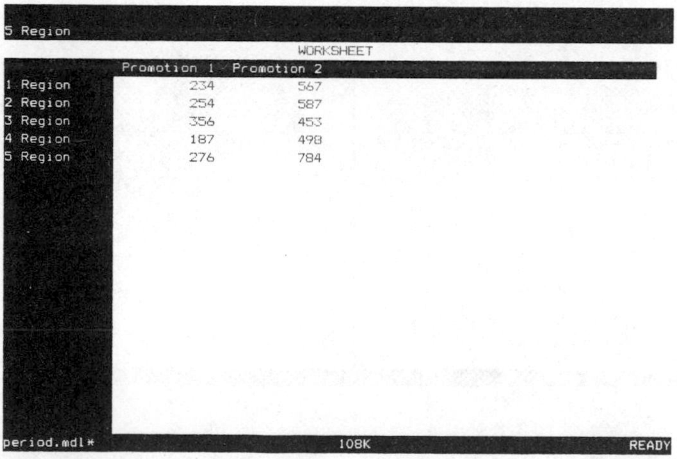

Fig. 4.17. WORKSHEET view with custom series independent of time.

To create a custom series as displayed in figures 4.16 and 4.17, begin by selecting /Define Time period. Next, select A or B when the Custom period name: prompt appears. When the Custom Period settings sheet appears, type the name of the series you want to attach to your variables. Figure 4.18, for example, shows Region as the series name. After assigning the variable name, select the *No base period* option on the Custom Period settings sheet to indicate that the series is not based on time. Finally, press Esc to save the series you have created.

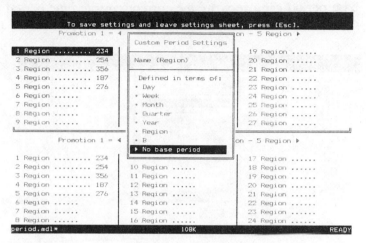

Fig. 4.18. Naming and defining a custom series independent of time.

To use your custom series, you need to attach it to specific variables. Select the Variable settings sheet for each variable you want to link to the custom series, move the cursor to the Period box, and choose the custom series that appears in the list of time periods. Notice, for example, that the Variable settings sheet in figure 4.19 contains the custom series *Region*. Once you have assigned a custom series to a variable, you can enter values for each item, as in figure 4.16. These tables display the number of responses from five regions of the country for the two promotions.

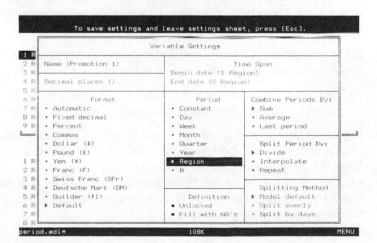

Fig. 4.19. Linking a custom series to a variable through the Variable settings sheet.

Note: If you want to clear a custom period or define a new one, select the /Define Time settings sheet (see fig. 4.20), change the period name back to the A or B default name (or to another of your own choosing), and select a new base period. When you select a new base period, Javelin indicates that the new base period can overwrite the current custom time period. Select *Yes* to overwrite the existing table. You are now ready to define a new custom period.

To save settings and leave settings sheet, press [Esc].

Custom Period Settings

Name (Bimonthly)

Defined in terms of:
- Day
- Week
▶ Month
- Quarter
- Year
- Bimonthly
- B
- No base period

Compactor Revenue

Compactor Units = ◀ Bimonthly period data ▶

timtime.mdl   109K   CALC READY

Fig. 4.20. You use the Custom Period settings sheet to clear custom time periods.

Converting Time Periods

If a formula contains time-series variables defined in different periods, the formula will not calculate without a time conversion function. Javelin's time conversion functions make it possible to mix periods in the same formula. In order for a formula to calculate, all variables on the right side of the formula must be converted to the same period.

After calculating *Blender Revenue* in weeks rather than months, for example, the original formula for *Total Revenue* will not calculate:

Total Revenue = Blender Revenue + Disposal
Revenue + Compactor Revenue

If you attempt to calculate this formula with its mixed periods, Javelin will display ERROR in the bottom right corner of the screen (see fig. 4.21). The ERRORS view (/View Errors) indicates that *Total Revenue* uses mixed periods (see fig. 4.22). Editing the *Total Revenue* formula so that *Blender Revenue* is converted to months will correct the error. One of Javelin's time-conversion functions solves the problem.

Fig. 4.21. Attempting calculation with mixed periods results in an error message.

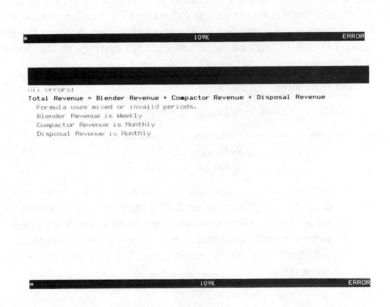

Fig. 4.22. ERRORS view showing mixed periods for variable *Total Revenue*.

Using Time Conversion Functions

When you need to mix variables with different time periods, use Javelin's time conversion functions. Javelin's list of time conversion functions includes DAILY, WEEKLY, MONTHLY, QUARTERLY, and YEARLY, plus two functions (A and B) for customized time periods. (See Appendix A for detailed explanations of each function.) To convert *Blender Revenue* (calculated in weeks) to monthly values, use the function MONTHLY. In our *Revenue* model, the formula for *Total Revenue* should be entered as:

    Total Revenue = MONTHLY(Blender Revenue) + Disposal
                    Revenue + Compactor Revenue

Choosing Methods and Settings for Converting Time Periods

A time conversion function like MONTHLY converts data from either a smaller to a larger period or a larger to a smaller period. For example, data entered as weeks for the variable *Blender Revenue* is converted into months through MONTHLY. Quarterly data could also be converted into months by the function MONTHLY.

The default method that Javelin uses to convert values from a smaller period to a larger period is to sum values. Javelin's default method for converting values for a larger to a smaller period is to divide values. Javelin provides, however, other methods for converting values from a smaller period to a larger or from a larger period to a smaller. You can change the method for either your whole model or for individual variables through settings in the Model and the Variable settings sheets:

Settings Sheet	*Settings*
Model	Splitting Method
Variable	Combine Periods By, Split Periods By, Splitting Method

As the names indicate, settings for *Splitting Method* and *Split Period By* affect conversions from a larger period to a smaller. The *Combine Periods By* setting, on the other hand, affects conversions from a smaller period to a larger, as in the *Blender Revenue* example above. The following sections describe the effect of the *Combine Periods By* setting, the *Splitting Method* setting and the *Split Period By* setting.

Converting from a Smaller to a Larger Period

The Variable settings sheet provides three options for controlling the way Javelin combines smaller time periods into larger ones (see fig. 4.23):

1. *Sum:* You can combine by simply summing values for periods.

2. *Average:* You can combine by having Javelin return the average of the values from the smaller period.

3. *Last Period:* You can combine by having Javelin return the value from the last smaller period within the larger period—the last week of the month, for example, when converting from weeks to months.

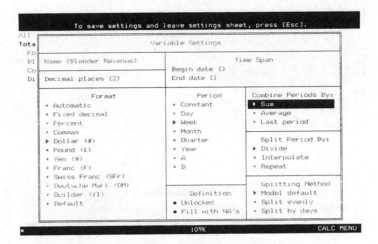

Fig. 4.23. Variable settings sheet.

Consider the differences between these three settings as they affect formulas based on the variable *Compactor Units*. First, if you wanted to create a variable for reporting quarterly compactor units, you would enter the variable:

Quarterly Compactor Units = QUARTERLY(Compactor Units)

As long as the *Combine Periods by* setting for *Compactor Units* is *Sum*, Javelin will return the total number of units sold for each quarter (see fig. 4.24). If, however, you change the setting to *Average*, Javelin then returns a value that is the average of the three months making up each quarter (see fig. 4.25). Finally, if you change the setting to *Last Period*, Javelin returns the value for the last month of each quarter (see fig. 4.26).

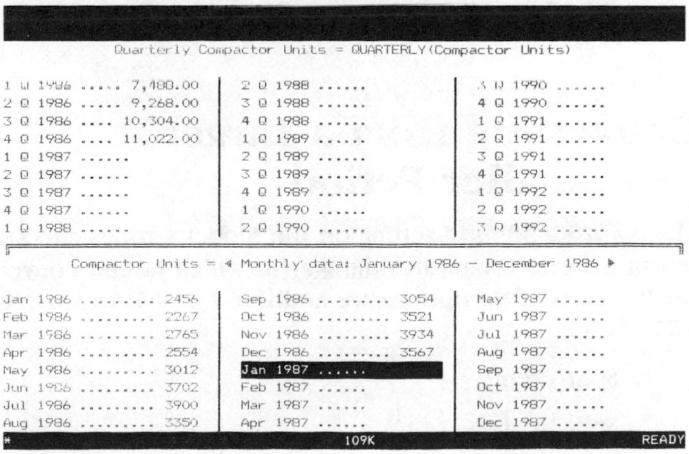

Fig. 4.24. Combining periods by summing values from smaller period.

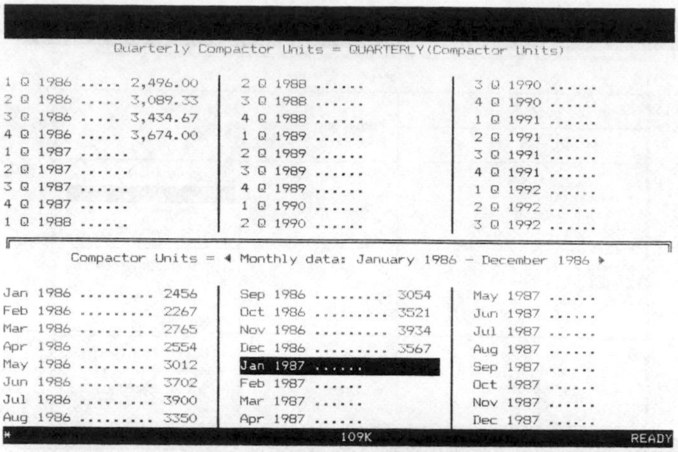

Fig. 4.25. Combining periods by averaging values for months making up each quarter.

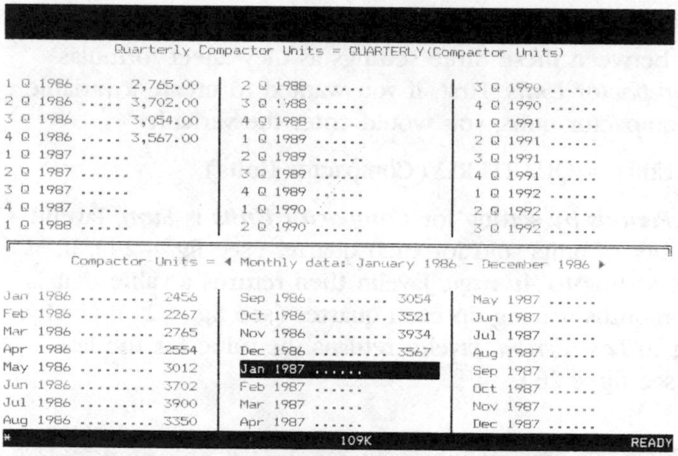

Fig. 4.26. Combining periods by taking the value of the last month for each quarter.

Converting from a Larger to a Smaller Period

The *Splitting Method* setting on the Model settings sheet and on the Variable settings sheets establishes the way in which Javelin converts larger periods to smaller ones. Two options are available for *Splitting Method* settings (see figs. 4.27–4.28):

1. Split evenly

2. Split by days

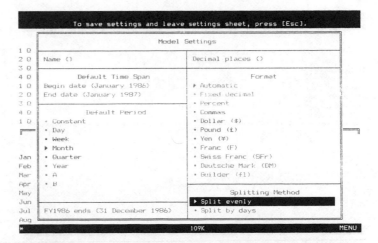

Fig. 4.27. The Model settings sheet gives you two options for the *Splitting Method* setting.

Fig. 4.28. Variable settings sheet gives you two options (plus Model default) for the *Splitting Method* setting.

Notice the difference between *Split evenly* and *Split by days* in the following example. Suppose that formulas for *Blender Revenue, Disposal Revenue,* and *Compactor Revenue* were calculated in months, but *Total Revenue* was calculated in weeks (see fig. 4.29). The *Split evenly* option would cause *Total Revenue* to be calculated by evenly dividing the values for each month by four or five, depending on the number of Saturdays in that month (see fig. 4.30). Notice that the values for each week in January (1 w 1986–4 w 1986) are the same. The *Split by days* option, on the other hand, would cause *Total Revenue* to be calculated by dividing the values according to the actual number of days in each month, then multiplying the daily value by the number of days of that particular week that fell within the given month (because weeks may cross monthly boundaries) (see fig. 4.31). Notice that the value for the first week of January is based on the actual number of days in the week.

```
Formulas for all variables:
Blender Price = 17
Blender Revenue = Blender Units * Blender Price
Blender Units = ◀ Monthly data: January 1986 - June 1986 ▶
Compactor Price = 175
Compactor Revenue = Compactor Units * Compactor Price
Compactor Units = ◀ Monthly data: January 1986 - June 1986 ▶
Disposal Price = 44
Disposal Revenue = Disposal Units * Disposal Price
Disposal Units = ◀ Monthly data ▶
Total Revenue = WEEKLY(Blender Revenue + Disposal Revenue + Compactor Revenue)
```

```
*                              108K                          READY
```

Fig. 4.29. List of formulas for *Total Revenue*.

```
52100
Total Revenue = WEEKLY(Blender Revenue + Disposal Revenue + Compactor Revenue)

 1 W 1986 .. $52,100.00    21 W 1986 .. $47,188.80    41 W 1986 ......
 2 W 1986 .. $52,100.00    22 W 1986 .. $47,188.80    42 W 1986 ......
 3 W 1986 .. $52,100.00    23 W 1986 .. $63,386.00    43 W 1986 ......
 4 W 1986 .. $52,100.00    24 W 1986 .. $63,386.00    44 W 1986 ......
 5 W 1986 .. $42,530.00    25 W 1986 .. $63,386.00    45 W 1986 ......
 6 W 1986 .. $42,530.00    26 W 1986 .. $63,386.00    46 W 1986 ......
 7 W 1986 .. $42,530.00    27 W 1986 ...... #RANGE    47 W 1986 ......
 8 W 1986 .. $42,530.00    28 W 1986 ......           48 W 1986 ......
 9 W 1986 .. $34,596.00    29 W 1986 ......           49 W 1986 ......
10 W 1986 .. $34,596.00    30 W 1986 ......           50 W 1986 ......
11 W 1986 .. $34,596.00    31 W 1986 ......           51 W 1986 ......
12 W 1986 .. $34,596.00    32 W 1986 ......           52 W 1986 ......
13 W 1986 .. $34,596.00    33 W 1986 ......            1 W 1987 ......
14 W 1986 .. $51,616.00    34 W 1986 ......            2 W 1987 ......
15 W 1986 .. $51,616.00    35 W 1986 ......            3 W 1987 ......
16 W 1986 .. $51,616.00    36 W 1986 ......            4 W 1987 ......
17 W 1986 .. $51,616.00    37 W 1986 ......            5 W 1987 ......
18 W 1986 .. $47,188.80    38 W 1986 ......            6 W 1987 ......
19 W 1986 .. $47,188.80    39 W 1986 ......            7 W 1987 ......
20 W 1986 .. $47,188.80    40 W 1986 ......            8 W 1987 ......
*                              108K                          READY
```

Fig. 4.30. TABLES view of *Total Revenue* showing effect of *Split evenly* option.

```
69640.8
Total Revenue = WEEKLY(Blender Revenue + Disposal Revenue + Compactor Revenue)

 1 W 1986 .. $94,032.52    21 W 1986 . $196,586.19    41 W 1986 ......
 2 W 1986 . $164,556.90    22 W 1986 . $196,586.19    42 W 1986 ......
 3 W 1986 . $164,556.90    23 W 1986 . $243,742.80    43 W 1986 ......
 4 W 1986 . $164,556.90    24 W 1986 . $243,742.80    44 W 1986 ......
 5 W 1986 . $164,652.92    25 W 1986 . $243,742.80    45 W 1986 ......
 6 W 1986 . $165,229.00    26 W 1986 . $243,742.80    46 W 1986 ......
 7 W 1986 . $165,229.00    27 W 1986 .. $69,640.80    47 W 1986 ......
 8 W 1986 . $165,229.00    28 W 1986 ......           48 W 1986 ......
 9 W 1986 . $165,314.70    29 W 1986 ......           49 W 1986 ......
10 W 1986 . $165,828.87    30 W 1986 ......           50 W 1986 ......
11 W 1986 . $165,828.87    31 W 1986 ......           51 W 1986 ......
12 W 1986 . $165,828.87    32 W 1986 ......           52 W 1986 ......
13 W 1986 . $165,828.87    33 W 1986 ......            1 W 1987 ......
14 W 1986 . $180,378.34    34 W 1986 ......            2 W 1987 ......
15 W 1986 . $186,198.13    35 W 1986 ......            3 W 1987 ......
16 W 1986 . $186,198.13    36 W 1986 ......            4 W 1987 ......
17 W 1986 . $186,198.13    37 W 1986 ......            5 W 1987 ......
18 W 1986 . $190,650.16    38 W 1986 ......            6 W 1987 ......
19 W 1986 . $196,586.19    39 W 1986 ......            7 W 1987 ......
20 W 1986 . $196,586.19    40 W 1986 ......            8 W 1987 ......
*                              108K                          READY
```

Fig. 4.31. TABLES view of *Total Revenue* showing effect of *Split by days* option.

You can change the *Splitting Method* setting from its default—*Split evenly*—to *Split by days*, and all variables will take on this setting. Or you can set *Splitting Method* for individual variables through the /**D**efine Variable command.

Three options are available under the *Split Period By* setting on the Variable settings sheet to provide a range of applications for converting from larger to smaller periods (see fig. 4.32):

1. Divide

2. Interpolate

3. Repeat

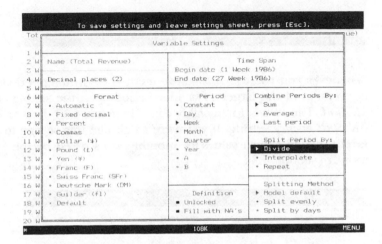

Fig. 4.32. Variable settings sheet gives you three options for the *Split Period By* setting.

Divide is the default setting for simply dividing the value for the larger period among smaller periods. Javelin calculates the values for *Total Revenue* by dividing the monthly values for blender, disposal, and compactor revenues between weeks.

Interpolate uses the difference between the current larger period and succeeding one to divide among smaller periods. Suppose that you have estimated year-end loans and want to estimate monthly loans based on those year-end figures. If year-end loan figures are estimated through the variable *Loans*, monthly loans can be estimated using the formula:

Monthly Loans = MONTHLY(Loans)

In order, however, for Javelin to return a monthly loan value that reflects the increase from one year to the next, you should choose the *Interpolate* option on the Variable settings sheet for *Loans*. Having selected *Interpolate* for *Loans*, Javelin will calculate *Monthly Loans*, as shown in figure 4.33.

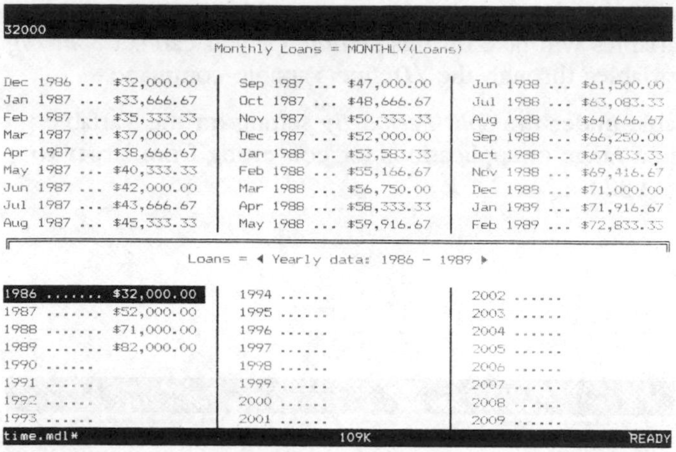

```
32000
                      Monthly Loans = MONTHLY(Loans)

Dec 1986 ... $32,000.00    Sep 1987 ... $47,000.00    Jun 1988 ... $61,500.00
Jan 1987 ... $33,666.67    Oct 1987 ... $48,666.67    Jul 1988 ... $63,083.33
Feb 1987 ... $35,333.33    Nov 1987 ... $50,333.33    Aug 1988 ... $64,666.67
Mar 1987 ... $37,000.00    Dec 1987 ... $52,000.00    Sep 1988 ... $66,250.00
Apr 1987 ... $38,666.67    Jan 1988 ... $53,583.33    Oct 1988 ... $67,833.33
May 1987 ... $40,333.33    Feb 1988 ... $55,166.67    Nov 1988 ... $69,416.67
Jun 1987 ... $42,000.00    Mar 1988 ... $56,750.00    Dec 1988 ... $71,000.00
Jul 1987 ... $43,666.67    Apr 1988 ... $58,333.33    Jan 1989 ... $71,916.67
Aug 1987 ... $45,333.33    May 1988 ... $59,916.67    Feb 1989 ... $72,833.33

               Loans = ◀ Yearly data: 1986 - 1989 ▶

1986 ....... $32,000.00    1994 ......        2002 ......
1987 ....... $52,000.00    1995 ......        2003 ......
1988 ....... $71,000.00    1996 ......        2004 ......
1989 ....... $82,000.00    1997 ......        2005 ......
1990 ......                1998 ......        2006 ......
1991 ......                1999 ......        2007 ......
1992 ......                2000 ......        2008 ......
1993 ......                2001 ......        2009 ......
time.mdl *                       109K                      READY
```

Fig. 4.33. Using the *Interpolate* method when converting from yearly to monthly loan figures.

Whenever you use the *Interpolate* method of dividing periods, Javelin bases the conversion of the larger to smaller period upon the setting entered for *Splitting Method*. The values for monthly loans in figure 4.33, for example, are based on the *Split evenly* setting. If you were to change this setting to *Split by days*, Javelin would return values for monthly loans based on the actual days in each month (see fig. 4.34).

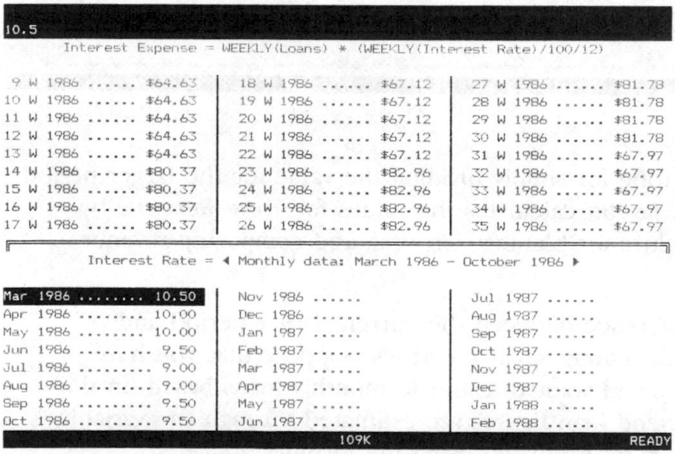

```
10.5
          Interest Expense = WEEKLY(Loans) * (WEEKLY(Interest Rate)/100/12)

 9 W 1986 ...... $64.63    18 W 1986 ...... $67.12    27 W 1986 ...... $81.78
10 W 1986 ...... $64.63    19 W 1986 ...... $67.12    28 W 1986 ...... $81.78
11 W 1986 ...... $64.63    20 W 1986 ...... $67.12    29 W 1986 ...... $81.78
12 W 1986 ...... $64.63    21 W 1986 ...... $67.12    30 W 1986 ...... $81.78
13 W 1986 ...... $64.63    22 W 1986 ...... $67.12    31 W 1986 ...... $67.97
14 W 1986 ...... $80.37    23 W 1986 ...... $82.96    32 W 1986 ...... $67.97
15 W 1986 ...... $80.37    24 W 1986 ...... $82.96    33 W 1986 ...... $67.97
16 W 1986 ...... $80.37    25 W 1986 ...... $82.96    34 W 1986 ...... $67.97
17 W 1986 ...... $80.37    26 W 1986 ...... $82.96    35 W 1986 ...... $67.97

            Interest Rate = ◀ Monthly data: March 1986 - October 1986 ▶

Mar 1986 ........ 10.50    Nov 1986 ......    Jul 1987 ......
Apr 1986 ........ 10.00    Dec 1986 ......    Aug 1987 ......
May 1986 ........ 10.00    Jan 1987 ......    Sep 1987 ......
Jun 1986 ......... 9.50    Feb 1987 ......    Oct 1987 ......
Jul 1986 ......... 9.00    Mar 1987 ......    Nov 1987 ......
Aug 1986 ......... 9.00    Apr 1987 ......    Dec 1987 ......
Sep 1986 ......... 9.50    May 1987 ......    Jan 1988 ......
Oct 1986 ......... 9.50    Jun 1987 ......    Feb 1988 ......
                                 109K                      READY
```

Fig. 4.34. The effect on *Monthly Loans* after changing the *Splitting Method* from *Split Evenly* to *Split by days*.

Repeat, the last method for splitting a time period, uses the value from the larger period when converting to the smaller. Using *Repeat* is necessary, for example, when you are calculating weekly interest expenses on loans, but using a variable for *Interest Rate* defined in months. The following formula for *Interest Expense* will return a weekly value:

Interest Expense = WEEKLY(Loans) * (WEEKLY(Interest Rate)/100/12)

To return the correct value, however, you must tell Javelin to repeat, rather than divide, the monthly values for *Interest Rate*. Setting the *Split Period By* setting to *Repeat* for the variable *Interest Rate* will return the correct values (see fig. 4.35).

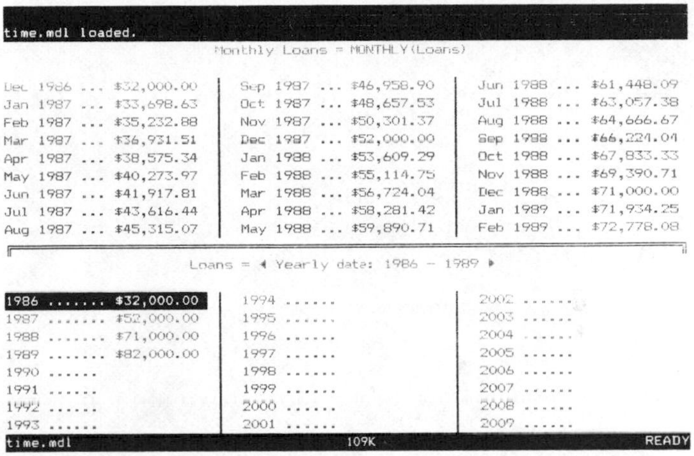

Fig. 4.35. Using the *Repeat* method to calculate weekly *Interest Expense*.

Conclusion

Javelin's capabilities for understanding time is one of the features that makes Javelin superior to conventional business applications programs. This chapter has shown how you can benefit most from this capability by understanding how to define the time period for your whole model and for specific variables. In addition, this chapter has covered how to convert from one time period to another by using Javelin's time functions and conversion methods.

5

Using the CHART, QUICK GRAPH, and WORKSHEET Views

Chapter 3 showed how to build a Javelin model using the DIAGRAM, FORMULAS, and TABLE views. In this chapter, we show you how to use three others, CHART, QUICK GRAPH, and WORKSHEET views. Specifically, you'll be introduced to:

- entering data in the CHART view by simply moving the cursor on the bar graph that Javelin displays when you choose /View Chart for any input variable

- entering data in the QUICK GRAPH view by moving the cursor on the line graph that Javelin displays when you choose /View Quick graph for time-series input variables

- using the WORKSHEET view for entering or displaying data when you choose /View Worksheet

These three views are powerful tools, not only for building models and entering data, but also for analyzing and presenting data. This chapter, though, concentrates on showing how they are model-building tools fitting your needs and your thinking. In particular, we emphasize how the WORKSHEET view can be used in conjunction with other views and how Javelin provides a full range of worksheet commands that enable you to produce professional reports. As part of introducing the CHART, QUICK GRAPH, and WORKSHEET views as model building and data entry tools, we discuss in this chapter the following commands and function keys:

Using the CHART View

The CHART view, like the TABLE view, displays values associated with one variable. The CHART view, however, represents values as a bar graph (see fig. 5.1). This view not only displays data for a single variable in a bar graph but also lets you change values for input variables either by typing in the exact value or by using the cursor keys. The CHART view can be used to enter data for input variables. Note: You can't use the CHART view to change values derived from formulas.

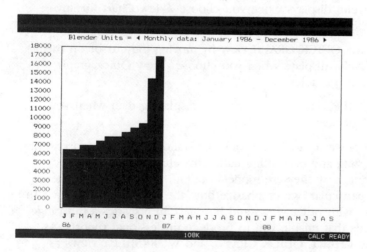

Fig. 5.1. The CHART view represents the value of an input variable as a bar graph.

Entering and Editing Data with the CHART View Displayed

In Chapter 1, we introduced Javelin by illustrating its features through the example of an Income Statement created for the New York office of Future Home Appliances, Inc. Chapter 3 introduced the DIAGRAM, FORMULAS, TABLE, and NOTES views through the Revenue model for the New York office. In this chapter, you see how the CHART, QUICK GRAPH, and WORKSHEET views are used to edit and enter data for a Cost of Goods and Operating Expense model for Future Home Appliances, Inc.

Suppose that you have begun to enter the formulas shown in figure 5.2 for the Cost of Goods model. The variables listed in the FORMULAS view of figure 5.2 were entered using the DIAGRAM, FORMULAS, and TABLES views we became familiar with in Chapter 3. There are three types of variables shown in figure 5.2: calculated variables, input variables defined as constants, and input variables defined as time-series variables.

Calculated Variables

   Total Cost = Blender Cost + Disposal Cost + Compactor Cost
   Blender Cost = Blender Unit Cost * Blender Units
   Disposal Cost = Disposal Unit Cost * Disposal Units
   Compactor Cost = Compactor Unit Cost * Compactor Units

Input Variables Defined as Constants

   Blender Unit Cost
   Disposal Unit Cost
   Compactor Unit Cost

Input Variables Defined as Time-Series Variables

   Blender Units
   Disposal Units
   Compactor Units

To see each of the variables listed above through the CHART view, divide the full screen shown in figure 5.2 into a two-window screen (/Window **2** windows). Make sure the cursor is highlighted in the top window by pressing the WINDOW key (F6). Then select /View Chart. By moving the cursor back to the FORMULAS view (press the WINDOW key, F6) and pressing the SYNC key (F3) to synchronize views, you can view each variable in the CHART view as it is highlighted in the FORMULAS view.

Look at the CHART view displayed for *Compactor Cost, Compactor Units*, and *Compactor Unit Cost* (see figs. 5.3, 5.4, and 5.5). Calculated and time-series

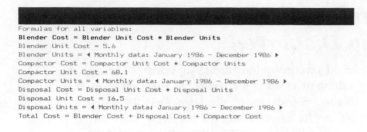

```
Formulas for all variables:
Blender Cost = Blender Unit Cost * Blender Units
Blender Unit Cost = 5.6
Blender Units = ◄ Monthly data: January 1986 - December 1986 ►
Compactor Cost = Compactor Unit Cost * Compactor Units
Compactor Unit Cost = 68.1
Compactor Units = ◄ Monthly data: January 1986 - December 1986 ►
Disposal Cost = Disposal Unit Cost * Disposal Units
Disposal Unit Cost = 16.5
Disposal Units = ◄ Monthly data: January 1986 - December 1986 ►
Total Cost = Blender Cost + Disposal Cost + Compactor Cost
```

Fig. 5.2. FORMULAS view of the Cost of Goods model.

variables like *Compactor Cost* and *Compactor Units* represent each value over time. The scale for values is represented along the y axis; the scale for time is along the x axis. Constants, like *Compactor Unit Cost*, are represented by a single bar next to the y axis. Javelin provides all labels and scaling automatically. If, for example, a time-series variable is defined in quarters rather than months, the CHART view for that variable will indicate quarters along the x axis.

Javelin's CHART view does much more than just display a bar graph of values entered for a single variable. Javelin's CHART view can also be used to input data. When you move your cursor to the CHART view (WINDOW key, F6), you can then edit or enter values in this view with the arrow keys (→, ←, ↑, ↓). However, you can only change *input* variables in the CHART view, not calculated variables. If you asked Javelin to display a chart of *Compactor Cost*,

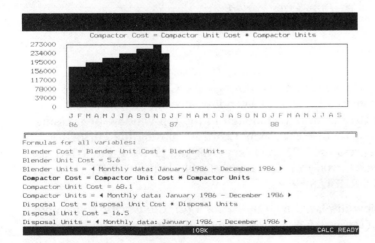

Fig. 5.3. CHART and FORMULAS views synchronized for calculated variable *Compactor Cost*.

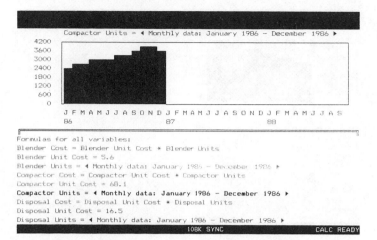

Fig. 5.4. CHART and FORMULAS views sychronized for time-series variable *Compactor Units*.

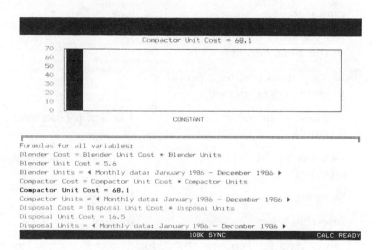

Fig. 5.5. CHART and FORMULAS views synchronized for constant variable *Compactor Unit Cost*.

for example, which is a calculated variable, it would display the chart shown in figure 5.3. If you attempted to move the cursor in this chart, however, Javelin would respond with this message (see fig. 5.6):

> Cannot add or change data; variable is already defined by formula.

To enter new data or edit existing data for any input variable in the CHART view, use the following keys:

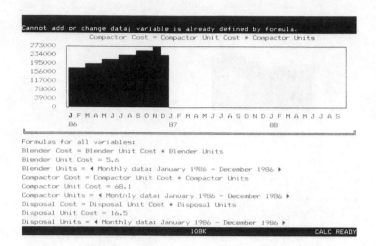

```
Cannot add or change data; variable is already defined by formula.
                Compactor Cost = Compactor Unit Cost * Compactor Units
273000
234000
195000
156000
117000
 78000
 39000
      0
      J F M A M J J A S O N D J F M A M J J A S O N D J F M A M J J A S
      86                        87                        88

Formulas for all variables:
Blender Cost = Blender Unit Cost * Blender Units
Blender Unit Cost = 5.6
Blender Units = ◀ Monthly data: January 1986 - December 1986 ▶
Compactor Cost = Compactor Unit Cost * Compactor Units
Compactor Unit Cost = 68.1
Compactor Units = ◀ Montnly data: January 1986 - December 1986 ▶
Disposal Cost = Disposal Unit Cost * Disposal Units
Disposal Unit Cost = 16.5
Disposal Units = ◀ Monthly data: January 1986 - December 1986 ▶
                                        108K                    CALC READY
```

Fig. 5.6. Attempting to change the value of a calculated variable in the CHART view results in an error message.

Function	Key
Moving from one time period to the next period	→
Moving from one time period to the previous period	←
Increasing the value for a period	↑ or PgUp (increments are twice those of ↑)
Decreasing the value for a period	↓ or PgDn (increments are twice those of ↓)
Deleting a bar	Del key
Inserting a bar	Ins key

To enter data for February, 1987, for *Compactor Units*, for example, move the cursor to F above 87 and press the Up-arrow key (↑) (see fig. 5.7). Moving the cursor to February of 1987 enters the value of the previous month, 3567 for January in this case. Pressing the Up-arrow key (↑) once increases that value to 3867. You may also change the data by highlighting the bar, typing the new value in the edit line, and pressing Enter.

Figure 5.7 shows the CHART and TABLE views. Note how the values change in the TABLE view as you change the CHART view.

You can change the scaling for values by simply pressing the arrow or PgUp and PgDn keys. As shown in figure 5.8, the CHART view represents negative as well as positive values.

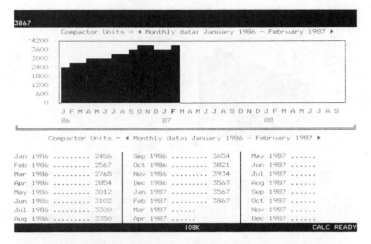

Fig. 5.7. Changing the value of a variable in the CHART view is reflected in the TABLE view.

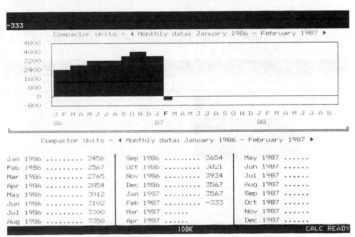

Fig. 5.8. The CHART view represents negative as well as positive values.

If you wish to have a smaller scale, expand the window (/Window Adjust) or use the CHART view alone on a single window screen (/Window 1 window) (see fig. 5.9).

Displaying the CHART View with the TABLE View

The CHART view can be displayed with other views, but is an especially effective tool when used with the TABLE view. When you use the CHART view with the TABLE view, for example, the screen displays both the individual numeric values and a bar graph of those values (see fig. 5.10). To display the CHART view with the TABLE view, simply move the cursor to the bottom

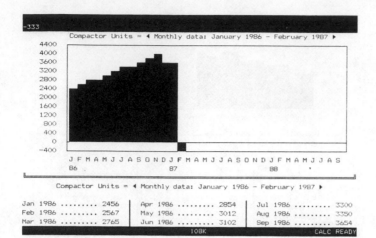

Fig. 5.9. Expanding the CHART
view to show a smaller scale.

window and select /View Table. Remember that you can choose the variable
you want to view in the TABLE view by using the SPELL key (Tab).

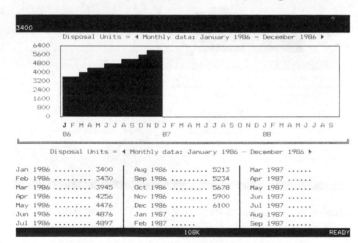

Fig. 5.10. CHART view displayed
with the TABLE view.

You can enter data in either view and have it immediately reflected in the
other. If, for example, you were to display the CHART view with the TABLE
view for the variable *Disposal Units*, as in figure 5.10, you could enter the value
7200 for January, 1987, and it would be reflected in the CHART view. The same
is true if you delete a value (see fig. 5.11).

In addition to displaying different views, you can make instant comparisons of
data by using the CHART view for one variable with the CHART view for
another. You can, of course, compare data on a single graph by using Javelin's
/View Graph option, but this requires entering a series of settings in order to

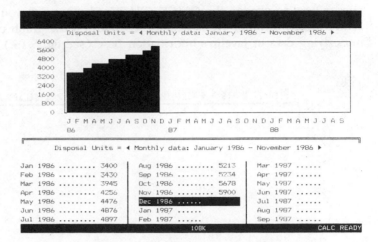

Fig. 5.11. Change in CHART view when values are deleted through TABLE view.

produce the graph. Displaying two variables in the CHART view, on the other hand, can be done in seconds. Comparing *Total Cost* with *Total Revenue* of Future Home Appliance, Inc.'s three products for a one-year period shows a greater change in costs than in revenue (see fig. 5.12).

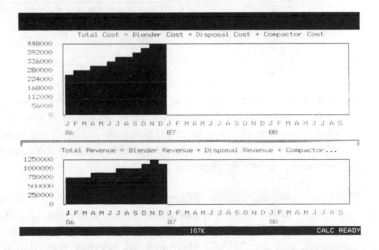

Fig. 5.12. The CHART view allows you to compare two variables.

Using the QUICK GRAPH View

The QUICK GRAPH view is another instant graph of your variables. When you identify a specific variable, and select /View Quick graph, Javelin produces a line graph of that variable over time. As with the CHART view, you can define new values and edit existing values for time-series input variables by using the cursor keys to change the QUICK GRAPH. Changes that you make to the graph are reflected in other views because changes on the graph change the underlying data in Javelin's Information Base (see fig. 5.13.).

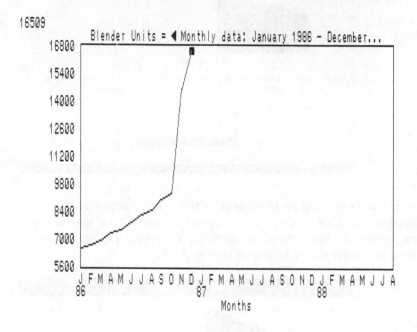

Fig. 5.13. Cursor in the QUICK GRAPH view allows you to change data for a time-series input variable.

Note that like the CHART view, the QUICK GRAPH view can be used to enter or edit input variables (time-series variables), but not to edit or enter data for variables that are defined through formulas (calculated variables). For example, attempting to change a calculated variable such as *Blender Cost* will result in the message shown in figure 5.14.

There are two significant differences between the QUICK GRAPH and CHART views that make certain applications more suited for one than the other. First, the QUICK GRAPH view cannot display constants. If you need to show constants, use the CHART view instead. Second, the QUICK GRAPH view uses a graphics driver to display a full-screen view; you cannot display a QUICK GRAPH in one window of a two-window screen.

Note: Because QUICK GRAPH uses a graphics driver, you can only see the QUICK GRAPH view if your computer is capable of displaying graphs.

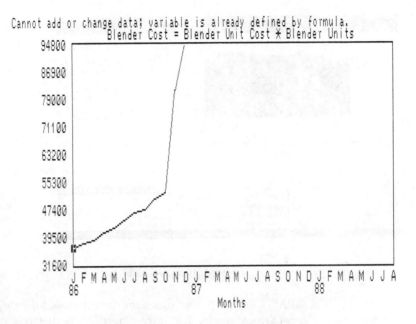

Fig. 5.14. You cannot change
data for a calculated variable.

Entering and Editing Data with the QUICK GRAPH View Displayed

You can use the QUICK GRAPH view as your electronic "scratch pad" to enter actual values and see them represented immediately in the line graph or to make a freehand representation of a trend in values over time. Unlike the paper scratch pad, though, QUICK GRAPH immediately stores your freehand graph as data in Javelin's Information Base. Any change made to the QUICK GRAPH can be viewed in another Javelin view—TABLE, WORKSHEET, CHART, or GRAPH.

Imagine, for example, that in July, 1986, Future Home Appliances, Inc., opens a new plant for producing blenders. Before opening the new plant, cost per unit for producing blenders had climbed from $5.80 in February, 1986, to $7.35 in July, 1986. Future Home Appliances predicts that new automated equipment will reduce the cost per unit to $6.25 over a 12-month period. Javelin's QUICK GRAPH provides an easy way of representing graphically the expected change.

The TABLE and CHART views shown in figure 5.15 illustrate the quick rise in cost and the initial decrease with the opening of the new plant. With the QUICK GRAPH view displayed, you can visually estimate the rate at which costs might decrease over the next six months. Changing from the TABLE-CHART screen to the QUICK GRAPH view involves simply selecting /View Quick Graph or pressing the QUICK GRAPH key (F8).

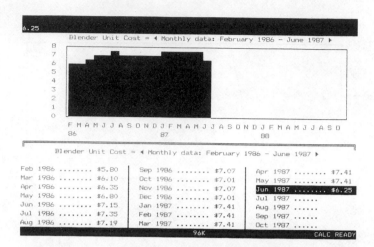

Fig. 5.15. TABLE and CHART views showing a quick rise in *Blender Unit Cost* over a six-month period.

The QUICK GRAPH Key (F8)

The QUICK GRAPH key performs the same function as selecting the command /View Quick graph. The only difference is that you must have selected the variable you want to display as a graph before using F8. When you use /View Quick Graph, on the other hand, you can select the command, then enter the variable when the prompt appears in the edit line.

With the QUICK GRAPH view displayed, you can visually estimate the rate at which cost might decrease over the next six months from January, 1987, to June, 1987 (see fig. 5.16).

You can change a QUICK GRAPH by typing a value in the edit line or by moving the cursor (the small box appearing on the graph line) using the following keys:

Function	Keys
Increase the value	↑ or PgUp (PgUp increases the value by five times the increment of the ↑.)
Decrease the value	↓ or PgDn (PgDn decreases the value by five times the reduction of the ↓.)

Javelin automatically provides labels and scaling for the y axis of the QUICK GRAPH and provides the range of time periods for the x axis. As you continue to increase or decrease values and expand the graph line to the right of the screen, Javelin automatically adjusts scaling along the y axis and the range of time periods along the x axis.

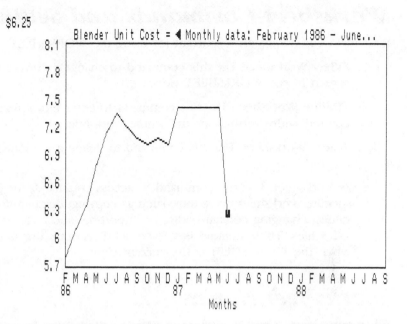

Fig. 5.16. Using the QUICK
GRAPH view to estimate
decrease in costs.

Using the WORKSHEET View

The WORKSHEET view is the view that will be most familiar to spreadsheet users because the display is similar. Keep in mind, however, that Javelin's worksheet is only one of the program's 10 views. The WORKSHEET view displays variables and data stored in Javelin's Information Base and can be effectively used in combination with other views.

When you use the WORKSHEET view along with other views, you realize how much quicker and easier creating a worksheet with Javelin is than creating worksheets in 1-2-3. The WORKSHEET view also demonstrates Javelin's incredible capabilities for linking variables and data to time.

The WORKSHEET view is a powerful instrument for building, analyzing, and presenting models. Using the WORKSHEET view, you can enter formulas and data, easily create a worksheet display of any variables and data previously entered into Javelin's Information Base, and readily print the data in your worksheet for presentation to others. This section introduces the WORKSHEET view as another tool for entering and editing formulas and data. In Chapter 9, you learn how valuable the WORKSHEET view is for analysis; you also learn about using the WORKSHEET view for presenting your models in electronic and printed form.

Worksheet Commands and Settings Sheet

Four main commands are important for using the WORKSHEET view:

1. /View Worksheet: Use this command to change a current view on screen to the WORKSHEET view.

2. /Define Worksheet: Use this command to enter global format and column width settings for the whole worksheet.

3. /Clear Worksheet: Use this command to delete a worksheet you have created.

4. /*Worksheet: Use this command to access commands for performing specific worksheet operations, such as copying, deleting, formatting values, changing column width, or importing labels and data from 1-2-3 files. The command is a "view-sensitive" one that is only available when the WORKSHEET is the current view.

Worksheet Names

When you select /View Worksheet or /Define Worksheet, Javelin prompts you to name the worksheet. Javelin keeps track of the worksheets you've created by the names you've assigned them. (If you do not provide a name, Javelin assigns the default name "WORKSHEET.") As with variable names, the SPELL key (Tab) can help you access worksheet names. When you must supply a worksheet name in response to the name prompt, simply press the SPELL key (Tab) or type the first few characters and then press the SPELL key (Tab). Javelin will enter the exact name or provide a list of worksheet names from which you can choose.

Suppose, for example, that you had created a Javelin model containing one worksheet displaying your company's Total Revenue, one worksheet displaying your company's Cost of Goods, and one worksheet displaying Operating Expenses. If you have given a worksheet name to each one, you can display each worksheet by selecting /View Worksheet, pressing the SPELL key (Tab), and selecting the worksheet name (see fig. 5.17).

To assign a name to a new worksheet, use /View Worksheet. You might, for example, enter *NY Operating Expense*. The name that you enter for a worksheet will appear above the worksheet's top border (see fig. 5.18). You should, therefore, choose names that would be appropriate titles for display.

To change a worksheet name, select /Define Worksheet. This brings up the worksheet settings sheet (see fig. 5.19).

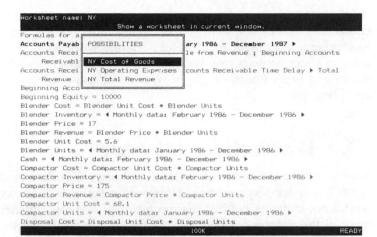

Fig. 5.17. Using SPELL key (Tab) to access a list of worksheet names.

```
Worksheet name: NY
                     Show a worksheet in current window.
Formulas for a
Accounts Payab  POSSIBILITIES          ary 1986 - December 1987 ▶
Accounts Recei                         le from Revenue ; Beginning Accounts
    Receivabl    NY Cost of Goods
Accounts Recei   NY Operating Expenses  counts Receivable Time Delay ▶ Total
    Revenue      NY Total Revenue
Beginning Acco
Beginning Equity = 10000
Blender Cost = Blender Unit Cost * Blender Units
Blender Inventory = ◀ Monthly data: February 1986 - December 1986 ▶
Blender Price = 17
Blender Revenue = Blender Price * Blender Units
Blender Unit Cost = 5.6
Blender Units = ◀ Monthly data: January 1986 - December 1986 ▶
Cash = ◀ Monthly data: February 1986 - December 1986 ▶
Compactor Cost = Compactor Unit Cost * Compactor Units
Compactor Inventory = ◀ Monthly data: February 1986 - December 1986 ▶
Compactor Price = 175
Compactor Revenue = Compactor Price * Compactor Units
Compactor Unit Cost = 68.1
Compactor Units = ◀ Monthly data: January 1986 - December 1986 ▶
Disposal Cost = Disposal Unit Cost * Disposal Units
                              100K                              READY
```

Fig. 5.18. The name you enter for a worksheet appears above the worksheet's top border.

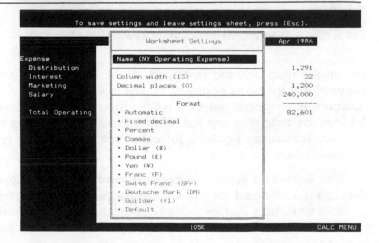

```
                      NY Operating Expense
                  Jan 1986    Feb 1986    Mar 1986    Apr 1986

Expense
  Distribution      1,108       1,139       1,224       1,291
  Interest                          0          23          32
  Marketing           800         800         800       1,200
  Salary          240,000     240,000     240,000     240,000
                  -------     -------     -------     -------
  Total Operating  81,968      81,968      81,960      82,601
                              105K                     CALC READY
```

Fig. 5.19. Use the Worksheet settings sheet to change worksheet names.

```
          To save settings and leave settings sheet, press [Esc].
                      Worksheet Settings            Apr 1986
Expense
  Distribution    Name (NY Operating Expense)         1,291
  Interest                                                32
  Marketing       Column width (13)                   1,200
  Salary          Decimal places (0)               240,000
                                                    -------
  Total Operating           Format                   82,601
                  • Automatic
                  • Fixed decimal
                  • Percent
                  ▶ Commas
                  • Dollar ($)
                  • Pound (£)
                  • Yen (¥)
                  • Franc (F)
                  • Swiss Franc (SFr)
                  • Deutsche Mark (DM)
                  • Guilder (fl)
                  • Default
                              105K                    CALC MENU
```

Worksheet names can be up to 79 characters long and can include any character (except the slash) on the alphanumeric keyboard. Whenever you want to change a worksheet name, select /Define Worksheet. When the Worksheet settings sheet appears, you can either press the EDIT key (F2), edit the existing name, and press Enter, or simply type a new name to replace the existing one and press Enter.

The Worksheet Display

After you have defined a name, Javelin displays a worksheet view that looks much like a 1-2-3 spreadsheet. However, as figure 5.20 shows, Javelin's worksheet contains neither column headings nor row numbers—an important mark of the differences between the two programs. In Javelin, information appearing on the worksheet is not stored in reference to cell locations. All information is stored in Javelin's Information Base.

Fig. 5.20. The Javelin worksheet display.

For display purposes, the appearance of the Javelin worksheet is much like conventional spreadsheet programs. The row and column borders in Javelin, however, have special purposes related to variables and data stored in the Information Base. The top and left borders are for entering variables or time periods. The corner border is for entering a name or date to control the entire worksheet (see fig. 5.21).

Javelin's worksheet is like conventional spreadsheet programs in that it displays data in the traditional form of a columnar pad. But the similarity between Javelin's worksheet and spreadsheet programs is, for the most part, limited to appearance, cursor movement, formatting commands, and "cut and paste"

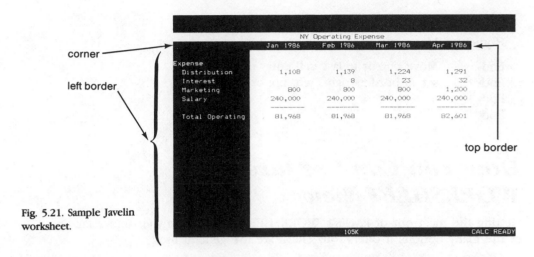

corner

left border

top border

Fig. 5.21. Sample Javelin
worksheet.

operations. Commands in Javelin's worksheet menu (/*Worksheet) that appear
to function like commands in 1-2-3 or Symphony perform operations related to
the display of information, not operations related to how information is stored
or linked.

Moving About the Worksheet (Cursor Keys for the Worksheet)

Making the transition from a spreadsheet program like 1-2-3 to Javelin is made
easier by similarities not only in the display, but also in keys used to move
about the worksheet:

Key	Function
→	Move cursor one cell right (when not entering or editing data)
←	Move cursor one cell left (when not entering or editing data)
→	Move cursor one character right when entering or editing data
←	Move cursor one character left when entering or editing data
↑	Move cursor up one row
↓	Move cursor down one row
Ctrl- →	Move cursor right one page
Ctrl- ←	Move cursor left one page
PgUp	Move cursor up one page

PgDn	Move cursor down one page
Home	Move cursor to upper left corner of worksheet
End- →	Move cursor to last cell entry or next
End- ←	set of borders right, left, up, or down
End- ↑	
End- ↓	

How You Can Use Javelin's WORKSHEET View

Getting the most out of Javelin's WORKSHEET depends on your understanding of the many options it offers you. There are five general uses:

1. You can use the WORKSHEET view as a display and reporting tool by instructing Javelin to display variables and data from the Information Base in worksheet form. Using the WORKSHEET view this way is as simple as entering the variables and time periods for which you want data displayed.

2. You can use the WORKSHEET view to enter and/or edit values for input variables already defined and stored in Javelin's Information Base.

3. You can use the WORKSHEET view to define new formulas and enter new data into Javelin's Information Base.

4. You can use the WORKSHEET view to display labels and values that appear in the worksheet but are not stored in the Information Base.

5. You can use the WORKSHEET to import labels and values from 1-2-3 worksheets or to import text (ASCII) files.

In the following sections, we look at each of the five ways of using the WORKSHEET view.

The WORKSHEET View as a Display/Reporting Tool

Possibly the best illustration of Javelin's power is the ease with which you can display data from the Information Base. Setting up a Javelin worksheet is as easy as entering variable names and dates.

Suppose that you had been developing a model for Future Home Appliances, Inc., that consisted of the variables needed to compute *Total Operating Expense* and which contained data for each of the input variables (see fig. 5.22). You could easily create a worksheet displaying data for the variables.

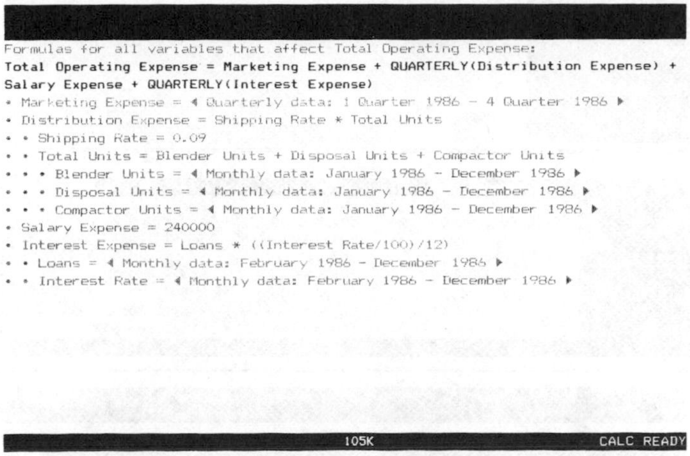

```
Formulas for all variables that affect Total Operating Expense:
Total Operating Expense = Marketing Expense + QUARTERLY(Distribution Expense) +
Salary Expense + QUARTERLY(Interest Expense)
• Marketing Expense = ◄ Quarterly data: 1 Quarter 1986 – 4 Quarter 1986 ►
• Distribution Expense = Shipping Rate * Total Units
• • Shipping Rate = 0.09
• • Total Units = Blender Units + Disposal Units + Compactor Units
• • • Blender Units = ◄ Monthly data: January 1986 – December 1986 ►
• • • Disposal Units = ◄ Monthly data: January 1986 – December 1986 ►
• • • Compactor Units = ◄ Monthly data: January 1986 – December 1986 ►
• Salary Expense = 240000
• Interest Expense = Loans * ((Interest Rate/100)/12)
• • Loans = ◄ Monthly data: February 1986 – December 1986 ►
• • Interest Rate = ◄ Monthly data: February 1986 – December 1986 ►
```

```
                                                                 105K                              CALC READY
```

Fig. 5.22. FORMULAS view showing variables for *Total Operating Expense*.

To display the WORKSHEET view, select /View Worksheet. When you select /View Worksheet, Javelin will prompt you for a worksheet name. After you have named your worksheet, you are ready to display variables and data from the Information Base. Because relationships among variables and data are stored in Javelin's Information Base, you do not have to define those relationships or enter this data manually on the worksheet.

Creating a worksheet display of variables and data already existing in Javelin's Information Base involves a few simple operations. Javelin not only makes it easy to create a worksheet from existing variables and data, but also gives you the flexibility of designing your worksheet in multiple ways (see figs. 5.23-5.25).

First, you can enter variable names in the left border of the worksheet and specify time periods in the top border or vice versa with variable names across the top, and time periods in the left border. Javelin then will supply the data, as in figure 5.23.

Second, you can enter variable names in both the left and top borders, specify a time period in the worksheet's corner, or specify dates in the left border and parts of the variable name in the corner (see fig. 5.24) and Javelin will supply the data.

Third, you can expand the top border in order to define time periods and to define the initial part of a variable name. The remaining parts of the variable name are defined in the left border (see fig. 5.25).

```
                          New York Revenue
                    Jan 1986    Feb 1986    Mar 1986    Apr 1986

Blender Revenue       109,752     113,271      96,730     163,778
Disposal Revenue      193,500     154,350     157,275     191,520
Compactor Revenue     429,800     396,725     483,875     446,950
```

```
                          Product Revenue
                  Blender Revenue  Disposal Revenue  Compactor Revenue

Jan 1986            109,752.00       193,500.00        429,800.00
Feb 1986            113,271.00       154,350.00        396,725.00
Mar 1986             96,730.00       157,275.00        483,875.00
Apr 1986            163,778.00       191,520.00        446,950.00
May 1986            126,752.00       221,670.00        527,100.00
Jun 1986            162,418.00       239,670.00        647,850.00
Jul 1986            160,769.00       260,865.00        682,500.00
                             83K                              READY
```

Fig. 5.23. Two worksheets: one with variable names in the left border and dates in the top border (top window) and the other with the reverse (bottom window).

```
1986
                           NY Revenue
1986                  Blender      Disposal      Compactor

Units                99,597.00     58,305.00      38,082.00
Price                    17.00        45.00         175.00

Revenue          $1,693,149.00 $2,623,725.00  $6,664,350.00
```

```
                        NY Product Revenue
Revenue               Blender      Disposal      Compactor

Jan 1986              109,752       193,500        429,800
Feb 1986              113,271       154,350        396,725
Mar 1986               96,730       157,275        483,875
Apr 1986              163,778       191,520        446,950
May 1986              126,752       221,670        527,100
Jun 1986              162,418       239,670        647,850
Jul 1986              160,769       260,865        682,500
                             83K                              READY
```

Fig. 5.24. Two worksheets showing variable names in top and left borders and a time period in the worksheet's corner.

```
                      New York Product Revenue
                      ---------1986---------
                      Blender    Disposal    Compactor

Units              112,452.00     58305       38082
Price                      17        45         175

Revenue             1,911,684   2,623,725   6,664,350
```

```
                           NY Revenue 3
                       ---------Blender---------
                    Jan 1986    Feb 1986    Mar 1986    Apr 1986

Units                6,456.00    6,663.00    5,690.00    9,634.00
Price                      17          17          17          17

Revenue               109,752     113,271      96,730     163,778
                             80K                              READY
```

Fig. 5.25. Two worksheets showing variable names in top and left borders and time period specified in top border.

To create a worksheet of *Total Operating Expense* from the variables and data already in Javelin's Information Base, for example, you would complete the following steps:

1. Select /View Worksheet and name the worksheet, as described above.

2. If your present screen has two windows and you want a full-screen worksheet, select /Window **1** window.

3. If you want to view the worksheet along with another view, move the cursor to the window where you want the other view to appear, select /View, then choose the view you want.

4. With the cursor in the WORKSHEET view, indicate what labels are to appear in the worksheet borders. Methods of doing this are described in the following section, "Entering Variable Names in Worksheet Borders."

Entering Variable Names in Worksheet Borders

You can enter variable names by typing each one into its appropriate border cell. You can also use the SPELL key (Tab) or the /*Worksheet Border Variable names command to automate this for you.

Suppose, for example, that you want to display values for *Marketing, Overhead, Salaries, Net Interest*, and *Total Operating Expense.* To use the SPELL key (Tab) to enter these names, move the cursor to the left border where you want a variable name to appear, press the SPELL key (Tab), select the variable, and press Enter. Or type a few characters and use the SPELL key (Tab) to help you enter the name.

To enter a series of variable names (all of which are identified by the same beginning or end part), use the /*Worksheet Border Variable names command from Javelin's /*Worksheet menu. Suppose, for example, that you want to enter the following variable names into the worksheet's left border:

> Marketing Expense
> Distribution Expense
> Salary Expense
> Interest Expense
> Total Operating Expense

Because all five variable names use the word *Expense*, you can tell Javelin to enter all variables containing *Expense* simultaneously. Just move the cursor to the location where you want to enter the word *Expense* as the main heading. Type *Expense* and press Enter (see fig. 5.26). With the cursor highlighting Expense, select /*Worksheet Border Variable names and press Enter.

Javelin will enter all variable names containing *Expense*, indented under the main heading (see fig. 5.27). As figure 5.27 shows, Javelin displays only as many characters as fit the column width. You can change the column width by using either the /Define Worksheet Column width command, which sets column width for the whole worksheet, or the /*Worksheet Width command, which sets width for a single cell, column, or row.

Fig. 5.26. Using the /*Worksheet Border Variable names command to enter all the *Expense* variable names.

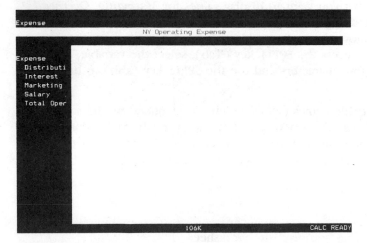

Fig. 5.27. Using the /*Worksheet Border Variable names command to enter variable names.

Defining the Time Period for Variables

Once you have selected the variable names you want to appear in the worksheet's left border, you can complete the worksheet by specifying the time period. (See the "Formats for Defining Time Periods in the Worksheet" section for a complete list of formats.) For example, you can specify that Javelin display values for each quarter of 1986 and totals for all of 1986. As soon as you indicate the time period, Javelin displays values for each period (see fig. 5.28).

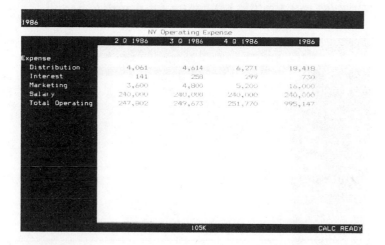

Fig. 5.28. After you indicate the time period for worksheet variables, Javelin displays values for each period.

You can specify time period in the borders in one of two ways:

1. Move the cursor to the column or row for the beginning period, type the period, and press Enter. Javelin displays the first period date and supplies values for each variable. To enter all succeeding dates, simply move the cursor to the next column or row and continue to press Enter until Javelin has automatically entered the time periods and values you want.

2. Move the cursor to the column or row for the beginning period, and select the /*Worksheet Border Dates command. When you select this command, Javelin responds with a prompt that also indicates begin date from the current period (refer to fig. 5.23).

If the begin date you want entered in the worksheet is the one displayed in the parentheses, simply press Enter. If you want another date, type the date after the prompt. Suppose, for example, that you want the worksheet for *NY Operating Expense* to display values for a period beginning in July, 1986. Type any of the following:

July 1986
Jul 1986
Jul86 (for dates between 1950 and 2049)

After you have indicated the beginning date for the top worksheet border and pressed Enter, Javelin will respond with a prompt for the last date you want entered (see fig. 5.29). If the last worksheet date is the one displayed in parentheses, press Enter; if not, supply the end date using one of the formats listed below. With the end date specified, Javelin will display values for all variables listed in the left border for that time period.

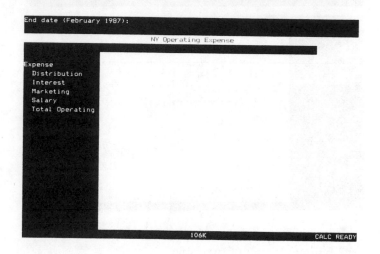

Fig. 5.29. After you enter a beginning date for the top worksheet border, Javelin prompts you for an end date.

Formats for Defining Time Periods in the Worksheet

When you enter time periods, use one of the following formats. You can mix uppercase and lowercase letters when entering time periods. Javelin will read both.

For Days:	1 January 1986
	1 Jan 1986
	1ja86 (for dates between 1950 and 2049)
For Weeks:	1 week 1986
	1 w 1986
	1w86 (for dates between 1950 and 2049)
For Months:	January 1986
	Jan 1986
	ja86 (for dates between 1950-2049)
For Quarters:	1 quarter 1986
	1 Q 1986
	1 Q86 (for 1950-2049)

For Years: 1986

86 (for dates between 1950 and 2049)

For custom   1 A Jan 1986 (when A is defined in terms of months)
time periods: 1 AJa86 (for 1950-2049)

1 A (when A is not based on standard periods)

Changing Time Periods in the Worksheet Border

If you change the time periods displayed in the top border of your worksheet, Javelin adjusts the values, displaying the values for the new periods. Suppose, for example, that you decide to display expenses in quarters rather than months. To change from months, as shown in figure 5.29, to quarters (see fig. 5.30), simply move the cursor to the beginning month and either type manually *1 q 1986* or use Javelin's /*Worksheet Border Dates command to enter the new time periods.

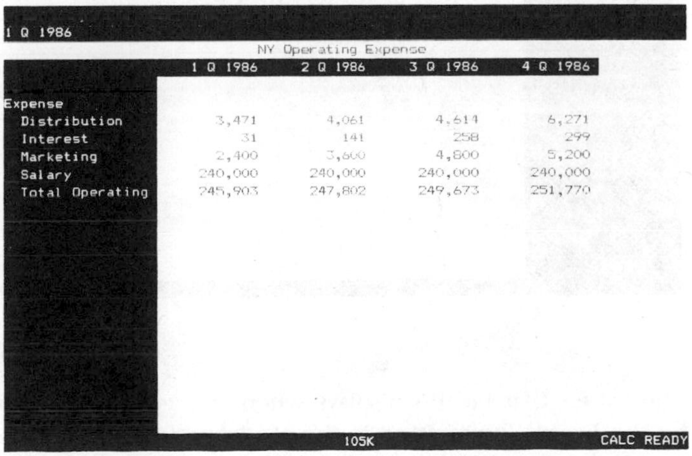

Fig. 5.30. Changing the time period in the top border from months to quarters.

The new time periods replace the existing periods and Javelin displays new values for blender, compactor, and disposal units. You can delete any remaining original periods and values by moving the cursor to the unwanted period and pressing the Del key. You can also delete periods and their values by using the /*Worksheet Range Delete command.

Mixing Time Periods on the Same Worksheet

The example in the preceding section shows that you can easily change a worksheet displaying values for one period to one displaying values for a different period. You can also mix periods on the same worksheet.

Suppose, for example, that you want to display not only individual expenses for each quarter, but also total expenses for the whole year. To display units for the year, you would move your cursor to the empty cell in the top border directly to the right of 4 Q 1986 in figure 5.31, type *1986*, and press Enter. Javelin then displays total 1986 values for each variable in the left border. You can also mix months with quarters or years or even mix a custom period with a standard one on the same worksheet.

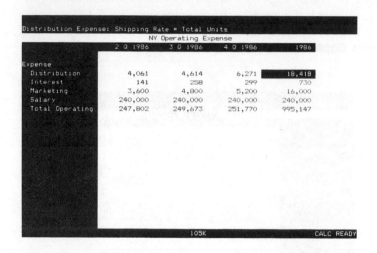

Fig. 5.31. Reporting quarterly and yearly values on the worksheet.

The values that Javelin displays when you ask for 1986 expenses are determined by the Fiscal Year setting in the Model settings sheet. The totals for 1986 will be for January, 1986, to December, 1986, if the Fiscal Year setting is

   FY1986 ends {31 December 1986}

If the fiscal year setting is different than this, Javelin displays values based on the particular setting. Notice how the values displayed in the worksheet in figure 5.31 change when you change the fiscal year setting to

   FYends {30 June 1986}

Using the WORKSHEET View for Data Input

You can use the WORKSHEET view as a model-building tool to input data for variables and formulas that you have defined. You can also use the WORKSHEET view as an analysis and presentation tool to display in seconds data for variables specified in worksheet borders. In this section, we look at the WORKSHEET view as an input tool. No matter how you use the worksheet view, though, remember that it's most powerful when used along with Javelin's other views.

To use the WORKSHEET view as an input tool, consider the following example. Suppose that, as a manager of Future Home Appliances, Inc., you have begun to develop a model for reporting your New York division's total operating expense. This model includes all of the variables shown in figure 5.32. You begin your task by completing the following steps:

1. You enter variables and formulas using Javelin's FORMULAS and DIAGRAM views to check relationships between formulas as you enter them.

2. After entering formulas, you use the TABLE view to enter data for the variables *Loans*, *Marketing Expense*, and *Salary Expense*, and define *Shipping Rate* as .09.

3. You use the WORKSHEET view to enter data for the *Blender Units*, *Disposal Units*, and *Compactor Units* variables.

```
Formulas for all variables:
Blender Units = ◀ Monthly data: January 1986 - December 1986 ▶
Compactor Units = ◀ Monthly data: January 1986 - December 1986 ▶
Disposal Units = ◀ Monthly data: January 1986 - December 1986 ▶
Distribution Expense - Shipping Rate * Total Units
Interest Expense = Loans * ((Interest Rate/100)/12)
Interest Rate = ◀ Monthly data: February 1986 - December 1986 ▶
Loans = ◀ Monthly data: February 1986 - December 1986 ▶
Marketing Expense = ◀ Quarterly data: 1 Quarter 1986 - 4 Quarter 1986 ▶
Salary Expense - 240000
Shipping Rate = 0.09
Total Operating Expense = Marketing Expense + QUARTERLY(Distribution Expense) +
       Salary Expense + QUARTERLY(Interest Expense)
Total Units = Blender Units + Disposal Units + Compactor Units
```
```
                                        105K                            READY
```

Fig. 5.32. FORMULAS view showing all the variables for New York division's total operating expense.

To use the WORKSHEET view for entering data for the three variables, enter the variable names in one of the worksheet borders. You can use one of the methods described previously in "Entering Variable Names in the Worksheet

Borders." For example, enter variable names by using the /*Worksheet **B**order **V**ariable names command (see fig. 5.33). With names entered in the left border, enter the dates for each variable in the top border. Whenever you use the worksheet as an input tool, you must use the same period in the worksheet that is defined for each variable. For example, if *Blender Units*, *Disposal Units*, and *Compactor Units* are all defined in terms of months, you must then use months as your worksheet time period.

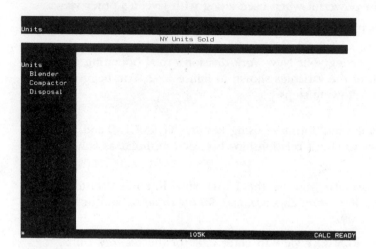

Fig. 5.33. Entering each complete variable name in the worksheet.

Once dates have been specified in the worksheet's top border, you can begin to enter data. To enter data, move the cursor to the cell at the intersection of the name and date, type the value, and press Enter or move the cursor. (Moving the cursor after you type data enters data, as does pressing Enter. See "Moving About the Worksheet.") If you synchronize the WORKSHEET view with the TABLE view as you enter values, the values are immediately displayed in both views (see fig. 5.34). Even though data is displayed on the worksheet, keep in mind that it is stored in Javelin's Information Base, not in the worksheet.

After you have entered values, you can move to the left border and enter the variable name *Total Units*. Either type *Total Units* manually or use the SPELL key (Tab) to enter it. Next, you can create a formula for *Total Units*. (See the section "Defining Formulas While Working in the WORKSHEET View.") Notice that as soon as you enter the formula *Total Units* and press the CALC key (F9), Javelin automatically displays the values for each (see fig. 5.35).

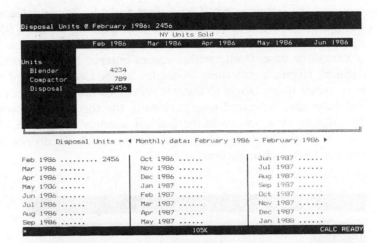

Fig. 5.34. Values entered into the
WORKSHEET view are reflected
in the TABLE view.

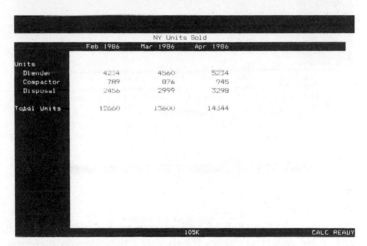

Fig. 5.35. Displaying totals for
values in the worksheet.

Entering New Variables and Formulas
in the WORKSHEET View

Just as you can enter data in the worksheet for variables that already exist in
Javelin's Information Base, you can also define new variables and formulas with
the WORKSHEET view displayed. Suppose, for example, that you are displaying a
new, blank worksheet on screen and have not yet created the variables *Blender
Units*, *Compactor Units*, *Disposal Units*, or *Total Units*. With the WORKSHEET
view displayed, you can define these variables as you would with another view
displayed. You also can simultaneously create worksheet labels and tell Javelin
to create new variables for your model.

Notice what happens when we create variables *Blender Units*, *Disposal Units*, *Compactor Units*, and *Total Units* while working in the WORKSHEET view. Remember that as soon as you define variables they become part of Javelin's Information Base. Until variable names entered in the WORKSHEET view are defined, Javelin treats them as display labels. Observe figure 5.38, where we have typed three labels in the left border of the worksheet (in the top window) and have also indicated time periods in the top border. If you look at the FORMULAS view shown in the bottom window of figure 5.36, you notice that *Blender Units*, *Disposal Units*, and *Compactor Units* do not appear; they have not yet been defined as variables.

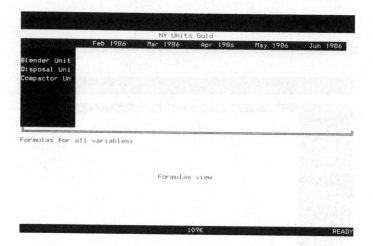

Fig. 5.36. Entering labels into the worksheet does not define the associated variables in Javelin's Information Base.

The labels in figure 5.36 will remain worksheet labels until you define them either by entering values for them or by entering formulas. If, for example, you move the cursor to the cell in the left border directly beneath Compactor Units and type *Total Units = Blender Units + Disposal Units + Compactor Units*, the formula displayed in the FORMULAS view now shows your original labels as variables. Note also in figure 5.37 that the worksheet indicates that Javelin is ready to calculate data.

Defining Formulas while Working in the WORKSHEET View

You can enter a formula in Javelin's WORKSHEET view in one of two ways. The formula for *Total Units*, for example, can be entered in either of these ways:

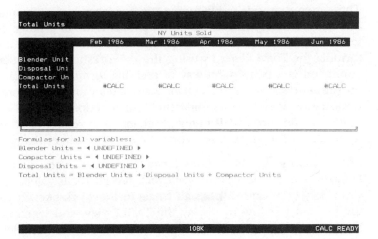

Fig. 5.37. Worksheet labels
become variables when you
define them with a formula.

1. You can define the formula by placing the cursor in the left border
   and typing the formula:

   Total Units = Blender Units + Disposal Units + Compactor Units

2. You can move the cursor to a cell in the worksheet in the same row
   as the label *Total Units* and enter the formula. For example, if you had
   entered the label *Total Units* in the left border, you could enter the
   formula by moving your cursor to the next adjacent cell in the same
   row (see fig. 5.38), and typing the following:

   Blender Units + Disposal Units + Compactor Units

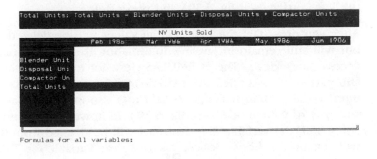

Fig. 5.38. Entering a formula for
Total Units into a worksheet cell.

These two methods apply to any type of formula. For formulas that sum, average, or define maximum or minimum value of a range of cells, you can use Javelin's /*Worksheet Range command. For example, you could enter the formula for *Total Units* by using the /*Worksheet Range Sum command. This command is a convenient way of creating formulas to total long columns of data on the worksheet. The command calculates values and stores them in Javelin's Information Base, just as using the SUM function or plus (+) operator will; however, the formula can only be changed in reference to the worksheet (see Appendix B for more discussion of the /*Worksheet Range Sum command).

After entering the *Total Units* formula, you can enter values for *Blender Units*, *Disposal Units*, and *Compactor Units*. Javelin totals values when you press the CALC key (F9) and displays all totals in the worksheet. If you were to change the bottom window to display the TABLE view and synchronize the TABLE and WORKSHEET views, you could see data for all four variables in both worksheet and table.

Displaying Labels and Values in the WORKSHEET View

As illustrated by the example above, you can enter worksheet labels that, although displayed in the WORKSHEET view, are not defined as model variables in Javelin's Information Base. You realize the difference between worksheet labels and model variables when you observe the effect of using the Del key versus using Javelin's /Clear Variable command. If, for example, you have created a formula such as the one for *Total Units* cited previously and want to delete the label and values from your worksheet but not from Javelin's Information Base, use the Del key. Move the cursor to the Total Units label in the left border (see fig. 5.39) and press Del.

After you press Del the label and all values will be deleted from the worksheet but will still remain in Javelin's Information Base, as you can see when you access other views. The FORMULAS view, for example, shows that *Total Units* is still part of your model; the TABLE view for *Total Units* or any of the three input variables that make up *Total Units* also indicates that these variables are still part of your model (see fig. 5.39). If, however, you use the /Clear Variable command, the variable and its values will be deleted from the model. The label will remain on the worksheet. Using /Clear Variable for *Total Units*, for example, results in deletion of the variable and values but not the *Total Units* label (see fig. 5.40).

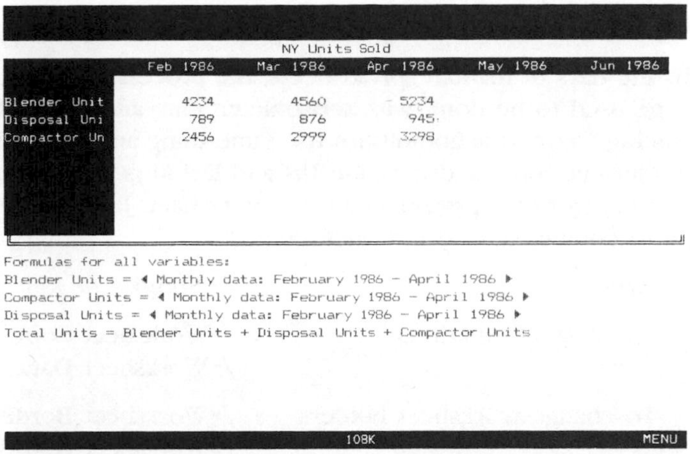

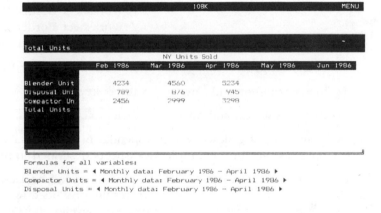

Fig. 5.39. Deleting *Total Units*
from the worksheet.

Fig. 5.40. Using /Clear Variable
deletes the variable and its value
from the worksheet, but the label
remains.

Changing and Improving the Worksheet Display

Once you have entered labels, variable names, time periods, and data into your worksheet, you may need to move, copy, or delete information originally displayed. You may need also to widen worksheet columns so that complete variable names and values can be seen, and values can be displayed in the correct format. Javelin contains a full set of commands and keys that enable you to change the worksheet layout as needed to improve the display. The following sections cover these commands along with the Ins and Del keys for inserting and deleting columns and rows.

Commands and Keys for Cutting and Pasting

In the days of manual spreadsheets, the process of moving data around on the page used to be done with scissors and glue and was called "cutting and pasting." Javelin accomplishes the same thing automatically with several worksheet commands and the Ins and Del keys. With these commands and keys, you control the appearance of the worksheet. Javelin's complete list of cut and paste commands and keys includes:

Function	*Command or Key*
To copy information	/*Worksheet **Copy**
	/*Worksheet **Data** copy
To change worksheet borders	/*Worksheet **Border Insert** border
	/*Worksheet **Border Remove** border
	/*Worksheet **Border Expand** border
	/*Worksheet **Border Shrink** border
To delete ranges	/*Worksheet **Range Delete**
To insert columns and rows	Insert key (Ins)
To delete columns and rows	Delete key (Del)

These commands are described in Appendix B, but let's take a look at how each one would operate in the sample worksheets described in previous sections.

Although these commands may be familiar to spreadsheet users, the results of using them are not always identical to results produced by similar commands in 1-2-3, Symphony, or SuperCalc. For example, Javelin contains two different copy commands, /*Worksheet **Copy** and /*Worksheet **Data** copy, while 1-2-3 contains only one. Using /*Worksheet **Data** copy when you need to use /*Worksheet **Copy** may not give you the results you want. See the "Copying" section.

The cut and paste commands /*Worksheet **Copy**, /*Worksheet **Data** copy, and /*Worksheet **Range Delete**, like 1-2-3 commands, require that you identify a range when used. A range is a rectangular group of worksheet cells. The size of the range you define can be as large as the worksheet itself or as small as a single cell, but must be rectangular (see fig. 5.41). Whenever Javelin asks you to designate a range that you want copied or deleted, you must indicate the range by anchoring a corner cell, then highlighting the remaining area. When Javelin prompts you for the location on the worksheet where you want information copied to, you need only indicate the top left corner cell where you want the information copied.

```
Press arrows to show range, then press ◄┘ to select it.
                                  WORKSHEET
                     Jan 1986    Feb 1986    Mar 1986    Apr 1986    May 1986

Inventory
  Blender              9000        9000        9000       10000       10000
  Compactor            3000        3000        3000        3500        4200
  Disposal             7500        7500        7500        8200        8200

Unit Cost
  Blender             15.20       15.10       14.72       12.79       11.85
  Compactor           84.60       84.60       68.28       68.35       68.39
  Disposal            23.75       23.75       24.07       24.20       23.57

Interest rat        10.500      10.000      10.000       9.500       9.000
Plant and Eq       800,000     800,000     800,000     800,000     800,000

beginning ca         5,000       5,000       5,000       5,000       5,000


newyork.mdl                                    82K                          POINT
```

Fig. 5.41. The shape of a range in the WORKSHEET must be rectangular.

Copying

Javelin provides two commands for copying information from one part of the worksheet to another: /*Worksheet Copy and /*Worksheet Data copy. The method for using each command is the same. However, /*Worksheet Data copy will only copy data (not formulas, for example,) while /*Worksheet Copy will duplicate formulas, relationships, names, exception cells, and data. /*Worksheet Copy will not create a formula where a variable already exists.

Copying a range from one part of a worksheet to another part, or to an entirely different worksheet consists of four operations:

1. Select the /*Worksheet Copy or /*Worksheet Data copy command.

2. Define the range you want to copy.

3. Place the cursor at the beginning of the new range.

4. Press Enter.

Suppose, for example, that you want to copy the variable names Units, Price, and Revenue from the cells located beneath Blender in figure 5.42 to the cells beneath Disposal. Using the /*Worksheet Copy command, you would move the cursor to the cell containing Units, select /*Worksheet Copy, identify the range by pressing the period key (.) and moving the cursor so that it highlights all three variable names. After pressing Enter to indicate the end of the "Copy from" range, move the cursor to the cell beneath Disposal and press Enter. All three variable names will be copied.

Keep in mind the difference between the /*Worksheet Copy and /*Worksheet Data copy commands. While /*Worksheet Copy will copy any type of

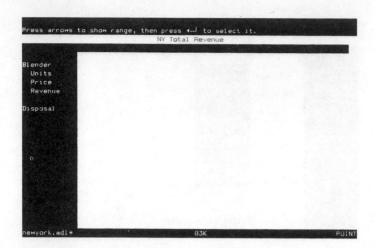

Fig. 5.42. Using the /*Worksheet
Copy command to enter variable
names.

information displayed on the worksheet (variable names, dates, exception cells,
labels), /*Worksheet **Data** copy will not copy formulas. /*Worksheet **Data** copy
should be used to copy data from an input or calculated variable to another
input variable.

Suppose, for example, that you are developing a model for *Total Revenue* and
are using the WORKSHEET view as you define variables and enter formulas.
First, you might begin by entering labels into the left border. Second, you could
define *Blender Revenue* by entering the formula:

   Blender Revenue = Blender Units * Blender Price

To continue with the rest of your model, you would enter the labels *Disposal
Units, Price*, and *Revenue* and *Compactor Units, Price*, and *Revenue* as shown in
figure 5.43. If you want to copy the formula you entered for *Blender Revenue* to
Disposal Revenue and *Compactor Revenue*, you must use the /*Worksheet **Copy**
command.

To copy the *Blender Revenue* formula, for example, select the /*Worksheet
Copy command. When the prompt Specify range to copy from: appears, move
your cursor to the cell containing the *Blender Revenue* formula and press Enter.
When the prompt Specify range to copy to: appears, move the cursor to the
cell directly to the right of *Disposal Revenue* and press Enter. The formula
should now be copied. You can then enter data into the *Disposal Price* and
Disposal Units cells, press CALC (F9), and Javelin will display *Disposal Revenue*.

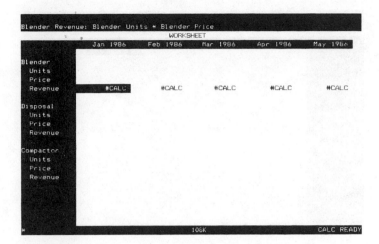

Fig. 5.43. Defining variables
through the WORKSHEET view.

Inserting and Deleting Rows and Columns

Inserting and deleting rows and columns in a Javelin worksheet is quite simple.
These operations only involve moving the cursor to the row in the left border
or column in the top border that you want to insert or delete and pressing the
Ins or Del key, respectively. Using the Ins and Del keys for row and column
insertion and deletion is a definite convenience over 1-2-3 and Symphony, which
require using Insert Row and Column and Delete Row and Column commands
to perform the operations.

You should keep two things in mind concerning inserting or deleting rows or
columns in Javelin. First, in order to insert or delete a row or column, you must
move the cursor to the left border (if you are inserting or deleting rows) or
the top border (if you are inserting or deleting columns). The Ins and Del keys
will not work within the body of the worksheet to insert or delete whole rows
and columns. (Del will work, however, on single exception cells.) Second,
when you delete a row or column, you are merely deleting the variable and
data from the worksheet view, not from the model. 1-2-3 users who have
accidentally deleted data with the Delete Row or Column command will
appreciate the protection this provides.

Suppose, for example, that you only want to display data for January, February,
and March on the worksheet shown in figure 5.44. To delete the columns
containing the data for the other months, simply move the cursor to the cell in
the top border displaying Apr 1986 and press the Del key. Suppose that, on the
other hand, you want to insert a column after Mar 1986 in order to display a
quarterly total. Press the Ins key. This will insert a new column; you can then
indicate the quarter period in the top border and Javelin will display the quarter
values.

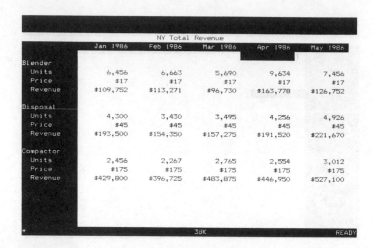

	Jan 1986	Feb 1986	Mar 1986	Apr 1986	May 1986
NY Total Revenue					
Blender					
Units	6,456	6,663	5,690	9,634	7,456
Price	$17	$17	$17	$17	$17
Revenue	$109,752	$113,271	$96,730	$163,778	$126,752
Disposal					
Units	4,300	3,430	3,495	4,256	4,926
Price	$45	$45	$45	$45	$45
Revenue	$193,500	$154,350	$157,275	$191,520	$221,670
Compactor					
Units	2,456	2,267	2,765	2,554	3,012
Price	$175	$175	$175	$175	$175
Revenue	$429,800	$396,725	$483,875	$446,950	$527,100

Fig. 5.44. Worksheet before deleting or inserting columns.

Deleting Single Cells and Ranges of Cells

In addition to deleting rows and columns, you can also delete individual cells and a range of cells. The Del key deletes individual exception cells; the /*Worksheet Range Delete command deletes a range of cells. If you have used a spreadsheet program, you will find that deleting individual cells or ranges of cells in the worksheet body is much different in Javelin from deleting cells and ranges in a program like 1-2-3.

In Javelin, deleting cells or ranges of cells depends on the location of the cursor and the contents of the cell. Within the top or left border of the worksheet you can delete any single cell or range from the worksheet. In the body of the worksheet, however, Del and /*Worksheet Range Delete operations are limited. You cannot, for example, delete in the body of the worksheet data linked to variable names and time periods set up in the worksheet borders.

In the left and top borders, Del will delete rows and columns. /*Worksheet Range Delete will delete a complete range of cells. Suppose, for example, that you want to change the worksheet shown in figure 5.44 so that only *Revenue* and its data are displayed. You need, therefore, to delete all variables names and values for *Price* and *Units*. To delete the range of values displayed for *Blender Units* and *Blender Price*, select /*Worksheet Range Delete, move the cursor to Units beneath Blender, and press the period key (.) to indicate the beginning of the range to be deleted. Next, press the Down-arrow key (↓) to indicate the end of the range. Finally, press Enter to complete the range delete operation. To delete price and unit data for disposals and compactors, repeat the operations described for deleting blender price and unit information.

The Del key and /*Worksheet Delete Range command will work on cells in the body of the worksheet if the information is not linked to variable names and dates specified in the worksheet borders. Suppose, for example, that you have imported a 1-2-3 worksheet into Javelin, have not entered variable names for that data, and want to delete information in individual cells or in a range. Del and /*Worksheet Range Delete can be used to delete any of the imported data. After you have imported the 1-2-3 worksheet shown in figure 5.45, for example, you can use Del to delete any individual label or value or use /*Worksheet Range Delete to delete any range of information.

Fig. 5.45. An unmodified 1-2-3 worksheet imported into a Javelin worksheet.

In most Javelin worksheets, however, deleting cells and ranges in the body will be more restricted. Only labels and exception cells may be freely deleted. Labels are those cells that contain headings or documentation for the worksheet. You can use Del to delete the NY Total Revenue heading from the worksheet in figure 5.46. An exception cell is a single location on a worksheet that is not bound by the definitions of other cells and is independent of border references. Exception cells are created by positioning the cursor on the cell you wish to "mark" and selecting /*Worksheet Exception. When the Cell should show prompt appears, enter a formula (one not yet entered in the model), the name of an existing variable, or a specific value.

Changing the Worksheet Borders

1-2-3 is capable of displaying more than one worksheet application on screen at one time. 1-2-3's /Worksheet Window command enables you to divide the worksheet horizontally with a second column border or vertically with a row border (see figs. 5.47 and 5.48). Javelin, too, provides the capability for adding borders and displaying different applications on a single worksheet through its /*Worksheet Border command. In addition, the /*Worksheet Border command enables you to expand or shrink borders for entering titles, variables names, and dates.

```
                                    NY Total Revenue
                          Jan 1986    Feb 1986    Mar 1986    Apr 1986    May 1986

Blender
  Units                   6,456       6,663       5,690       9,634       7,456
  Price                     $17         $17         $17         $17         $17
  Revenue               $109,752    $113,271     $96,730    $163,778    $126,752

Disposal
  Units                   4,300       3,430       3,495       4,256       4,926
  Price                     $45         $45         $45         $45         $45
  Revenue               $193,500    $154,350    $157,275    $191,520    $221,670

Compactor
  Units                   2,456       2,267       2,765       2,554       3,012
  Price                    $175        $175        $175        $175        $175
  Revenue               $429,800    $396,725    $483,875    $446,950    $527,100

Total Revenu            $733,052    $664,346    $737,880    $802,248    $875,522

                                        67K                              READY
```

Fig. 5.46. The Del key can be used to delete the heading NY Total Revenue.

A83:   Debt Equity Ratio   READY

```
          A    B    C      D         A    B    C      D      E
54                                81  ==================================
55                                82  INDICATORS OF SOLVENCY
56   Gross Sales        $732,730  83     Debt Equity Ratio       0.52
57      Less: Returns      4,167  84     Times Interest Ear      6.61
58                  -----------   85
59   Net Sales            728,563 86  INDICATORS OF LIQUIDITY
60   Cost of Goods        468,947 87     Net Working Capita $1,233,000
61                  -----------   88     Net Working Capita      0.38
62   Gross Margin         259,616 89     Current Ratio           2.59
63   Operating Expenses   201,042 90     Quick Ratio             2.01
64   Depreciation          12,016 91     Cash Ratio              0.4
65                                92
66   Earnings before Int.  46,558 93  FUNDS MANAGEMENT RATIO
67   Interest Expense       7,043 94     Receivable Sales        0.14
68                  -----------   95     Days Sales Outstan       52
69   Earnings before Taxes 39,515 96     Payables/Cost of G      0.07
70   Income Taxes          10,342 97     Days Purchases in        25
71                  -----------   98     Inventory Turnover    15.68
72   Earnings after Taxes  29,173 99     Days Sales in Inve       23
73   Cash Dividends            0 100     Sales/Fixed Assets    10.56
```

Fig. 5.47. Dividing the worksheet vertically with 1-2-3's /Worksheet Window command.

A118:   (D1) [W10] @DATE(86,1,31)   READY

```
        A          B           C           D          E           F          G
86   INDICATORS OF LIQUIDITY
87     Net Working Capital                           $1,233,000
88     Net Working Capital/Assets                          0.38
89     Current Ratio                                        2.59
90     Quick Ratio                                          2.01
91     Cash Ratio                                           0.40
92
93   FUNDS MANAGEMENT RATIOS
94     Receivables/Sales (Annualized)                       0.14
95     Days Sales in Receivables                             52
        A          B           C           D          E           F
111  Record                            Working     Gross      Month
112  Date      Tot Assets  Cur Assets  Capital     Sales      EAT
113  31-Jan-86 $3,202,976  1,907,543  $1,160,483  $729,652    26,612
114  28-Feb-86 $3,194,328  1,902,393  $1,157,350  $727,682    26,540
115  31-Mar-86 $3,185,703  1,897,256  $1,154,225  $725,717    26,468
116  30-Apr-86 $3,177,102  1,892,134  $1,151,108  $723,758    26,397
117  31-May-86 $3,168,524  1,887,025  $1,148,000  $721,804    26,326
118  31-Jan-86 $3,159,969  1,881,930  $1,144,901  $719,855    26,255
119
23-Jan-86   02:34 PM                              CALC
```

Fig. 5.48. Dividing the worksheet horizontally with 1-2-3's /Worksheet Window command.

Four commands are available for changing Javelin's worksheet borders:

/*Worksheet **B**order **I**nsert border
/*Worksheet **B**order **R**emove border
/*Worksheet **B**order **E**xpand border
/*Worksheet **B**order **S**hrink border

The first command enables you to divide the worksheet area with additional borders, and the second command removes additional borders. The /*Worksheet **B**order **E**xpand border command allows you to make additional rows in the top border for headings and subheadings, and for defining variable names or time periods. The last command deletes extra rows in the top border.

Suppose, for example, that you want to display two sets of data on the same worksheet: product revenue for January, 1986, and cost of goods. The worksheet displayed in figure 5.49 contains both of these. To create this worksheet, you use /*Worksheet **B**order **E**xpand to increase the top border so that both variable names and the January date can be included. You also use /*Worksheet **B**order **I**nsert to add the borders needed to display the Cost of Goods information.

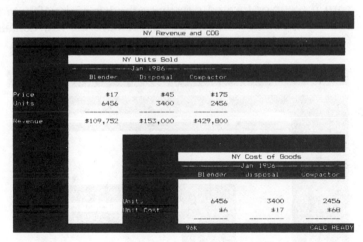

Fig. 5.49. Javelin allows you to display two spreadsheets on the same worksheet area.

To create a new border for the Cost of Goods worksheet, you moved the cursor two cells beneath the revenue total for Disposal, selected /*Worksheet **B**order **I**nsert, and pressed Enter. In order to expand the additional border to include heading, date, and variable names, you used the /*Worksheet **B**order **E**xpand command in the new top border.

You can also use /*Worksheet **B**order **I**nsert to create additional headings for your worksheet. In figure 5.49, for example, /*Worksheet **B**order **I**nsert was used to create a row reserved for a worksheet heading above the variable names and the date. If you need to include such a row, first create the extra border using /*Worksheet Border Insert, and then enter variable names and the date in the border closest to your worksheet area.

To delete additional worksheet borders that you have created with /*Worksheet Insert, use /*Worksheet Border Remove border. Whenever you remove the border you also remove any variable names or dates defined in that border, which means removing data displayed in the the worksheet.

To expand the top border, you simply move the cursor to the top border, select /*Worksheet Border Expand and press Enter. You can then enter variable names, labels, or dates. Both of the worksheets in figure 5.49 have expanded borders. The top row shows the date; the row beneath it identifies part of the variable name. *Blender*, for example, in conjunction with *Price*, *Units*, and *Revenue* identifies three variables in our model: *Blender Price*, *Blender Units*, and *Blender Revenue*.

To delete a row that you have added to the top border with /*Worksheet Border Expand, use /*Worksheet Border Shrink. When you use /*Worksheet Border Shrink, Javelin removes the row closest to the work area. For example, with the cursor located directly to the left of *Jan 1986* in figure 5.50, selecting /*Worksheet Border Shrink would remove the row containing *Blender*, *Disposal*, and *Compactor*.

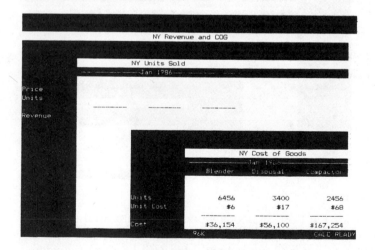

Fig. 5.50. Shrinking the top worksheet border using /*Worksheet Border Shrink.

Worksheet Format

Four different settings can determine the format in which values appear when displayed in the WORKSHEET view:

- **/Define Settings**, which establishes the global format for your model (see Chapter 3)

- **/Define Variable** settings to provide a format setting for individual variables

- **/Define Worksheet Format**, a setting for the worksheet you are working with

- **/*Worksheet Format**, a setting for specific rows, columns, or cells in a worksheet

Whenever values are displayed for variables, they are automatically displayed in the default format, as shown on the Model settings sheet. Unless you design your own model default setting, Javelin assigns the Automatic format to your model, which displays values with as many decimal places as needed and without commas separating numerals. The Automatic format and the other formats listed in the Model settings sheet (see fig. 5.51) determine how values linked with model variables are displayed in the WORKSHEET view.

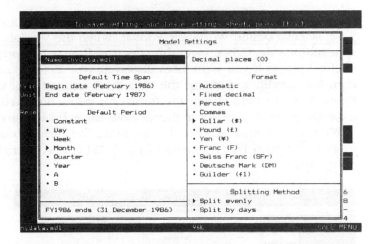

Fig. 5.51. Format options on the Model settings sheet.

You can override a model format setting in a Javelin worksheet with one of the other three settings. For example, the values in figure 5.52 appear in Dollar format because this is the setting for the whole model. If, however, you want to display the first three rows of values in comma format and the last row in Dollar format, you can assign a global comma format to the worksheet using the **/Define Worksheet Format** setting, and then assign a Dollar format to values displayed for *Total Operating Expense* using the **/*Worksheet Format Dollar** command. Both worksheet format commands will override format settings in **/Define Variable** and **/Define Settings**. Also, setting format for a single worksheet cell will override the format setting for a group of cells or the worksheet.

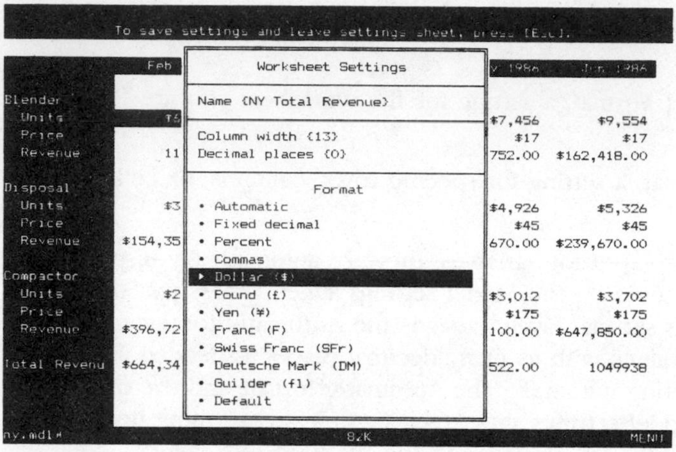

To save settings and leave settings sheet, press [Esc].

	Feb			y 1986	Jun 1986

Worksheet Settings

Name (NY Total Revenue)

Column width (13)
Decimal places (0)

Format
• Automatic
• Fixed decimal
• Percent
• Commas
▶ Dollar ($)
• Pound (£)
• Yen (¥)
• Franc (F)
• Swiss Franc (SFr)
• Deutsche Mark (DM)
• Guilder (fl)
• Default

Fig. 5.52. These worksheet values in Dollar format reflect a setting for the whole model.

To change the format from dollar to commas for all values displayed in figure 5.52, select /Define Worksheet Format. When the Worksheet settings sheet appears (see fig. 5.53), move the cursor to Commas and press Enter. Next, enter decimal places if you want them displayed; type 2, for example, press Enter, then Esc. Javelin will change the worksheet format for all values, as shown in figure 5.54. To then change the format for values displayed for *Total Operating Expense*, move the cursor to the variable name Total Operating, select /*Worksheet Format, choose Dollar, move the cursor to decimal places, type 2, press Enter, then Esc. All values in the Total Operating row will appear in dollar format.

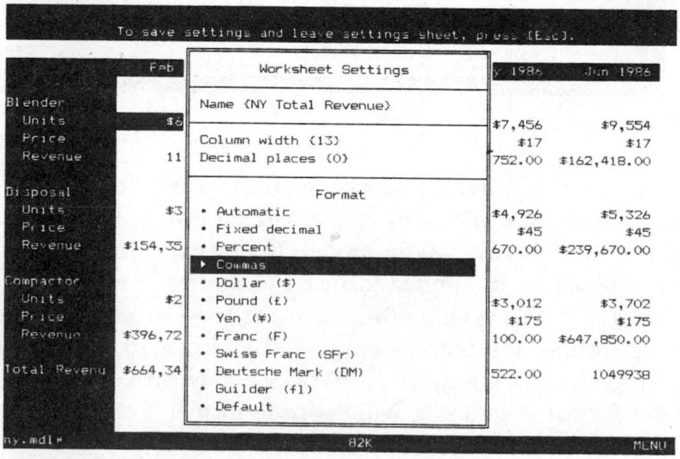

Fig. 5.53. Worksheet settings sheet.

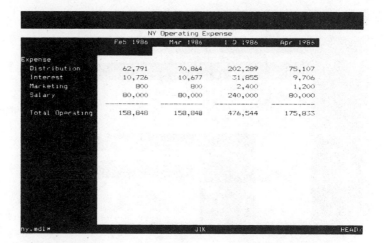

```
                              NY Operating Expense
                     Feb 1986        Mar 1986       1 Q 1986      Apr 1986

Expense
  Distribution        62,791          70,864        202,289        75,107
  Interest            10,726          10,677         31,855         9,706
  Marketing              800             800          2,400         1,200
  Salary              80,000          80,000        240,000        80,000
                    ----------      ----------     ----------     ----------
  Total Operating    158,848         158,848        476,544       175,833
```

Fig. 5.54. The worksheet now reflects settings for fixed decimal and commas.

The /*Worksheet Format command doesn't require that you "paint" a range to indicate what group of values you want to format. The command allows you to indicate cells to format by positioning the cursor as described in the following:

- *To format a whole row*, move the cursor to the appropriate row in the left border.

- *To format a whole column*, move the cursor to the appropriate column in the top border.

- *To format a cell*, move the cursor to the specific cell.

- *To format all cells within a worksheet's borders*, move the cursor to the corner where the top and left borders intersect. If, for example, you wanted to change the format for all cells in the *NY Cost of Goods* spreadsheet but not in the *NY Total Revenue* spreadsheet, you would move the the cursor to the corner, as in figure 5.55, select /*Worksheet Format, select Commas and press Esc.

Adjusting Column Width

Like conventional spreadsheet programs, the column width on Javelin's worksheet can be adjusted for the whole worksheet or for specific columns. Javelin's default column width for the worksheet is 13 characters. All 13 can be displayed in any column in the body of the worksheet; in the left and top borders 12 characters are displayed since Javelin reserves a 1-character space for a margin. If you enter numeric values that are longer than the column width, Javelin displays as many characters as permitted by the column width setting,

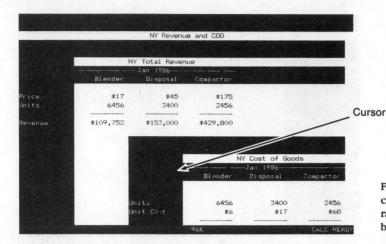

Fig. 5.55. Cursor position for changing format for worksheet range within a single pair of borders.

assuming that there is an appropriate format for Javelin to use. Otherwise, Javelin displays asterisks (***). If you enter text that is longer than the column width, Javelin displays all characters unless interrupted by numbers or text in adjacent cells (see fig. 5.56).

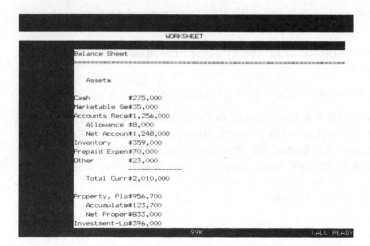

Fig. 5.56. Text display is limited if interrupted by numbers or text in an adjacent worksheet cell.

You can change column width globally for the whole worksheet or for an individual column. Both commands can narrow column width to 1 character or expand it to 40 characters. To change column width for the whole worksheet, use the /Define Worksheet command (see fig. 5.57). Move the cursor to Column width, type the new width, press Enter and press Esc to lock in the setting. Whenever you change column width in the worksheet settings sheet, the width applies only to the specific worksheet indicated by the *Name* in the settings sheet.

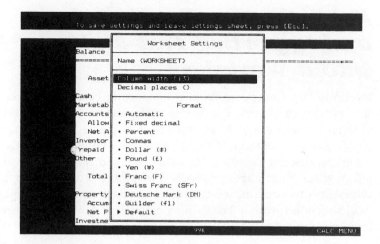

Fig. 5.57. Use the Worksheet
settings sheet (/Define
Worksheet) to change column
width for the whole worksheet.

On worksheets that contain more than one border, as in figure 5.58, the
/Define Worksheet Column width setting affects columns in each worksheet
area. If you want to change a specific column width in the worksheet, use the
/*Worksheet Width command. For example, to change the *Compactor* column
width in the *NY Cost of Goods* worksheet in figure 5.58, move the cursor to
the column, select /*Worksheet Width, and either type in the new width or use
the Left-arrow key (←) or Right-arrow key (→) to adjust width. Finally, press
Enter. The /*Worksheet Width setting for individual columns overrides the
/Define Worksheet Column width setting. Pressing the Del or Esc key will
return you to the default column width.

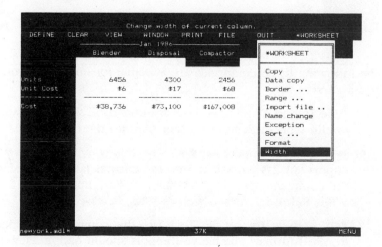

Fig. 5.58. Using the /*Worksheet
Width command to change a
specific column width.

Importing Javelin Worksheets
and Importing Text and 1-2-3 Files
into a Worksheet

Javelin is far more powerful in its importing capabilities than conventional
spreadsheet programs. The Javelin /File Import command alone provides seven
options for importing. As the submenu in figure 5.59 shows, /File Import allows
you to import complete files (models) as well as specific parts of files—
variables, macros, or values. In Chapter 6 and Appendix A, you can find more
information on importing models, variables, building blocks, time periods, and
values; in this section, we introduce Javelin's capabilities for importing
worksheets into other Javelin files, importing 1-2-3 worksheets, and importing
text into a worksheet.

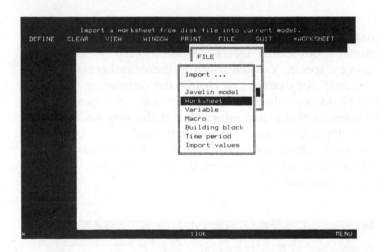

Fig. 5.59. The /File Import
command gives you seven
options for importing files into
Javelin.

The following three commands are available for importing worksheets and text
into a current file:

- /File Import Worksheet: Use this command when you want to import a
  Javelin worksheet from another file into the current file.

- /*Worksheet Import file WKS: Use this command when you want to
  import a 1-2-3 worksheet into the current Javelin worksheet. Although
  the command specifies WKS files, /*Worksheet Import file will import
  WK1, Release 2 files as well as WKS, Release 1A files.

- /*Worksheet Import file Text: Use this command to import text saved
  in ASCII format. The file you import should have a .PRN extension.

Importing Worksheets from Other Javelin Models

Javelin's /File Import Worksheet command enables you to import worksheets from other files to your current file. When you use this command, Javelin does not import onto an existing worksheet that you may have displayed, even if that worksheet is blank. Javelin merely adds the outside worksheet to the set of worksheets in your file. You can use /File Import Worksheet from any current view; you need not be working in the WORKSHEET view to import another Javelin worksheet. /File Import Worksheet imports headings in the borders, labels, exception cells, and range operations in the original worksheet to the current file. It does not import actual variables and associated values from the original worksheet. If you want to import variables, you must use the /File Import Variable command (see Appendix B).

Do not confuse /File Import Worksheet with commands in spreadsheet programs that consolidate worksheets by combining one with another. /File Import Worksheet merely copies a worksheet, as described above, from one Javelin file to the current file. The command will not combine the values of the current worksheet with the values of the imported worksheet. Note also that when the worksheet you are importing has the same name as an existing worksheet, Javelin will ask if you want to replace the existing worksheet with the imported one, and will give you a chance to cancel the operation.

Importing Text Files into a Worksheet

The first option from Javelin's /*Worksheet Import File command enables you to import characters from .PRN (ASCII format) files for use in Javelin worksheets. When you use the /*Worksheet Import file Text command, however, Javelin will import text only if it is enclosed in quotation marks. Otherwise, Javelin will only import numeric characters.

Consider, for example, the database in figure 5.60. If this database were saved as a text file (.PRN) and then imported into a Javelin worksheet, the import would produce the worksheet displayed in figure 5.61. Notice that not only does Javelin restrict the imported data to numeric characters (and the hyphen), it also places numerals originally set off by commas in individual columns.

To have values appear in individual columns, you need to change the format of the numbers in the original file from comma to general format. And if you want to import the labels, they must be enclosed in quotation marks. An imported file like that in figure 5.62 would be displayed in a Javelin worksheet as shown in figure 5.63. After you have imported numeric characters, you can easily make

Record Date	Tot Assets	Cur Assets	Working Capital	Gross Sales	Month EAT
31-Jan-86	$3,202,976	1,907,543	$1,160,483	$729,652	26,612
28-Feb-86	$3,194,328	1,902,393	$1,157,350	$727,682	26,540
31-Mar-86	$3,185,703	1,897,256	$1,154,225	$725,717	26,468
30-Apr-86	$3,177,102	1,892,134	$1,151,108	$723,758	26,397
31-May-86	$3,168,524	1,887,025	$1,148,000	$721,804	26,326
31-Jan-86	$3,159,969	1,881,930	$1,144,901	$719,855	26,255

Fig. 5.60. Sample database before importing into a Javelin worksheet.

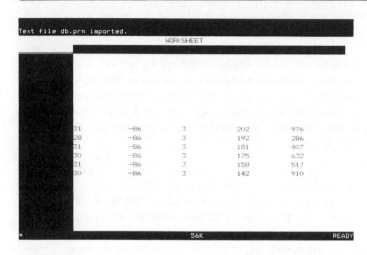

Fig. 5.61. What happens when you import a database saved as a text file into a Javelin worksheet.

use of this data as values by assigning variable names and dates to the worksheet.

"Record" "Date"	"Tot Assets"	"Cur Assets"	"Working" "Capital"	"Month" "Gross" "Sales"	"Month" "EAT"
31443	3202976	1907543	1160483	729652	26612
31471	3192286	1893724	1167836	726572	24269
31502	3181407	1843487	1118712	722683	24833
31532	3175632	1875261	1091880	717947	25481
31563	3158517	1888461	1154019	714820	22582
31593	3142910	1821474	1085296	713267	23201

Fig. 5.62. Changing the number format and enclosing the labels in quotation marks to import a database file into a Javelin worksheet.

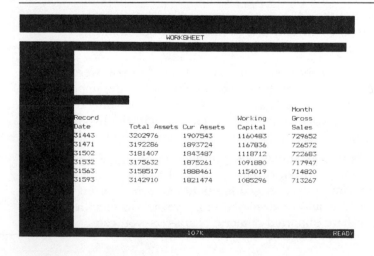

Fig. 5.63. Both numbers and labels imported into a Javelin worksheet.

Importing 1-2-3 Files

For users converting from 1-2-3 to Javelin, the /*Worksheet Import file WKS command will save time that might be spent re-creating and reentering models originally developed with 1-2-3. Importing 1-2-3 spreadsheet data into a Javelin worksheet is similar to importing text files into the worksheet because both can only be done from the WORKSHEET view and because completing command operations for both are similar. The primary difference is that Javelin imports both text and numbers from the 1-2-3 file.

Like importing text with the /*Worksheet Import Text command, though, importing a 1-2-3 spreadsheet has certain limitations. First, you cannot control where in the Javelin worksheet 1-2-3 data is imported. Javelin will import the 1-2-3 file so that it begins in the upper left corner of the worksheet, at the intersection of the left and top borders. Second, Javelin does not import 1-2-3 formulas; it only imports the values representing cell formulas. Third, 1-2-3 data is imported to the body of the Javelin worksheet in the same location where it appeared in 1-2-3.

Suppose, for example, that you want to import the 1-2-3 balance sheet pictured in figure 5.64. You would begin by creating a "shell worksheet" that is prepared to receive the imported data. (A "shell worksheet" contains the necessary variable names or names and dates for defining information as variables in Javelin's Information Base.) The body of the "shell worksheet" should remain blank, ready to receive the imported data from a .WKS (or a .WK1) file. To create a "shell worksheet," select /View Worksheet, and then enter the variable names in the left border, as in figure 5.65. With the "shell worksheet" prepared, you are ready to import the 1-2-3 file.

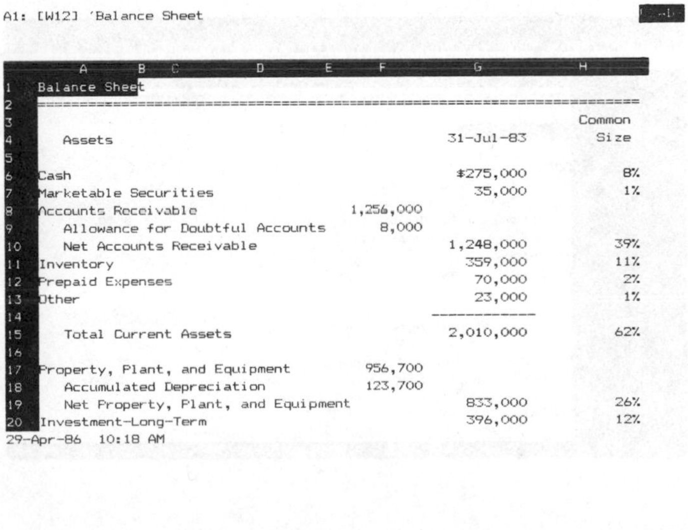

Fig. 5.64. Sample balance sheet created with 1-2-3.

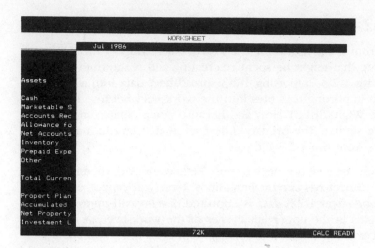

Fig. 5.65. "Shell worksheet" in Javelin ready for imported data from a 1-2-3 .WKS file.

To import the 1-2-3 file, select the /*Worksheet Import file **WKS** command and press Enter. Javelin responds with a prompt asking for the name of the 1-2-3 file. If the .WKS file you want to import is stored in the Javelin default drive and directory, you can use the SPELL key (Tab) to indicate the file. Otherwise, you need to specify the correct drive and directory. After you indicate the .WKS file, Javelin imports the file into the current worksheet (see fig. 5.66). To then make use of the data you've imported into Javelin, delete 1-2-3 labels and finish the worksheet by entering any other variable names and dates for the data to be used in your Javelin model. As mentioned previously, Javelin does not import 1-2-3 formulas; only the values resulting from these formulas are imported. You need, therefore, to re-create these formulas as Javelin formulas.

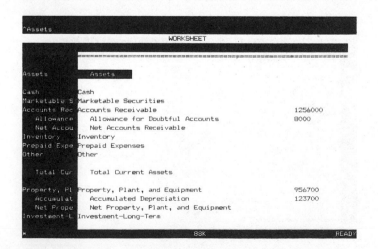

Fig. 5.66. After you indicate the .WKS file, Javelin imports the file into the current worksheet.

Although importing your 1-2-3 files will require some extra work, once you've converted your 1-2-3 models to Javelin models, you realize Javelin's conveniences for entering new data and editing existing data. You also benefit from having Javelin's 10 views for analyzing and reporting data that in 1-2-3 could only be presented through the spreadsheet and graphs.

Conclusion

The WORKSHEET view is one of Javelin's most important views. And users of conventional spreadsheet programs will find it particularly easy to use for inputting data and for defining variables and formulas. Spreadsheet users, however, will find that Javelin's incredible worksheet capability goes far beyond conventional spreadsheets in flexibility of formats and speed of producing reports.

The WORKSHEET view is a powerful model-building tool when it's used along with other views covered in this chapter—CHART and QUICK GRAPH—and in Chapter 3—DIAGRAM, TABLE, and FORMULAS. Used together, these views provide a full complement of tools for model building.

6

Importing and Consolidating among Javelin Models

In Javelin, importing and consolidating cover a wide range of operations. Commands accessed through /File Import, /Define Building block, and /*Worksheet Import provide capabilities for:

- importing a complete Javelin model into another

- importing part of a Javelin model, such as macros, individual variables, or data associated with variables

- consolidating part of or a complete Javelin model with another model

- importing a 1-2-3 worksheet into a Javelin worksheet

- importing a text (ASCII) file into a Javelin worksheet

In Chapter 5, we discussed the commands to import 1-2-3 and text (ASCII) files into Javelin worksheets. This chapter introduces you to the commands for importing and consolidating *among* Javelin models.

Commands Emphasized in this Chapter

/File Import Variable
/Define Building block Import data
/Define Building block Rollup
/File Import Import values
/File Import Javelin model
/File Import Macro
/File Import Building block
/File Import Time period

Importing and Consolidating: Javelin versus 1-2-3 and Symphony

If you're making the transition from 1-2-3 or Symphony to Javelin, you'll find Javelin's capabilities for importing and consolidating models quite different from those in 1-2-3 and Symphony. Keeping the following three major differences in mind will help you to make this transition.

First, although /File Import with Javelin and **/File** Import with Symphony and 1-2-3 have the same command name, they do not have the same functions. Importing refers to a much broader range of operations in Javelin than in 1-2-3 and Symphony. For example, 1-2-3's and Symphony's /File Import commands are limited to copying standard text (ASCII) files to specific locations in a 1-2-3 or Symphony worksheet; Javelin's /File Import command, on the other hand, imports information between Javelin .MDL files only. (Javelin's /*Worksheet Import **Text** command is more directly comparable to 1-2-3 and Symphony /File Import commands. See Chapter 5.)

Second, because Javelin imports and consolidates data stored in its Information Base, formulas and data are not anchored to worksheet cells. This feature eliminates the problems experienced with 1-2-3 or Symphony when you import formulas from one worksheet to another. When you import or consolidate with Javelin, for example, you cannot accidentally overwrite formulas and data in your current model. 1-2-3's and Symphony's /File Combine Copy and /File Combine Add commands, on the other hand, provide no security to protect users from overwriting current formulas and data.

Third, Javelin's Import data and Rollup building blocks allow Javelin to go far beyond 1-2-3's and Symphony's consolidation capabilities. These building blocks have no counterparts in 1-2-3 or Symphony. They allow consolidation and rollups to be done in Javelin based on variable names and time periods. This is a significant advance over 1-2-3's and Symphony's techniques of consolidating data by its position in the spreadsheet.

Javelin's Commands for Importing and Consolidating

Learning to use all of Javelin's importing capabilities will take some time, but you can begin by learning the differences between the importing and consolidating commands. /Define, /File, and /*Worksheet, from Javelin's main command menu (see fig. 6.1), lead directly to the specific commands for importing or consolidating:

/Define Building block
/File Import
/*Worksheet Import

Fig. 6.1. Javelin's main menu with the /File Import command highlighted.

/Define Building block enables you to import through the Import data and Rollup options. **/File Import** provides options for importing complete Javelin models, worksheets, individual variables, macros, building blocks, customized time periods, and values. **/*Worksheet Import** lets you import 1-2-3 .WKS files and text (ASCII) files into an active worksheet.

These commands differ in two ways. First, they differ according to whether you can import from another Javelin file or from a file created with another program. **/Define Building** block and **/File Import** provide options for importing only between Javelin models (.MDL files). **/*Worksheet Import**, on the other hand, lets you import an ASCII or 1-2-3 file. **/*Worksheet Import** is the only command, in fact, that can import files other than Javelin .MDL files.

Second, commands for importing and consolidating also differ according to the type of information and the way it is imported. When you use **/File Import Variable**, for example, Javelin imports the values, the formula, and the settings associated with the variable imported and retains the original variable name. On the other hand, when you use **/Define Building** block Import data, Javelin imports only the values of the original variable and assigns (or lets you assign) a new name to the imported data. The list in table 6.1 explains the specific functions of each command available for importing and consolidating.

Table 6.1
Commands for Importing and Consolidating

1. Commands for importing and consolidating variables and data

Function	Command
To import individual variables, keeping the original names, relationships, settings	**/F**ile Import **V**ariable
To import variable data alone and assign new variable names to the imported data	
To import variables and values and consolidate them	**/D**efine **B**uilding block **R**ollup
To import values for variables in Import data or Rollup building blocks	**/F**ile Import **I**mport values

2. Commands for importing part of or a complete Javelin model into your current model

Function	Command
To import a complete Javelin model	**/F**ile Import **J**avelin model
To import a worksheet from another Javelin model	**/F**ile Import **W**orksheet
To import a macro from another Javelin model	**/F**ile Import **M**acro
To import a building block from another Javelin model	**/F**ile Import **B**uilding block
To import a custom time period from another Javelin model	**/F**ile Import **T**ime period

3. Commands for importing text and 1-2-3 files into a Javelin worksheet

Function	Command
To import text (ASCII) files	**/∗W**orksheet Import **T**ext
To import 1-2-3 worksheet files	**/∗W**orksheet Import **1-2-3**

Importing Individual Variables with /File Import Variable

Javelin's /File Import Variable command imports individual variables into your current model. Suppose, for example, that in order to complete a model for calculating your company's operating expenses, you need to import variables from another model. You need, for example, to import variables and data for blender, compactor, and disposal unit sales (see fig. 6.2). You can use /File Import Variable to import these variables into your current model. After the variables are imported, you can use them to calculate total operating expense.

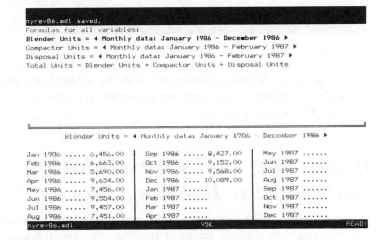

Fig. 6.2. Variables needed to calculate total operating expense.

To import variables with their formulas, settings, and data, select /File Import Variable. At the prompt, enter the name of the file containing the variable. You can enter the name by pressing the SPELL key (Tab) to locate the file containing the variables, or by typing the name. After the file name is entered, Javelin prompts you for the variable names. Again, you can use the SPELL key (Tab) for a list of variables, or you can type the full name.

After the variables are imported, you can complete your model and calculate results. Figure 6.3 shows the variables *Blender Units*, *Compactor Units*, and *Disposal Units* after they have been imported into the current model. Figure 6.2 displays the same variables in the original model. Notice that the imported variables in figure 6.3 appear in the same form as the variables in the original model.

Whenever you import a variable from another model into the current model, remember that you also import everything related to the variable in the original

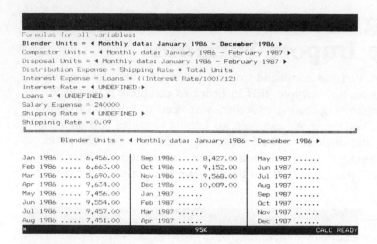

```
Formulas for all variables:
Blender Units = ◄ Monthly data: January 1986 - December 1986 ►
Compactor Units = ◄ Monthly data: January 1986 - February 1987 ►
Disposal Units = ◄ Monthly data: January 1986 - February 1987 ►
Distribution Expense = Shipping Rate * Total Units
Interest Expense = Loans * ((Interest Rate/100)/12)
Interest Rate = ◄ UNDEFINED ►
Loans = ◄ UNDEFINED ►
Salary Expense = 240000
Shipping Rate = ◄ UNDEFINED ►
Shippinig Rate = 0.09
```

```
              Blender Units = ◄ Monthly data: January 1986 - December 1986 ►

Jan 1986 ..... 6,456.00    Sep 1986 ..... 8,427.00    May 1987 ......
Feb 1986 ..... 6,663.00    Oct 1986 ..... 9,152.00    Jun 1987 ......
Mar 1986 ..... 5,690.00    Nov 1986 ..... 9,568.00    Jul 1987 ......
Apr 1986 ..... 9,634.00    Dec 1986 .... 10,089.00    Aug 1987 ......
May 1986 ..... 7,456.00    Jan 1987 ......            Sep 1987 ......
Jun 1986 ..... 9,554.00    Feb 1987 ......            Oct 1987 ......
Jul 1986 ..... 9,457.00    Mar 1987 ......            Nov 1987 ......
Aug 1986 ..... 7,451.00    Apr 1987 ......            Dec 1987 ......
                                    95K                          CALC READY
```

Fig. 6.3. Variables *Blender Units*, *Compactor Units*, and *Disposal Units* imported into the current model.

file. Not only are values imported along with the variable but also settings, notes, and other formulas associated with the variable. Be aware, however, that although the values of the total are imported, the values of the variables that make up the formula are not.

Importing and Consolidating with Javelin Building Blocks

Javelin building blocks represent complex relationships among variables simply and accurately as a single graph or diagram. The tremendous advantage of Javelin building blocks is that they treat relationships (lookup tables, time-delay curves, consolidated models) without requiring that you enter complicated formulas. Five building block applications are possible with Javelin's /**Define Building** block command; two of these provide capabilities for importing and consolidating. First, you can import data associated with variables from other models by using the /**Define Building** block **Import** data command. Second, you can import and consolidate variables with the /**Define Building** block **Rollup** command.

Importing with /Define Building Block Import Data

Although the /**File Import Variable** command lets you import variables and all associated data, formulas, and settings, the /**Define Building** block **Import** data command is limited to importing only data linked to variables in other models.

Once you have indicated what data should be imported and assigned a new variable name (or used Javelin's default name) for the data, Javelin imports data alone, without the original associated variables or settings.

Consider, for example, what happens when you use /File Import Variable and /Define Building block Import data on the same variable from another Javelin model. Importing *Blender Revenue*, for example, through /File Import results in importing the complete formula, as illustrated in the FORMULAS view in figure 6.4. Importing *Blender Revenue* through the /Define Building block Import data command, on the other hand, only imports the data associated with *Blender Revenue*, assigns a new name (*Corp Blender Revenue*) to the data, and displays the variable as the output of a Javelin building block (see fig. 6.5).

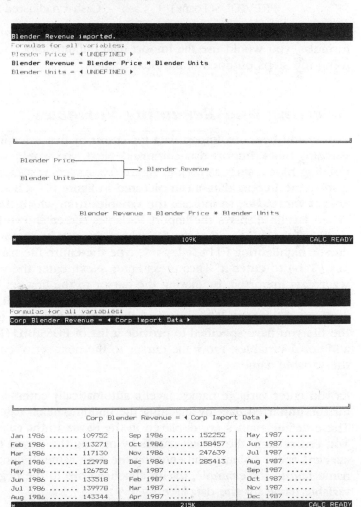

Fig. 6.4. The /File Import command imports complete formulas.

Fig. 6.5. The /Define Building block Import data command is used to import the data associated with a variable.

The Import data building block is especially useful when you want to use data originally entered through a formula as input data in a new model. The Import data building block "frees" the data originally linked to variable relationships and formulas. Suppose, for example, that you want to create the following formula in your current model:

Interest Expense = Loans * ((Interest Rate/100)/12)

The data for the variable *Loans*, however, is stored within another model, which calculates the values for *Loans* with the formula:

Loans = IF(PREVIOUS(Loans) + Cash - Cash Unadjusted <0, 0,
            PREVIOUS(Loans) + Cash - Cash Unadjusted) ; Beginning Loans.

If, in your current model, you need only the data for *Loans* rather than its formulas, you would use the Import data building block to import the data using the steps outlined in the next section.

Selecting and Renaming Variables

You would begin to import data for *Loans* by first selecting the /Define Building block Import data command. Next, you would supply a name for the building block, such as Corp in figure 6.6. Assigning a name causes Javelin to display the Import data menu pictured in figure 6.7. Choose the first item, Select variables, to indicate the variables from which data should be imported. When Javelin displays the Import Variables screen shown in figure 6.8, you would enter the name of the file where the data to import is stored. With the cursor highlighting File to import, type the entire file name or use the SPELL key (Tab) to enter it. Then press Enter. Next, enter the variables for which you want data imported, by moving the cursor to the first set of braces within the Variables to Import column and typing or using the SPELL key (Tab) to define each variable name. When you use the SPELL key (Tab), it actually looks into the file you have specified to provide a list of POSSIBILITIES. To enter additional variables, move the cursor to the next set of empty braces and enter the variable name.

As you enter variable names, Javelin automatically enters a new variable name for the imported data by attaching the building block name to each original. These default names are displayed in the Names in the current model column. You can rename the default names by moving the cursor to the Names in the current model column and entering the new name. When you enter the variable name *Loans,* for example, Javelin attaches *Corp* to the beginning to create a variable name for the data (see fig. 6.9).

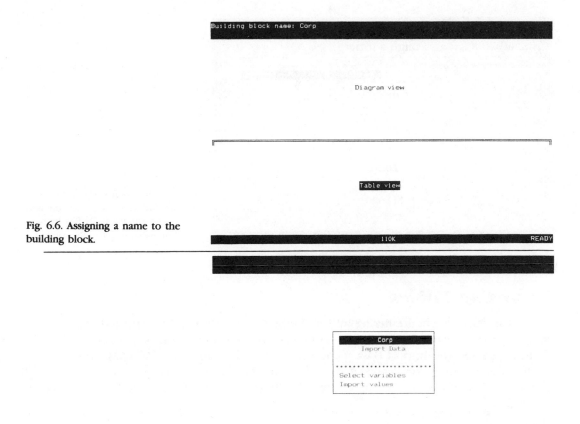

Fig. 6.6. Assigning a name to the building block.

Fig. 6.7. Entering the filename for Importing Variables.

Fig. 6.8. Import Data variables list.

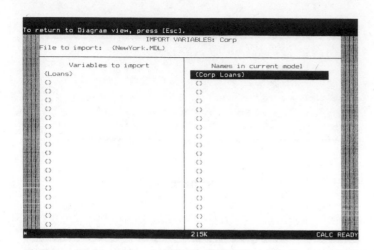

Fig. 6.9. When you enter a variable name in the left column, Javelin automatically fills in a new name in the right column.

Importing Values

When you have finished entering all variable names for data to be imported and have renamed variables, press Esc to complete the *Select variables* step. You should then see the Import Data menu screen, which displays a DIAGRAM view of all variable names for imported data. To complete the final step necessary for importing data, move the cursor to Import values and press Enter (see figure 6.10).

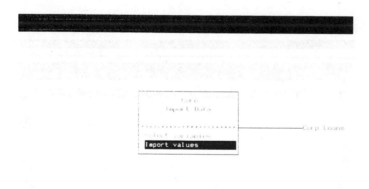

Fig. 6.10. Choosing the *Import values* option on the Import Data menu.

Consolidating Data with /Define Building Block Rollup

Whenever you want to combine variables and data from two or more Javelin models into a single consolidated model, use the /Define Building block Rollup command. With this command, you can combine values for any variables from different files but with the same variable names. Javelin's /Define Building block Rollup is ideal, for example, when companies want to consolidate data from different departments or divisions. As long as variable names are the same in all the models, Javelin totals values from original models and creates variables in the current model for both original and consolidated data.

Javelin's /Define Building block Rollup command makes consolidation easy, quick, and reliable. You don't need to worry about the confusion and errors that plague spreadsheet users when they try to consolidate several large models into one.

Consider how you would consolidate product revenues for the two regional offices of Future Home Appliances, Inc.—New York and Los Angeles. To consolidate data with Javelin's /Define Building block Rollup command, two criteria must be met. First, each office must have models containing the same variables for storing and calculating revenue data. In other words, each office must use the list of formulas and variables shown in figure 6.11. Second, in order to consolidate variables, each office must use a different file name. The New York office, for example, uses the file name NYREV.MDL for its revenue model; the Los Angeles office uses LAREV.MDL for its revenue model.

```
Formulas for all variables:
Blender Price = 17
Blender Revenue = Blender Price * Blender Units
Blender Units = ◀ Monthly data: January 1986 – December 1986 ▶
Compactor Price = 175
Compactor Revenue = Compactor Price * Compactor Units
Compactor Units = ◀ Monthly data: January 1986 – December 1986 ▶
Disposal Price = 45
Disposal Revenue = Disposal Price * Disposal Units
Disposal Units = ◀ Monthly data: January 1986 – December 1986 ▶
Total Revenue = Blender Revenue + Disposal Revenue + Compactor Revenue
```

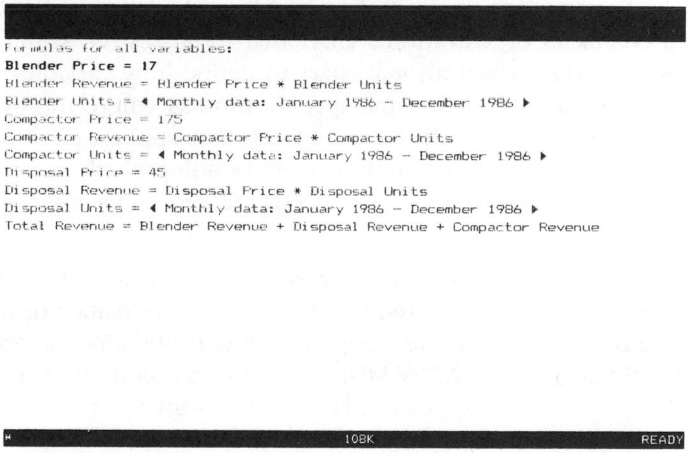

Fig. 6.11. To consolidate, variable names must be the same in different models.

`W                                        108K                            READY`

With the criteria for variable and file names met, you can create a consolidated model that imports all variables and data and then consolidates that data into

corporate totals. To consolidate NYREV.MDL and LAREV.MDL, begin by selecting
/Define Building block Rollup. When the prompt Building block name: appears,
supply a name that Javelin can attach to the new building block. The building
block consolidating NYREV.MDL and LAREV.MDL, for example, is named *Future
Home*.

Once you enter a building block name and press Enter, Javelin displays a menu
for completing the consolidation (see figure 6.12) with options for editing the
organizational chart, selecting the variables, and importing values.

```
┌─────────────────────────┐
│▌   Future Home          │
│       Rollup            │
│                         │
│ .......................  │
│ Edit org chart          │
│ Select variables        │
│ Import values           │
└─────────────────────────┘
```

Fig. 6.12. A Rollup building block
menu.

Telling Javelin Which Variables To Consolidate

The first option on the Rollup building block menu, Edit org chart, enables you
to create an organizational chart that indicates the structure of the rollup. You
also use the organizational chart to define how variables are identified when
imported and to define the specific models where the original variables are
stored. Figure 6.13 shows the screen that appears after you select Edit org
chart. The single box indicates the building block name that also identifies the
consolidated variables. You can change this name if you want by typing a new
name.

Your next step is to indicate how variables from other models should be
identified when imported and to indicate the names of the files where these
variables are stored. Because you are consolidating variables from the files
NYREV.MDL and LAREV.MDL, you can complete the organizational chart by
pressing the Ins key to tell Javelin you want to create a new box to enter a
variable identifier and a file name. Javelin then displays a box (see fig. 6.14)
where you can enter both the variable identifier and the file name. To indicate
that you want all variables from NYREV.MDL identified by *NY* at the beginning
of the variable name, enter *NY* in the first row of the box.

Fig. 6.13. The organizational
chart before adding more boxes.

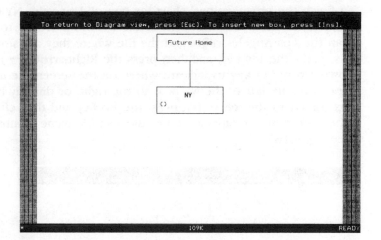

Fig. 6.14. The organizational
chart after one box has been
added.

Within the braces below NY in figure 6.14, you should enter the name of the
file (model) where the variables are stored. File names must be given for the
models from which you want to consolidate variables. Whenever you enter a file
name in braces in the boxes of the organizational chart, you can use any of the
following formats:

1. First part of file name without extension: *NYREV*

2. Complete file name: *NYREV.MDL*

3. File name with path name: *\JAV\NYREV*

To indicate to Javelin which file the variables are stored in, move the cursor to
the second row of the box and type *NYREV.MDL* (see fig. 6.15).

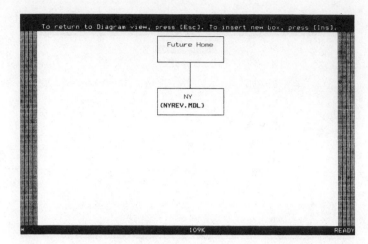

Fig. 6.15. File name in braces indicates the model to be imported and consolidated.

To finish the organizational chart for consolidating the NYREV.MDL and LAREV.MDL files, you must next create a box for LAREV to identify the variables from the Los Angeles office and the file where they are stored. To create a new box, press the Ins key, and then press the Right-arrow (→), Left-arrow (←), or Down-arrow (↓) key to indicate where on the screen the new box should appear: to the left of the NY box, to the right, or directly below. To create a box for LA to the left of NY, press the Ins key and the Left-arrow key (←). When the new box appears, enter the variable name identifier and the file name (see fig. 6.16).

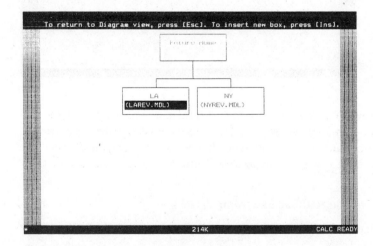

Fig. 6.16. Adding a box to the left.

If necessary, Javelin enables you to create multiple levels in the organizational chart, as shown in figure 6.17. If you need to delete a box, move the cursor to the box you want to delete and press the Del key. You can, however, delete a box only when no other boxes are attached beneath it. When you place a box directly beneath another box, the lower box becomes a subtotal or total box. Only boxes with no boxes attached to them can refer to file names.

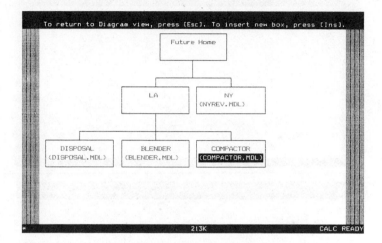

Fig. 6.17. The organizational chart with multiple levels.

Selecting Variables for Consolidating

Once you have created the complete organizational chart for consolidating the files you want, press the Esc key. Javelin returns to the main Rollup menu where you can select the variables you want to rollup on the *Select variables* screen displayed in figure 6.18. On the screen, enter each variable you want to consolidate by either typing the variable name or using the SPELL key (Tab). Remember that Javelin consolidates only variables that have the same names as those in the files from which you want to rollup. If you need to delete a variable name you've entered, move the cursor to the variable you want to delete and press the Del key.

With the complete list of variables supplied, Javelin creates the DIAGRAM view pictured in figure 6.19, displaying all variables to be imported and consolidated. Notice that variables imported from the NYREV.MDL file are identified with NY preceding the variable name; variables from the LAREV file are identified with LA.MDL. Variables that consolidate the two are identified with the name Future Home.

If you check all the variables imported and consolidated through the Rollup building block in the FORMULAS view, you'll find, as the list in figure 6.20 indicates, that Javelin identifies each variable in terms of the rollup. Once variables are defined through the Rollup building block, you cannot redefine them by editing the variables. If you were to try to edit the variable *Future*

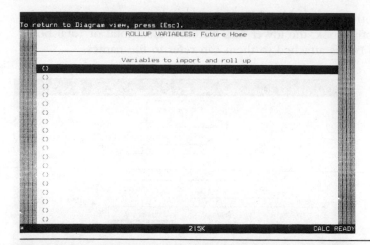

Fig. 6.18. The Select variables screen for Rollup variables.

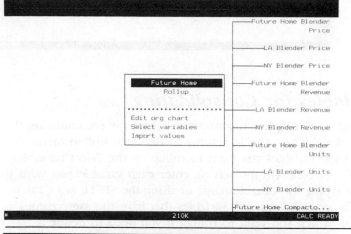

Fig. 6.19. The DIAGRAM view displays all variables in rollup.

```
Formulas for all variables:
Future Home Blender Price = ◀ Future Home Rollup ▶
Future Home Blender Revenue = ◀ Future Home Rollup ▶
Future Home Blender Units = ◀ Future Home Rollup ▶
Future Home Compactor Price = ◀ Future Home Rollup ▶
Future Home Compactor Revenue = ◀ Future Home Rollup ▶
Future Home Compactor Units = ◀ Future Home Rollup ▶
Future Home Disposal Price = ◀ Future Home Rollup ▶
Future Home Disposal Revenue = ◀ Future Home Rollup ▶
Future Home Disposal Units = ◀ Future Home Rollup ▶
Future Home Total Revenue = ◀ Future Home Rollup ▶
LA Blender Price = ◀ Future Home Rollup ▶
LA Blender Revenue = ◀ Future Home Rollup ▶
LA Blender Units = ◀ Future Home Rollup ▶
LA Compactor Price = ◀ Future Home Rollup ▶
LA Compactor Revenue = ◀ Future Home Rollup ▶
LA Compactor Units = ◀ Future Home Rollup ▶
LA Disposal Price = ◀ Future Home Rollup ▶
LA Disposal Revenue = ◀ Future Home Rollup ▶
LA Disposal Units = ◀ Future Home Rollup ▶
LA Total Revenue = ◀ Future Home Rollup ▶
NY Blender Price = ◀ Future Home Rollup ▶
H                                          209K                          CALC READY
```

Fig. 6.20. The FORMULAS view showing the Rollup building block variables.

Home Blender Price by pressing the Edit key (F2), indicating the variable to be edited, and then typing = *27*, Javelin would display the following error message:

`Cannot redefine the output of a building block.`

Importing Values

After you have entered all the variables you want to import and consolidate, the final step is to select *Import values* from the Rollup building block menu. Move the cursor to `Import values` and press Enter. The `WAIT` message flashes while Javelin is importing values, then the program indicates that the model needs to be calculated. To calculate all formulas, press the CALC key (F9).

Once you have imported and calculated values, you can view variables and data in Javelin views or create worksheets, graphs, macros, etc. You can also import parts of other Javelin models—macros, worksheets, variables—into the file containing your Rollup building block. Note that with Javelin's **/File** Import Variable command you can import variables that are the same as the original variables you imported into the rollup. For example, you can import *Blender Revenue* from the original NYREV.MDL file into the model although the rollup variable *NY Blender Revenue* and *Blender Revenue* are linked to the same data. With the rollup complete, the original *Blender Revenue* is identified as a new variable. Javelin distinguishes only between the variable names. The screen in figure 6.21, for example, shows the same data for `Blender Revenue` and `NY Blender Revenue`.

```
109752
              Blender Revenue = Blender Price * Blender Units

   Jan 1986 ....... 109752   Oct 1986 ....... 158457   Jul 1987 ......
   Feb 1986 ....... 113271   Nov 1986 ....... 247639   Aug 1987 ......
   Mar 1986 ....... 117130   Dec 1986 ....... 285413   Sep 1987 ......
   Apr 1986 ....... 122978   Jan 1987 ......           Oct 1987 ......
   May 1986 ....... 126752   Feb 1987 ......           Nov 1987 ......
   Jun 1986 ....... 133518   Mar 1987 ......           Dec 1987 ......
   Jul 1986 ....... 139978   Apr 1987 ......           Jan 1988 ......
   Aug 1986 ....... 143344   May 1987 ......           Feb 1988 ......
   Sep 1986 ....... 152252   Jun 1987 ......           Mar 1988 ......

          NY Blender Revenue = ◄ Future Home Rollup ►

   Jan 1986 ....... 109752   Sep 1986 ....... 152252   May 1987 ......
   Feb 1986 ....... 113271   Oct 1986 ....... 158457   Jun 1987 ......
   Mar 1986 ....... 117130   Nov 1986 ....... 247639   Jul 1987 ......
   Apr 1986 ....... 122978   Dec 1986 ....... 285413   Aug 1987 ......
   May 1986 ....... 126752   Jan 1987 ......           Sep 1987 ......
   Jun 1986 ....... 133518   Feb 1987 ......           Oct 1987 ......
   Jul 1986 ....... 139978   Mar 1987 ......           Nov 1987 ......
   Aug 1986 ....... 143344   Apr 1987 ......           Dec 1987 ......
                                 208K                      CALC READY
```

Fig. 6.21. Importing variables that are linked to the same data.

Keep in mind the differences among **/Define Building block Rollup**, **/Define Building block Import**, **/File Import Javelin**, and **/File Import Variable**. Only with the /Define Building block Rollup can you import and consolidate variables; the other three commands import variables but provide no option for consolidation.

Updating Values in a Rollup or Import Data Building Block

Once you have created a Rollup or an Import data building block, you will need to update it whenever data changes or is added to the original models that you've imported into the building block. You can update values two different ways in a Rollup or Import data building block.

First, you can update values by returning to the main menu of the specific building block and selecting Import values. Suppose, for example, that you need to update values in a Rollup building block which consolidates product revenue. To access the main menu of the Rollup building block, either press the GO TO key (F5) and indicate the building block or select Javelin's DIAGRAM view and move the cursor to the building block. When the menu appears, move the cursor to Import values and press Enter. Javelin replaces existing values with new values, making the building block current with data from original files.

Second, you can also update data in a building block by using the /File Import Import values command. To update values in a Rollup or Import data building block, select /File Import Import values. As soon as you have selected the command, Javelin imports values from the original files containing those variables for all building blocks. Javelin again replaces all existing values.

Note that there are two important differences whenever you use /File Import Import values instead of the *Import values* option from a building block. First, you can select the /File Import Import values command from anywhere in your model; in other words, you do not need to be working within the building block to operate the command. Second, whenever you use the /File Import Import values command, Javelin updates *all* building blocks within a model. If you want to preserve the original values for some building blocks but update the values for others, you should choose the *Import values* option from the building block menu.

Importing Complete Javelin Models and Parts

Javelin's importing options allow you to import as much of an existing model as you need, from the complete model to segments of a model. To help save you the time and trouble of having to re-create a model, several commands in the /File Import menu let you use all or the following parts of Javelin models in your current model:

1. You can use the /File Worksheet command to import worksheets already created in other Javelin models for use in your current model. (See Chapter 5 for more information on importing worksheets.)

2. You can import macros already existing in other Javelin files.

3. You can import building blocks from other files and use them in your current file.

4. You can use the /File Import command to borrow custom time periods that you created in another model and use those time periods in your current model.

Importing Complete Models into the Current Model

If you want to import all variables, formulas, values, worksheets, and settings from one model to another, use Javelin's /File Import Javelin command. With this command, you add to the existing variables, formulas, and values in your current file. You would use /File Import Javelin, for example, to import smaller models into one larger one. Importing three models—an individual revenue model, operating expense model, and cost of goods model—is necessary to build a larger income statement and a balance sheet that use variables and data from all three.

To import three different models into your current model, for example, choose /File Import Javelin model. When the prompt appears asking you to identify the model name, enter the name by either typing it or using the SPELL key (Tab) and press Enter. Repeat the import operation until you have imported all three models. Like the /File Import Variable command, /File Import Javelin model imports everything associated with a variable including values, notes, settings, and formulas. But in addition, /File Import Javelin model imports worksheets, macros, and settings with all model variables, formulas, and data.

If there are conflicts among the model being imported and the current model—duplicate variable names, for example—Javelin will prompt you for a decision to continue or to abort the import process.

Importing Macros

Javelin facilitates using macros with the /File Import Macro command. And if you've used a spreadsheet program, you'll find that using macros across files with Javelin is much easier than with programs like 1-2-3 or Symphony. Importing macros with 1-2-3 or Symphony requires either importing the worksheet range containing a macro in another 1-2-3 or Symphony file or maintaining a separate macro library file that can be imported.

If you create macros that you can use for any model, the /File Import Macro command lets you easily import the macro into your current file. Macros like the one for creating graphs described in Chapter 11 can be imported into any model in which you want to create a graph. To import the *Grapher* macro, select /File Import Macro. When Javelin displays the prompt for file name, enter the name of the file containing the macro you want to use, then enter the macro name. As soon as Javelin imports the macro, you can use it.

Building Macro Library Files with /File Import

As you continue to create macros within your Javelin models, having a single file reserved for collecting these macros will save you the trouble of trying to remember file names for models containing original macros. You'll find it particularly helpful to create a macro library file storing those generic macros you could use in many types of models. And when you need to use a generic macro, simply use /File Import Macro to import the macro into the current model.

To create a macro library file, begin with a new Javelin file and select /File Import Macro. Enter the file and macro name to complete the import operation, and repeat the process for as many macros as you want to store in your library file. Save this library file under a name that indicates its function and continue adding macros to the file as they are created.

A macro library file saves you time because it eliminates the need to search through a long list of file names when you want to import a macro. In addition, a macro library file can free up extra memory for other elements in your Javelin model. You conserve memory used by your model because you avoid storing too many macros in the model. With a library file, you can easily import macros when needed and clear them from the model when no longer needed.

Importing Javelin Building Blocks

Javelin building blocks represent complex relationships among variables simply and accurately without requiring that you show these relationships by building complicated formulas. Lookup tables, model consolidation, and time delay curves, for example, can be done simply with Javelin building blocks. And once you have created a building block in one model, the /File Import Building block command lets you import it into other models as well.

The concept of Javelin building blocks is covered in more detail in Chapter 7, but consider here how the /File Import Building block command functions. Suppose, for example, that you have three Rollup building blocks in three different models. You want to bring these building blocks together in a single model. In one file, you have a Rollup building block consolidating corporate marketing expenses; in another file, a Rollup building block consolidating corporate salary expense; and in a third file, a Rollup building block consolidating product distribution expenses. You would use the /File Import Building block command to incorporate all three building blocks into one model.

To import building blocks, follow these steps. First, select /File Import Building block. When Javelin displays the prompt for file name, enter the file name of the model containing the original Rollup building block. You can enter the file name by either typing it or using the SPELL key (Tab). Second, when Javelin asks for the building block name, enter the name, again either by typing it or using the SPELL key (Tab), then press Enter. Javelin will import the building block, making it possible for you to use it in your current model.

Importing Custom Time Periods

You can import custom time periods created in other models into any Javelin file. (See Chapter 4 for more on custom time periods.) Suppose, for example, that you have created a custom time period for entering inventory bimonthly. In a second model, you need to use the same custom period to enter product shipping data bimonthly. With the /File Import Time command, you can import the custom period from the first model to use in the second.

To import a custom time period, select /File Import Time period. Javelin will ask you for the file name containing original custom period. Enter the file name by typing it or by using the SPELL (Tab) key. Next, Javelin will prompt you to identify the period name (A or B). Enter A or B, and press Enter. The custom period will then be imported.

Keep in mind when you use /File Import Time period that imported periods will overwrite existing periods in the current model. For example, you may have created a bimonthly period for the current model, entering this period as the *A* period. If you then direct Javelin to import an *A* biweekly period from another model into the current model, Javelin will replace the current *A* bimonthly period with the biweekly period.

Conclusion

Javelin's commands for importing and consolidating can be powerful assets for building your models. As you continue to develop models, you'll save time and simplify model creation by importing variables, worksheets, data, macros, and custom time periods you have created in other models. And with Javelin's /Define Building block Rollup command, you can consolidate smaller models into larger companywide or corporate models.

7

Using the Time Delay, Lookup Table, and Curve Building Blocks

Javelin building blocks allow you to define complex relationships between variables simply and effectively. These variables can be in the same model or in different models. This chapter focuses on three Javelin building blocks that define relationships between variables in the current model: the Time delay building block, the Lookup table building block, and the Curve building block.

Commands Emphasized in this Chapter

/**Define Building block**
/**Define Building block Name change**
/**Define Building block Time delay**
/**Define Building block Lookup table**
/**Define Building block Curve**
/**Clear Building block**

The Time delay building block defines a relationship between a variable and the current as well as the previous values of another variable. You can use this building block in many of the same applications where you would use Javelin's PREVIOUS function. You can use the Time delay building block to forecast accounts receivable and cash collections, project new product sales as well as warranty costs and spare parts requirements, and perform statistical smoothing of data to uncover trends.

Like the Time delay building block, the Lookup table building block defines a relationship between two variables, but uses a lookup table format to establish an input range and corresponding output values. This building block provides

223

the same capabilities as the @VLOOKUP and @HLOOKUP commands in 1-2-3. You can use the Lookup table building block to show tax tables, volume discount schedules, production cost as a function of operating rate, and production learning curves.

Similar in capability to the Lookup building block, the Curve building block represents the relationship between two variables with a graph rather than a table. The Curve building block is particularly useful for describing economic relationships, such as quantity sold versus selling price, where you know what the relationship looks like but don't know the exact numbers required to build a lookup table.

Before taking a closer look at these three building blocks, let's review some general principles about defining and using building blocks.

- Define a building block with the /Define Building block command. After you specify the type of building block and enter its name, Javelin changes the current window to the DIAGRAM view and displays the building block being defined. You then specify the input and output pairs of variables and the relationship to be shown.

- Modify a building block by returning to the DIAGRAM view and highlighting the building block with the cursor. You can then add or remove input and output variables or change the relationship defined by the building block.

- Delete a building block by using the /Clear Building block command.

Warning! When you delete a building block, all output variables defined by the building block are deleted.

- Change the name of a building block with the /Define Building block Name change command. Javelin prompts you for the existing name, then for the new name. You can also use Javelin's SPELL key (Tab) to fill in the existing name.

The Time Delay Building Block

The Time delay building block defines the relationship between a variable and the current and previous values of another variable. The Time delay building block lets you create relationships that have a fixed time dependence.

Using the Time Delay Building Block

You can use the Time delay building block for any of the following:

- to project both accounts receivable and cash collections as a function of current and previous sales

- to project a new product's sales as a function of the time period since product introduction

- to project product service and spare part needs as a function of sales over time

- to project production requirements based on a sales forecast and the flow of product through various stages of production to final sales distribution

- to analyze trends in data

Determining Cash Receipts

As an example of using the Time delay building block, suppose that you are developing a financial model of your company's cash receipts and accounts receivable. Your company typically experiences the following collection schedule:

    5% payment at time of sale
15% payment after one month
30% payment after two months
10% payment after three months
35% payment after four months

By entering this collection schedule into a Time delay building block, you can determine cash receipts for a given month as a function of sales in that month and in the four previous months. (Your collections add up to 95 percent of sales in a given month. After four months, five percent of the outstanding balance is assumed to be uncollectable.) Figure 7.1 shows an example of collections versus billings using this time delay schedule. Notice that after a jump in billings, collections require several months to catch up.

Showing Uncollected Amounts

The company's accounts receivable balance consists of uncollected amounts at the end of each month. This includes amounts uncollected for this month's sales

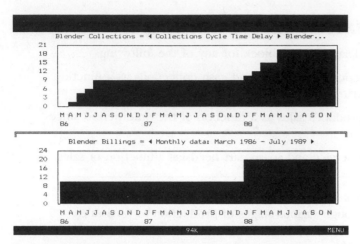

Fig. 7.1. Collections as a time-delayed function of billings.

as well as for sales made in previous months. Based on the collection schedule shown previously, the company's accounts receivable consist of:

    95% of the current month's sales
    80% of last month's sales
    50% of sales two months ago
    40% of sales three months ago

By entering this schedule in a Time delay building block, you can project *Accounts Receivable* at the end of any month based on sales from that month and from the three previous months. Note that the percentages in this schedule add up to 265 percent of sales. One way to understand this percentage is that, on average, receivables remain outstanding for 2.65 months after the sale is made.

Statistical Analysis

The Time delay building block can also be used to smooth data. Although Javelin's RAVG function performs a rolling average (the smoothed current value is the simple average of the past *n* values), the Time delay building block can perform data smoothing using weighted averages of past values.

Creating a Time Delay Building Block

You set up a Time delay building block by choosing the /Define Building block Time delay command. Next, you give the Time delay building block a name; for this example we use *Collections Cycle* (see fig. 7.2). Javelin responds by switching to a DIAGRAM view and showing the building block.

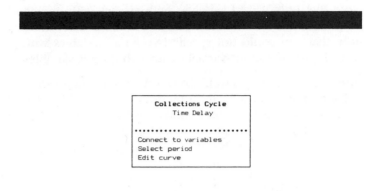

Fig. 7.2. *Collections Cycle* time
delay building block.

To define the variables, move the cursor from Collections Cycle to Connect to variables and press Enter. The Connections settings sheet appears on the screen (see fig. 7.3). You use this settings sheet to indicate which variables are time delays of other variables. The cursor marks the empty Inputs column where you begin to enter your settings. Type *Blender Billings* in this column, move the cursor to the Outputs column, and type *Blender Collections*.

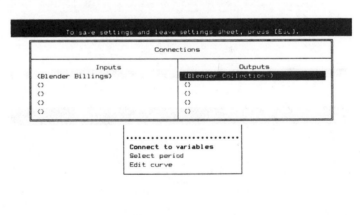

Fig. 7.3. You specify the input
and output variables for a table
on the Connections settings
sheet.

You can enter up to five pairs of input and output variables for each Time delay building block. For the purpose of our example, add *Compactor Billings*, *Compactor Collections*, *Disposal Billings*, and *Disposal Collections*. After typing the variable names, press Esc to leave the settings sheet.

Note that only paired variables will interact with one another. Each input/output pair in a Time delay building block is calculated independently. Also note that you could not specify two input variables with just one output variable, or one input variable with two output variables.

After you press Esc, Javelin shows the connecting variables attached to the Time delay building block in the DIAGRAM view (see fig. 7.4). If we had listed five variable pairs on the Connections settings sheet for the *Collections Cycle* Time delay building block, all five would appear. If, however, you have two windows on the screen and if the block is too big to fit in one window, figure 7.5 shows what you will see on the screen.

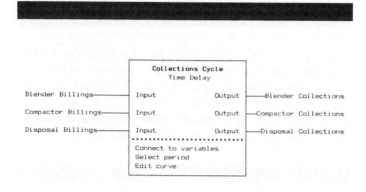

Fig. 7.4. DIAGRAM view of Time delay building block showing input and output variables.

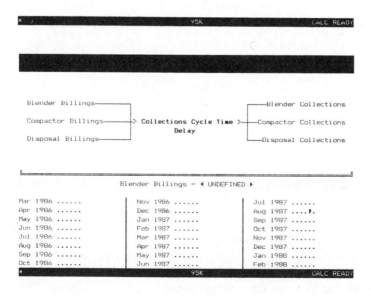

Fig. 7.5. Javelin shows only the name of the building block itself when room in the view is limited.

Indicating the Base Time Period

Because you're working with a time delay, you must indicate the time delay's base period. Begin by moving the cursor to the Select Period line in the Time delay building block. Pressing Enter activates the *Period for Delay* box, which resembles the *Period* box on the Variable settings sheet (see fig. 7.6).

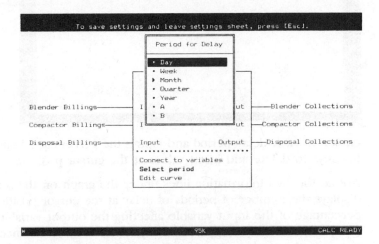

Fig. 7.6. Entering the base period into the Time delay building block.

Any valid Javelin time period (including custom time periods) can be used as a period for delay. If the time delay is in days, the base period would be *Day*. Likewise, if the delay is weeks, you would select *Week*. In this example, because the company collects its billings in one-month intervals, the base time delay is *Month*.

Selecting a period for delay is the same as choosing other options in Javelin. Move the cursor to the appropriate choice, press Enter, then press Esc to return to the DIAGRAM view.

Editing the Time Delay Curve

The next part of defining a Time delay building block involves editing the curve that represents the time delay. Move the cursor to the Edit Curve option in the *Collections Cycle* Time delay building block and press Enter. The Time delay curve screen appears (see fig. 7.7). The vertical axis represents the percentage of the input variable affecting the output variable. The horizontal axis shows the number of periods of delay.

You define the actual time delay curve by using the cursor keys to build the curve graphically. You can also create the time delay curve by moving the

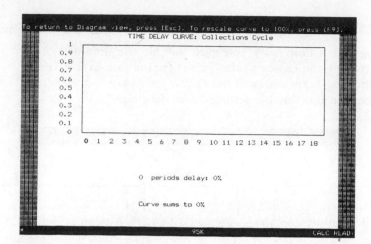

Fig. 7.7. The Time delay curve before editing.

cursor to each delay period and typing the percentage. You can use the Del and Ins keys to delete and insert values at the cursor position.

Notice the two information lines under the graph on the screen. The first line displays the number of periods of delay at the cursor position followed by the percentage of the input variable affecting the output variable at that period (output variable = 10 percent of input variable, for instance). The second line indicates the total percentage effect of the input variable on the output variable over the entire time delay (see fig. 7.8).

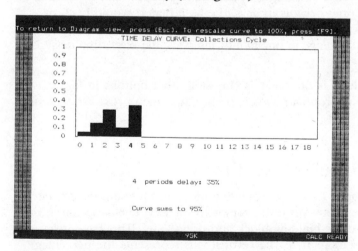

Fig. 7.8. The Time delay building block screen showing the time delay curve.

Use the cursor keys to create the curve shown in figure 7.8. Before you start entering data, the two lines read:

0 periods delay: 0%
Curve sums to 0%

As you build the curve, notice how the two information lines change. After the value is entered for five-percent billings as cash collections, the two lines read:

0 periods delay: 5%
Curve sums to 5%

After you enter the second delay value (corresponding to 15 percent of billings collected in 1 month's time), the two lines read:

1 periods delay: 15%
Curve sums to 20%

When you finish building the complete curve for the time delay, you should have the same screen as figure 7.8. Why does the curve only sum to 95 percent? Recall that five percent of billings remain uncollected after four months and are written off.

Keep in mind that only one time delay curve can be created for each Time delay building block, no matter how many variable pairs are linked to it. This single time delay curve applies to all variable pairs in a particular building block. You can create several Time delay building blocks and link up to five variable pairs to each building block, but each pair of variables would be linked to only one time delay curve in its respective building block.

Summary of Steps for the Time Delay Building Block

To create a Time delay building block, you follow these steps:

1. Select the /Define Building block Time delay command.

2. Move the cursor to the Connect to variables line in the building block and press Enter to display the Connections settings sheet. On this sheet, enter the names of the variable pairs (up to five pairs are allowed per building block) to be linked by this particular time delay. Press Esc to return to the DIAGRAM view.

3. Move the cursor to the Select periods line in the building block and press Enter. On the Period for Delay menu, move the cursor to the period for delay you want and press Enter. Press Esc to return to the DIAGRAM view.

4. Move the cursor to the Edit curve line in the building block and press Enter. The screen shows a blank graph where you create the time delay curve with the cursor keys or by typing the exact percentage values. After completing the curve, press Esc to return to the DIAGRAM view.

Rescaling to 100 Percent

At times you will know the shape of your time delay curve and that the curve sums to 100 percent, but you won't be able to supply specific data. Javelin lets you create a curve in the proportions you want and then scale it to 100 percent. You choose the rescaling option by pressing the CALC key (F9) when the time delay curve is displayed (see fig. 7.9).

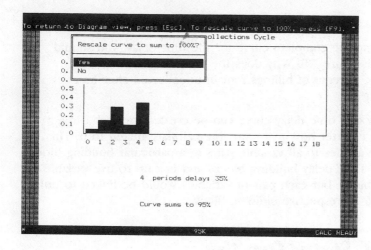

Fig. 7.9. You have the option to rescale a time delay curve to 100 percent.

When Javelin scales your curve to 100 percent, be aware that the shape of the curve remains in proportion while the values included in the curve change. For instance, in the time delay curve example we have been looking at, we have coordinate pairs of (0,5), (1,15), (2,30), (3,10), and (4,35). The curve sums to 95 percent, as intended.

If you incorrectly choose to rescale the sample curve to 100 percent, the coordinate pairs of (0,5), (1,16), (2,32), (3,11), and (4,37) would allow the curve to sum to 100 percent. Javelin rescales by retaining the shape of the curve but adjusting each value in the curve so that the values total to 100 percent. In this case, the sum of y values is 101 (5+16+32+11+37+0 = 101) due to round-off error.

The Lookup Table Building Block

The Lookup table building block defines a relationship between two variables and uses a lookup table format to establish an input range and corresponding output values. This particular building block should be familiar to experienced spreadsheet users because it provides the same capabilities as the @VLOOKUP and @HLOOKUP commands in 1-2-3.

A lookup table will be familiar also to anyone who has ever used a tax table, done volume discounting, made purchases based on current inventory, determined livestock-feed ratios based on animal weight, calculated insurance premiums based on rate and face amount, determined distribution spreads for sales commissions, or determined office- or building-rental rates based on price per square foot of floor space.

The basic format of a lookup table can be seen in figures 7.10 and 7.11. Figure 7.10 shows a lookup table for volume discounting of sales. Figure 7.11 shows the Internal Revenue Service Schedule Y for married taxpayers filing joint returns for 1985.

Fig. 7.10. A volume discounting lookup table.

```
Top of interval:
To return to Diagram view, press [Esc]. To interpolate rates, press [F9].
                  LOOKUP TABLE: Volume Discounts

        Input Interval                Output Value
        Over      But not over     Base amount    Rate (optional)

                    -       0.00         0.00
        0.00     -       100.00       100.00           0.00
      100.00     -       250.00        95.00           0.00
over 250.00                            70.00           0.00




                                                  94K              CALC READY
```

Fig. 7.11. Another typical lookup table (IRS Schedule Y for 1985).

```
Rate on excess over base value:
To return to Diagram view, press [Esc]. To interpolate rates, press [F9].
                  LOOKUP TABLE: Schedule Y

        Input Interval                Output Value
        Over      But not over     Base amount    Rate (optional)

                    -         0.00        0.00
        0.00     -       3540.00          0.00          0.00
     3540.00     -       5720.00          0.00          0.11
     5720.00     -       7910.00        239.80          0.12
     7910.00     -      12390.00        502.60          0.14
    12390.00     -      16650.00       1129.80          0.16
    16650.00     -      21020.00       1811.40          0.18
    21020.00     -      25600.00       2598.00          0.22
    25600.00     -      31120.00       3605.60          0.25
    31120.00     -      36630.00       4985.60          0.28
    36630.00     -      47670.00       6528.40          0.33
    47670.00     -      62450.00      10171.60          0.38
    62450.00     -      89090.00      15788.00          0.42
    89090.00     -     113860.00      26976.80          0.45
   113860.00     -     169020.00      38123.30          0.49
over 169020.00                        65151.70          0.50

                                          95K        NUM        CALC READY
```

A Lookup table building block is defined in terms of input intervals (ranges). For each input interval, you define a base output value and a rate. The rate is applied to the difference between the actual input value and the lower limit of the input interval. For a given input value, the lookup table finds the input interval that contains this input value and returns an output value equal to the corresponding base value plus the rate times the difference between the actual input value and the lower limit of the input interval.

Applications for the Lookup Table Building Block

Javelin's Lookup table building block can be used to define a wide range of functional relationships between an input variable and an output variable. The two most common types of relationships in business modeling are a step function and a piecewise-linear function.

The volume-discount lookup table in figure 7.10 is an example of a step function. Note that the output value is defined as the corresponding base value over each input interval. Figure 7.12 shows the volume price as a function of the input value. Note that the output does not change while the input remains in the same input interval. Another example of a step function in business analysis is modeling production capacity as a function of the number of shifts.

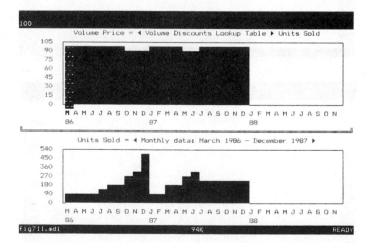

Fig. 7.12. *Volume Price* as a function of *Units Sold*.

The IRS tax table in Figure 7.11 is an example of a piecewise-linear (or arbitrary) function. The output variable is defined in terms of base plus rate, and the output value at the top of an input range (base plus rate times width of interval) is equal to the base value of the next input range. Figure 7.13 shows an example of *Income Tax* versus *Taxable Income* for several values of *Taxable Income*. Note that *Income Tax* varies with *Taxable Income* even when *Taxable Income* stays within the same input interval.

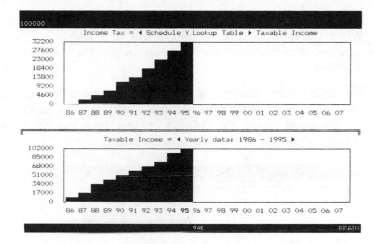

Fig. 7.13. *Income Tax* as a function of *Taxable Income*.

Creating a Lookup Table Building Block

Suppose that you wanted to create a Lookup table building block for *Volume Discounts*. Use the /Define Building block Lookup table command and assign the name *Volume Discounts* to the building block. The initial screen of the *Volume Discounts* Lookup table building block is shown in figure 7.14.

Fig. 7.14. Initial screen for the *Volume Discounts* Lookup table building block.

The Lookup table building block operates much the same as all the other building blocks we have seen. To define the input and output variables, move the cursor down to Connect to variables and press Enter. As with the Time delay building block, the Lookup table building block requires input and output variables in pairs.

In volume discounting, *Units Sold* and *Volume Discount* are a matched pair. When the number of units sold in one time period reaches a specified amount, a discount is extended on the entire order. The more units sold, the greater the discount.

To enter these variables, move the cursor to the first pair of braces under Inputs on the Connections settings sheet (see fig. 7.15). Type *Units Sold*, move the cursor across to the Outputs column, type *Volume Price*, and press Enter. Finally, press Esc to exit the settings sheet.

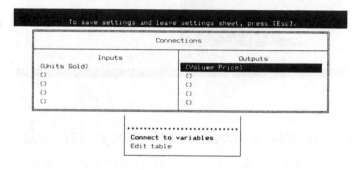

Fig. 7.15. The Connections settings sheet for the Lookup table building block.

After linking variables as pairs, you define the actual lookup table. Move the cursor to the Edit table line in the Lookup table building block and press Enter. As you can see in figure 7.16, the lookup table is divided into two distinct areas marked Input Interval (the leftmost column) and Output Value (the two columns on the right of the screen).

In the *Input Interval* area, you specify the values of the input variable (*Units Sold*, in our example) that affect the output variable (*Volume Price*). Figure 7.16 indicates that any purchase of up to 100 units will be sold at the undiscounted price of $100 per unit. Because some customers will order less than 100 units and pay the full price, the *Volume Price* corresponding to the input interval 0 – 100 is 100. Purchases totaling more than 100 units but less than 250 units will be sold at a price of $95 (5 percent discount), and so on.

```
Top of interval:
To return to Diagram view, press [Esc]. To interpolate rates, press [F9].
                        LOOKUP TABLE: Volume Discounts

              Input Interval                      Output Value
              Over        But not over     Base amount    Rate (optional)

                       -            0.00           0.00
              0.00     -          100.00         100.00            0.00
            100.00     -          250.00          95.00            0.00
      over  250.00                                90.00            0.00
```

Fig. 7.16. The Lookup table building block is divided into *Input Interval* and the *Output Value*.

You can fill in the table by moving the cursor to the entry and typing the necessary values. Note that input intervals must progress in order from the least amount to greatest amount. Because Javelin does not allow a decreasing range in a Lookup table building block, the following input intervals would result in the display of an error message:

                    – 0.00
           0.00 – 1000.00
        1000.00 – 500.00

The program prompts you with the following error message followed by a request that you place the intervals in their proper order:

Lookup table interval limits must go from lowest to highest

The second column under the *Output Value* section of the lookup table lets you specify any incremental change relating the input value to the output value. In other words, if the *Rate* column in figure 7.16 were blank, Javelin would assume a unit price of $100 for any orders of 100 units or less, a unit price of $95 for any orders between 101 and 250, and a unit price of $90 for all orders over 250.

Javelin, however, gives you the option of letting the program determine the rates for the lookup table. To use this option, press the CALC key (F9) while the lookup table is on screen (see fig. 7.17).

Javelin computes the rates for the lookup tables by straight-line interpolation. That is, Javelin calculates rates for the output values by determining a steady increase between base values. You can see the results of the calculations in figure 7.18. In this case, Javelin has interpolated a sliding-scale volume discount.

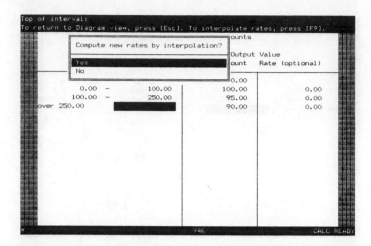

Fig. 7.17. The prompt to
compute new rates by
interpolation after pressing the
CALC key (F9).

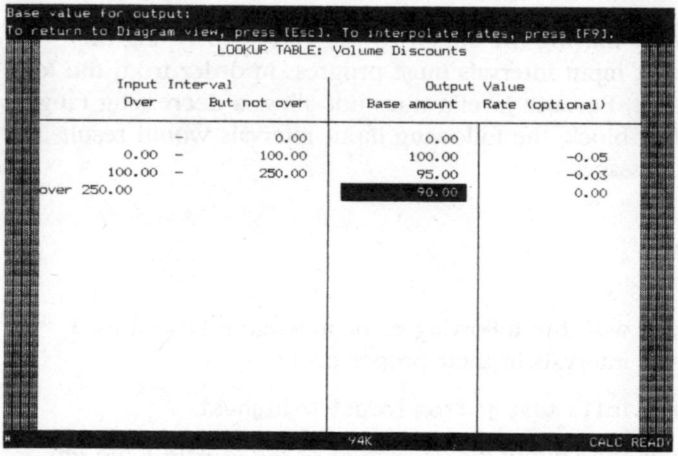

Fig. 7.18. The results of Javelin's
rate interpolation.

For example, if you purchased 50 units, your rate would be $97.50 per unit.
After the interpolation, you can customize the rates to your own particular
needs.

The best use of Javelin's rate scaling is when you have base numbers but would
like to establish rates to make a piecewise-linear function. If you don't like the
numbers supplied by Javelin, you can delete them wholly or selectively. The IRS
table in figure 7.11 was built this way. The input intervals and base amounts
were defined when Javelin interpolated the rates.

Note that you can place up to five input-output variable pairs into a Lookup
table building block. The Lookup table building block functions like the Time
delay building block in one important way: all variable pairs will be linked by
the one lookup table. You can create as many Lookup table building blocks as

you need for any one model, but all variable pairs in any one lookup Table building block will use the same lookup table.

You can also use the Lookup table building block to place specific flags in your model. For example, you may want to know when input values go outside a certain range. You can enter *#ERROR* or *#NA* (no value available) as the output value for input values outside that range. When the Inputs go below the threshold, your model responds with an #ERROR or CANNOT BE CALCULATED message. You could use this technique for several variable pairs. Placing an ERRORS view window on the screen would instantly show you any problems occurring in your model. Finally, you can use this technique to build automatic input validation into a model.

Summary of Steps for Lookup Table Building Block

To create a Lookup table building block, you follow these steps:

1. Select the /Define Building block Lookup table command and enter the name of your building block.

2. Move the cursor to the Connect to variables line in the building block and press Enter to display the Connections settings sheet. Enter the variable pairs that are to be linked through this Lookup table building block. When you are through, press Esc to return to the DIAGRAM view.

3. Move the cursor to the Edit table line in the building block, and press Enter to display the lookup table screen. Enter the ranges and output values in columns one and two, respectively. You can also enter the rate of change in column three or let Javelin compute the rate of change that will yield a piecewise-linear function. You don't have to enter any rate of change. Type Esc to return to the DIAGRAM view.

The Lookup table building block provides a tabular format for defining one variable as a function of another. This is particularly useful when the values that go into the table are known and when there are relatively few input ranges. If, however, you do not know the exact numerical relationship between the input variable and the output variable, or if you have a detailed piecewise-linear approximation, you may prefer to define the output variable with a graph. Javelin provides such a format in the Curve building block.

The Curve Building Block

Javelin's Curve building block provides a graph format for defining an output variable as a piecewise-linear function of an input variable. Although both the Curve and the Lookup table building blocks can be used for such a definition, the Curve building block has the advantage of using a graph to illustrate the shape of the functional relationship being defined.

The Time delay building block creates a curve that shows one variable's interaction with another variable over time. The Curve building block allows you to develop a similar type of curve showing one variable as a piecewise-linear function of another variable in the model. The Curve building block allows you to represent the relationship between two variables by sketching a "freehand" curve describing the relationship.

The Curve building block is particularly useful for defining variables in economic analysis and strategic planning models. You often know the general shape of the relationship between critical variables in these models without knowing the exact functional relationship. The Curve building block provides an efficient way to define such a relationship in graph form.

For example, suppose that you want to project unit sales as a function of selling price. You know the current and past unit sales and selling prices, but you want to examine what might happen if you raised or lowered your price outside this range. Using the Curve building block, you can sketch a curve showing the possible relationship between price and unit sales. You can use this curve for "What if" analysis by quickly changing the curve to reflect other relationships. Figure 7.19 shows such a curve relating the variables *Price* and *Quantity* for a product in a market where you have some flexibility about pricing.

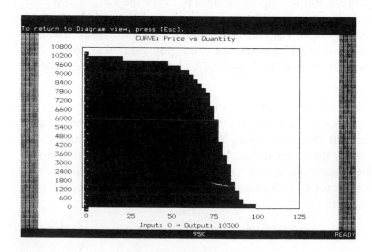

Fig. 7.19. Curve relating *Price* and *Quantity* for a product.

Suppose that the production and distribution cost for the product is $50 per unit. What price will maximize the profit on this product? Figure 7.20 shows how you might investigate this question using the *Price vs Quantity* Curve building block and the following formula:

Profit (Price-Cost)*Quantity

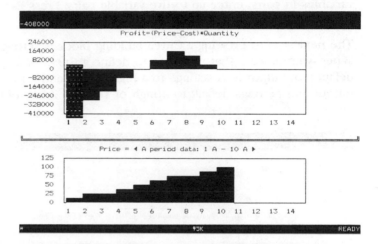

Fig. 7.20. Determining the profit-maximizing price.

Figure 7.20 shows that the price that maximizes profit is about $80 per unit if you use the relationship between price and quantity shown in figure 7.19. Any lower price does not generate enough additional volume to offset the lower margins. A higher price causes volume to fall off too much. You can test the sensitivity of this profit-maximizing price to a change in the price-to-volume relationship by editing the Curve building block and retrying the profit calculation.

More complex relationships between variables can be constructed by combining the output variables from several Curve building blocks together in a formula. In such a compound formula, each Curve building block describes graphically how the final output variable depends on one input variable with all others held constant.

Creating the Curve Building Block

Like all the other building blocks, you must first define the Curve building block. Begin by selecting the /Define Building block Curve command. Name the building block *Price vs Quantity* and press Enter.

The three items on the Curve building block (see fig. 7.21) lead to the following screens: the Connections settings sheet (see fig. 7.22); the Curve settings sheet (see fig. 7.23); and the graph for building the curve (see fig. 7.24).

To create a Curve building block, you must first connect the variables to the building block. Move the cursor to the `Connect to variables` line in the building block and press Enter. Keeping in mind that Javelin allows only variables in pairs, enter up to five variable pairs. Press Esc to return to the DIAGRAM view.

The next step to creating a Curve building block is setting the graph scale. When you indicate that you want to define a Curve building block, Javelin defaults the input axis settings to a high of 100 and a low of 0. Likewise, the output axis settings default to a high of 100 and a low of 0. Any of these

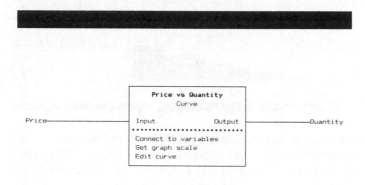

Fig. 7.21. The Curve building block.

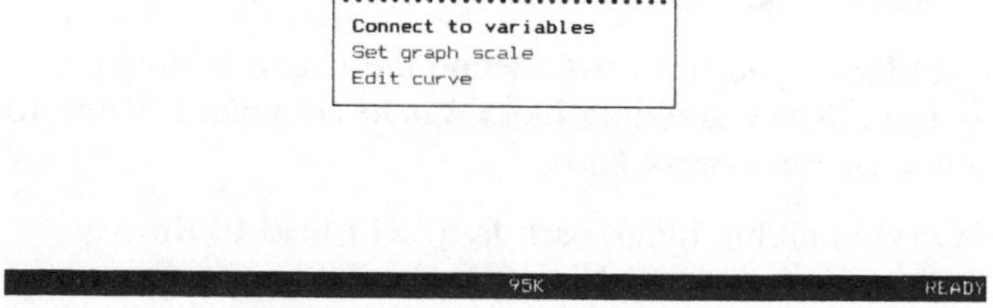

Fig. 7.22. The Connections settings sheet for the Curve building block.

Fig. 7.23. The Curve settings
sheet for the Curve building
block.

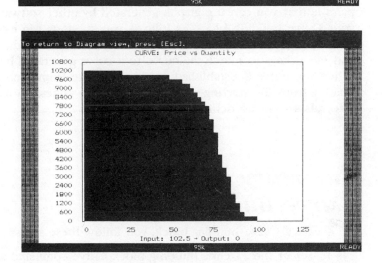

Fig. 7.24. The curve for the
Curve building block.

defaults can be changed by moving the cursor to the Set graph scale line in the
Curve building block and pressing Enter. This produces the Curve settings sheet
(see fig. 7.23). You change the graph scale by moving the cursor to the setting
you would like to change, typing your number, and pressing Enter. Press Esc to
return to the DIAGRAM view when you're done.

By default, Javelin uses an interval of 2.5 on the input axis. If you want to enter
variables using a different input interval, you must change the input-axis default
maximum. In general, the interval that Javelin uses is roughly 1/30th of the
input interval specified in the Curve settings sheet.

The final step in creating the Curve building block is to build the curve itself.
Move the cursor to Edit curve in the building block and press Enter. You can

edit and build the curve two different ways. With the first method, you use the Up-arrow (↑), Down-arrow (↓), PgUp, and PgDn keys to create the bars that relate input to output variables. With the second method, you use the Left-arrow (←) and Right-arrow (→) keys to move to a specific input value and then type a specific output value. You can use the Del and Ins keys to delete and insert values at the cursor position.

The Curve building block's real strength is that it can find correct matches of input and output variables for you. For example, you may have an input value that falls between the points of the input scale. Javelin interpolates the corresponding point on the curve (and hence the output value) although no exact point has been defined. Keep in mind that Javelin interprets values outside the defined range as "no value available" and displays the message #NA.

Another advantage to using the Curve building block method of relating variable pairs is that you can use graphs generated by other software as the basis for your Curve building block. As long as you know or can estimate the beginning and ending values of your variable pairs, you can move the cursor and the PgUp and PgDn keys to match the curve to a curve generated by other software. When the curve is established, you can use the Home and End keys to move quickly from the starting values to the ending values, no matter how many intervals are in the definition of the curve.

Summary of Steps for Curve Building Block

To create a Curve building block, you follow these steps:

1. Select the /Define Building block Curve command and enter the name you want to assign the building block.

2. Move the cursor to the Connect to variables line in the building block and press Enter. The screen now displays the Connections settings sheet, where you enter the variable pairs for the building block. You can enter up to five pairs per building block. Press Esc to return to the DIAGRAM view.

3. Move the cursor to the Set graph scale line and press Enter. This step is necessary only if you want to change Javelin's default scale settings. Enter the values you want and press Esc to return to the DIAGRAM view.

4. Move the cursor to the Edit curve line and press Enter. This brings up a screen showing the curve before editing. You can create and edit the curve with the cursor or PgUp and PgDn keys, or you can type values at each input interval. Press Esc to return to the DIAGRAM view.

Conclusion

This chapter has shown you how to use three of Javelin's most powerful model building tools: the Time delay building block, the Lookup table building block, and the Curve building block. Each of these building blocks lets you specify certain types of complex relationships between the variables in your model. Although the Lookup table building block is comparable to the @VLOOKUP and @HLOOKUP functions found in 1-2-3 and other spreadsheet packages, the Time delay and Curve building blocks provide capabilities that go well beyond those available in other spreadsheet products.

Although you could use Javelin's formulas and functions to emulate the use of these building blocks in the model, the great advantage of these building blocks is that they provide you with an easy way to define complex relationships between the variables in your models. The graphing capabilities of the Time delay and Curve building blocks mean that you can see the relationship defined between the input and output variables, something difficult to do with a spreadsheet full of complex formulas.

Part **III**

Checking Your Javelin Model

8

Using the ERRORS and FORMULAS Views for Model Checking

Regardless of what software you use for business analysis, when you create a financial model, you must be able to identify, isolate, and correct errors. Checking popular spreadsheet software for errors remains difficult and time-consuming. To check a 1-2-3 or Symphony model, for example, you need a good memory and sharp eyes to inspect a printout of the formulas, range names, and values stored in each spreadsheet cell. But a printout alone falls short of making the relationships between formulas and data explicit. An auditing utility program may help, but this means extra expense, learning, and time.

Javelin provides a built-in means of checking models for errors. Whether you choose to check before completing and calculating your model or after you've finished, the ERRORS and FORMULAS views make error checking easy and thorough. This chapter describes how these views help you find errors. The chapter also provides examples and tips to facilitate regular checking of your models.

First, this chapter shows the value of using the ERRORS view for detecting undefined, time-period, and time-span errors. Next, you see how combining the FORMULAS view with the ERRORS view can help you spot certain types of errors. Finally, the chapter discusses the /*Formulas Circular command.

Commands Emphasized in this Chapter

/View Errors
/*Errors All errors
/*Errors Undefined
/*Errors Time period
/View Formulas
/View Formulas All
/View Formulas Roots
/View Formulas Branches
/*Formulas Undefined
/*Formulas Circular

Model Checking: What Kinds of Errors Can Occur?

First, your model may give incorrect results because of improper logic or poor problem formulation; your assumptions cause problems, not your use of the software. You may consider a variable as monthly data when really it is quarterly data, for example, or you may forget to include a factor in some formula. Like misspelled words, these types of errors can show up no matter what you do, and your only hope is to catch them before using the report to make decisions.

Second, errors can come from incompletely defining the problem in your model or from poor modeling techniques. Javelin can often catch these types of errors and bring them to your attention. Most often such errors result from:

- failing to define one or more variables
- attempting to combine variables with different time periods
- time-span conflicts between variables
- using a constant in a function argument when a time-series variable is preferred or vice versa
- circular references in formulas

Javelin's ERRORS and FORMULAS views can help you avoid or catch such errors.

Checking with the ERRORS View

The ERRORS view helps you check your model by displaying a complete list of errors in the model or just certain types of errors. Assume, for example, that you have constructed the Income Statement model for Future Home Appliances, Inc., introduced in Chapter 1. After you have entered all formulas and data for the model and pressed the CALC key (F9), Javelin indicates that there are errors in your model.

The **ERROR** indicator appears at the bottom right of the screen on the status line. Javelin is indicating that it has detected errors. If you select /View Errors to see the ERRORS view at this point, Javelin will display a complete list of errors (see fig. 8.1).

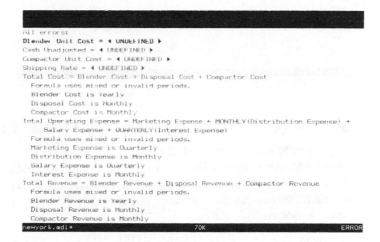

Fig. 8.1. Javelin helps you clear up errors in your model.

Notice in figure 8.1 that Javelin lists each formula that contains an error. These errors include several types of errors indicated by the ERRORS view, including variables that are undefined and formulas that have mixed or invalid time periods. Indented information, such as that following the formula for *Total Cost*, explains what causes the error. In this case, Javelin cites mixed time periods and lists the period for each variable in the formula.

In addition to the main ERRORS view menu, a view-sensitive menu is available that provides options for viewing all errors or for viewing a certain type of error. This view-sensitive menu is similar to those available through the WORKSHEET and FORMULAS views. The /*Errors command option appears to the right of the QUIT option and is available only when you are using the ERRORS view. When you select /*Errors, you can view a complete list of errors (the same option available with the /View Errors command); you can view errors caused only by undefined variables; or you can view errors caused by mixing time periods (see fig. 8.2).

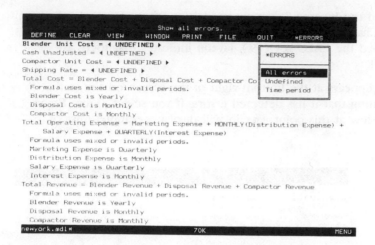

```
                          Show all errors.
 DEFINE   CLEAR   VIEW      WINDOW  PRINT    FILE      QUIT    *ERRORS
Blender Unit Cost = ◄ UNDEFINED ►
Cash Unadjusted = ◄ UNDEFINED ►
Compactor Unit Cost = ◄ UNDEFINED ►          *ERRORS
Shipping Rate = ◄ UNDEFINED ►
Total Cost = Blender Cost + Disposal Cost + Compactor Co   All errors
   Formula uses mixed or invalid periods.                  Undefined
   Blender Cost is Yearly                                  Time period
   Disposal Cost is Monthly
   Compactor Cost is Monthly
Total Operating Expense = Marketing Expense + MONTHLY(Distribution Expense) +
     Salary Expense + QUARTERLY(Interest Expense)
   Formula uses mixed or invalid periods.
   Marketing Expense is Quarterly
   Distribution Expense is Monthly
   Salary Expense is Quarterly
   Interest Expense is Monthly
Total Revenue = Blender Revenue + Disposal Revenue + Compactor Revenue
   Formula uses mixed or invalid periods.
   Blender Revenue is Yearly
   Disposal Revenue is Monthly
   Compactor Revenue is Monthly
newyork.mdl*                    70K                    MENU
```

Fig. 8.2. The /View Errors command activates the ERRORS view.

Getting a List of Undefined Variables

Using the /*Errors command allows you to focus on a single type of error. /*Errors Undefined lets you, for example, isolate any undefined variables from a list of errors (see fig. 8.1). An undefined variable is a variable without assigned data or formulas. Javelin indicates undefined variables as errors because the value cannot be calculated.

Whenever the TABLE, DIAGRAM, WORKSHEET, CHART, or QUICK GRAPH views are displayed, Javelin alerts you to undefined variables. In the TABLE, DIAGRAM, CHART, and QUICK GRAPH views, these variables are identified by:

   (variable name) = < UNDEFINED >

For undefined variables in the WORKSHEET view, Javelin displays an #UNDEF message. If, for example, you build a model using the WORKSHEET view and then calculate the model by pressing the CALC key (F9), Javelin alerts you to all undefined variables by placing an #UNDEF message where a value would normally be displayed (see fig. 8.3). You can get a complete list of undefined variables through the /*Errors Undefined command. To use this command, first select /View Errors, then choose /*Errors Undefined. You will find the /*Errors Undefined command particularly valuable when you are creating large models. With the /*Errors Undefined command, you can make certain that all variables needed for calculating formulas have been defined before you calculate the model.

You will soon realize how much time and trouble the ERRORS view saves you when you are building complex models. Consider, for example, how valuable the ERRORS view is when you are developing a balance sheet like that in figure

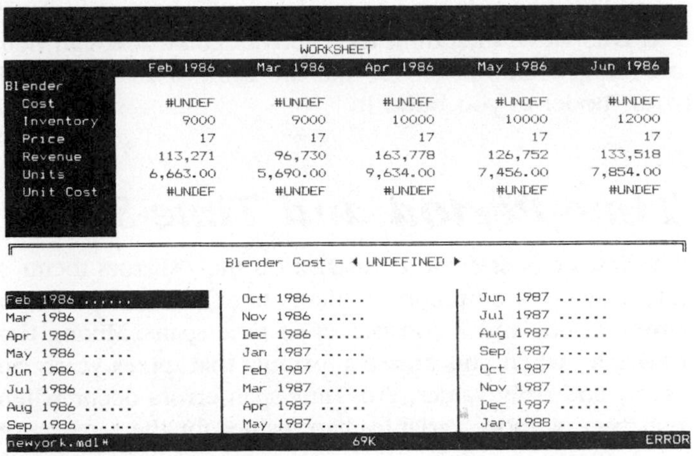

Fig. 8.3. Javelin warns you when there are undefined terms in the formulas and the model.

8.4. Although only a few variable names appear in the worksheet, these variables are dependent on many other variables in the model. Forgetting to define one can affect others, although that single variable may be directly linked to only one other variable. For example, forgetting to enter data for the variable *Interest Expense*—directly linked to only one variable—causes six undefined variables on the worksheet (see fig. 8.4).

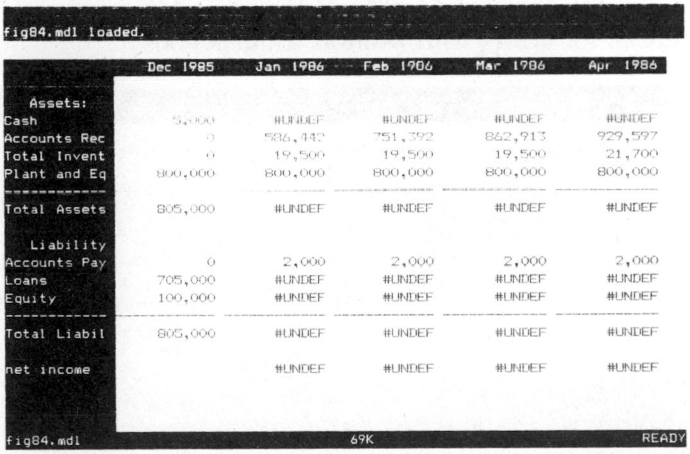

Fig. 8.4. A balance sheet worksheet indicating that variables are undefined.

Without the ERRORS view, it would be difficult to find the single undefined variable *Interest Expense* among the many variables that are used for developing the balance sheet.

In addition to helping you catch errors when you calculate your model, Javelin's ERRORS view, including the /*Errors command, can help you develop good modeling techniques. Get into the habit of using the ERRORS view to debug your model as you build it.

Time-Period and Time-Span Errors

The last error-specific command on the /*Errors menu, /*Errors Time period, addresses two common problems new Javelin users encounter: the mixing of time periods and inconsistency in time spans. Mixing time periods occurs, for example, when you create a formula that mixes yearly and monthly values, yearly and daily values, etc. Time-span errors occur when a formula requires that two or more variables have values for the same period.

As discussed in Chapter 4, Javelin lets you assign whatever period you want to a variable—daily, weekly, monthly, quarterly, yearly, or custom period—using the Variable settings sheet. Problems occur when time periods are mixed in formulas that don't contain a time conversion function (such as WEEKLY or MONTHLY). For example, the list of errors in figure 8.1 shows that the formula for *Total Operating Expense* mixes monthly with quarterly data. If you tried to calculate the model by pressing the CALC key (F9), Javelin would display the ERROR indicator. The /View Errors command indicates whether the error is caused by mixed periods. /*Errors Time periods identifies only mixed time period errors (see fig. 8.5). If your models use several different time periods, check for errors with /*Errors Time periods.

```
Time period errors:
Total Operating Expense = Marketing Expense + Distribution Expense + Salary
        Expense + Interest Expense
   Formula uses mixed or invalid periods.
   Marketing Expense is Quarterly
   Distribution Expense is Monthly
   Salary Expense is Quarterly
   Interest Expense is Monthly
```

```
newyork.mdl*                          69K                              ERROR
```

Fig. 8.5. Javelin notes time-period errors by telling you that there are mixed time periods in a formula.

Javelin cannot completely calculate a model if it contains mixed or invalid time periods. Like errors caused by undefined variables, this type of error is indicated

by the message CANNOT BE CALCULATED displayed in the TABLE and CHART views.
The TABLE view in figure 8.6, for example, displays the CANNOT BE CALCULATED
message.

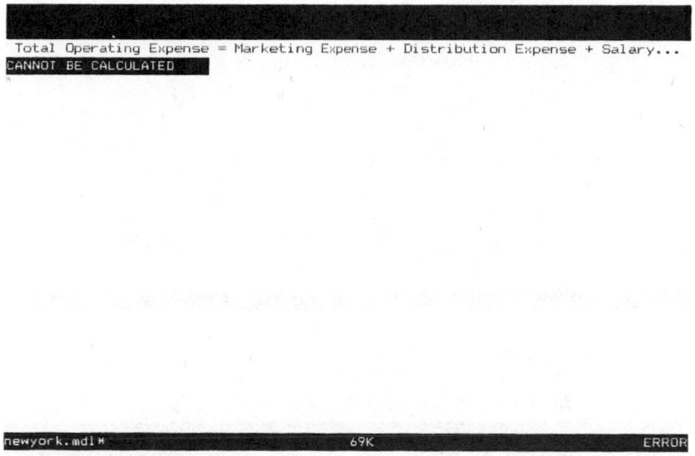

```
████████████████████████████████████████████████████████████████████████
  Total Operating Expense = Marketing Expense + Distribution Expense + Salary...
CANNOT BE CALCULATED
```

Fig. 8.6. Javelin detects time-
period errors.

```
newyork.mdl*                                    69K                          ERROR
```

When you determine the problem with mixed time periods, you can easily
correct your model by editing the formula. To edit the *Total Operating Expense*
formula in figure 8.5 while in the ERRORS view, move the cursor to the formula
and press the EDIT key (F2). Next, move the cursor to the first character of the
variable you want to convert to another time period, type the time conversion
function, and place parentheses around the variable to convert (see fig. 8.7).
The *Total Operating Expense* formula mixes monthly with quarterly variables.
The formula, therefore, should convert all values to either quarterly or monthly
values. To correct the error, edit the formula so that the function QUARTERLY
is used with both *Distribution Expense* and *Marketing Expense*.

Time-Period Errors Involving
Custom Time Periods

Invalid time periods can also occur when you use custom period A or B defined
in terms of *No base period*. You will recall that the /Define Time period
command brings up a Custom period settings sheet (see fig. 8.8). Use this
settings sheet to define the custom period in terms of a common time period
(using the common time period as a base period) or to define the custom
period with no base period. If you decide to define the custom period in terms

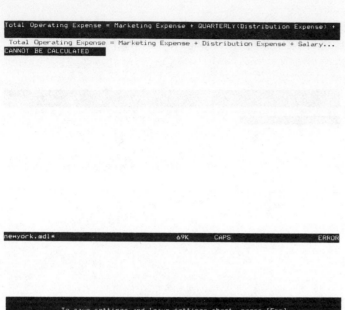

```
Total Operating Expense = Marketing Expense + QUARTERLY(Distribution Expense) +

 Total Operating Expense = Marketing Expense + Distribution Expense + Salary...
CANNOT BE CALCULATED
```

```
newyork.mdl*                          69K        CAPS                    ERROR
```

Fig. 8.7. Editing a formula with mixed periods by adding a time conversion function.

```
         To save settings and leave settings sheet, press [Esc].
Formulas for all variables:
Accounts Payable = ◀ Monthl ┌─ Custom Period Settings ─┐ cember 1987 ▶
Accounts Receivable = Accou │                           │ e ; Beginning Accounts
   Receivable               │  Name (A)                 │
Accounts Receivable from Re │                           │ ble Time Delay ▶ Total
   Revenue                  │  Defined in terms of:     │
Beginning Accounts Receivab │  • Day                    │
Beginning Cash = 5000       │  • Week                   │
Beginning Equity = 100000   │  • Month                  │
Beginning Loans = 705000    │  • Quarter                │
Blender Cost = Blender Unit │  • Year                   │
Blender Inventory = ◀ Month │  • A                      │ ecember 1986 ▶
Blender Price = 17          │  • B                      │
Blender Revenue = Blender P │  ▶ No base period         │
Blender Shipping Rate = 1.5 └───────────────────────────┘
Blender Unit Cost = ◀ Monthly data: January 1986 - December 1987 ▶
Blender Units = ◀ Monthly data: January 1986 - December 1986 ▶
Cash = IF( AND(Cash Unadjusted>Cash min, Cash Unadjusted<Cash max), Cash
   Unadjusted, IF(Cash Unadjusted<Cash min, Cash min, IF(PREVIOUS(Loans) +
   Cash max - Cash Unadjusted >=0, Cash max, Cash Unadjusted - PREVIOUS(Loans)
   ))) ; Beginning Cash
Cash max = 10000
newyork.mdl                          69K                               READY
```

Fig. 8.8. The Custom period settings sheet.

of a given time period, define the new period in the Custom time period table. In figure 8.9, custom period A is defined as an hour by directing Javelin to divide the built-in time period *Day* by 24.

If a variable uses a custom time period that is not defined in terms of a common time period, this variable produces an error when used in a formula with variables based on any other custom period or any of the regular periods. This happens because Javelin is unable to determine how the custom time period fits into the other time periods. Suppose, for example, that you have created two variables for tracking sales: one variable for telephone sales and another for mail order sales (see fig. 8.10). Using the *Telephone Sales* variable defined in a weekly period and the *Mail Order Sales* defined in a custom period (allowing you to track sales by region) together in a formula causes an error. Selecting /View Errors would indicate that the formula uses mixed periods (see fig. 8.11).

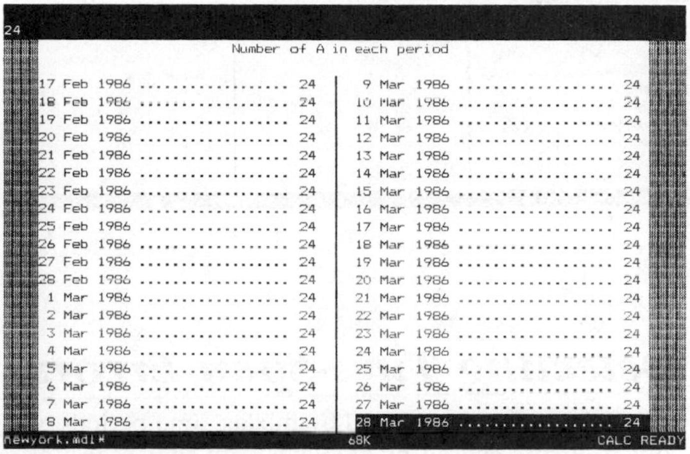

Fig. 8.9. The Custom period table.

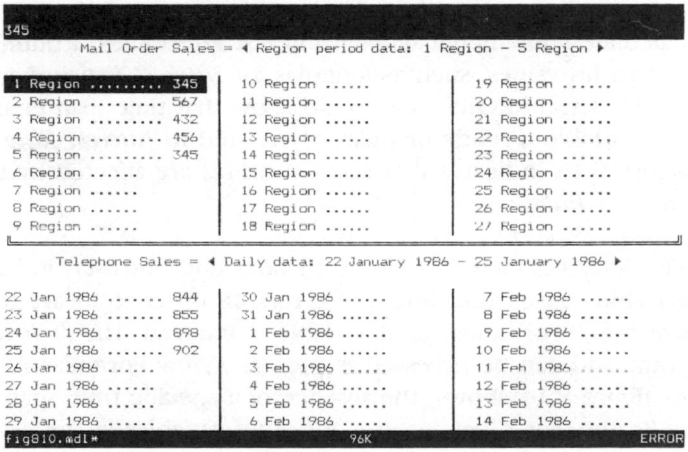

Fig. 8.10. Using a custom time period and a daily time period for sales variables creates an error message.

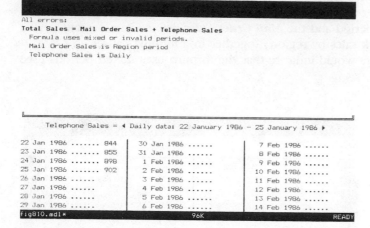

All errors:
Total Sales = Mail Order Sales + Telephone Sales
  Formula uses mixed or invalid periods.
  Mail Order Sales is Region period
  Telephone Sales is Daily

Telephone Sales = ◄ Daily data: 22 January 1986 – 25 January 1986 ►

22 Jan 1986 844	30 Jan 1986	7 Feb 1986 ......
23 Jan 1986 855	31 Jan 1986	8 Feb 1986 ......
24 Jan 1986 898	1 Feb 1986	9 Feb 1986 ......
25 Jan 1986 902	2 Feb 1986	10 Feb 1986 ......
26 Jan 1986	3 Feb 1986	11 Feb 1986 ......
27 Jan 1986	4 Feb 1986	12 Feb 1986 ......
28 Jan 1986	5 Feb 1986	13 Feb 1986 ......
29 Jan 1986	6 Feb 1986	14 Feb 1986 ......

fig810.mdl *   96K   READY

Fig. 8.11. /View Errors indicates that variables cannot be mixed.

Detecting Time-Span Errors

In addition to errors caused by mixing time periods, your model may also contain errors caused by problems with time spans for variables. Time-span errors occur when data is not available for a defined variable used in a formula. Suppose, for example, that the *Interest Rate* variable used in formulas for our balance sheet model is defined but contains no values. If you attempt to calculate your model without interest rate values, a number of formulas would return no values, such as formulas for *Interest Expense* and *Net Income* (see fig. 8.12). The ERRORS view would show that time-span errors had occurred for any variable directly or indirectly related to *Interest Rate*. The ERRORS view in figure 8.13 indicates that seven variables are affected by the absence of data for *Interest Rate*.

The ERRORS view in figure 8.13 does not, however, indicate specifically which variable caused the time-span errors. In order to locate the source, you need to use the /*Formulas Input Variables command. The /*Formulas Input Variables command can be accessed as soon as /View Formulas All is the current view. As figure 8.14 shows, the absence of a specific time span for *Interest Rate* indicates that it has no data. All other variables in the list contain dates marking the period for which data is available.

Another type of time-span error occurs when variables with no common dates are added together. Suppose, for example, that the variable *Blender Units* contains data for January through June, 1986, but *Disposal Units* contains data

```
                    Interest Expense = Loans * ((Interest Rate/100)/12)

      Dec 1985 ......        Sep 1986 ......        Jun 1987 ......
      Jan 1986 ......        Oct 1986 ......        Jul 1987 ......
      Feb 1986 ......        Nov 1986 ......        Aug 1987 ......
      Mar 1986 ......        Dec 1986 ......        Sep 1987 ......
      Apr 1986 ......        Jan 1987 ......        Oct 1987 ......
      May 1986 ......        Feb 1987 ......        Nov 1987 ......
      Jun 1986 ......        Mar 1987 ......        Dec 1987 ......
      Jul 1986 ......        Apr 1987 ......        Jan 1988 ......
      Aug 1986 ......        May 1987 ......        Feb 1988 ......

   Total Operating Expense = Marketing Expense + QUARTERLY(Distribution Expense)...

      4 Q 1985 ......        4 Q 1987 ......        4 Q 1989 ......
      1 Q 1986 ......        1 Q 1988 ......        1 Q 1990 ......
      2 Q 1986 ......        2 Q 1988 ......        2 Q 1990 ......
      3 Q 1986 ......        3 Q 1988 ......        3 Q 1990 ......
      4 Q 1986 ......        4 Q 1988 ......        4 Q 1990 ......
      1 Q 1987 ......        1 Q 1989 ......        1 Q 1991 ......
      2 Q 1987 ......        2 Q 1989 ......        2 Q 1991 ......
      3 Q 1987 ......        3 Q 1989 ......        3 Q 1991 ......
   fig812.mdl                              71K                           READY
```

Fig. 8.12. TABLE view shows that no values can be returned for formulas affected by *Interest Rate*.

```
   All errors:
   Income Before Taxes = Total Revenue - Total Cost - MONTHLY(Total Operating
       Expense)
     Time-span error: no dates can be computed for formula.
   Interest Expense = Loans * ((Interest Rate/100)/12)
     Time-span error: no dates can be computed for formula.
   Net Income = Income Before Taxes - Taxes
     Time-span error: no dates can be computed for formula.
   Taxes = IF(Month = 1, YTD Taxes, YTD Taxes - PREVIOUS(YTD Taxes))
     Time-span error: no dates can be computed for formula.
   Total Cost Per Unit = ◀ UNDEFINED ▶
   Total Operating Expense = Marketing Expense + QUARTERLY(Distribution Expense) +
       Salary Expense + QUARTERLY(Interest Expense)
     Time-span error: no dates can be computed for formula.
   YTD IBT = YTD(Income Before Taxes)
     Time-span error: no dates can be computed for formula.
   fig813.mdl                              70K                           READY
```

Fig. 8.13. The ERRORS view indicates that seven variables are affected by the absence of data for *Interest Rate*.

```
   Formulas for input variables:
   Blender Shipping Rate = 1.5
   Blender Unit Cost = ◀ Monthly data: January 1986 - December 1987 ▶
   Blender Units = ◀ Monthly data: January 1986 - December 1986 ▶
   Cash max = 10000
   Cash min = 5000
   Compactor Inventory = ◀ Monthly data: December 1985 - December 1986 ▶
   Compactor Price = 175
   Compactor Shipping Rate = 18.75
   Compactor Unit Cost = ◀ Monthly data: January 1986 - February 1988 ▶
   Compactor Units = ◀ Monthly data: January 1986 - December 1986 ▶
   Disposal Inventory = ◀ Monthly data: December 1985 - December 1986 ▶
   Disposal Price = 45
   Disposal Shipping Rate = 3
   Disposal Unit Cost = ◀ Monthly data: January 1986 - October 1987 ▶
   Disposal Units = ◀ Monthly data: January 1986 - December 1986 ▶
   Interest Rate = ◀ Monthly data ▶
   Marketing Expense = ◀ Quarterly data: 1 Quarter 1986 - 4 Quarter 1986 ▶
   Month = ◀ Monthly data: January 1986 - January 1989 ▶
   Plant and Equipment = ◀ Monthly data: December 1985 - January 1988 ▶
   Salary Expense = ◀ Quarterly data: 4 Quarter 1985 - 4 Quarter 1987 ▶
   Total Cost Per Unit = ◀ UNDEFINED ▶
   fig814.mdl                              70K                           READY
```

Fig. 8.14. /*Formulas Input Variables helps you locate variables that are defined by have no data available.

only for July through December, 1986 (see fig. 8.15). You create the following formula:

Total Units = Blender Units + Disposal Units + Compactor Units

After you calculate the model, the ERRORS view will indicate that no dates can be computed for the variables in figure 8.16—those affected by *Total Units* or using *Blender Units* and *Disposal Units* in the same formula.

To detect the specific variables causing this type of error, you again need to use the /*Formulas command. In this instance, the /*Formulas Time span command isolates all time-series variables so you can scan the list for any incongruous time spans. As figure 8.17 shows, *Blender Units* and *Disposal Units* are the only variables with time spans less than 12 months. In addition, *Disposal Units* is the only variable without a beginning date of January, 1986.

Both types of time-span errors mentioned above—those caused by the absence of values and those caused by mixing incongruous time spans in the same formula—may not be as clearly identified as other types of errors. That is, you won't get an ERROR message when you calculate these formulas. Nonetheless, the ERRORS and FORMULAS views help you debug your model to find such errors.

Detecting Function Argument Errors

Besides using Javelin's /View Errors command to detect problems with time periods and time spans, this command can also inform you of another type of error occurring in the formulas you create. The /View Errors command detects problems caused by including a constant in a function requiring a time-series variable and vice versa.

Suppose, for example, that you want to determine the change in total product cost in the Income Statement model. If a variable for total cost per unit already exists, you could calculate the change in cost over time by entering the following formula, using Javelin's CHANGE function:

Total Cost Change = CHANGE(Total Cost Per Unit)

If the variable *Total Cost Per Unit* is a constant rather than a time-series variable, Javelin indicates that an error has occurred by displaying an ERROR message in the lower right corner of your screen. Selecting the ERRORS view (/View Errors) will display the following message: Argument 1 to CHANGE function is constant. Should be time series.

Fig. 8.15. The variables *Blender Units* and *Disposal Units* have no common time span.

```
5797
            Blender Units = ◀ Monthly data: January 1986 - June 1986 ▶

Jan 1986 ..... 9,434.00    Oct 1986 ......    Jul 1987 ......
Feb 1986 .... 10,832.00    Nov 1986 ......    Aug 1987 ......
Mar 1986 .... 7,756.00     Dec 1986 ......    Sep 1987 ......
Apr 1986 ..... 9,321.00    Jan 1987 ......    Oct 1987 ......
May 1986 .... 14,567.00    Feb 1987 ......    Nov 1987 ......
Jun 1986 .... 16,789.00    Mar 1987 ......    Dec 1987 ......
Jul 1986 ......            Apr 1987 ......    Jan 1988 ......
Aug 1986 ......            May 1987 ......    Feb 1988 ......
Sep 1986 ......            Jun 1987 ......    Mar 1988 ......

        Disposal Units = ◀ Monthly data: July 1986 - December 1986 ▶

Jul 1986 ........ 5797     Mar 1987 ......    Nov 1987 ......
Aug 1986 ........ 5213     Apr 1987 ......    Dec 1987 ......
Sep 1986 ........ 4784     May 1987 ......    Jan 1988 ......
Oct 1986 ........ 5678     Jun 1987 ......    Feb 1988 ......
Nov 1986 ........ 5900     Jul 1987 ......    Mar 1988 ......
Dec 1986 ........ 5200     Aug 1987 ......    Apr 1988 ......
Jan 1987 ......            Sep 1987 ......    May 1988 ......
Feb 1987 ......            Oct 1987 ......    Jun 1988 ......
fig815.mdl                        70K                     READY
```

Fig. 8.16. The ERRORS view shows the effect on the model when you attempt to add *Blender Units* and *Disposal Units*.

```
All errors:
Distribution Expense = (Blender Shipping Rate * Blender Units) + (Compactor
    Shipping Rate * Compactor Units) + (Disposal Shipping Rate * Disposal
    Units)
  Time-span error: no dates can be computed for formula.
Income Before Taxes = Total Revenue - Total Cost - MONTHLY(Total Operating
    Expense)
  Time-span error: no dates can be computed for formula.
Net Income = Income Before Taxes - Taxes
  Time-span error: no dates can be computed for formula.
Taxes = IF(Month = 1, YTD Taxes, YTD Taxes - PREVIOUS(YTD Taxes))
  Time-span error: no dates can be computed for formula.
Total Cost = Blender Cost + Disposal Cost + Compactor Cost
  Time-span error: no dates can be computed for formula.
Total Cost Per Unit = ◀ UNDEFINED ▶
Total Operating Expense = Marketing Expense + QUARTERLY(Distribution Expense) +
    Salary Expense + QUARTERLY(Interest Expense)
  Time-span error: no dates can be computed for formula.
Total Revenue = Blender Revenue + Disposal Revenue + Compactor Revenue
  Time-span error: no dates can be computed for formula.
Total Units = Blender Units + Disposal Units + Compactor Units
  Time-span error: no dates can be computed for formula.
fig816.mdl                        70K                     READY
```

Fig. 8.17. /*Formulas Time Span indicates the discrepancy in time span for *Blender Units* and *Disposal Units*.

```
                    Show time spans for all variables.
   DEFINE   CLEAR   VIEW    WINDOW   PRINT   FILE    QUIT    *FORMULAS
Blender Units = ◀ Monthly data: January 1986 - June 1986 ┌──────────────┐
Cash = ◀ Monthly calculated: December 1985 - December 19 │ *FORMULAS    │
Cash max = ◀ CONSTANT ▶                                  │              │
Cash min = ◀ CONSTANT ▶                                  │ All formulas │
Cash Unadjusted = ◀ Monthly calculated: December 1985 -  │ Inputs       │
Compactor Cost = ◀ Monthly calculated: January 1986 - Fe │ Results      │
Compactor Inventory = ◀ Monthly data: December 1985 - De │ Undefined    │
Compactor Price = ◀ CONSTANT ▶                           │ Circular     │
Compactor Revenue = ◀ Monthly calculated: January 1986 - │ Notes        │
Compactor Shipping Rate = ◀ CONSTANT ▶                   │ Time spans   │
                                                         └──────────────┘
Time spans for all variables:
Disposal Units = ◀ Monthly data: July 1986 - December 1986 ▶
Distribution Expense = ◀ Monthly calculated: January 1986 - February 1987 ▶
Equity = ◀ Monthly calculated: December 1985 - December 1987 ▶
Income Before Taxes = ◀ Monthly calculated: December 1985 - December 1986 ▶
Interest Expense = ◀ Monthly calculated: January 1986 - December 1987 ▶
Interest Rate = ◀ Monthly data: January 1986 - December 1987 ▶
Loans = ◀ Monthly calculated: December 1985 - December 1987 ▶
Marketing Expense = ◀ Quarterly data: 1 Quarter 1986 - 4 Quarter 1986 ▶
Month = ◀ Monthly data: January 1986 - January 1989 ▶
newyork.mdl*                       68K                  CALC MENU
```

An opposite type of error occurs whenever you use a time-series variable in a function argument where a constant is required. Using a time-series variable for principal, for example, in Javelin's PMT function will result in the following message: Argument 1 to PMT function is time series. Should be constant.

Checking with the FORMULAS View

As we have already indicated, the FORMULAS view is extremely valuable for checking errors when used along with the ERRORS view. As the previous examples show, you can detect some types of time-span errors only when using /*Formulas Input Variables and /*Formulas Time Span commands. Other options available through the FORMULAS view will help you check you model.

The /View Formulas command submenu has three options: /View Formulas All, /View Formulas Roots, and /View Formulas Branches (see fig. 8.18). The /View Formulas All command provides a listing of every formula in the model and includes all input variables (see fig. 8.19). The /View Formulas Roots command first prompts for a variable (see fig. 8.20). Javelin then uses this variable as the top of a pyramid. Everything in the pyramid is a part of the model that contributes to the variable at the top of the pyramid. The /View Formulas Branches command shows the other side of the Roots option (see fig. 8.21), prompting for a variable that Javelin will use in an inverted pyramid. This variable becomes the apex of the pyramid. The rest of the pyramid is filled with all the variables to which the apex variable contributes.

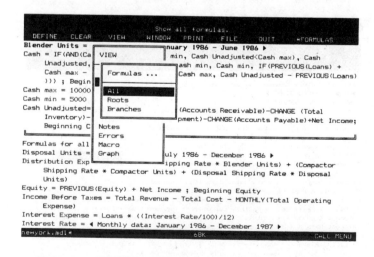

Fig. 8.18. The /View Formulas submenu.

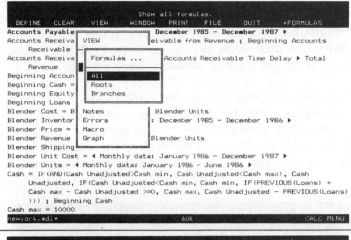

Fig. 8.19. The /View Formulas
All formulas command shows all
the formulas for a model.

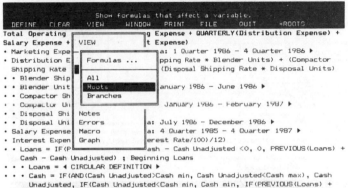

Fig. 8.20. The /View Formulas
Roots command shows the roots
of a variable.

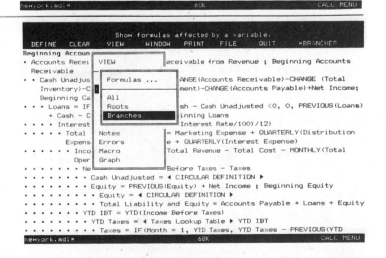

Fig. 8.21. The /View Formulas
Branches command.

Note that the *All*, *Roots*, and *Branches* options of the /View Formulas command menu have their own view-sensitive menus. You access these menus through /*Formulas, /*Roots, and /*Branches, respectively. These menus become active only when their particular aspect of the FORMULAS view is active; you can see them at the far right of the menu line (see figs. 8.22-24).

Note that you must activate the FORMULAS view to access any of the /*Formulas, /*Roots, or /*Branches commands from the menu line, as well as any /View Formulas options. You cannot access any /*Branches options from the /View Formulas Roots view; you cannot access any /*Formulas options from the /View Formulas Branches view, and so on.

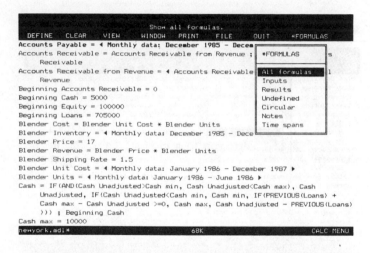

Fig. 8.22. The /*Formulas menu.

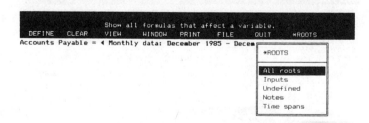

Fig. 8.23. The /*Roots menu.

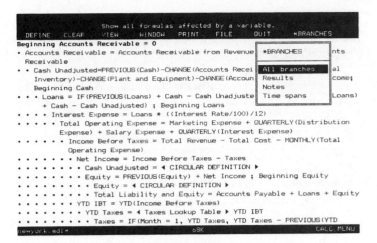

Fig. 8.24. The /*Branches menu.

Circular References

The circular reference, another common error, occurs when you define a variable as a function of itself. Javelin alerts you to a circular reference in the TABLE view or WORKSHEET view through the message #CIRC (see fig. 8.25). To display a complete list of all circular references, select /View Formulas All and then /*Formulas Circular (see fig. 8.26).

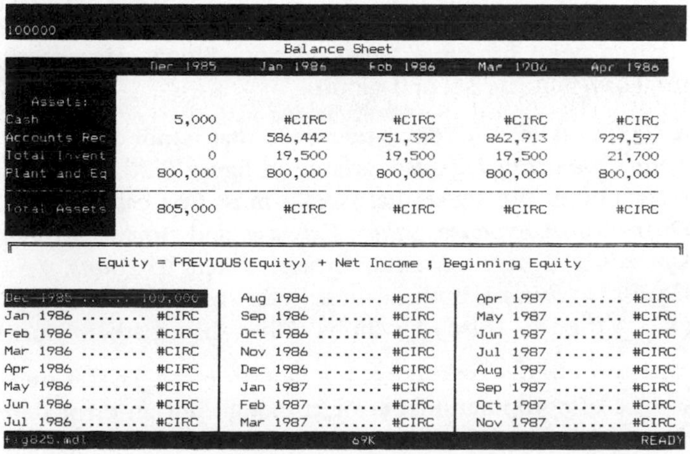

Fig. 8.25. Javelin alerts you to a circular reference in the TABLE view or WORKSHEET view.

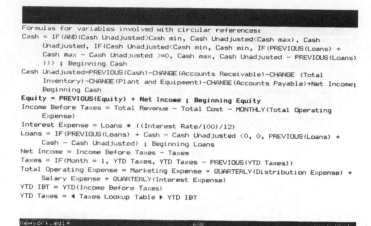

```
Formulas for variables involved with circular references:
Cash = IF(AND(Cash Unadjusted>Cash min, Cash Unadjusted<Cash max), Cash
     Unadjusted, IF(Cash Unadjusted<Cash min, Cash min, IF(PREVIOUS(Loans) +
     Cash max - Cash Unadjusted >=0, Cash max, Cash Unadjusted - PREVIOUS(Loans)
     ))) ; Beginning Cash
Cash Unadjusted=PREVIOUS(Cash)-CHANGE(Accounts Receivable)-CHANGE (Total
     Inventory)-CHANGE(Plant and Equipment)-CHANGE(Accounts Payable)+Net Income;
     Beginning Cash
Equity = PREVIOUS(Equity) + Net Income ; Beginning Equity
Income Before Taxes = Total Revenue - Total Cost - MONTHLY(Total Operating
     Expense)
Interest Expense = Loans * ((Interest Rate/100)/12)
Loans = IF(PREVIOUS(Loans) + Cash - Cash Unadjusted <0, 0, PREVIOUS(Loans) +
     Cash - Cash Unadjusted) ; Beginning Loans
Net Income = Income Before Taxes - Taxes
Taxes = IF(Month = 1, YTD Taxes, YTD Taxes - PREVIOUS(YTD Taxes))
Total Operating Expense = Marketing Expense + QUARTERLY(Distribution Expense) +
     Salary Expense + QUARTERLY(Interest Expense)
YTD IBT = YTD(Income Before Taxes)
YTD Taxes = ◀ Taxes Lookup Table ▶ YTD IBT
```

```
newyork.mdl ▪                              68K                        CALC READY
```

Fig. 8.26. Use the /*Formulas Circular reference command to see all the variables that are functions of themselves.

Circular references are not always errors. The formula *Equity* = Equity contains an error because no other variable is included in the definition of *Equity*. To correct this type of circular reference, you edit the formula to eliminate the circular definition. You can do this by equating the variable to one of its previous values or by assuming some starting point value for the variable. In this case, the proper equation would be

Equity PREVIOUS(Equity) + Net Income; Beginning Equity

Javelin first looks at the part of the equation preceding the semicolon. Because there are no previous values for *Equity*, the first part of the equation can't be evaluated or calculated. Javelin then looks at the second part of the equation where there is a value for *Beginning Equity*. This value is used to form a starting point for the *Equity* equation, allowing Javelin to evaluate the equation for *Equity* in the second month.

A second type of circular reference that is not an error is illustrated by the *Total Operating Expense* variable in figure 8.26. This variable is a circular reference in the sense that Javelin must first calculate *Marketing Expense*, *Distribution Expense*, *Salary Expense*, and *Interest Expense* to calculate *Total Operating Expense*. *Interest Expense* refers to *Loans*, which refers to *Cash* and *Cash Unadjusted*. Both of these refer to one another, but through logical (If . . . then . . . else) functions rather than mathematical functions.

This is a circular reference, but not an error. Javelin merely indicates a possible source of computational error, although not an error detected when calculating the model.

Conclusion

Whether you are in the process of developing a Javelin model or calculating an existing model, Javelin's ERRORS and FORMULAS views are essential for ensuring that your model is error free, that it is complete, and that the logic is sound. Javelin encourages you to make checking for errors a routine step in creating models.

## Part IV

Analyzing and Presenting with Javelin

9

Analysis and Presentation with Views and Building Blocks

Chapters 3 through 8 provide the basic groundwork for using Javelin views and building blocks for creating and checking a Javelin model. Chapter 3, for example, explains how to begin developing Javelin models by using the FORMULAS and DIAGRAM views to help you enter variables, create formulas, and keep track of relationships between variables as your model develops. And when you're ready to enter data for variables you have defined, Chapter 3 describes how the TABLE view assists with this task.

Chapter 5 introduces the CHART, QUICK GRAPH, and WORKSHEET views and shows how they can be used for building models and inputting data. Chapter 6 explains how you can take advantage of Javelin's many options for importing and consolidating data. Chapter 7 introduces those building blocks essential for models using lookup tables, time delay curves, or curves for approximating relationships between variables. And in Chapter 8 you learn about checking your model with the FORMULAS and ERRORS views. In this chapter, we use a sales forecast model to illustrate some of the many ways to use Javelin views and building blocks for analysis and presentation.

When you use Javelin for analysis, you take advantage of the program's many options for displaying data—in table, graph, or worksheet, for example—to help you think through a business problem. By allowing you to view data in many ways and compare different views of data on one screen, Javelin helps you make business decisions.

When you use Javelin for presentation—either orally or on paper—you take advantage of the program's capability of displaying data in multiple ways to support your conclusions. Like conventional spreadsheet software, Javelin provides many options for printing reports and graphs to summarize data effectively. But Javelin also makes it easy for you to summarize data electronically for presenting conclusions in meetings. No matter what the focus—sales, forecasting, planning for company growth, or product planning—Javelin can help you present data clearly and convincingly.

Using Javelin for Analysis

Imagine that you are the marketing and sales manager for Future Home's New York office and have prepared the following:

1. Forecast of blender sales for 1987

2. Report of actual blender sales for 1987

3. Comparison of the 1987 forecast with actual 1987 sales

4. Comparison of actual 1987 sales with actual 1986 sales

You've been asked not only to provide data for all four items but also to summarize this information in one final report. Javelin can help you build a model with all the data you need, analyze this data easily, and then present it to others.

Methods for Creating a Sales Forecast Model

Before looking at how powerful Javelin is for analysis, consider the different ways you can create a sales forecast model. You have a number of options for designing a model that will provide the forecasts, reports, and comparisons you need.

For example, you can use either of the following two methods to design a sales forecast application with Javelin. First, you can create one Javelin model containing all the variables you need to report each particular type of information. Second, you can create three separate models:

- one model containing the forecast for 1987

- one model containing actual sales figures for 1986-87

- one model combining variables for all three models and containing new formulas for comparing forecast sales with 1987 actual sales and actual sales with 1986 sales

The method you choose depends on how data will be entered. You may find it convenient to control all data within a single model, copy the model for others to enter actual sales data, and then analyze the single model and create reports whenever needed. You may find it more effective (and possibly more secure) to keep data in separate models, and then combine models into a larger model by using Javelin's /File Import Variable and /Define Building block Import commands. The following description shows how you might forecast sales by creating a single model or a consolidated model.

Creating a Single Sales Forecast Model

First, if you wanted to create a single model for entering, storing, displaying, and reporting both forecasted and actual sales data, you would begin by developing a model with the variables and formulas listed in figure 9.1.

Fig. 9.1. List of variables and formulas for forecasting and reporting actual blender sales.

Notice the types of variables listed in figure 9.1. The first three variables can be used for entering blender price and the number of blenders sold each month and for calculating monthly blender revenue. These variables are

Actual Blender Units
Actual Blender Price
Actual Blender Revenue

Actual Blender Units is a time-series variable using Javelin's default time period of a month. *Actual Blender Price* is a constant. *Actual Blender Revenue* is a calculated variable defined as follows:

Actual Blender Revenue = Actual Blender Units * Actual
                        Blender Price

In addition to the variables for the actual number of blenders sold each month and for monthly blender revenue, the FORMULAS view in figure 9.1 lists variables for both actual and projected sales. Data for actual sales is available for January, 1986, through December, 1986; data for projections is available for January, 1987, through December, 1987.

    Projected Blender Units
    Projected Blender Price
    Projected Blender Revenue

Projected Blender Price is a constant, but both *Projected Blender Units* and *Projected Blender Revenue* are calculated variables:

Projected Blender Units = (Percent Change * TREND(Actual
                        Blender Units, Jan 1987, Dec 1987))
                        + TREND(Actual Blender Units, Jan
                        1987, Dec 1987)

Notice that Javelin's TREND function estimates the number of blender units sold for each month in 1987. This function's estimates are based on the past trend of blender sales. You can see the results of the *Projected Blender Units* formula in the top window of the screen in figure 9.2 with a table of estimated monthly sales from January, 1987, through December, 1987. The bottom half of the screen displays a table of the actual number of blenders sold in the previous year. *Projected Blender Revenue* is calculated from the *Projected Blender Units* values.

In addition to the variables for actual and projected blender sales, four other variables are part of the model. First, two variables compare monthly data for actual versus projected blender sales:

    Actual vs Projected Blender Units
    Actual vs Projected Blender Revenue

The data resulting from these variables can be used in numerous ways from setting sales goals to determining a marketing budget. Second, two variables compare monthly data for this year's blender sales with last years blender sales:

    Actual vs Last Years Blender Units
    Actual vs Last Years Blender Revenue

```
[illegible]
 Projected Blender Units = (Percent Change  * TREND(Actual Blender Units,Jan...

Jan 1987 .... [illegible] | Oct 1987 .... 12,914.85 | Jul 1988 ......
Feb 1987 .... 11,095.37   | Nov 1987 .... 15,203.16 | Aug 1988 ......
Mar 1987 .... 11,097.13   | Dec 1987 .... 17,134.88 | Sep 1988 ......
Apr 1987 .... 11,662.93   | Jan 1988 ......         | Oct 1988 ......
May 1987 .... 12,142.88   | Feb 1988 ......         | Nov 1988 ......
Jun 1987 .... 12,130.84   | Mar 1988 ......         | Dec 1988 ......
Jul 1987 .... 10,060.49   | Apr 1988 ......         | Jan 1989 ......
Aug 1987 .... 16,588.72   | May 1988 ......         | Feb 1989 ......
Sep 1987 .... 12,533.02   | Jun 1988 ......         | Mar 1989 ......

      Actual Blender Units = ◄ Monthly data: January 1986 - December 1986 ►

Jan 1986 ..... 4,989.00   | Sep 1986 ..... 7,456.00  | May 1987 ......
Feb 1986 ..... 5,210.00   | Oct 1986 ..... 7,854.00  | Jun 1987 ......
Mar 1986 ..... 5,460.00   | Nov 1986 ..... 9,434.00  | Jul 1987 ......
Apr 1986 ..... 5,979.00   | Dec 1986 .... 10,832.00  | Aug 1987 ......
May 1986 ..... 6,456.00   | Jan 1987 ......          | Sep 1987 ......
Jun 1986 ..... 6,663.00   | Feb 1987 ......          | Oct 1987 ......
Jul 1986 ..... 5,690.00   | Mar 1987 ......          | Nov 1987 ......
Aug 1986 ..... 9,634.00   | Apr 1987 ......          | Dec 1987 ......
planz.mdl                          [illegible]                          READY
```

Fig. 9.2. TABLE views showing actual sales for 1986 and forecasted sales for 1987.

Note that the variable names for this model are designed to be highly descriptive for ease of use when you need to recall a name or develop worksheets to display data.

Creating a Consolidated Sales Forecast Model

In the model in the last example, we entered and calculated all data in the same file. With Javelin, it's just as easy to develop the application in different models as it is in one. One method for developing an application to report and compare actual, projected, and previous year's sales data might consist of:

- one model for entering and calculating actual sales
- one model for projecting sales
- one model for containing projected and actual sales data, comparing actual against projections, and comparing this year's actual sales to last year's

You would design such an application by beginning with a model for entering and calculating blender sales. The model might consist of only those variables necessary for indicating price, reporting number of units, and calculating revenue, as in the FORMULAS view displayed in figure 9.3. Next, a model for estimating blender sales could consist of the variables shown in figure 9.4. This model uses Javelin's Import data building block to import data for blender price, revenue, and units.

A third model brings both actual and projected sales information together and contains formulas for comparisons. To develop this model, you would import

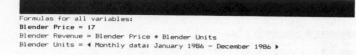

```
Formulas for all variables:
Blender Price = 17
Blender Revenue = Blender Price * Blender Units
Blender Units = ◄ Monthly data: January 1986 - December 1986 ►
```

Fig. 9.3. Variables for reporting price, actual sales units, and revenue.

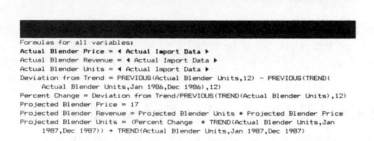

```
Formulas for all variables:
Actual Blender Price = ◄ Actual Import Data ►
Actual Blender Revenue = ◄ Actual Import Data ►
Actual Blender Units = ◄ Actual Import Data ►
Deviation from Trend = PREVIOUS(Actual Blender Units,12) - PREVIOUS(TREND(
     Actual Blender Units,Jan 1986,Dec 1986),12)
Percent Change = Deviation from Trend/PREVIOUS(TREND(Actual Blender Units),12)
Projected Blender Price = 17
Projected Blender Revenue = Projected Blender Units * Projected Blender Price
Projected Blender Units = (Percent Change  * TREND(Actual Blender Units,Jan
     1987,Dec 1987)) + TREND(Actual Blender Units,Jan 1987,Dec 1987)
```

Fig. 9.4. Variables for forecasting blender sales and revenue.

data for actual blender price, units, and sales by using Javelin's /Define Building block Import data command. The data that this command imports is then assigned a new variable name by Javelin. In the original model, price, units, and revenue data were linked to variables named *Blender Price*, *Blender Units*, and *Blender Revenue*. The Import data building block places NY Actual before each original name to create a new name for the imported data for actual sales (see fig. 9.5). The third model also uses Javelin's /Define Building block Import data command to import original variables for projected blender sales.

Once imported as an Import data building block, actual blender sales data cannot be changed, although imported variables can be used in other formulas. You can, however, update data in an Import data building block when data is

```
Formulas for all variables:
NY Actual Blender Price = ◄ NY Import Data ►
NY Actual Blender Revenue = ◄ NY Import Data ►
NY Actual Blender Units = ◄ NY Import Data ►
NY Actual vs Last Years Blender Revenue = NY Actual Blender Revenue - PREVIOUS(
     NY Actual Blender Revenue,12)
NY Actual vs Last Years Blender Units = NY Actual Blender Units - PREVIOUS(NY
     Actual Blender Units,12)
NY Actual vs Projected Blender Revenue = NY Actual Blender Revenue - NY
     Projected Blender Revenue
NY Actual vs Projected Blender Units = NY Actual Blender Units - NY Projected
     Blender Units
NY Deviation from Trend = ◄ NY Import Data ►
NY Percent Change = ◄ NY Import Data ►
NY Projected Blender Price = ◄ NY Import Data ►
NY Projected Blender Revenue = ◄ NY Import Data ►
NY Projected Blender Units = ◄ NY Import Data ►
```

```
frimp.mdl                                        93K        CAPS                         READY
```

Fig. 9.5. Sales forecast model created through /Define Building block Import data.

changed in the original model by using the /File Import Import values command or the Import values command from Javelin's Import data building block menu.

In addition to the imported data and variables, the third model includes four formulas to compare actual with projected units sold and revenue as well as to compare this year's sales with last year's:

NY Actual vs Last Years Blender Revenue
NY Actual vs Last Years Blender Units
NY Actual vs Projected Blender Revenue
NY Actual vs Projected Blender Units

Analyzing with Javelin Views

For any model you build, Javelin's 10 views give you numerous perspectives on the information. TABLE, CHART, QUICK GRAPH, GRAPH, and WORKSHEET, for example, are powerful views that help you analyze data, such as that in the blender sales model. The following sections emphasize how you can use these views to aid your analysis of projected and actual blender sales data.

Using the TABLE View for Analysis

Javelin's TABLE view provides a quick view of the data for any variable in your model, whether the variable was imported or entered directly into the model. In our model for forecasting blender sales, for example, the TABLE view provides a quick comparison of the actual number of blenders sold versus the number projected for the months of January, 1987, through December, 1987 (see fig. 9.6).

```
10980
     Actual Blender Units = ◄ Monthly data: January 1986 - December 1987 ►

  Jan 1987 ....... 10,980    Oct 1987 ....... 11,240    Jul 1988 ......
  Feb 1987 ....... 11,023    Nov 1987 ....... 15,900    Aug 1988 ......
  Mar 1987 ....... 13,567    Dec 1987 ....... 18,034    Sep 1988 ......
  Apr 1987 ....... 11,900    Jan 1988 ......            Oct 1988 ......
  May 1987 ....... 12,789    Feb 1988 ......            Nov 1988 ......
  Jun 1987 ....... 13,002    Mar 1988 ......            Dec 1988 ......
  Jul 1987 ....... 14,005    Apr 1988 ......            Jan 1989 ......
  Aug 1987 ....... 16,890    May 1988 ......            Feb 1989 ......
  Sep 1987 ....... 13,045    Jun 1988 ......            Mar 1989 ......

     Projected Blender Units = (Percent Change  * TREND(Actual Blender Units,Jan...

  Jan 1987 ....... 11,913    Sep 1987 ....... 12,831    May 1988 ......
  Feb 1987 ....... 11,691    Oct 1987 ....... 13,195    Jun 1988 ......
  Mar 1987 ....... 11,614    Nov 1987 ....... 15,505    Jul 1988 ......
  Apr 1987 ....... 12,139    Dec 1987 ....... 17,448    Aug 1988 ......
  May 1987 ....... 12,582    Jan 1988 ......            Sep 1988 ......
  Jun 1987 ....... 12,522    Feb 1988 ......            Oct 1988 ......
  Jul 1987 ....... 10,352    Mar 1988 ......            Nov 1988 ......
  Aug 1987 ....... 17,023    Apr 1988 ......            Dec 1988 ......
plan2.mdl                          85K                              READY
```

Fig. 9.6. Comparison of actual and projected blender sales, using Javelin's TABLE view.

The TABLE view, however, also gives you a quick numeric summary of data for many other variables in your model. The TABLE views shown in figure 9.7, for example, contrast dollar amounts for actual revenue from blenders sold with forecasted revenue. And when you need to analyze specific value differences over time of actual versus projected sales, the TABLE views in figure 9.8 tell you how close you came to your forecast in number of products sold and dollar return. As indicated in the tables, January, February, April, August, and October fell below estimated sales, while actual sales for March and July greatly exceeded the projected sales.

```
186660
     Actual Blender Revenue = Actual Blender Price * Actual Blender Units

  Jan 1987 .. $186,660.00    Oct 1987 .. $191,080.00   Jul 1988 ......
  Feb 1987 .. $187,391.00    Nov 1987 .. $270,300.00   Aug 1988 ......
  Mar 1987 .. $230,639.00    Dec 1987 .. $306,578.00   Sep 1988 ......
  Apr 1987 .. $202,300.00    Jan 1988 ......           Oct 1988 ......
  May 1987 .. $217,413.00    Feb 1988 ......           Nov 1988 ......
  Jun 1987 .. $221,034.00    Mar 1988 ......           Dec 1988 ......
  Jul 1987 .. $238,085.00    Apr 1988 ......           Jan 1989 ......
  Aug 1987 .. $287,130.00    May 1988 ......           Feb 1989 ......
  Sep 1987 .. $221,765.00    Jun 1988 ......           Mar 1989 ......

     Projected Blender Revenue = Projected Blender Units * Projected Blender Price

  Jan 1987 .. $202,518.81    Sep 1987 .. $218,123.41   May 1988 ......
  Feb 1987 .. $198,747.59    Oct 1987 .. $224,312.56   Jun 1988 ......
  Mar 1987 .. $197,439.24    Nov 1987 .. $263,589.05   Jul 1988 ......
  Apr 1987 .. $206,370.15    Dec 1987 .. $296,617.77   Aug 1988 ......
  May 1987 .. $213,892.50    Jan 1988 ......           Sep 1988 ......
  Jun 1987 .. $212,874.65    Feb 1988 ......           Oct 1988 ......
  Jul 1987 .. $175,981.12    Mar 1988 ......           Nov 1988 ......
  Aug 1987 .. $289,385.80    Apr 1988 ......           Dec 1988 ......
plan1.mdl                          85K                              READY
```

Fig. 9.7. TABLE view showing actual blender revenue and forecasted blender revenue.

```
-932.8714291413
Actual vs Projected Blender Units = Actual Blender Units - Projected Blender...

Jan 1987 ...... (932.87)    Oct 1987 .... (1,954.86)    Jul 1988 ......
Feb 1987 ...... (668.03)    Nov 1987 ....... 394.76     Aug 1988 ......
Mar 1987 ..... 1,952.93     Dec 1987 ....... 585.90     Sep 1988 ......
Apr 1987 ...... (239.42)    Jan 1988 ......             Oct 1988 ......
May 1987 ....... 207.09     Feb 1988 ......             Nov 1988 ......
Jun 1987 ....... 479.96     Mar 1988 ......             Dec 1988 ......
Jul 1987 ..... 3,653.17     Apr 1988 ......             Jan 1989 ......
Aug 1987 ...... (132.69)    May 1988 ......             Feb 1989 ......
Sep 1987 ....... 214.21     Jun 1988 ......             Mar 1989 ......

   Actual vs Projected Blender Revenue = Actual Blender Revenue - Projected...

Jan 1987 ... (15,858.81)    Sep 1987 ..... 3,641.59     May 1988 ......
Feb 1987 ... (11,356.59)    Oct 1987 ... (33,232.56)    Jun 1988 ......
Mar 1987 .... 33,199.76     Nov 1987 ..... 6,710.95     Jul 1988 ......
Apr 1987 .... (4,070.15)    Dec 1987 ..... 9,960.23     Aug 1988 ......
May 1987 .... 3,520.50      Jan 1988 ......             Sep 1988 ......
Jun 1987 ..... 8,159.35     Feb 1988 ......             Oct 1988 ......
Jul 1987 .... 62,103.88     Mar 1988 ......             Nov 1988 ......
Aug 1987 ... (2,255.80)     Apr 1988 ......             Dec 1988 ......
plan1.mdl                                  86K                            READY
```

Fig. 9.8. TABLE view showing differences between actual and forecasted blender sales.

Comparing Actual and Projected Sales

Suppose that you want to know the percentage differences rather than amount sold between actual and projected sales. You can calculate percentage by editing the formula for *Actual vs. Projected Blender Units* and then displaying a TABLE view for the information, as shown in figure 9.9. Editing the formula to calculate percentage difference between the monthly amount forecasted and actual sales, you would make the TABLE view displaying *Actual vs. Projected Blender Units* your current window, press the EDIT key (F2), and edit the formula as indicated below:

Actual vs Projected
Blender Units Percent = (Actual Blender Units - Projected
                                 Blender Units)/Actual Blender Units

To complete the operation, press Enter and then press the CALC key (F9). The TABLE view is displayed with values formatted like those originally set for the variable *Actual vs. Projected Blender Units*. If you want to display values in percent format, select /Define Variable Settings, move the cursor to Percent in the format box of the settings sheet, and press Esc. Javelin now displays percentage differences between actual and forecasted sales (see fig. 9.9). The table displayed in figure 9.9 indicates that July sales were 26.08% higher than forecasted, whereas October sales were a painful 17.39% below those projected.

In addition to viewing the percentage difference between actual and forecasted sales, you can display another window that shows the difference in units sold and units forecasted. Figure 9.10 shows unit differences in the top window and shows percentage differences in the bottom.

```
-0.0849609680456
Actual vs Projected Blender Units Percent = (Actual Blender Units - Projected...

Jan 1987 ........ -8.50%    Sep 1988 ......        May 1990 ......
Feb 1987 ........ -6.06%    Oct 1988 ......        Jun 1990 ......
Mar 1987 ........ 14.39%    Nov 1988 ......        Jul 1990 ......
Apr 1987 ........ -2.01%    Dec 1988 ......        Aug 1990 ......
May 1987 ......... 1.62%    Jan 1989 ......        Sep 1990 ......
Jun 1987 ......... 3.69%    Feb 1989 ......        Oct 1990 ......
Jul 1987 ........ 26.08%    Mar 1989 ......        Nov 1990 ......
Aug 1987 ........ -0.79%    Apr 1989 ......        Dec 1990 ......
Sep 1987 ......... 1.64%    May 1989 ......        Jan 1991 ......
Oct 1987 ....... -17.39%    Jun 1989 ......        Feb 1991 ......
Nov 1987 ......... 2.48%    Jul 1989 ......        Mar 1991 ......
Dec 1987 ......... 3.25%    Aug 1989 ......        Apr 1991 ......
Jan 1988 ......             Sep 1989 ......        May 1991 ......
Feb 1988 ......             Oct 1989 ......        Jun 1991 ......
Mar 1988 ......             Nov 1989 ......        Jul 1991 ......
Apr 1988 ......             Dec 1989 ......        Aug 1991 ......
May 1988 ......             Jan 1990 ......        Sep 1991 ......
Jun 1988 ......             Feb 1990 ......        Oct 1991 ......
Jul 1988 ......             Mar 1990 ......        Nov 1991 ......
Aug 1988 ......             Apr 1990 ......        Dec 1991 ......
plan2.mdl*                              85K                          READY
```

Fig. 9.9. TABLE view displaying percentage differences between forecasted and actual blender sales.

```
-932.8714291413
Actual vs Projected Blender Units = Actual Blender Units - Projected Blender...

Jan 1987 ........ (933)     Oct 1987 ....... (1,955)    Jul 1988 ......
Feb 1987 ........ (668)     Nov 1987 .......... 395     Aug 1988 ......
Mar 1987 ........ 1,953     Dec 1987 .......... 586     Sep 1988 ......
Apr 1987 ........ (239)     Jan 1988 ......            Oct 1988 ......
May 1987 .......... 207     Feb 1988 ......            Nov 1988 ......
Jun 1987 .......... 480     Mar 1988 ......            Dec 1988 ......
Jul 1987 ........ 3,653     Apr 1988 ......            Jan 1989 ......
Aug 1987 ........ (133)     May 1988 ......            Feb 1989 ......
Sep 1987 .......... 214     Jun 1988 ......            Mar 1989 ......

Actual vs Projected Blender Units Percent = (Actual Blender Units - Projected...

Jan 1987 ........ -8.50%    Sep 1987 ......... 1.64%    May 1988 ......
Feb 1987 ........ -6.06%    Oct 1987 ....... -17.39%    Jun 1988 ......
Mar 1987 ........ 14.39%    Nov 1987 ......... 2.48%    Jul 1988 ......
Apr 1987 ........ -2.01%    Dec 1987 ......... 3.25%    Aug 1988 ......
May 1987 ......... 1.62%    Jan 1988 ......            Sep 1988 ......
Jun 1987 ......... 3.69%    Feb 1988 ......            Oct 1988 ......
Jul 1987 ........ 26.08%    Mar 1988 ......            Nov 1988 ......
Aug 1987 ........ -0.79%    Apr 1988 ......            Dec 1988 ......
plan2.mdl*                              85K                          READY
```

Fig. 9.10. TABLE view showing percent and unit differences in forecasted versus actual blender sales.

At this point, if you want to determine quickly whether total sales for 1987 are above or below forecast, you can rapidly determine the total difference between 1987 forecasted sales and 1987 actual sales by editing the formula for *Actual vs Projected Blender Units*. To display a year-end total, select the formula for *Actual vs Projected Blender Units*, press the EDIT key (F2), and enter the function YEARLY at the beginning of the right side of the formula, as follows:

Actual vs Projected Blender Units = YEARLY(Actual Blender
Units - Projected
Blender Units)

The TABLE view in figure 9.11 shows that 3,560 blender units were sold above the projected figures for 1987. If you want to see the difference between forecasted and actual sales in dollar amounts, add the function YEARLY to the *Actual vs Projected Blender Revenue* formula (see fig. 9.12).

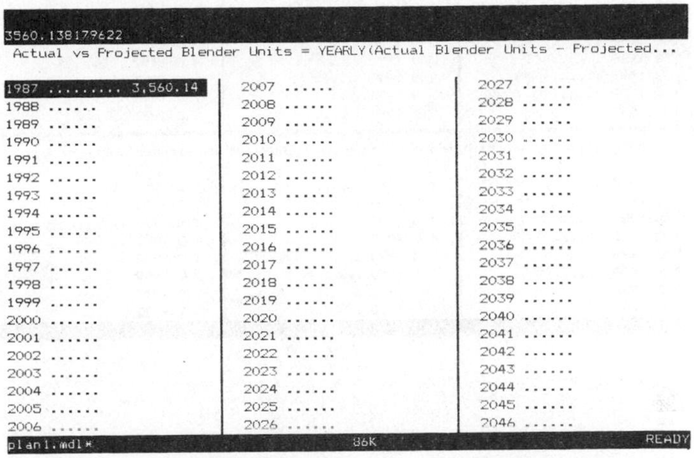

```
3560.138179622
Actual vs Projected Blender Units = YEARLY(Actual Blender Units - Projected...

1987 ........ 3,560.14    2007 ......    2027 ......
1988 ......               2008 ......    2028 ......
1989 ......               2009 ......    2029 ......
1990 ......               2010 ......    2030 ......
1991 ......               2011 ......    2031 ......
1992 ......               2012 ......    2032 ......
1993 ......               2013 ......    2033 ......
1994 ......               2014 ......    2034 ......
1995 ......               2015 ......    2035 ......
1996 ......               2016 ......    2036 ......
1997 ......               2017 ......    2037 ......
1998 ......               2018 ......    2038 ......
1999 ......               2019 ......    2039 ......
2000 ......               2020 ......    2040 ......
2001 ......               2021 ......    2041 ......
2002 ......               2022 ......    2042 ......
2003 ......               2023 ......    2043 ......
2004 ......               2024 ......    2044 ......
2005 ......               2025 ......    2045 ......
2006 ......               2026 ......    2046 ......
plan1.mdl*                      86K                       READY
```

Fig. 9.11. Total yearly difference between forecasted units sold and actual units sold.

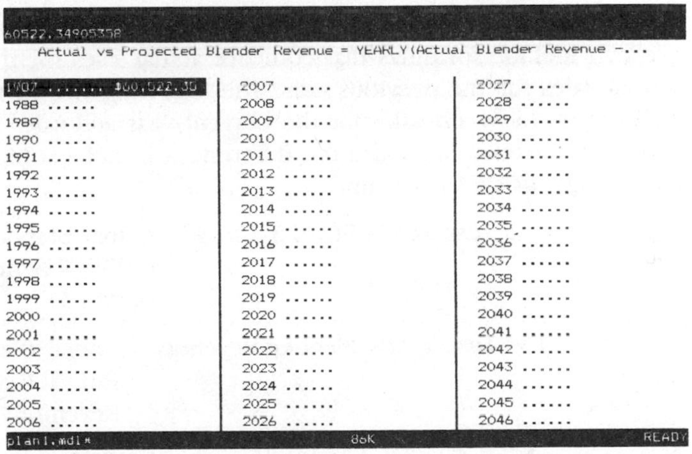

```
60522.34905358
Actual vs Projected Blender Revenue = YEARLY(Actual Blender Revenue -...

1987 ....... $60,522.35    2007 ......    2027 ......
1988 ......                2008 ......    2028 ......
1989 ......                2009 ......    2029 ......
1990 ......                2010 ......    2030 ......
1991 ......                2011 ......    2031 ......
1992 ......                2012 ......    2032 ......
1993 ......                2013 ......    2033 ......
1994 ......                2014 ......    2034 ......
1995 ......                2015 ......    2035 ......
1996 ......                2016 ......    2036 ......
1997 ......                2017 ......    2037 ......
1998 ......                2018 ......    2038 ......
1999 ......                2019 ......    2039 ......
2000 ......                2020 ......    2040 ......
2001 ......                2021 ......    2041 ......
2002 ......                2022 ......    2042 ......
2003 ......                2023 ......    2043 ......
2004 ......                2024 ......    2044 ......
2005 ......                2025 ......    2045 ......
2006 ......                2026 ......    2046 ......
plan1.mdl*                      86K                       READY
```

Fig. 9.12. Total yearly difference between forecasted revenue and actual revenue.

Javelin makes analyzing data in monthly, yearly, or quarterly totals quite simple. Forming a quarterly report comparing actual and forecasted blender sales is as easy as adding the function QUARTERLY to the formula for *Actual vs. Projected Blender Units* and for *Actual vs. Projected Blender Revenue*. Figure 9.13 shows a table displaying quarter-by-quarter differences in units and dollar amount between actual and forecasted sales.

```
5984.355004898
Actual vs Projected Blender Revenue = QUARTERLY(Actual Blender Revenue -...

1 Q 1987 .... $5,784.36    2 Q 1989 ......    3 Q 1991 ......
2 Q 1987 .... $7,609.70    3 Q 1989 ......    4 Q 1991 ......
3 Q 1987 ... $63,489.67    4 Q 1989 ......    1 Q 1992 ......
4 Q 1987 .. ($16,561.38)   1 Q 1990 ......    2 Q 1992 ......
1 Q 1988 ......            2 Q 1990 ......    3 Q 1992 ......
2 Q 1988 ......            3 Q 1990 ......    4 Q 1992 ......
3 Q 1988 ......            4 Q 1990 ......    1 Q 1993 ......
4 Q 1988 ......            1 Q 1991 ......    2 Q 1993 ......
1 Q 1989 ......            2 Q 1991 ......    3 Q 1993 ......

       Actual vs Projected Blender Units = QUARTERLY(Actual Blender Units -...

1 Q 1987 ....... 352.02    1 Q 1989 ......    1 Q 1991 ......
2 Q 1987 ....... 447.63    2 Q 1989 ......    2 Q 1991 ......
3 Q 1987 ..... 3,734.69    3 Q 1989 ......    3 Q 1991 ......
4 Q 1987 ...... (974.20)   4 Q 1989 ......    4 Q 1991 ......
1 Q 1988 ......            1 Q 1990 ......    1 Q 1992 ......
2 Q 1988 ......            2 Q 1990 ......    2 Q 1992 ......
3 Q 1988 ......            3 Q 1990 ......    3 Q 1992 ......
4 Q 1988 ......            4 Q 1990 ......    4 Q 1992 ......
blah1.edit                           65K                       READY
```

Fig. 9.13. TABLE view displaying quarterly differences between forecasted and actual blender sales.

Comparing Yearly Sales

In addition to entering formulas to compare forecasted sales with actual sales, we can include formulas that compare actual sales for the current year with actual sales for the previous year. The following two formulas can calculate differences between sales for the current year and sales for the previous year. The first formula calculates the differences in units sold; the second calculates differences in dollar amount.

- Actual vs Last Year's Blender Units = Actual Blender Units - PREVIOUS(Actual Blender Units,12)

- Actual vs Last Year's Blender Revenue = Actual Blender Revenue - PREVIOUS(Actual Blender Revenue,12)

Notice that both formulas use the function PREVIOUS. In the first formula, PREVIOUS indicates that Javelin should return the value twelve months ago from any given month (January, 1987 - January, 1986; February, 1987 - February, 1986, etc.) The TABLE view results of both formulas are displayed in figure 9.14. A quick analysis of the two tables shows that 1987 sales were above 1986 sales for every month.

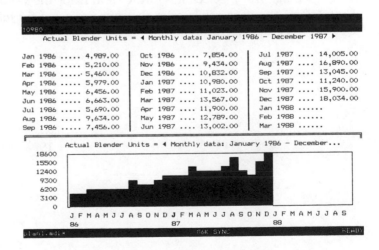

```
101847
Actual vs Last Years Blender Units = Actual Blender Units - PREVIOUS(Actual...

Jan 1987 ..... 5,991.00    Oct 1987 ..... 3,386.00    Jul 1988 ......
Feb 1987 ..... 5,813.00    Nov 1987 ..... 6,466.00    Aug 1988 ......
Mar 1987 ..... 8,107.00    Dec 1987 ..... 7,202.00    Sep 1988 ......
Apr 1987 ..... 5,921.00    Jan 1988 ......            Oct 1988 ......
May 1987 ..... 6,333.00    Feb 1988 ......            Nov 1988 ......
Jun 1987 ..... 6,339.00    Mar 1988 ......            Dec 1988 ......
Jul 1987 ..... 8,315.00    Apr 1988 ......            Jan 1989 ......
Aug 1987 ..... 7,256.00    May 1988 ......            Feb 1989 ......
Sep 1987 ..... 5,589.00    Jun 1988 ......            Mar 1989 ......

Actual vs Last Years Blender Revenue = Actual Blender Revenue -...

Jan 1987 ... 101,847.00    Sep 1987 .... 95,013.00    May 1988 ......
Feb 1987 .... 98,821.00    Oct 1987 .... 57,562.00    Jun 1988 ......
Mar 1987 ... 137,819.00    Nov 1987 ... 109,922.00    Jul 1988 ......
Apr 1987 ... 100,657.00    Dec 1987 ... 122,434.00    Aug 1988 ......
May 1987 ... 107,661.00    Jan 1988 ......            Sep 1988 ......
Jun 1987 ... 107,763.00    Feb 1988 ......            Oct 1988 ......
Jul 1987 ... 141,355.00    Mar 1988 ......            Nov 1988 ......
Aug 1987 ... 123,352.00    Apr 1988 ......            Dec 1988 ......
plan1.mdl*                          86K                              READY
```

Fig. 9.14. TABLE views displaying current year's sales with previous year's sales.

Using the CHART and QUICK GRAPH Views for Analysis

When you use the TABLE view by itself or with other views, you can quickly see trends or spot any aberrations in your data. Displaying *Actual Blender Units* in a TABLE view at the top half of the screen with a CHART view in the bottom half, for example, enables you to spot easily those months with dramatic changes in units sold. As figure 9.15 shows, sales of blender units in September and October of 1986 and 1987 dip dramatically from sales in August of 1986 and 1987.

```
10980
Actual Blender Units = ◀ Monthly data: January 1986 - December 1987 ▶

Jan 1986 ..... 4,989.00    Oct 1986 ..... 7,854.00    Jul 1987 .... 14,005.00
Feb 1986 ..... 5,210.00    Nov 1986 ..... 9,434.00    Aug 1987 .... 16,890.00
Mar 1986 ..... 5,460.00    Dec 1986 .... 10,832.00    Sep 1987 .... 13,045.00
Apr 1986 ..... 5,979.00    Jan 1987 .... 10,980.00    Oct 1987 .... 11,240.00
May 1986 ..... 6,456.00    Feb 1987 .... 11,023.00    Nov 1987 .... 15,900.00
Jun 1986 ..... 6,663.00    Mar 1987 .... 13,567.00    Dec 1987 .... 18,034.00
Jul 1986 ..... 5,690.00    Apr 1987 .... 11,900.00    Jan 1988 ......
Aug 1986 ..... 9,634.00    May 1987 .... 12,789.00    Feb 1988 ......
Sep 1986 ..... 7,456.00    Jun 1987 .... 13,002.00    Mar 1988 ......
```

Fig. 9.15. TABLE and CHART views of actual blender units sold.

Displaying CHART views of two different variables on the same screen can also help you analyze data. Compare, for example, the CHART views in figure 9.16. The CHART view of *Actual Blender Units* for January, 1986, through December, 1987, is displayed in the top window; the CHART view of *Projected Blender Units* for January, 1987, through December, 1987, is displayed in the bottom. Notice that actual sales for September and October decline just as predicted in the projected figures over the same period.

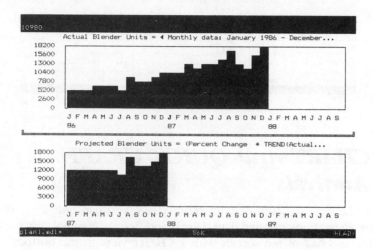

Fig. 9.16. CHART views showing actual and forecasted blender sales.

An even more dramatic indication of a trend in actual blender sales is provided by a QUICK GRAPH view of units sold between January, 1986, and December, 1987 (see fig. 9.17). Selecting QUICK GRAPH for the variable *Projected Blender Units* shows the decrease in sales that was projected for July, September, and October (see fig. 9.18).

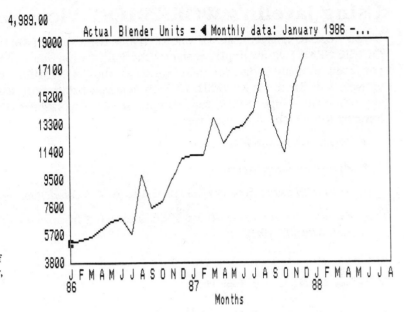

Fig. 9.17. QUICK GRAPH view of
actual blender sales from January,
1986, to December, 1987.

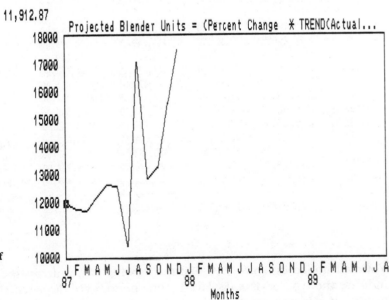

Fig. 9.18. QUICK GRAPH view of
forecasted blender sales from
January, 1987, to December,
1987.

Using Javelin's WORKSHEET View for Analysis

If you need to analyze data for one or two variables, the TABLE, CHART, or QUICK GRAPH views display instantly the information you need. If, however, you want to analyze data for many variables, the WORKSHEET view is the best view to use. Javelin's WORKSHEET view lets you bring more data together than any other view. Figure 9.19, for example, shows a worksheet that displays information for the following variables:

- *Projected Blender Revenue*

- *Actual Blender Revenue*

- *Actual Blender Revenue* subtracted from *Projected Blender Revenue*

- *Actual Blender Revenue* for 1986 subtracted from *Actual Blender Revenue* for 1987

Future Home Appliances, Inc. 5 Mar 1986

| | | | -----------------------Blender Revenue----------------------- | |
	Projected	Actual	Actual vs Projected	Actual vs Last Years
Jan 1987	$202,518.81	$186,660.00	($15,858.81)	$101,847.00
Feb 1987	$198,747.59	$187,391.00	($11,356.59)	$98,821.00
Mar 1987	$197,439.24	$230,639.00	$33,199.76	$137,819.00
Apr 1987	$206,370.15	$202,300.00	($4,070.15)	$100,657.00
May 1987	$213,892.50	$217,413.00	$3,520.50	$107,661.00
Jun 1987	$212,874.65	$221,034.00	$8,159.35	$107,763.00
Jul 1987	$175,981.12	$238,085.00	$62,103.88	$141,355.00
Aug 1987	$289,385.80	$287,130.00	($2,255.80)	$123,352.00
Sep 1987	$218,123.41	$221,765.00	$3,641.59	$95,013.00
Oct 1987	$224,312.56	$191,080.00	($33,232.56)	$57,562.00
Nov 1987	$263,589.05	$270,300.00	$6,710.95	$109,922.00
Dec 1987	$296,617.77	$306,578.00	$9,960.23	$122,434.00
	------------	-----------	------------	------------
1987	$2,699,853	$2,760,375	$60,522	$1,304,206

Fig. 9.19. WORKSHEET view displaying projected, actual, and the differences between actual and projected and between current year's and previous year's actual sales.

You will notice in figure 9.19 that the variable names across the top border indicate the type of data displayed. Time periods are displayed along the left border. If you want to analyze actual and projected sales data in a more typical spreadsheet format, however, figure 9.20 shows a worksheet designed with dates in the top border and variable names in the left. You can display data for any time period you need, simply by changing the dates in the top border. You can analyze totals by quarter and year as well as by month, as the worksheet in figure 9.20 shows. A simple quarterly summary of actual and projected blender sales is presented in the worksheet shown in figure 9.21.

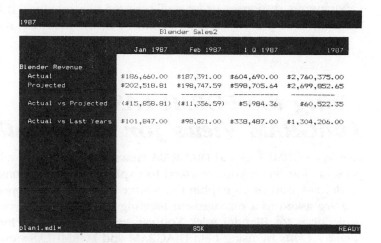

Fig. 9.20. WORKSHEET view displaying monthly, quarterly, and yearly values for forecasted and actual blender sales.

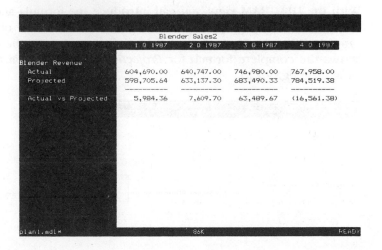

Fig. 9.21. WORKSHEET view displaying quarterly summary of actual and forecasted blender sales.

Using Javelin for Presentations

With the right equipment—a large-screen monitor or projection system—you can use Javelin in meetings and formal presentations to clarify points about your data or to support your conclusions. By controlling the display of data in different Javelin views, you can support your points by selecting the view or combination of views with the greatest impact on your audience. Javelin is particularly valuable when you are faced with impromptu "What if?" questions or "Please explain" requests. And if you want to automate your presentation, macros let you build "slide-show" presentations displaying graphs, worksheets, tables, and even diagrams of your model's variables. Whether you use Javelin for spontaneous responses or for well-scripted presentations, it is an excellent tool for electronic presentations as described in the following section.

Using the FORMULAS and DIAGRAM Views for Presentation

Javelin's FORMULAS and DIAGRAM views are particularly valuable in a presentation when you are asked to explain the assumptions on which your model is based or to explain the source of your data. Suppose, for example, that you are asked in a management meeting to explain how you developed the projections for Blender sales. You can easily describe the formula for *Projected Blender Units* by using both DIAGRAM and FORMULAS views.

With the DIAGRAM view, you can introduce the formula and quickly identify the variables making up the formula. The DIAGRAM view of the formula for *Projected Blender Units* displays those items making up the formula. It also shows the complete formula for *Projected Blender Units* at the bottom of the view (see fig. 9.22).

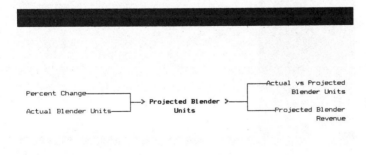

```
Percent Change                          ┌─Actual vs Projected
                                        │    Blender Units
              ──> Projected Blender >────┤
Actual Blender Units─┘         Units     └─Projected Blender
                                                    Revenue
```

```
Projected Blender Units = (Percent Change  * TREND(Actual Blender Units,Jan
     1987,Dec 1987)) + TREND(Actual Blender Units,Jan 1987,Dec 1987)
```

Fig. 9.22. DIAGRAM view of *Projected Blender Units*.

The /View /Formulas Roots command provides a more detailed view of the formula for *Projected Blender Units*. As figure 9.23 shows, *Projected Blender Units* is calculated by adding the following two amounts:

1. Forecasted difference in sales between one month and the next

2. Forecasted straight-line trend of sales

All variables making up *Projected Blender Units* are displayed in the FORMULAS
Roots view.

```
Formulas for all variables that affect Projected Blender Units:
Projected Blender Units = (Percent Change  * TREND(Actual Blender Units,Jan
  1987,Dec 1987)) + TREND(Actual Blender Units,Jan 1987,Dec 1987)
• Percent Change = Deviation from Trend/PREVIOUS(TREND(Actual Blender Units),12)
• • Deviation from Trend = PREVIOUS(Actual Blender Units,12) − PREVIOUS(TREND(
    Actual Blender Units,Jan 1986,Dec 1986),12)
• • • Actual Blender Units = ◄ Monthly data: January 1986 − December 1987 ►
• • Actual Blender Units = ◄ Monthly data: January 1986 − December 1987 ►
• Actual Blender Units = ◄ Monthly data: January 1986 − December 1987 ►
```

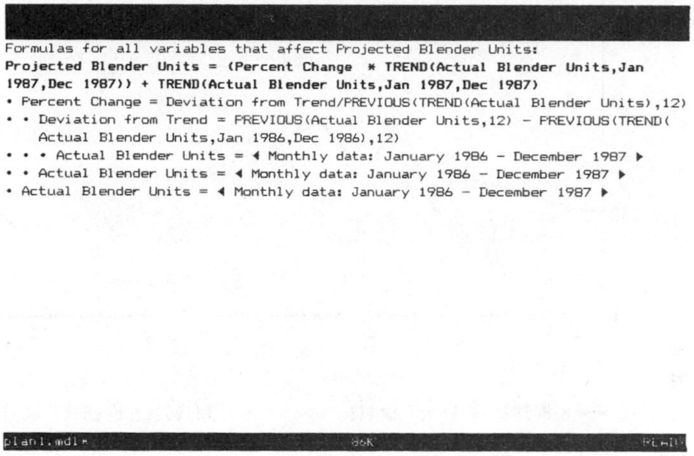

Fig. 9.23. FORMULAS Roots view
showing all variables making up
the formula for forecasting
blender units.

```
plan1.mdl *                              86K                          PLAIN
```

Using the GRAPH View for Presentations

Using the FORMULAS and DIAGRAM views helps you to reveal the underlying
logic and sources for data of your model. In some instances, however, depicting
data through one of the graphs in Javelin's GRAPH view can better support your
conclusions and possibly even the logic of your model. For example, although
the FORMULAS Roots view of the variable *Projected Blender Units* outlines how
the formula was created, a line graph can more clearly show the relationship
between actual units sold and forecasted sales. The line graph in figure 9.24, for
example, displays the curve for units sold in 1986 and the sales projected
for 1987.

In addition to using Javelin's GRAPH view to compare a sales forecast with
actual sales for a previous period, you can display a graph comparing the year's
forecast with actual sales as ongoing totals become available. The line graph in
figure 9.25, for example, depicts forecasted blender sales with actual blender
sales for January, 1987, to December, 1987. To create this graph, you would
enter the settings indicated in the Graph settings sheet shown in figure 9.26. If
you want a clearer picture of the specific monthly differences between *Actual
Blender Units* and *Projected Blender Units*, changing the line graph to a bar
graph provides a comparison of each month's actual versus projected sales (see
fig. 9.27).

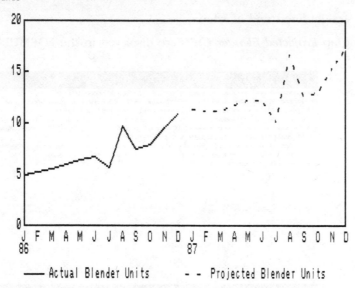

Fig. 9.24. Line graph displaying the curve for actual and projected blender sales.

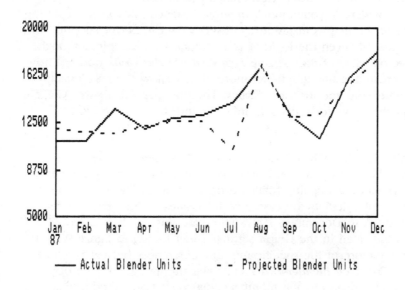

Fig. 9.25. Line graph depicting forecasted blender sales compared with actual blender sales.

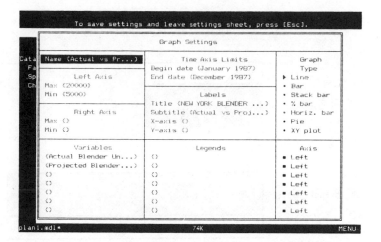

Fig. 9.26. Graph settings sheet for line graph comparing forecasted and actual blender sales.

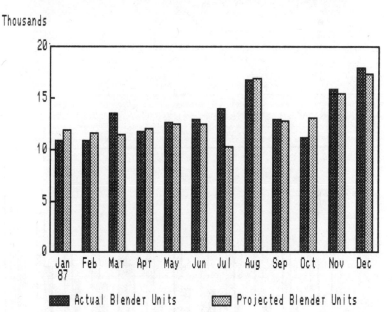

Fig. 9.27. Bar graph comparing actual blender sales with projected blender sales.

If you need to compare sales for the current month to sales for the same month in the prior year, the horizontal bar graph in figure 9.28 gives a single-month comparison of January, 1987 sales. A comparison of monthly blender revenue for the current year with every month of the previous year's revenue is shown in figure 9.29.

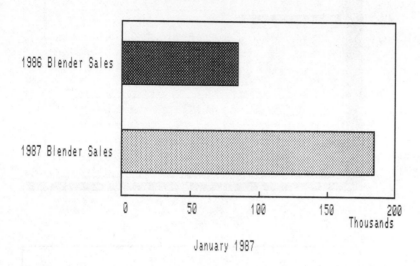

Fig. 9.28. Horizontal bar graph comparing January, 1987, blender sales with January, 1986, blender sales.

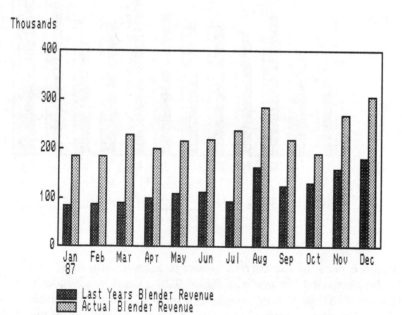

Fig. 9.29. Bar graph comparing current year's blender sales with prior year's blender sales.

Using the QUICK GRAPH View To Answer "What If?"

For planned presentations, Javelin's GRAPH view gives you many options for displaying your data. Javelin's CHART and QUICK GRAPH views are ideal if you are asked to change data quickly and show the change in a graph.

Suppose, for example, that in addition to forecasting blender sales, you have also forecasted material and production cost per unit for blenders manufactured in your New York plant. As shown in figures 9.30 and 9.31, the blender forecast model contains a variable for entering the actual cost each month and a variable for projecting costs for 12 months. As the TABLE view of actual blender cost indicates (see fig. 9.30), costs have steadily increased over the past 36 months from January, 1984, to December, 1986. The TABLE view of projected costs reflects this steady increase (see fig. 3.31).

Javelin's QUICK GRAPH view represents the steady increase in both actual and projected costs (see figs. 9.32 and 9.33). You can use this view effectively in a meeting to show the trend in cost increase. QUICK GRAPH is perfect for answering questions such as "What would be the effect on our forecast of costs for 1987 if we purchase new equipment and reduce costs in the second half of 1986?" You can respond quickly by changing the QUICK GRAPH view of actual blender costs to reflect the decrease, pressing the CALC key (F9), and then displaying the TABLE view of the newly calculated forecasted costs (see figs. 9.34 and 9.35).

15.21		
Blender Unit Cost = ◀ Monthly data: January 1984 – December 1986 ▶		
Jan 1984 .... 15.21	Sep 1985 .... 15.29	May 1987 ......
Feb 1984 .... 15.23	Oct 1985 .... 15.29	Jun 1987 ......
Mar 1984 .... 15.23	Nov 1985 .... 15.32	Jul 1987 ......
Apr 1984 .... 15.25	Dec 1985 .... 15.33	Aug 1987 ......
May 1984 .... 15.25	Jan 1986 .... 15.37	Sep 1987 ......
Jun 1984 .... 15.24	Feb 1986 .... 15.37	Oct 1987 ......
Jul 1984 .... 15.24	Mar 1986 .... 15.39	Nov 1987 ......
Aug 1984 .... 15.24	Apr 1986 .... 15.41	Dec 1987 ......
Sep 1984 .... 15.25	May 1986 .... 15.45	Jan 1988 ......
Oct 1984 .... 15.25	Jun 1986 .... 15.43	Feb 1988 ......
Nov 1984 .... 15.25	Jul 1986 .... 15.41	Mar 1988 ......
Dec 1984 .... 15.27	Aug 1986 .... 15.38	Apr 1988 ......
Jan 1985 .... 15.27	Sep 1986 .... 15.37	May 1988 ......
Feb 1985 .... 15.28	Oct 1986 .... 15.36	Jun 1988 ......
Mar 1985 .... 15.28	Nov 1986 .... 15.36	Jul 1988 ......
Apr 1985 .... 15.30	Dec 1986 .... 15.35	Aug 1988 ......
May 1985 .... 15.30	Jan 1987	Sep 1988 ......
Jun 1985 .... 15.30	Feb 1987	Oct 1988 ......
Jul 1985 .... 15.30	Mar 1987	Nov 1988 ......
Aug 1985 .... 15.29	Apr 1987	Dec 1988 ......
cost.mdl	94K	READY

Fig. 9.30. TABLE view of actual blender costs for January, 1984, through December, 1986.

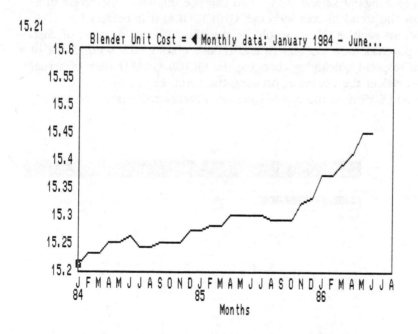

```
15.44027050984

Projected Blender Unit Cost = (Percent Change * TREND(Blender Unit Cost,Jan...

Jan 1987 ........ 15.44    Sep 1988 ......    May 1990 ......
Feb 1987 ........ 15.44    Oct 1988 ......    Jun 1990 ......
Mar 1987 ........ 15.46    Nov 1988 ......    Jul 1990 ......
Apr 1987 ........ 15.48    Dec 1988 ......    Aug 1990 ......
May 1987 ........ 15.52    Jan 1989 ......    Sep 1990 ......
Jun 1987 ........ 15.52    Feb 1989 ......    Oct 1990 ......
Jul 1987 ........ 15.45    Mar 1989 ......    Nov 1990 ......
Aug 1987 ........ 15.44    Apr 1989 ......    Dec 1990 ......
Sep 1987 ........ 15.44    May 1989 ......    Jan 1991 ......
Oct 1987 ........ 15.44    Jun 1989 ......    Feb 1991 ......
Nov 1987 ........ 15.47    Jul 1989 ......    Mar 1991 ......
Dec 1987 ........ 15.48    Aug 1989 ......    Apr 1991 ......
Jan 1988 ......            Sep 1989 ......    May 1991 ......
Feb 1988 ......            Oct 1989 ......    Jun 1991 ......
Mar 1988 ......            Nov 1989 ......    Jul 1991 ......
Apr 1988 ......            Dec 1989 ......    Aug 1991 ......
May 1988 ......            Jan 1990 ......    Sep 1991 ......
Jun 1988 ......            Feb 1990 ......    Oct 1991 ......
Jul 1988 ......            Mar 1990 ......    Nov 1991 ......
Aug 1988 ......            Apr 1990 ......    Dec 1991 ......
cost.mdl*                            94K                          READY
```

Fig. 9.31. TABLE view of projected blender costs for January, 1987, through December, 1987.

Blender Unit Cost = ◀ Monthly data: January 1984 – June...

15.21

Months

Fig. 9.32. QUICK GRAPH view of actual blender costs for January, 1984, through June, 1986.

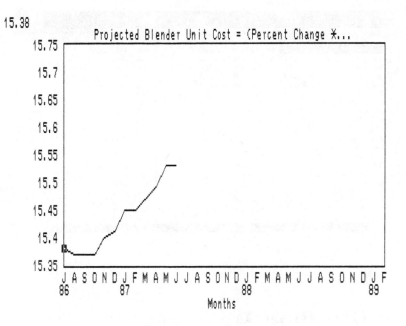

15.38

Fig. 9.33. QUICK GRAPH view of forecasted blender costs for July, 1986, through June, 1987.

Fig. 9.34. QUICK GRAPH view of estimated decrease in costs for January, 1987, through December, 1987.

```
15.4361642975
Projected Blender Unit Cost = (Percent Change * TREND(Blender Unit Cost,Jan...

Jan 1987 ........ 15.44    Sep 1988 ......    May 1990 ......
Feb 1987 ........ 15.44    Oct 1988 ......    Jun 1990 ......
Mar 1987 ........ 15.46    Nov 1988 ......    Jul 1990 ......
Apr 1987 ........ 15.48    Dec 1988 ......    Aug 1990 ......
May 1987 ........ 15.52    Jan 1989 ......    Sep 1990 ......
Jun 1987 ........ 15.50    Feb 1989 ......    Oct 1990 ......
Jul 1987 ........ 15.48    Mar 1989 ......    Nov 1990 ......
Aug 1987 ........ 15.45    Apr 1989 ......    Dec 1990 ......
Sep 1987 ........ 15.44    May 1989 ......    Jan 1991 ......
Oct 1987 ........ 15.43    Jun 1989 ......    Feb 1991 ......
Nov 1987 ........ 15.43    Jul 1989 ......    Mar 1991 ......
Dec 1987 ........ 15.42    Aug 1989 ......    Apr 1991 ......
Jan 1988 ......            Sep 1989 ......    May 1991 ......
Feb 1988 ......            Oct 1989 ......    Jun 1991 ......
Mar 1988 ......            Nov 1989 ......    Jul 1991 ......
Apr 1988 ......            Dec 1989 ......    Aug 1991 ......
May 1988 ......            Jan 1990 ......    Sep 1991 ......
Jun 1988 ......            Feb 1990 ......    Oct 1991 ......
Jul 1988 ......            Mar 1990 ......    Nov 1991 ......
Aug 1988 ......            Apr 1990 ......    Dec 1991 ......
cost.mdl*                        83K                        READY
```

Fig. 9.35. TABLE view of forecasted blender costs for January, 1987, through December, 1987, reflecting estimated decrease in July-December, 1986.

Conclusion

Javelin's capabilities for helping you analyze and present data go far beyond conventional spreadsheet programs. Javelin views allow numerous perspectives of the data in your model, helping you draw conclusions and make decisions. But Javelin is also a very powerful tool for sharing your data and conclusions in formal or informal presentations. For formal presentations, Javelin enables you to link tables, graphs, and worksheets to support and clarify points in your presentation. For informal presentations, Javelin helps you answer "What if" questions.

10

Creating Graphs

Graphs are the most dramatic way to present information to your audience. The QUICK GRAPH and CHART views let you see and manipulate the data for a single variable. If you want a printed graph or a graph showing more than one variable, use the GRAPH view to create graphs in seven possible formats:—line, bar, stacked bar, percent bar, horizontal bar, pie, XY-scatter plot. With Javelin's GRAPH view, you can display high quality graphs to present to others in printed form, in slides, on a large-screen monitor, or on a projection system.

Javelin's powerful GRAPH view is discussed in detail in this chapter. The other two graphics views, QUICK GRAPH and CHART, are not discussed except to illustrate the differences between them and the GRAPH view. (See Chapter 5 for the QUICK GRAPH and CHART views.) The information in this chapter shows you how to use the Graph settings sheets to create presentation-quality graphs.

Commands Emphasized in this Chapter

/View Graph
/Define Graph
/Print Graph

CHART and QUICK GRAPH Views versus GRAPH View

Three of the ten Javelin views display data in graphic form: CHART, QUICK GRAPH, and GRAPH.

297

Each type of graph view has its own special capabilities for model building, analysis, and presentation. With the CHART and QUICK GRAPH views, creating graphs is easy. You can use either to look at a single variable in an interactive graph. Both views allow you to enter and change data in Javelin's Information Base by changing the graph. You can view the CHART view along with another view on a two-window screen. When analyzing your model, for example, you can view data in the CHART view and in the WORKSHEET or TABLE view at the same time.

Neither the CHART nor the QUICK GRAPH view, however, provides options for adding legends or labels or for graphing more than one variable at a time. If you want to produce presentation-quality graphs or compare data for more than one variable, use Javelin's GRAPH view. With the CHART and QUICK GRAPH views, you can produce a bar and line graph of a single variable; with the GRAPH view, you can produce seven types of graphs displaying data for up to seven different variables.

Creating a New Graph with Javelin

To begin creating a Javelin graph, you use the /Define Graph command and specify a graph name. The name appears in the *Name* box. (If you don't specify a name, Javelin gives the graph the name *GRAPH*. Anytime you want, you can rename a graph by changing the name in the *Name* box.) After pressing Enter, you see the Graph settings sheet (see fig. 10.1). The two default settings in Javelin's GRAPH view are (1) a default name *GRAPH* assigned to the Graph settings sheet and (2) *Bar* graph selected as the type of graph. Each Graph settings sheet can be assigned a name that will appear in the *Name* box at the top left of the Graph settings sheet. This sheet contains nine categories of settings, each category located in a separate box. You can change the name of a graph by entering a new name when the cursor is in the *Name* box.

To change a setting within any box, you move the cursor to the appropriate setting. The nine boxes of settings marked in figure 10.2 are

1. Graph settings sheet name

2. Values for the left axis scale

3. Values for the right axis scale

4. Variable names for data to be graphed

5. Beginning and end date for x axis

6. Labels

7. Legends for variable data

8. Graph type

9. Setting for displaying left or right axis alone or displaying both left and right axes

Exit the Graph settings sheet by pressing the Esc key.

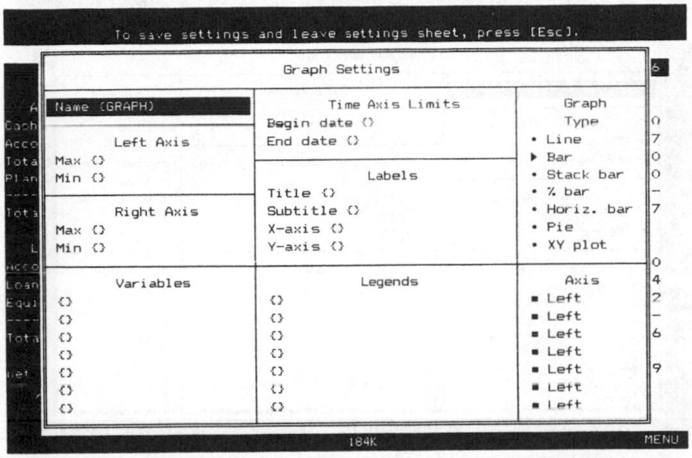

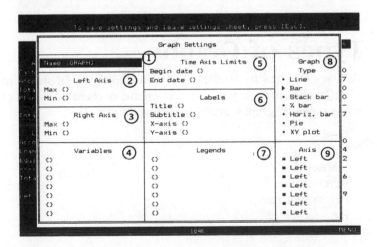

Fig. 10.1. The Graph settings sheet for a bar graph.

Fig. 10.2. The nine categories of settings for a bar graph.

If you want to create a line, stacked-bar, or percent bar graph, the settings sheet for each is identical to the settings sheet for a bar graph. If, however, you choose to create a horizontal bar graph, a pie graph, or an XY plot, when you make your selection from the settings in the *Graph Type* box (box #8 in fig. 10.2), some of the boxes on the settings sheet change. For example, if you change the *Graph Type* setting from *Bar* to *Pie*, the settings sheet in figure 10.3 is displayed. Notice that four boxes are different from those on the bar graph settings sheet displayed in figure 10.2. Special settings for pie graphs include settings for the date shown, number display, date display, and location of wedges, which replace the axis settings used for line, bar, stacked-bar, and percent bar graphs.

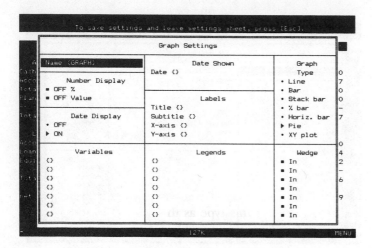

Fig. 10.3. Graph settings sheet for a pie graph.

Types of Graphs

The types of graphs available in Javelin compare favorably with those of 1-2-3. With Javelin, in fact, you can also create percent or horizontal bar graphs. The seven types of graphs available in Javelin are

> Line
> Bar
> Stacked bar
> Percent bar
> Horizontal bar
> Pie
> XY plot

The settings sheets for the types of graphs are similar, so you'll find it easy to learn how to create different kinds of graphs. Because the settings sheet is identical for line, bar, stacked-bar, and percent bar graphs, the following sections discuss all four together. Horizontal bar graphs, pie graphs, and XY plots are covered separately in the second half of this chapter.

Creating a Simple Line, Bar, Stacked-Bar, or Percent Bar Graph

Javelin's Graph settings sheet makes it convenient to create graphs quickly and add labels and legends and change scaling at any point. You can, for example, create a simple line, bar, stacked-bar, or percent bar graph by entering just a few settings. Suppose that you want to create one of these graphs to display all blender and compactor sales data available in your model. To create the four types of graphs in figures 10.4, 10.5, 10.6, and 10.7, you would complete the following steps:

1. Go to the Graph settings sheet by selecting /Define Graph.

2. When the prompt Graph name: appears, provide a unique name for the settings sheet (if you want to save the settings for multiple graphs in one model) or use Javelin's default name, *GRAPH*, by pressing Enter.

3. When the settings sheet is displayed as in figure 10.2, move the cursor to the Graph Type box (box #8 in fig. 10.2) and select the type of graph you want to create. Press Enter. If you want to create a bar graph, Javelin has already chosen this type as the default, indicated by the triangle. If you want another type of graph, use the Down-arrow (↓) or Up-arrow (↑) key to move the cursor to your selection and press Enter.

4. Indicate which variables are to be shown in the graph by moving the cursor to the braces in the Variables box (box #4 in fig. 10.2) and entering the names of the variables (type the names or use the SPELL key). You can show up to seven variables in each graph (see fig. 10.8). These variables may be any variables in the current model whether they are constant through time, functions of other variables, or data values.

   Javelin only allows you to enter the names of variables already defined in the model; you cannot enter the name of a variable on the settings sheet and then define that variable after you have left the settings sheet. Remember that the SPELL key (Tab) can recall the names of all the variables in your model if you are not sure what you called them.

5. Press the Esc key to save settings on the Graph settings sheet or just press the GRAPH key (F10) to see the graph. To return to the settings sheet, press the GRAPH key (F10) again.

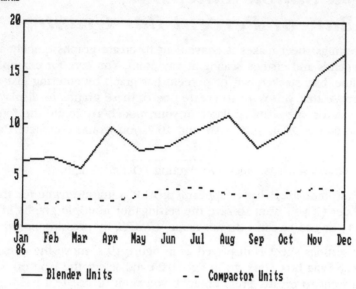

Fig. 10.4. Simple line graph displaying blender and compactor sales.

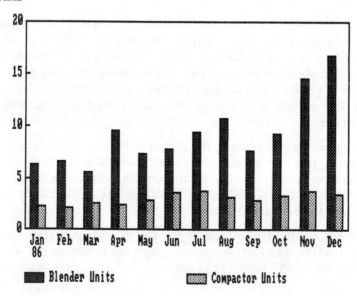

Fig. 10.5. Simple bar graph displaying blender and compactor sales.

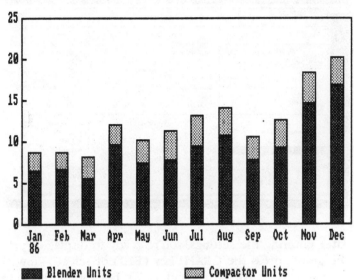

Fig. 10.6. Simple stacked-bar
graph displaying blender and
compactor sales.

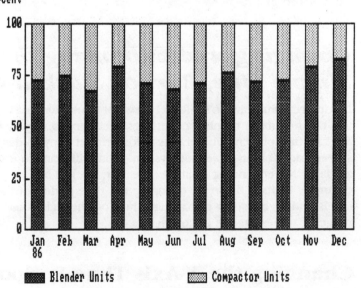

Fig. 10.7. Simple percent bar
graph displaying blender and
compactor sales.

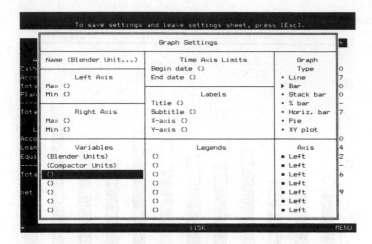

Fig. 10.8. Graph settings sheet with variable names entered.

After entering the settings, you're ready to display or print the graph. To display the graph, press the GRAPH key (F10) or select /View Graph and press Enter (see figs. 10.4, 10.5. 10.6, and 10.7). Both show the last graph defined or viewed. Notice that these graphs were created by entering just two variable names and by indicating the type of graph. Javelin supplies the left axis values and the legends for data automatically. You can change both of the these, but if you want to create a graph quickly, you only need to enter the names of the variables to graph.

Changing and Enhancing the Simple Line, Bar, or Stacked-Bar Graph

If you are using Javelin's GRAPH view for your own analysis, you may want to use the minimum number of settings necessary to display the graph. But if you are creating presentation graphs— for printed copy, slides, or display on a large-screen monitor or projection system—you will want to enhance them. Settings available for enhancing a simple line, bar, stacked-bar, or percent bar graph, for example, include those for changing the time period of the x-axis; for adding labels and legends; for displaying values on the right axis; and for changing the range of values on the left or right axis.

Changing the X-Axis Time Period

If you want your graph to display a different period or a shorter time range for your data, you can change the time-period settings in the *Time Axis Limits* box

(box #5 in figure 10.2). The bar graph in figure 10.9, for example, displays only 3 months of data rather than the 12 months of data available for the variables. This graph was created by entering January, 1986, for the beginning period and March, 1986, for the ending period. To enter these periods, move the cursor to **Begin date** and enter *January 1986*, move the cursor to **End date** and enter *March 1986*, and press Esc to save the new *Time Axis Limits* settings. To view the new graph, select **/View Graph** and press Enter.

Fig. 10.9 Bar graph displaying only part of the data stored for variables.

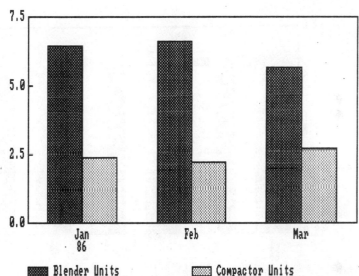

Fig. 10.10. The Graph settings sheet highlighting the *Time Axis Limits* box.

If you want to graph data in any of the regular or custom periods available in your model other than the default period, indicate the beginning and end period in the *Time Axis Limits* box, and Javelin automatically converts the values to that period. If, for example, you want to graph *Blender Units* and *Compactor Units* for the first six weeks of 1986, you would enter *1 w 1986* for the *Begin Date* setting and enter *6 w 1986* for the *End Date* setting. After saving these settings and selecting /View Graph, you can display the graph in figure 10.11.

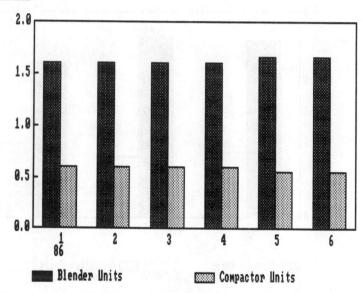

Fig. 10.11 Bar graph depicting blender and compactor sales for the first six weeks of 1986.

Adding Labels and Legends to a Line, Bar, Stacked-Bar, or Percent Bar Graph

In Javelin you can add four types of labels to any graph: title, subtitle, x-axis label, and y-axis label. The graphs in figures 10.12, 10.13, 10.14, and 10.15 contain labels added in the *Labels* box (box #6 in figure 10.2). To add labels to a graph, move the cursor to the appropriate setting in the Labels box and type the label. Although it's possible to include up to 119 total characters and spaces in a label, only the first 51 will appear when you display the graph on the screen.

Unless you supply legends, Javelin shows the variable names as the legends. *Blender Units* and *Compactor Units*, for example, are the legends supplied in

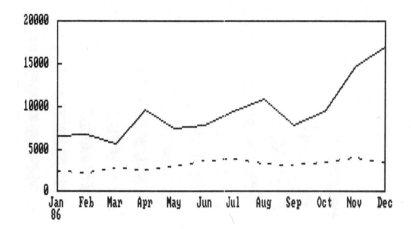

Fig. 10.12. Line graph with labels.

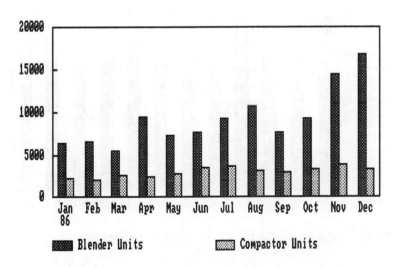

Fig. 10.13. Bar graph with labels.

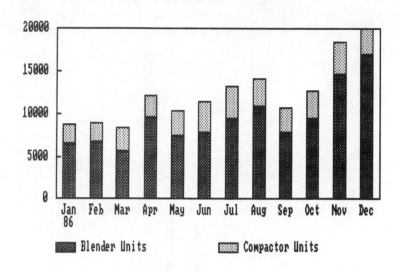

Fig. 10.14. Stacked-bar graph with labels.

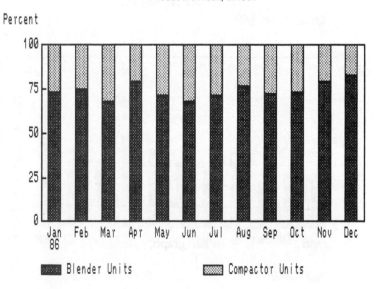

Fig. 10.15. Percent bar graph with labels.

the graphs in figures 10.4, 10.5, 10.6, and 10.7. If you want to change legends, move the cursor to the Legends box in the Graph settings sheet (see box #7 in fig. 10.2) and enter new legends. Legends are entered exactly like labels, and may also contain up to 119 total characters and spaces, although only 51 will appear when the graphs are displayed on the screen. The bar graph in figure 10.16 uses the legends *New York Blender Sales* and *New York Compactor Sales* in place of the original variable names.

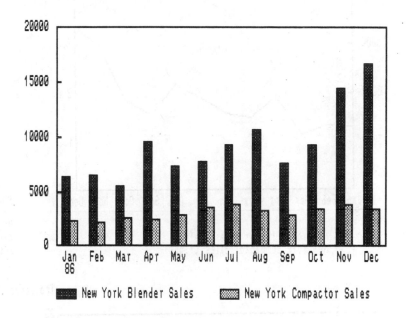

Fig. 10.16. Bar graph with special legends.

Settings for Displaying and Changing Y-Axis Values: Line, Bar, and Stacked-Bar Graphs

Three types of settings are available on the Graph settings sheet (see fig. 10.2) for displaying and changing y-axis values: the *Axis* settings (see box #9), the *Left Axis* setting (see box #2), and the *Right Axis* setting (see box #3).

When you create a line graph or any type of bar graph, Javelin displays data values along the left axis automatically. You can, however, display y-axis values along the right side as well, or along the right side alone, by using the *Axis* setting. To indicate that you want y-axis values displayed on the right for one or all variables, move the cursor to Left in the Axis box and press Enter. If you

change the default setting from Left to Right for one variable, Javelin displays
the y-axis values on the right side of the graph for that variable (see fig. 10.17).
If you change the *Axis* settings from *Left* to *Right* for all variables, Javelin
displays values on the right side only of your graph (see figure 10.18).

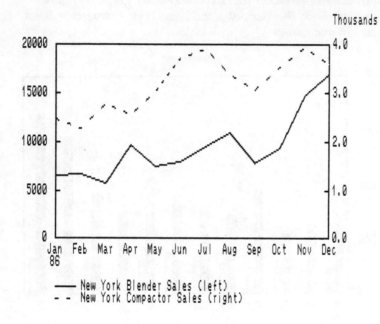

Fig. 10.17. Displaying values for
New York Blender Sales on the
left and values for *New York
Compactor Sales* on the right
sides of a line graph.

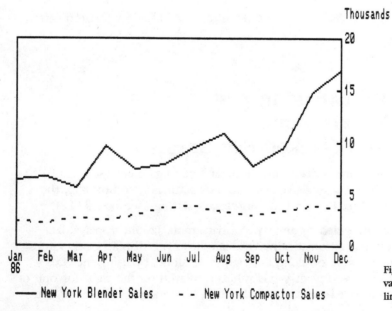

Fig. 10.18. Displaying y-axis
values on only the right side of a
line graph.

Switching an axis from the left side of the graph to right side gives you an opportunity to change the scaling for one of the variables. You can look at variables that are functions of each other or that show similar functions. Figure 10.19 shows the variables *Compactor Revenue* and *Blender Revenue* scaled on the same axis. In figure 10.20, when *Compactor Revenue* is scaled on or graphed on the left axis and *Blender Revenue* is graphed on the right axis, you can see that the two variables show similar trends. Moving the second variable to another axis helps you determine the validity of the data or formulas on which you have based your assumptions. Moving the second variable to another axis is also useful if one of your variables is a percentage, such as market share.

You can change the limits displayed for either the left or the right axis by entering your own settings in the *Left Axis* or *Right Axis* boxes (see boxes #2 and #3 in fig. 10.2). If you do not enter settings, Javelin automatically sets the y-axis lower limit value at 0 and determines the upper limit according to the highest value of the data you are graphing.

To change maximum and minimum limits for both right and left axes, move the cursor to Max or Min in the Left Axis or Right Axis box, type the desired value, then press Enter. Keep in mind the following when you are entering maximum and minimum values:

1. Javelin does not indicate if a variable is beyond the range of your settings. You must be careful to make sure that the values of the variables are within the limits you set.

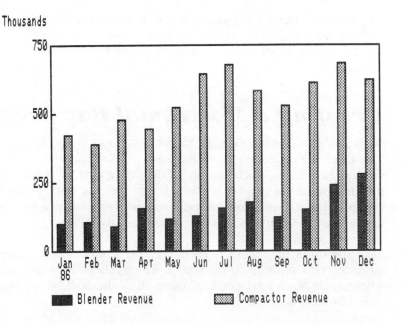

Fig. 10.19. *Compactor Revenue* and *Blender Revenue* scaled on the same axis.

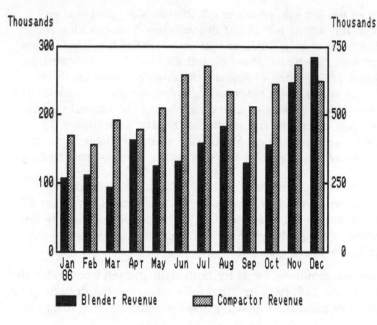

Fig. 10.20. *Compactor Revenue* scaled on the left axis, and *Blender Revenue* scaled on the right axis.

2. If you do not enter a minimum value, Javelin sets it at 0; if you do not enter a maximum value, Javelin determines the maximum based on the highest value for the data you are graphing.

Javelin automatically supplied the y-axis scale in figure 10.21, for example, when no settings were entered for either minimum or maximum settings. In figure 10.22, on the other hand, settings were entered for *Max* (7000) and *Min* (1500).

Creating a Horizontal Bar Graph

With Javelin's /Define Graph command, you can create four types of bar graphs. The three we've already discussed—bar, stacked-bar, and percent bar—are all vertical bar graphs, each capable of displaying data for a range of times. The fourth type of bar graph—horizontal bar—lets you display data for up to seven variables for a single time period. The horizontal bar graph in figure 10.23 displays sales revenue for the month of January, 1986.

Like the other graphs we've seen, creating a horizontal bar graph is as simple as entering two settings on the Graph settings sheet. However, you can polish and change any horizontal graph by using all of the available settings discussed in the following sections.

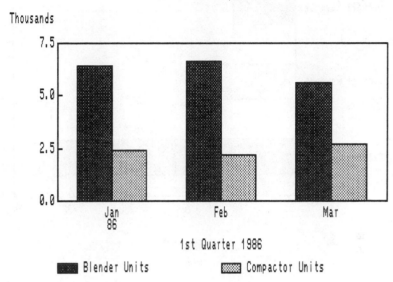

Fig. 10.21. Bar graph displaying
y-axis values entered
automatically by Javelin.

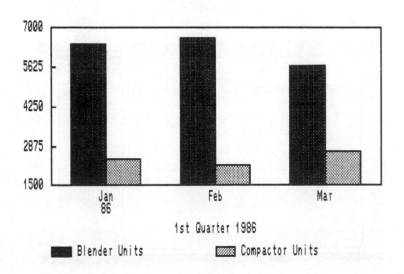

Fig. 10.22. Bar graph displaying
y-axis values set by the user.

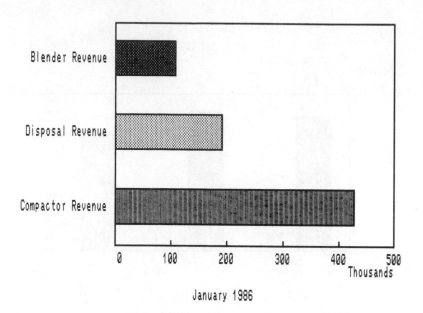

Fig. 10.23. Horizontal bar graph showing blender, compactor, and disposal revenue for January, 1986.

Settings for Horizontal Bar Graphs

When you select the *Horiz. bar* option on the Graph settings sheet, a settings sheet for horizontal bar graphs appears (see fig. 10.24). Three settings are special to the horizontal bar graph: *Horizontal Axis* (box #2), *Date Display* (box #3), and *Date Shown* (box #5).

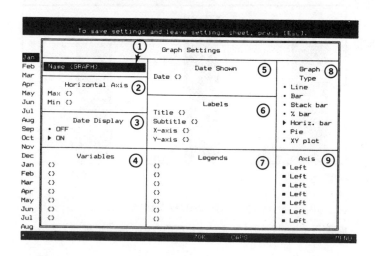

Fig. 10.24. Settings sheet for horizontal bar graphs.

Entering a Date for Horizontal Bar Graph Data

The most significant difference between the horizontal bar graph and other bar graphs is that data is displayed for only a single date. Instead of choosing beginning and ending dates for your data, you select a single period or let Javelin supply a single default period.

If you do not supply a date in the *Date Shown* box, Javelin uses the first date for which any of the variables you're graphing have data. The graph in figure 10.23 displays data for January 1986—the default beginning date for our model.

Note: If your model uses a custom time period, you must type the full, correct name. The SPELL key (Tab) does not do this for you. Javelin notifies you when you have entered an invalid time period by sounding a beep.

Suppose, for example, that you want to compare blender, disposal, and compactor revenues for the 3rd quarter of 1986. If data is available for that quarter for the variables, you can create a simple horizontal graph by entering the following three settings in the Graph settings sheet in figure 10.25:

1. Set the *Graph Type* to *Horiz. bar*.

2. Enter the variable names *Blender Revenue*, *Disposal Revenue*, and *Compactor Revenue* in the *Variables* box.

3. Enter the date *3 Quarter 1986* in the *Date Shown* box.

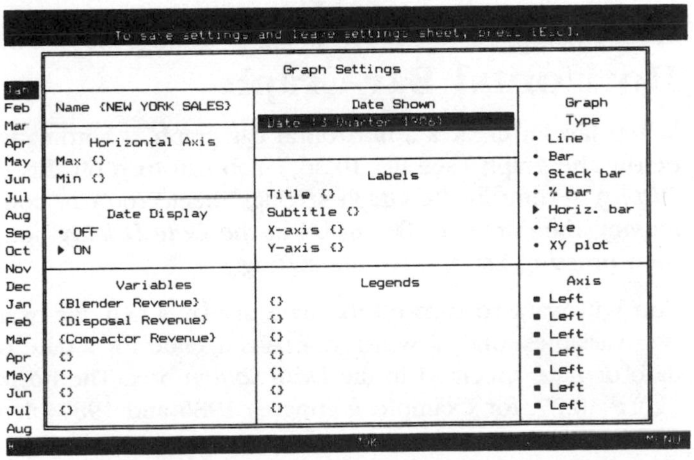

Fig. 10.25. Graph settings sheet for a horizontal bar graph.

To enter or change the date in the *Date Shown* box, move the cursor to the Date setting and type the date. You can use any of the accepted abbreviated date forms (see Chapter 4 for a complete list). Press Esc after entering the date. You can at this point view your graph using the /View Graph command or print it using the /Print Graph command (see "Printing a Graph with the /Print Graph Command"). Figure 10.26 shows the printed graph.

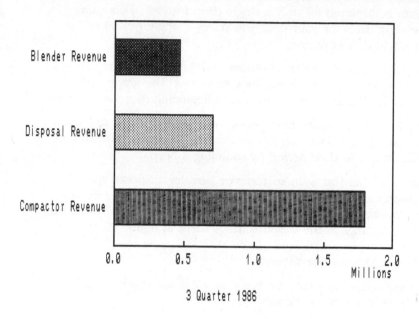

Fig. 10.26. A horizontal bar graph created by entering a specific date setting.

Turning Off the Date Display for a Horizontal Bar Graph

When Javelin creates a horizontal bar graph, it automatically shows the date below the graph (see fig. 10.26.) You can turn off this display with the *Date Display* setting in the Graph settings sheet. You can control the date display by moving the cursor to OFF or ON in the *Date Display* box, pressing Enter, and then pressing Esc to save the setting.

You will want to turn off the date display when, for example, you graph data for two variables, one of which contains a value for a date other than the default date or date specified in the *Date Shown* box. The horizontal bar graph in figure 10.27, for example, compares 1986 and 1987 blender sales.

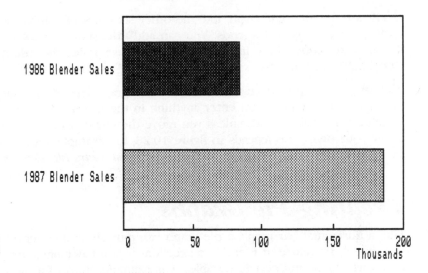

Fig. 10.27. Horizontal bar graph with the date display turned off.

Changing Data Values on a Horizontal Bar Graph

Because a horizontal bar graph is a graph in one plane, you need to define only one axis. You can use the *Horizontal Axis* box on the Graph settings sheet for horizontal graphs (see fig. 10.28) to set the maximum and minimum limits for the graph. You enter the limits by typing them and pressing Enter. By setting standard values for the horizontal axis, you can show changes over time.

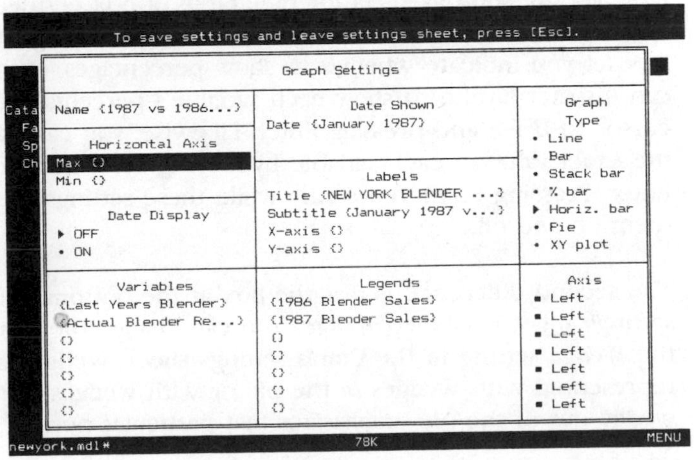

Fig. 10.28. Cursor marks the *Horizontal Axis* box on the settings sheet for horizontal bar graphs.

Adding Labels and Changing Legends on a Horizontal Bar Graph

Javelin's horizontal bar graph, like the other six types of graphs, can be created with special labels and legends. You can add title, subtitle, x-axis, or y-axis labels in the *Labels* box. In figure 10.28, we have added the title *NEW YORK BLENDER SALES* and the subtitle *January 1987 vs January 1986*.

As with other types of graphs, horizontal bar graph legends are supplied automatically if you do not enter anything in the *Legends* box. Javelin uses variable names as legends unless you move the cursor to the Legends box and enter your own. The legends in figure 10.28, for example, replace the original variable names *Actual Blender Revenue* and *Last Years Blender Revenue*.

Creating Pie Graphs

Like a horizontal bar graph, a pie graph can only show one period of time in the model; therefore, it is another excellent tool for demonstrating the relationships among certain variables. For example, think of a pie graph of *Blender Revenue*, *Disposal Revenue*, and *Compactor Revenue*. This pie graph is an excellent way of checking total revenue as new data is entered into your model.

Settings for Pie Graphs

The settings sheet for a pie graph (see fig. 10.29) is similar to that for a horizontal bar graph. Two differences between the settings sheets are apparent. First, on the settings sheet for pie graphs, a box entitled *Number Display* appears under the *Name* box. The two toggle settings in the *Number Display* box let you indicate whether to show percentages, exact values, or both. You can instruct Javelin to show each variable's percentage of the pie by moving the cursor to OFF % and pressing Enter. Likewise, you can have the pie graph reflect the exact value of each variable by moving the cursor to OFF Value and pressing Enter. Pressing Enter repeatedly while these settings are highlighted toggles them on and off.

The second difference is that the box at the bottom right on the pie graph settings sheet is labeled *Wedge*. You can change the position of a wedge using the *Wedge* setting in the Graph settings sheet. Wedges of a pie graph can be represented with wedges *in* the pie or with wedges *out* of the pie. Moving a wedge out of the pie emphasizes that particular portion of the graph.

```
           To save settings and leave settings sheet, press [Esc].

                              Graph Settings
Dec                                                                        000
Jan   Name {GRAPH}                    Date Shown              Graph         000
Feb                             Date ()                        Type        000
Mar        Number Display                                   • Line         000
Apr   ▪ OFF %                                               • Bar          000
May   ▪ OFF Value                        Labels             • Stack bar    000
Jun                             Title ()                    • % bar        000
Jul        Date Display         Subtitle ()                 • Horiz. bar
Aug   • OFF                      X-axis ()                   ▸ Pie
      ▸ ON                       Y-axis ()                  • XY plot

           Variables               Legends                  Wedge
Jan   ()                        ()                          ▪ In
Feb   ()                        ()                          ▪ In
Mar   ()                        ()                          ▪ In
Apr   ()                        ()                          ▪ In
May   ()                        ()                          ▪ In
Jun   ()                        ()                          ▪ In
Jul   ()                        ()                          ▪ In
Aug
                                         CAPS                        MENU
```

Fig. 10.29. The settings sheet for
pie graphs.

Figures 10.30 and 10.31 display two pie graphs, one with all in, the other with
the wedge for *Blender Revenue* exploded from the pie. These pie graphs show
the same three variables as the horizontal bar graph in figure 10.23. Notice that
the graph in figure 10.31 displays both percents and values for each wedge.
Percents and values appear when both the *%* and *Value* settings are toggled on
in the *Number Display* box of the Graph settings sheet.

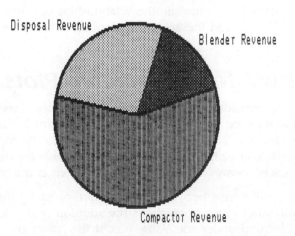

Fig. 10.30. Pie graph with all
wedges in the pie.

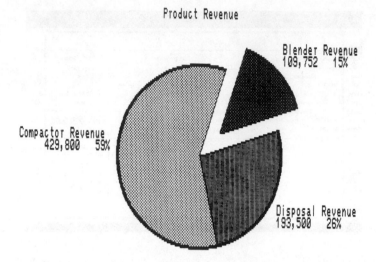

Fig. 10.31. Pie graph with one wedge exploded.

XY Scatter Plots

The final type of graph available in Javelin is the XY scatter plot. In an XY scatter plot, data from two or more variables can share the same x value. XY scatter plots help to illustrate the relationships between different attributes of data, such as age and income or educational achievements and salary.

Settings for XY Scatter Plots

The XY scatter plot is the last option in the *Graph Type* box on the Graph settings sheet (see fig. 10.32). The XY scatter plot is the only Javelin graph that lets you plot one variable against another without having to consider a time-period axis. You can, if you want, set *Time Limits* for the X and Y pairs on the settings sheet. However, this "hidden" time axis is not shown in the graph.

The major difference between the XY scatter-plot settings sheet and the settings sheets for other types of graphs is the addition of the *X Axis* and *Y Axis* settings, located under the *Name* box at the left of the screen. You can set maximum and minimum limits for each axis by typing a value and pressing Enter.

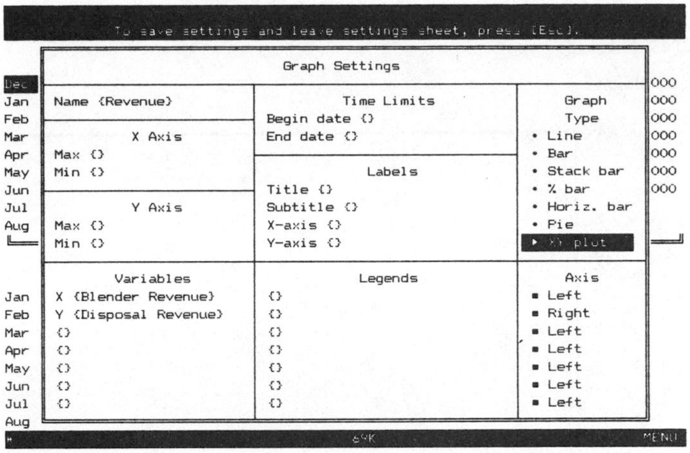

Fig. 10.32. Settings sheet for XY scatter-plot graph.

To create an XY scatter plot, begin by moving the cursor to the XY plot setting in the *Graph Type* box of the settings sheet. Next, move the cursor to the Variables box and enter the names of the two variables you want to plot. The XY scatter plot in figure 10.33, for example, plots *Blender Revenue* against *Disposal Revenue*. Notice on the settings sheet that the first two slots for entering variable names are preceded by an X and Y, indicating variables to plot. Javelin ignores variable names in any other slot. In addition to entering settings for *Graph Type* and *Variables*, you can include labels. Figure 10.33, for example, includes the title *New York Sales*, the y-axis label *Disposal Sales* and the x-axis label *Blender Sales*.

Printing a Graph with the /Print Graph Command

An individual or a small group can easily study relationships on a detailed graph on an ordinary monitor. Unless you have a large-screen monitor, however, a larger group of people will need printed graphs.

You can print any graph in the current model by selecting the /Print Graph command (see fig. 10.34) and entering the graph name. You can use the SPELL key (Tab) to list the names of graphs defined in the model.

A graph does not have to be on screen to be printed by Javelin, nor do you have to exit to another program as you do with 1-2-3 and Symphony to produce the graph. The /Print Graph command causes the graph you select to be sent to the printer "sideways" (horizontally). Printing does not have to interrupt your work session, unless you do not have a print buffer or a graphics printer.

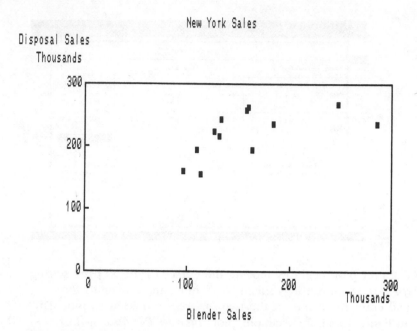

Fig. 10.33. XY scatter plot displaying blender and disposal sales.

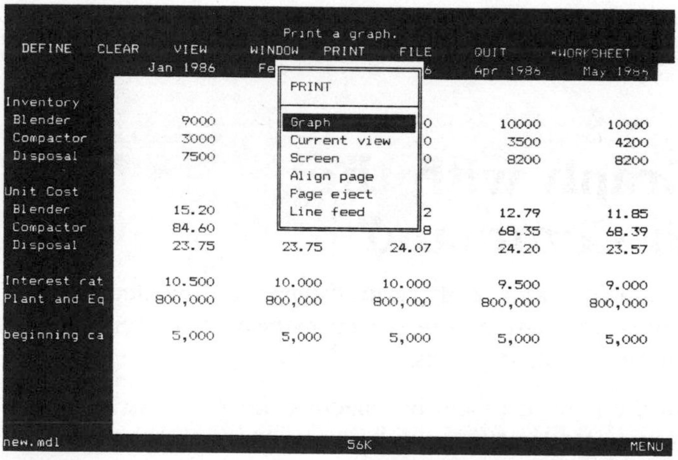

Fig. 10.34. The /Print Graph command.

Javelin will not print your graph if there isn't enough free random-access memory remaining in your system. Recall that the amount of available memory in the system is displayed in the center of the status line on the Javelin screen. This value decreases as your model grows. Usually this process is slow because Javelin places data in memory very efficiently.

However, when you elect to print a graph, Javelin first has to load in the driver for your particular printer before the graph can be printed. Printing graphs can require as many as several tens of kilobytes. In some instances, your system may not have enough memory for Javelin to load in the necessary driver files to print your graph. Javelin tells you when that has happened (see fig. 10.35).

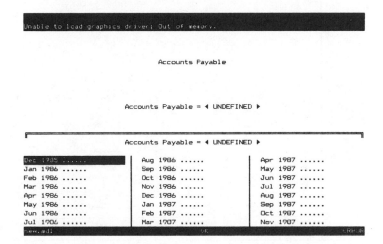

Fig. 10.35. Insufficient memory to
load printer drivers message.

There are two solutions you can choose. One solution is to free some of your computer's memory by clearing unused worksheets, building blocks, variables, other graphs, or data ranges. You should save your model before you do this if some of the data you plan to trim is important. When you have freed enough memory, you can load in the printer driver and print your graph. The second solution is to save your model to a file, then clear the model. After clearing the model, you can input only those variables needed to create the graph.

What follows is a step-by-step description of the second solution:

1. Save the file by selecting the /File Save command, typing the name of the file, and pressing Enter.

2. Use the /Clear All command to free all memory.

3. With the PC's memory blank, define the import data building block to access the variables from the previous model.

4. Create the graph in the current model. You can speed up this process up by using the /Define Macro command to copy the keystrokes used in creating the graph in the original model, then importing the macro to recreate the graph in the current model.

5. Print the graph (see fig. 10.36).

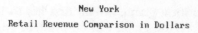

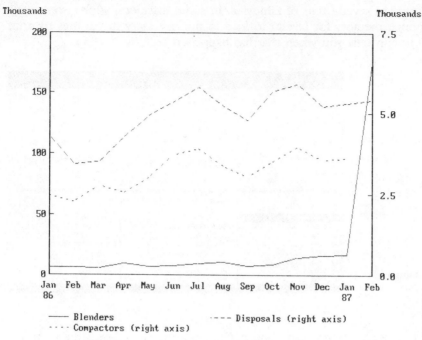

Fig. 10.36. The complex graph with the variables used in the building block.

Conclusion

Javelin's graph commands are valuable when you need to create simple graphs for analyzing your data or when you need to create presentation-quality graphs. In ease of use and in quality, you'll find that Javelin's graph capabilities give you all the power you need for sophisticated business graphics.

11

Printing Reports

Javelin's flexibility allows you to create a wide range of reports, including customized reports. You can print reports documenting the data and logic in your model, analytical reports highlighting key points in your analysis, and presentation-quality reports for customers, management, or investors.

To take full advantage of Javelin's printing capabilities, you need to know what you want printed, what device (printer or disk drive) will receive the output, and what form (graph, chart, diagram, formula list, table, etc.) you want the output to take. For example, if you want to print a customized report for presentation, you must design the report in the WORKSHEET view before printing.

This chapter demonstrates how Javelin reports are created and printed. After learning the types of reports Javelin can produce, you see how to modify printer settings to change the print style and destination of the reports. You then learn some important techniques for developing presentation-quality reports.

The /Print command capabilities are shown in the menu in figure 11.1. The first three menu options, *Graph*, *Current view*, and *Screen*, specify the part of your model that you want printed. The last three options (*Align page*, *Page eject*, *Line feed*) let you control where the printer begins printing on the paper and when the paper ejects from the printer.

In addition to the options for printing a graph, current view, or screen with the /Print command, you can print a worksheet range by using the /*Worksheet Range Print command (see fig. 11.2). This Javelin command works much the same way as the 1-2-3 and SuperCalc³ range print commands.

A subsequent section, "Entering Print Settings—The Printer Settings Sheet," describes how you can use Javelin to take advantage of your printer's special features. The /Define Printer command in the /Define submenu lets you

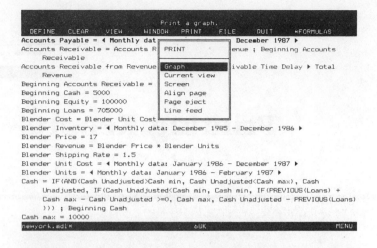

```
                          Print a graph.
 DEFINE    CLEAR    VIEW     WINDOW    PRINT    FILE       QUIT     *FORMULAS
Accounts Payable = ◀ Monthly dat┌──────────────┐  December 1987 ▶
Accounts Receivable = Accounts R│ PRINT        │enue ; Beginning Accounts
    Receivable                  │              │
Accounts Receivable from Revenue│ Graph        │ivable Time Delay ▶ Total
    Revenue                     │ Current view │
Beginning Accounts Receivable = │ Screen       │
Beginning Cash = 5000           │ Align page   │
Beginning Equity = 100000       │ Page eject   │
Beginning Loans = 705000        │ Line feed    │
Blender Cost = Blender Unit Cost└──────────────┘
Blender Inventory = ◀ Monthly data: December 1985 - December 1986 ▶
Blender Price = 17
Blender Revenue = Blender Price * Blender Units
Blender Shipping Rate = 1.5
Blender Unit Cost = ◀ Monthly data: January 1986 - December 1987 ▶
Blender Units = ◀ Monthly data: January 1986 - February 1987 ▶
Cash = IF(AND(Cash Unadjusted>Cash min, Cash Unadjusted<Cash max), Cash
    Unadjusted, IF(Cash Unadjusted<Cash min, Cash min, IF(PREVIOUS(Loans) +
    Cash max - Cash Unadjusted >=0, Cash max, Cash Unadjusted - PREVIOUS(Loans)
    ))) ; Beginning Cash
Cash max = 10000
newyork.mdl*                         68K                          MENU
```

Fig. 11.1. The /Print menu.

```
                      Print cells in a range.
 DEFINE    CLEAR    VIEW     WINDOW    PRINT    FILE      QUIT     *WORKSHEET
                  Jan 1986   Feb 1986   Mar 1986                        986
                                                ┌──────────────┐
Inventory                                       │  *WORKSHEET   │
 Blender            9000       9000       9000  │              │000
 Compactor          3000       3000       3000  │ Range ...    │200
 Disposal           7500       7500       7500  │              │200
                                                │ Sum          │
Unit Cost                                       │ Average      │
 Blender           15.20      15.10      14.72  │ High/Max     │
 Compactor         84.60      84.60      68.28  │ Low/Min      │.85
 Disposal          23.75      23.75      24.07  │ Delete       │.39
                                                │ Print        │.57
Interest rat       10.500     10.000     10.000 │              │
Plant and Eq      800,000    800,000    800,000 │ Width        │000
                                                └──────────────┘000
beginning ca       5,000      5,000      5,000     5,000     5,000

newyork.mdl                          82K                      CALC MENU
```

Fig. 11.2. The /*Worksheet Range Print command.

configure your printer while still in Javelin, to send your information to different printers or to a file. Once you have defined your printer settings, you can save them permanently using the /Define Configuration Save command.

Finally, "Creating Custom Reports Using the WORKSHEET View" discusses how you can use the WORKSHEET view to prepare presentation-quality reports. The WORKSHEET view lets you print exactly what you see on the screen for custom reports. You can think of the WORKSHEET view as Javelin's report generator.

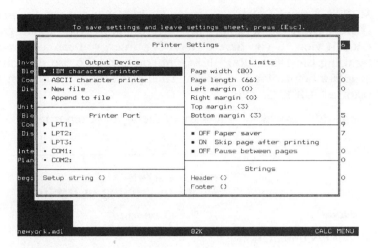

Fig. 11.3. The Printer settings
sheet.

Options for Printing

In Javelin, you can print a variety of reports, such as reports that present model results, analytical reports that display an important aspect of the model, or reports that document the logic and data of a model. The first section, "Options for Printing," describes Javelin's capability to print complete views, do graphic-style screen dumps, and print out selected portions of the WORKSHEET view. You can print a report from any of Javelin's views except the QUICK GRAPH view. You can also print the contents of the screen using the /Print command or the PrtSc (Print Screen) key.

The /Print Current view command prints all the information in the view containing the cursor. You can use the /Print Current view command to print model results or document your model by printing information from any of Javelin's views except the QUICK GRAPH. You can print a diagram of the model, a list of formulas in the model, tables of values for model variables, bar charts of model variables, worksheets showing values for all or selected variables, notes in the model, errors in the model, listings of macros in the model, and various graphs of the values of variables in the model. (For more information about presentation graphics, see Chapter 9.)

If you want to print only the contents of the current screen, use the /Print Screen command. Exceptions include line graphs displayed with QUICK GRAPH and settings sheets. This command is particularly useful for placing information from two Javelin views in one report.

To document the settings for your model, use the PrtSc key to print copies of Javelin's settings sheets. If you are using a graphics program like PRINT

SCREEN® from DOMUS Software Limited, you can use the PrtSc key to print QUICK GRAPH line graphs or rough drafts of presentation graphs from the GRAPH view. If you have a graphics printer, you can also print a QUICK GRAPH by using the DOS GRAPHICS.COM command. To use this command, type *graphics* before loading Javelin. Then press the PrtSc key whenever you want to print a QUICK GRAPH.

Table 11.1 provides a summary of the types of reporting possible with Javelin.

Table 11.1
Modes of Printing in Javelin

Mode	*Command*
Model documentation	
FORMULAS view	/**Print Current view** (from the FORMULAS view)
DIAGRAM view	/**Print Current view** (from the DIAGRAM view)
NOTES view	/**Print Current view** (from the NOTES view)
MACRO view	/**Print Current view** (from the MACRO view)
ERRORS view	/**Print Current view** (from the ERRORS view)
Settings sheets	Use the PrtSc key
Building block screens	Use the PrtSc key
Model data values (input or calculated)	/**Print Current view** (from the TABLE view)
Tabular reports	
Single variable	/**Print Current view** (from the TABLE view)
Multiple variables (draft or presentation)	/**Print Current view** (from the WORKSHEET view) or /***Worksheet Range Print** (from the WORKSHEET view)

Graphs

Draft	/**Print** Current view (from the CHART view) /**Print** Graph (a graph defined in the GRAPH view)
Presentation	/**Print** Graph (a graph defined in the GRAPH view)
QUICK GRAPH line graph	Use PrtSc key (requires a graphics screen dump package like DOMUS PRINT SCREEN)

Printing the Complete View

You can print the contents of 8 of the 10 Javelin views (all but the GRAPH and QUICK GRAPH views) with the /**Print** Current view command. When you use this command, you print the entire view, not just what is on the screen. (Only the visible portion of the diagram, however, is printed in the DIAGRAM view.) The /**Print** Current view command is Javelin's primary report command for model documentation, analytical reports, and presentation reports.

To use the /**Print** Current view command, the desired view must be the active view on the screen. If the desired view is not on screen, use the /**View** command to make it the current view.

1. In one-window mode, the current view is what is on the screen.

2. In two-window mode, the current view is indicated by the ends of the center bar (the cursor is in the active window). The end hooks point to the current window, up for the top half, down for the lower half of the screen (see fig. 11.4). To make the other window the current view, use the /**Window** Switch command or the WINDOW key (F6).

Selecting /**Print** Current view causes Javelin to print out what is on the screen and any additional information in the view that cannot fit on the screen.

Figures 11.5 through 11.12 show the results of using the /**Print** Current view command in the FORMULAS, DIAGRAM, NOTES, MACRO, ERRORS, TABLE, WORKSHEET, and CHART views.

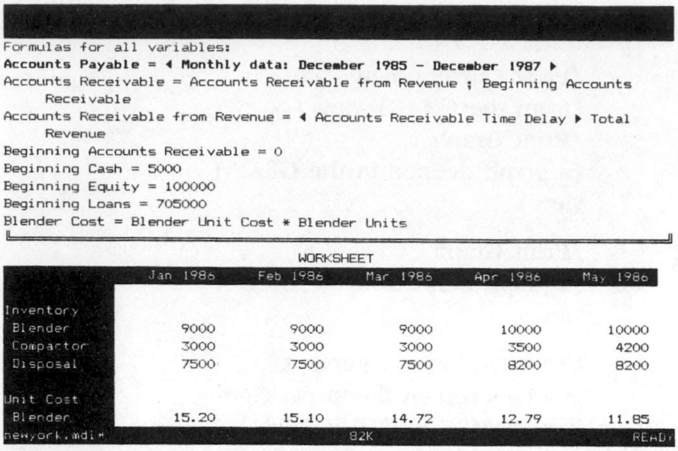

```
Formulas for all variables:
Accounts Payable = ◀ Monthly data: December 1985 - December 1987 ▶
Accounts Receivable = Accounts Receivable from Revenue ; Beginning Accounts
      Receivable
Accounts Receivable from Revenue = ◀ Accounts Receivable Time Delay ▶ Total
      Revenue
Beginning Accounts Receivable = 0
Beginning Cash = 5000
Beginning Equity = 100000
Beginning Loans = 705000
Blender Cost = Blender Unit Cost * Blender Units
```

```
                          WORKSHEET
                 Jan 1986    Feb 1986    Mar 1986    Apr 1986    May 1986

Inventory
 Blender            9000        9000        9000       10000       10000
 Compactor          3000        3000        3000        3500        4200
 Disposal           7500        7500        7500        8200        8200

Unit Cost
 Blender           15.20       15.10       14.72       12.79       11.85
newyork.mdl *                           82K                          READY
```

Fig. 11.4. Javelin screen in two-window mode with FORMULAS view active.

```
Formulas for all variables:

Accounts Payable = < Monthly data: December 1985 - December 1987 >
Accounts Receivable = Accounts Receivable from Revenue ; Beginning Accounts
      Receivable
Accounts Receivable from Revenue = < Accounts Receivable Time Delay > Total
      Revenue
Beginning Accounts Receivable = 0
Beginning Cash = 5000
Beginning Equity = 100000
Beginning Loans = 705000
Blender Cost = Blender Unit Cost * Blender Units
Blender Inventory = < Monthly data: December 1985 - December 1986 >
Blender Price = 17
Blender Revenue = Blender Price * Blender Units
Blender Shipping Rate = 1.5
Blender Unit Cost = < Monthly data: January 1986 - December 1987 >
Blender Units = < Monthly data: January 1986 - February 1987 >
Cash = IF(AND(Cash Unadjusted>Cash min, Cash Unadjusted<Cash max), Cash
      Unadjusted, IF(Cash Unadjusted<Cash min, Cash min, IF(PREVIOUS(Loans) +
      Cash max - Cash Unadjusted >=0, Cash max, Cash Unadjusted - PREVIOUS(Loans)
      ))) ; Beginning Cash
Cash max = 10000
Cash min = 5000
Cash Unadjusted=PREVIOUS(Cash)-CHANGE(Accounts Receivable)-CHANGE (Total
      Inventory)-CHANGE(Plant and Equipment)-CHANGE(Accounts Payable)+Net Income;
      Beginning Cash
Compactor Cost = Compactor Unit Cost * Compactor Units
Compactor Inventory = < Monthly data: December 1985 - December 1986 >
Compactor Price = 175
Compactor Revenue = Compactor Price * Compactor Units
Compactor Shipping Rate = 18.75
Compactor Unit Cost = < Monthly data: January 1986 - February 1988 >
Compactor Units = < Monthly data: January 1986 - February 1987 >
Cost Increase = CHANGE(Total Cost Per Unit)
Disposal Cost = Disposal Unit Cost * Disposal Units
Disposal Inventory = < Monthly data: December 1985 - December 1986 >
Disposal Price = 45
Disposal Revenue = Disposal Price * Disposal Units
Disposal Shipping Rate = 3
Disposal Unit Cost = < Monthly data: January 1986 - October 1987 >
Disposal Units = < Monthly data: January 1986 - February 1987 >
Distribution Expense = (Blender Shipping Rate * Blender Units) + (Compactor
      Shipping Rate * Compactor Units) + (Disposal Shipping Rate * Disposal
      Units)
Equity = PREVIOUS(Equity) + Net Income ; Beginning Equity
Income Before Taxes = Total Revenue - Total Cost - MONTHLY(Total Operating
      Expense)
Interest Expense = Loans * ((Interest Rate/100)/12)
Interest Rate = < Monthly data: January 1986 - December 1987 >
Loans = IF(PREVIOUS(Loans) + Cash - Cash Unadjusted <0, 0, PREVIOUS(Loans) +
      Cash - Cash Unadjusted) ; Beginning Loans
Marketing Expense = < Quarterly data: 1 Quarter 1985 - 4 Quarter 1986 >
Month = < Monthly data: January 1986 - January 1989 >
Net Income = Income Before Taxes - Taxes
Plant and Equipment = < Monthly data: December 1985 - January 1988 >
Predicted Blender Sales = TREND(Blender Units,Jan 1987,Dec 1987)
Salary Expense = < Quarterly data: 4 Quarter 1985 - 4 Quarter 1987 >
Taxes = IF(Month = 1, YTD Taxes, YTD Taxes - PREVIOUS(YTD Taxes))
Total Assets = Cash + Accounts Receivable + Total Inventory + Plant and
```

```
        Equipment
Total Cost = Blender Cost + Disposal Cost + Compactor Cost
Total Cost Per Unit = < UNDEFINED >
Total Inventory = Blender Inventory + Compactor Inventory + Disposal Inventory
Total Liability and Equity = Accounts Payable + Loans + Equity
Total Operating Expense = Marketing Expense + QUARTERLY(Distribution Expense) +
    Salary Expense + QUARTERLY(Interest Expense)
Total Revenue = Blender Revenue + Disposal Revenue + Compactor Revenue
Total Units = Blender Units + Disposal Units + Compactor Units
YTD IBT = YTD(Income Before Taxes)
YTD Taxes = < Taxes Lookup Table > YTD IBT
```

Fig. 11.5. Printout from the FORMULAS view.

```
Total Revenue------------+
                        |
                        |                    +-------------Net Income
Total Cost--------------+-> Income Before Taxes >---+
                        |                    +----------------YTD IBT
                        |
Total Operating Expense-+

  Income Before Taxes = Total Revenue - Total Cost - MONTHLY(Total Operating
                              Expense)
```

Fig. 11.6. Printout from the DIAGRAM view.

```
Notes for Cash:

Cash is calculated based on the previous cash balance plus the cash flow
from operations plus change in loans. If cash based on operating cash flow
is below the minimum balance, loans are increased to bring cash up to the
minimum. If the cash balance exceeds the maximum balance and there are
outstanding loans, these loans are paid off to reduce the cash balance to
the maximum.
```

Fig. 11.7. Printout from the NOTES view.

```
Macro 4 box:

@SLASH dbr
@PROMPT What is the name of this Rollup building block? @READ @ENTER
@DOWN @ENTER @INS @PROMPT What is the name of this box? @READ @ENTER
@DOWN @SPELL @PROMPT Please choose a file for this box. @READ @ENTER
@INS @RIGHT @PROMPT What is the name of this box? @READ @ENTER
@DOWN @SPELL @PROMPT Please choose a file for this box. @READ @ENTER
@INS @RIGHT @PROMPT What is the name of this box? @READ @ENTER
@DOWN @SPELL @PROMPT Please choose a file for this box. @READ @ENTER
@INS @RIGHT @PROMPT What is the name of this box? @READ @ENTFR
@INS @RIGHT @PROMPT What is the name of this box? @READ @ENTER
@DOWN @SPELL @PROMPT Please choose a file for this box. @READ @ENTER
@ESC @DOWN @DOWN @ENTER
@PROMPT Enter the variables you wish to use here. Press F7 to continue.
@PAUSE @ESC @DOWN @DOWN @DOWN @ENTER
```

Fig. 11.8. Printout from the MACROS view.

```
All errors:

Total Cost Per Unit = < UNDEFINED >
```

Fig. 11.9. Printout from the ERRORS view.

```
Cash = IF(AND(Cash Unadjusted>Cash min, Cash Unadjusted<Cash max), Cash...

Dec 1985 ...................... 5,000   !  Sep 1990 ......
Jan 1986 ...................... 5,000   !  Oct 1990 ......
Feb 1986 ...................... 5,000   !  Nov 1990 ......
Mar 1986 ...................... 10,000  !  Dec 1990 ......
Apr 1986 ...................... 10,000  !  Jan 1991 ......
May 1986 ...................... 10,000  !  Feb 1991 ......
Jun 1986 ...................... 10,000  !  Mar 1991 ......
Jul 1986 ...................... 10,000  !  Apr 1991 ......
Aug 1986 ...................... 10,000  !  May 1991 ......
Sep 1986 ...................... 10,000  !  Jun 1991 ......
Oct 1986 ...................... 10,000  !  Jul 1991 ......
Nov 1986 ...................... 10,000  !  Aug 1991 ......
Dec 1986 ...................... 110,765 !  Sep 1991 ......
Jan 1987 ...................... 10,000  !  Oct 1991 ......
Feb 1987 ...................... 10,000  !  Nov 1991 ......
Mar 1987 ...................... 10,000  !  Dec 1991 ......
Apr 1987 ...................... 10,000  !  Jan 1992 ......
May 1987 ...................... 10,000  !  Feb 1992 ......
Jun 1987 ...................... 10,000  !  Mar 1992 ......
Jul 1987 ...................... 10,000  !  Apr 1992 ......
Aug 1987 ...................... 10,000  !  May 1992 ......
Sep 1987 ...................... 10,000  !  Jun 1992 ......
Oct 1987 ...................... 10,000  !  Jul 1992 ......
Nov 1987 ...................... 10,000  !  Aug 1992 ......
Dec 1987 ...................... 10,000  !  Sep 1992 ......
Jan 1988 ......                         !  Oct 1992 ......
Feb 1988 ......                         !  Nov 1992 ......
Mar 1988 ......                         !  Dec 1992 ......
Apr 1988 ......                         !  Jan 1993 ......
May 1988 ......                         !  Feb 1993 ......
Jun 1988 ......                         !  Mar 1993 ......
Jul 1988 ......                         !  Apr 1993 ......
Aug 1988 ......                         !  May 1993 ......
Sep 1988 ......                         !  Jun 1993 ......
Oct 1988 ......                         !  Jul 1993 ......
Nov 1988 ......                         !  Aug 1993 ......
Dec 1988 ......                         !  Sep 1993 ......
Jan 1989 ......                         !  Oct 1993 ......
Feb 1989 ......                         !  Nov 1993 ......
Mar 1989 ......                         !  Dec 1993 ......
Apr 1989 ......                         !  Jan 1994 ......
May 1989 ......                         !  Feb 1994 ......
Jun 1989 ......                         !  Mar 1994 ......
Jul 1989 ......                         !  Apr 1994 ......
Aug 1989 ......                         !  May 1994 ......
Sep 1989 ......                         !  Jun 1994 ......
Oct 1989 ......                         !  Jul 1994 ......
Nov 1989 ......                         !  Aug 1994 ......
Dec 1989 ......                         !  Sep 1994 ......
Jan 1990 ......                         !  Oct 1994 ......
Feb 1990 ......                         !  Nov 1994 ......
Mar 1990 ......                         !  Dec 1994 ......
Apr 1990 ......                         !  Jan 1995 ......
May 1990 ......                         !  Feb 1995 ......
Jun 1990 ......                         !  Mar 1995 ......
Jul 1990 ......                         !  Apr 1995 ......
Aug 1990 ......                         !  May 1995 ......
```

Fig. 11.10. Printout from the TABLE view.

	1 Q 1986	2 Q 1986	3 Q 1986	4 Q 1986	1986
Revenue					
Blender	319,753.00	424,048.00	476,374.00	691,509.00	1,911,684.00
Compactor	1,310,400.00	1,621,900.00	1,803,200.00	1,928,850.00	6,664,350.00
Disposal	505,125.00	652,860.00	710,730.00	755,010.00	2,623,725.00
Total	2,135,278.00	2,698,808.00	2,990,304.00	3,375,369.00	11,199,759.00
Cost					
Blender	282,499.30	305,663.38	279,744.02	325,616.87	1,193,523.57
Compactor	588,360.00	633,773.38	677,308.58	715,927.81	2,615,369.77
Disposal	267,712.15	326,366.66	315,708.49	310,690.18	1,220,477.48
Total	1,138,571.45	1,265,803.42	1,272,761.09	1,352,234.86	5,029,370.82
Expense					
Distributi	202,288.50	254,715.00	282,615.00	318,012.00	1,057,630.50
Interest	31,958.43	26,567.40	16,363.96	3,020.85	77,910.65
Marketing	2,400.00	3,600.00	4,800.00	5,200.00	16,000.00
Salary	240,000.00	240,000.00	252,000.00	282,000.00	1,014,000.00
Total Oper	476,646.93	524,882.40	555,778.96	608,232.85	2,165,541.15
Income Befor	520,059.62	908,122.18	1,161,763.95	1,414,901.29	4,004,847.03
Taxes	211,026.83	408,654.98	522,793.78	636,705.58	1,779,181.16
Net Income	309,032.79	499,467.20	638,970.17	778,195.71	2,225,665.87

Fig. 11.11. Printout from the WORKSHEET view.

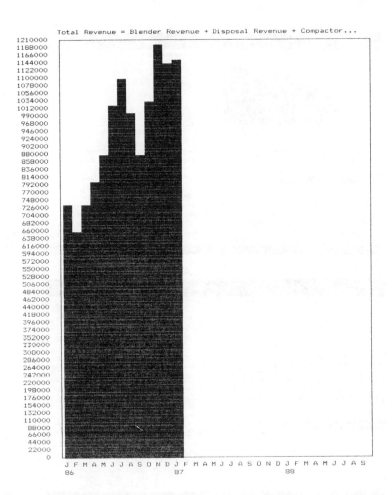

Fig. 11.12. Printout from the
CHART view.

Printing the Screen

The /**Print Current** view command lets you print reports from a single view.
You can also print reports showing two views together by using the /**Print
Screen** command or the PrtSc key with the desired views displayed in two
windows on the screen.

Printing the current screen lets you record a screen for documentation, analysis,
or presentation. For example, figure 11.13 shows a screen print with the
CHART view of *Total Revenue* in the top window and the TABLE view of the
same variable in the bottom window. This report presents *Total Revenue* both
graphically and numerically on the same page. In contrast, figure 11.14 shows
two TABLE views, documenting the behavior of *Predicted Blender Sales* versus
Blender Units, the variable used to define *Predicted Blender Sales*.

Total Revenue = Blender Revenue + Disposal Revenue + Compactor Revenue

Jan 1986 ..... $733,052	Sep 1986 ..... $881,582	May 1987 ......
Feb 1986 ..... $664,346	Oct 1986 ... $1,030,142	Jun 1987 ......
Mar 1986 ..... $737,880	Nov 1986 ... $1,201,589	Jul 1987 ......
Apr 1986 ..... $802,248	Dec 1986 ... $1,143,638	Aug 1987 ......
May 1986 ..... $875,522	Jan 1987 ... $1,157,517	Sep 1987 ......
Jun 1986 ... $1,021,038	Feb 1987	Oct 1987 ......
Jul 1986 ... $1,103,743	Mar 1987	Nov 1987 ......
Aug 1986 ... $1,004,979	Apr 1987	Dec 1987 ......

newyork.mdl 81K READY

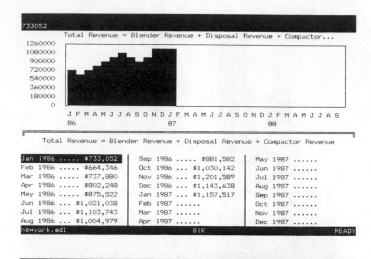

Fig. 11.13. Combined CHART and TABLE views of *Total Revenue*.

6456

Predicted Blender Sales = TREND(Blender Units,Jan 1987,Dec 1987)

Jan 1987 51,358	Oct 1987 99,812	Jul 1988 ......
Feb 1987 56,742	Nov 1987 105,196	Aug 1988 ......
Mar 1987 62,125	Dec 1987 110,580	Sep 1988 ......
Apr 1987 67,509	Jan 1988	Oct 1988 ......
May 1987 72,893	Feb 1988	Nov 1988 ......
Jun 1987 78,277	Mar 1988	Dec 1988 ......
Jul 1987 83,661	Apr 1988	Jan 1989 ......
Aug 1987 89,044	May 1988	Feb 1989 ......
Sep 1987 94,428	Jun 1988	Mar 1989 ......

Blender Units = ◀ Monthly data: January 1986 - February 1987 ▶

Jan 1986 ..... 6,456.00	Sep 1986 ..... 7,756.00	May 1987 ......
Feb 1986 ..... 6,663.00	Oct 1986 ..... 9,321.00	Jun 1987 ......
Mar 1986 ..... 5,690.00	Nov 1986 .... 14,567.00	Jul 1987 ......
Apr 1986 ..... 9,634.00	Dec 1986 .... 16,789.00	Aug 1987 ......
May 1986 ..... 7,456.00	Jan 1987 .... 17,001.00	Sep 1987 ......
Jun 1986 ..... 7,854.00	Feb 1987 ... 175,000.00	Oct 1987 ......
Jul 1986 ..... 9,434.00	Mar 1987	Nov 1987 ......
Aug 1986 .... 10,832.00	Apr 1987	Dec 1987 ......

newyork.mdl 81K READY

Fig. 11.14. TABLE views of *Predicted Blender Sales* and *Blender Units*.

The /**P**rint **S**creen command and the PrtSc key perform similar functions. The /**P**rint **S**creen command causes the program to print out whatever is on the screen. Pressing the PrtSc key on the PC keyboard gives you a printout of whatever is on the screen.

Javelin's /**P**rint **S**creen command differs from the PrtSc key in several ways, however. Only the command, for example, can be written into macros: @SLASH ps. The /**P**rint **S**creen command sends output to the device specified in the /**D**efine **P**rinter command; PrtSc, in contrast, goes to the DOS LPT1 (Line Printer 1) device. The PrtSc key can be used to print settings sheets, whereas /**P**rint **S**creen cannot. If you have a graphics printer and use DOMUS PRINT SCREEN, you can use the PrtSc key to print QUICK GRAPH graphs.

Printing a Worksheet

Worksheets are a valuable presentation tool because of their arrangement of variable names and formats of data values. Javelin provides several options for printing a worksheet as a report. You can print a worksheet range much the same as you can with 1-2-3 and SuperCalc³. In addition, Javelin lets you print the current screen and the entire WORKSHEET view, giving you greater flexibility than either 1-2-3 or SuperCalc³.

Printing the WORKSHEET View

The /Print Current view command works equally well with the WORKSHEET view, printing the entire worksheet. Javelin automatically prints large worksheets on multiple pages should their size require it.

The /Print Current view command in the WORKSHEET view prompts you to indicate whether you want to include the worksheet borders on each page of the printed report (see fig. 11.15). These borders typically include the worksheet title, variable names, and dates. You are asked simply if you want to include borders on each page of the written document.

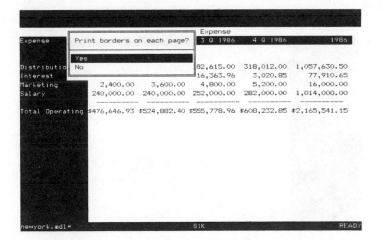

Fig. 11.15. The /Print Current view command gives you the option of including worksheet borders on every page of your printed report.

Printing Worksheet Ranges

To start printing the worksheet range, use the /*Worksheet Range Print command (see fig. 11.16). Javelin prompts you to place the cursor at the corner of the range to be printed. If you want to print only that single cell, press Enter.

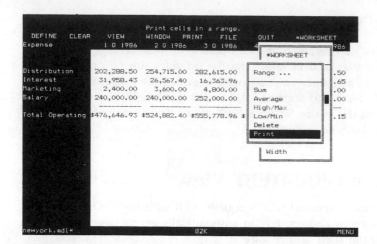

Fig. 11.16. /*Worksheet **Range**
Print lets you print selected
ranges of a worksheet.

To print a larger range, press the period key (.), move the cursor to the
opposite corner of the designated range, and press Enter. Using the sample data
in figure 11.17 as an example, begin defining the range to be printed by
entering the /*Worksheet **Range** **Print** command. Javelin then asks where you
want to begin defining the range to be printed.

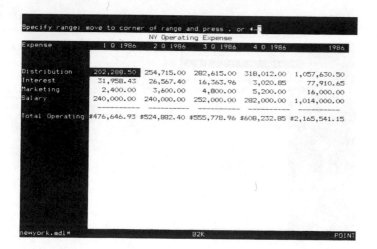

Fig. 11.17. Javelin prompts you to
specify the top left corner of the
worksheet range you want to
print.

You move the cursor to one end of the range to be printed (at the intersection
of the row labeled Distribution and the column labeled 1 Q 1986) and press
the period key (.). The program then asks for the other end of the range.

Now move the cursor to the opposite end of the range. Notice that Javelin
highlights the range as you move the cursor and indicates the cell contents on

the prompt line. When the cursor is in the correct end cell, press Enter (see fig. 11.18).

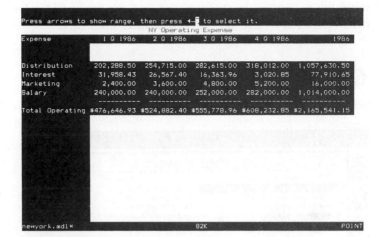

Fig. 11.18. Javelin prompts you to indicate the bottom right corner of the range you want to print.

Finally, Javelin asks whether you want to print the worksheet borders on each page (see fig. 11.19).

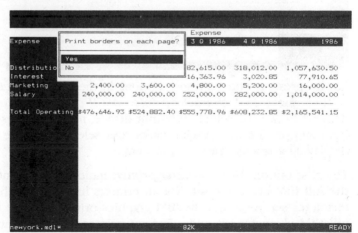

Fig. 11.19. After you indicate the range of cells to print, Javelin asks whether you want worksheet borders on each page.

Entering Print Settings— The Printer Settings Sheet

Suppose that you are working in your model and want to send data to a printer. Because you designated a printer when you ran the JCONFIG program during installation, sending data to that printer is relatively easy (see Chapter 2 for

installation procedures). However, imagine that you have borrowed a color
printer and want to use it at another port (LPT1, COM1, etc.). You could use
the JCONFIG program to reconfigure the Javelin system, but you probably
wouldn't reconfigure your system just for a borrowed printer. Therefore, your
next option is to use the /**Define Printer** command.

Output Device Settings

Select /**Define Printer** to see the Printer settings sheet (see fig. 11.20).

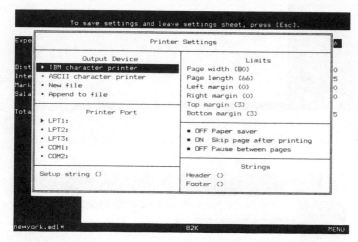

Fig. 11.20. Printer settings sheet
with first item in *Output Device*
box highlighted.

Javelin presents you with four options in the *Output Device* box on the Printer
settings sheet: *IBM character printer*, *ASCII character printer*, *New file*, and
Append to file. To select an output device, move the cursor to the appropriate
item and press Enter. Javelin marks your selection on the settings sheet by
displaying a triangle next to the item.

The first option, *IBM character printer*, indicates any printer capable of printing
the full IBM character set. Not all printers have the capability to print the full
character set. Although the IBM graphics printer and the Proprinter print the
full IBM character set, older Epson® printers do not print the complete set.
Some printers, such as the Okidata® line, come with special IBM adapters. If
you are not sure whether your printer prints the IBM characters, try both the
IBM character option and the ASCII character option to print data from the
CHART view or the DIAGRAM view, and use the option that produces the best
looking reports.

The second option, *ASCII character printer*, is for any printer that is not an IBM
character printer. If your printer does not print the full IBM character set,
choose this option.

Figure 11.21 shows a printout from the CHART view with the IBM character printer option; figure 11.22 shows the same chart printed with the ASCII character option. As the figures show, the IBM character printer option produces better CHART view printouts.

New file, the third choice, routes output to a file that can be sent to the printer later or saved for further use. When you choose this option, Javelin creates a file with a .PRN extension, similar to 1-2-3. .PRN files are created in ASCII format, a character-for-character representation. These files are not Javelin files and carry none of Javelin's internal file notation. Javelin can use them only as ASCII input files. The .PRN files are the only way to export data from Javelin to other software packages.

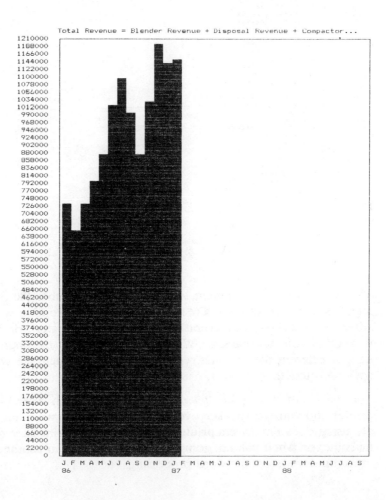

Fig. 11.21. CHART view printed with IBM character printer option.

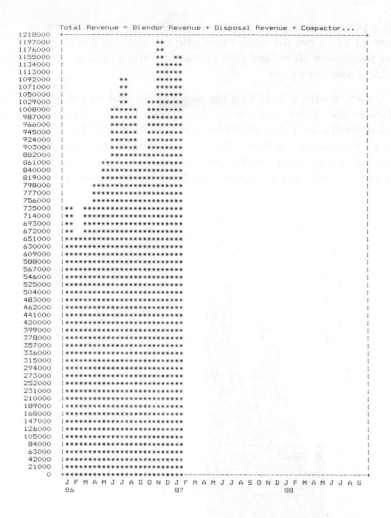

Fig. 11.22. CHART view printed with ASCII character option.

The last output device option, *Append to file*, is another file procedure that attaches new output to an already existing file. This option is particularly useful when you want to send several reports to a file for later printing or to export to another software package. Without the *Append to file* option, you would need a different file for each report rather than a single file with the reports appended together.

You may want to use the *Append to file option* when several computers share a printer and you want to keep your reports together, when the computer you are using does not have a printer and you plan to print later on another machine, or when you are going to export the data to another software package or computer system for word processing, etc.

After changing the output device to a file with the /Define Printer command and then calling up the /Print menu, you are asked the name of the file to use as an output device. A warning appears on the screen if a file already exists with that name (see fig. 11.23).

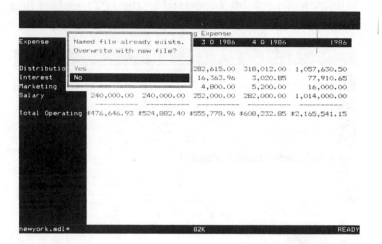

Fig. 11.23. Javelin warns you when you are about to write over a file.

If you want to overwrite the old file, press *Y*; otherwise, press *N*. If you use the *Append to file* option to send the output to disk, you are also asked for a filename. This time, however, if you use a preexisting filename, you create a longer and longer file that includes each of your printouts. You are then able to print the whole file together at your convenience. The *Append to file* option is especially useful for printing all notes in your model.

Printer Port Settings

Standard IBM PCs can have from zero to five output ports. If you have no output ports, you cannot attach a printer to your machine. If you have five output ports, you probably have three *parallel* ports and two *serial* ports. Most machines have some combination of output ports between these two extremes. Ask your dealer or technical support person, or check your owner's manual and purchase receipts if you need to find out how many ports of each kind your machine has.

Basically, parallel and serial ports are two different ways of sending information to the printer. On the PC a parallel port is identified as an *LPT* and a serial port as a *COM*. If you have a parallel printer, it is connected to an LPT port; likewise, a serial printer would be connected to a COM port. You should know to which LPT or COM port your printer is connected. If your operator's manual is

unclear or you are unable to check with your dealer, try the following steps to
determine the nature of your system.

When you first use the /Define Printer command, select the *Printer port* setting
to indicate what type of printer you have (see fig. 11.24). If you have a parallel
printer, it is probably connected to the LPT1 parallel port. A serial printer
should be connected to the COM1 or COM2 serial port.

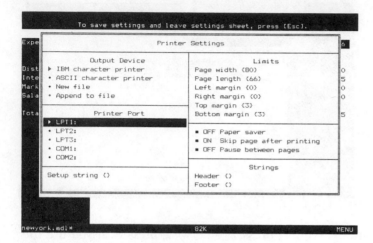

Fig. 11.24. Printer settings sheet
with highlight on the *LPT1:*
option.

Another possibility is to switch output between an existing parallel and existing
serial printer. For example, suppose that the parallel printer is attached to
LPT1, the serial printer to COM1. If this is the case, output can be sent to one
printer or the other by simply changing the printer port settings on the Printer
settings sheet. (This affects output produced by the /Print Current view, /Print
Screen, and /*Worksheet Range Print commands, but not the PrtSc key.)

Setup String Settings

Some printers are capable of a wide variety of fonts, character settings, and so
on. These options are usually triggered by a special set of instructions called a
setup string. This string is sent to the printer before any specialized print is sent
(see fig. 11.25).

If you have a printer capable of several types of printing styles and formats, a
setup string tells your printer which style and format you want. A setup string is
a list of decimal numeric codes sent to the printer to select fonts, pitches, line
and character widths, modes, and so on. These characters are entered into
Javelin's setup string option as a series of numeric ASCII codes preceded by a

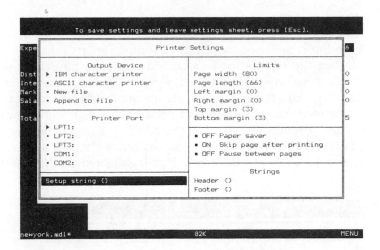

```
                   To save settings and leave settings sheet, press [Esc].
Expe                           Printer Settings                              6

                   Output Device                     Limits
Dist     ▶ IBM character printer          Page width  (80)              0
Inte     • ASCII character printer        Page length (66)              5
Mark     • New file                       Left margin  (0)              0
Sala     • Append to file                 Right margin (0)              0
                                          Top margin   (3)
Tota                 Printer Port         Bottom margin (3)             5
         ▶ LPT1:
         • LPT2:                           ▪ OFF Paper saver
         • LPT3:                           ▪ ON  Skip page after printing
         • COM1:                           ▪ OFF Pause between pages
         • COM2:
                                                     Strings
          Setup string ()                 Header ()
                                          Footer ()

newyork.mdl *                             82K                          MENU
```

Fig. 11.25. Printer settings sheet
with setup string option
highlighted.

backslash (\ ). A list of the ASCII setup-string codes for your printer should be available in your printer manual.

If your normal print setting is 10 pitch (10 characters per inch), you can print about 67 characters per horizontal line on 8 1/2-by-11-inch paper with standard letter margins, or 132 characters on 8 1/2-by-14-inch computer paper with .4-inch margins. The standard 8 1/2-by-11-inch sheet of paper allows 80 characters per horizontal line when no margins are set.

If you want to print a worksheet with 132 characters at 10 pitch on an 80-column printer, you might try condensing your print to 17 pitch (17 characters per inch). To condense print, you need to know the code that activates your printer's condensed print mode. If your printer activates the condensed print mode when you press Ctrl-O, for example, you would need to tell Javelin the ASCII code for Ctrl-O, which is *015*.

To enter the printer-setup codes, move the cursor to the Setup string box. After consulting your printer manual for the necessary codes, enter the codes for each character, preceded by a backslash (\ ). In Javelin, each ASCII code in the setup string must be preceded by a backslash. For example, to create the Javelin equivalent of the Ctrl-O key combination, you would type *015* and press Enter. To create the equivalent of an Esc followed by the characters *A H*, you would type *027**065**072* and press the Enter key.

Besides changing printer pitch settings, you can use setup strings to change the line height (the number of lines printed per inch). For example, if you are using 1/8-inch line spacing rather than the normal 1/6-inch line spacing, you print eight lines per inch instead of the normal six lines.

Page Limits

Page limits are used by Javelin to format reports into pages of output before sending the reports to the specified printer or file. These settings include page width, page length, left margin, right margin, top margin, and bottom margin. The page width and page length specify to Javelin the maximum number of characters that the printer can print on one horizontal line and the maximum number of lines that can be printed on one page. The margin settings tell Javelin what margins to leave on the left, right, top, and bottom of the page. Figure 11.26 shows the *Limits* box highlighted on the Printer settings sheet.

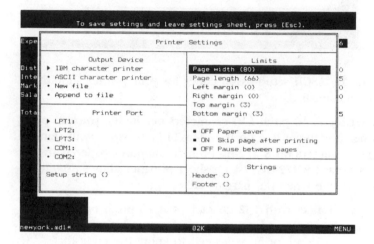

Fig. 11.26. The *Limits* box highlighted on the Printer settings sheet.

Setting Page Width and Length

When you change from 8 1/2-inch-wide paper to 14-inch-wide paper, or include a setup string to change the print pitch from 10 to 12 characters per inch, you have to change the page width setting. If you are unsure about the page width to use with a particular combination of paper width and character pitch, check your printer manual or with your dealer.

For example, suppose that you are using 8 1/2-inch paper but want to print a report with 132 columns on the page. You would change the character pitch to 17 characters per inch (compressed print on an IBM or Epson printer), and set the page width to 132.

As a second example, suppose that you have a wide-carriage printer (requiring 14-inch paper) and want to print a wide report in compressed print (17 characters per inch). You would switch the character pitch with the setup string and set the page width to 233 (this value is from an Epson printer manual).

The Printer settings sheet also contains settings for page length. A standard 8 1/2-by-11-inch page is 66 lines long (at a standard 6 lines per inch). Should you set the printer to 8 lines per inch with the setup string, you would have to set the page length to 88 lines per 8 1/2-by-11-inch page. Should you use longer paper, say 8 1/2-by-14-inch paper (legal-sized stationery), you could change Javelin's default page length to 84 lines per sheet.

Setting Margins

In most applications you want to leave margins at the top and bottom of the page, and at the left and right edges of the paper. The margin settings specify the amounts of blank space to leave at each edge of the paper. Javelin margin settings are in lines for the top and bottom margin, and characters for the left and right margins. If you want a specific top or bottom margin in inches, enter a top or bottom margin setting equal to the desired number of inches times the lines per inch (normally 6 lines per inch). If you want a specific right or left margin in inches, enter the right or left margin setting equal to the desired number of inches times the character pitch (normally 10 characters per inch).

Standard letter margins on 8 1/2-by-11-inch paper are top and bottom margins of 3 lines, and left and right margins of 10 characters. Of course, you can set the margins to whatever values you require. If you change the print pitch or the number of lines per inch with setup strings and you want to retain the same margins in inches, you have to change the margin settings corresponding to the new number of characters or lines per inch.

Miscellaneous Printer Settings

The middle-right section of the Printer settings sheet (see fig. 11.27) lists three miscellaneous functions: *Paper saver*, *Skip page after printing*, and *Pause between pages*. You can toggle these settings on or off by moving the cursor to them and pressing the Enter key.

Saving Paper

The first option, *Paper saver*, gives you some additional flexibility if your worksheet is too wide to fit on one page. If you cannot produce a good printout of your worksheet by using the *Page width* and *Setup string* options,

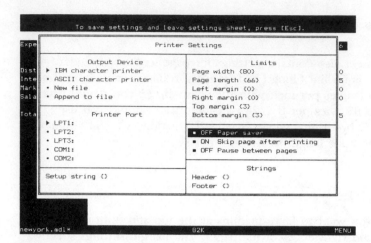

Fig. 11.27. Miscellaneous settings on the Printer settings sheet.

you can use the *Paper saver* option to print as much of the worksheet on one page as possible.

You can switch the *Paper saver* option to *ON* to print as many columns as will fit across the page and then continue printing underneath the first set of rows on the same page. Returning the *Paper saver* option to the default setting (*OFF*) causes the bottom half of the worksheet to be printed on the next page rather than underneath the first half on the same page.

Note: The *Paper saver* toggle works only when printing all or part of the WORKSHEET view.

Skipping a Page

The *Skip page after printing* setting tells Javelin to go to the top of the next sheet of paper after printing is completed. Normally, this feature can be left on, which is the default setting.

Pausing Between Pages

The last setting, *Pause between pages*, is usually inactive because Javelin assumes that you are using continuous paper rather than single sheets. If you want to insert paper a sheet at a time, you would move the cursor to Pause between pages and press Enter. In the ON mode, Javelin would alert you that more paper was needed after each sheet of paper was printed.

Note: If you are using a print spooler or other print buffering device, the *Pause between pages* toggle will not alert you at the time the printer has finished

printing a page. Instead, the toggle will indicate only that a page of information
has been sent to the spooler or buffer.

Headers and Footers

The last part of the Printer settings sheet controls the header and footer strings
(see fig. 11.28). These messages, placed at the top (header) and bottom
(footer) of the printed page, can provide additional information about printed
information. For instance, you can supply date and time information on a report
to be reviewed by others. You may also want to print the date and time on a
worksheet that is frequently updated. You can also add titles, such as
explanations of variables in TABLE view printouts.

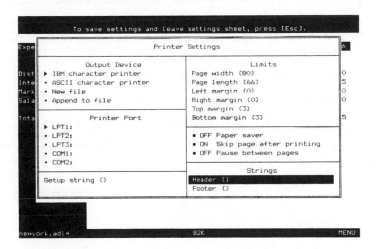

Fig. 11.28. The *Strings* box on
the Printer settings sheet.

Header and footer messages are entered either as straight text or as commands
with @DATE, @TIME, and @PAGE. For example, if you wanted to indicate the
date and time of the assumptions that went into a particular worksheet, you
could use the following as a header:

ASSUMPTIONS AS OF @TIME @DATE

For a longer printout, you could display page numbers as a footer, such as:

Page #@PAGE

These settings would cause Javelin to print out the following message at the top
of the page to the left:

ASSUMPTIONS AS OF 3:46PM 11 April 1986

At the bottom of the page to the left, `Page #` appears followed by the appropriate page number.

To center these messages, place one Javelin vertical bar place marker (|) before each message. To display these messages on the right edge of the page, place two vertical bars before the header or footer text. Each vertical bar tells Javelin that any text following the vertical bar should go one-third of the way across the page. Look at the following header line:

    |ASSUMPTIONS AS OF @TIME @DATE

These directions tell Javelin to go one-third of the way across the top line of the page, enter *ASSUMPTIONS AS OF* followed by the system time and date, and leave the last third of the top line blank (see fig. 11.29).

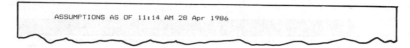

Fig. 11.29. Header positioned one-third of the way across the page.

Consider the following header:

    ||ASSUMPTIONS AS OF @TIME @DATE

These directions tell Javelin to go two-thirds of the way across the top line of the page and enter *ASSUMPTIONS AS OF* followed by the system time and date (see fig. 11.30).

Fig. 11.30. Header positioned two-thirds of the way across the page.

You can place separate messages on the left, in the center, and on the right of the header line. For example, consider the following header:

    @DATE @TIME|Future Home, Inc|Page @PAGE

This header displays the system date and time on the left, *Future Home, Inc.* in the center, and the page number on the right (see fig. 11.31).

You enter footer strings in exactly the same way.

Note: Any text setting or numeric setting on this sheet can be typed over or deleted, should you wish to change the entry or leave it blank.

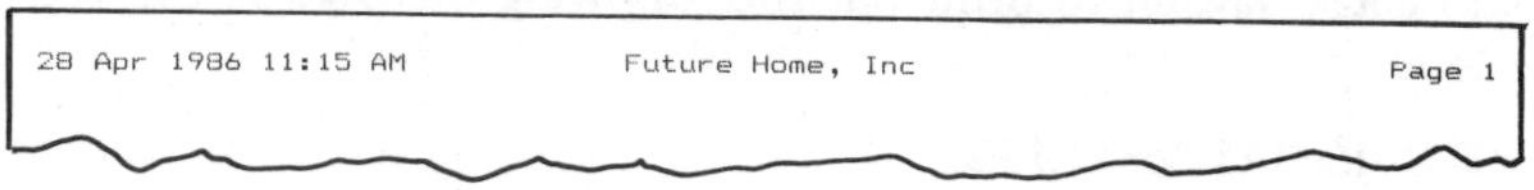

Fig. 11.31. Header showing separate messages on the left, in the center, and on the right.

Saving Print Settings

You must save printer settings to use them again. To save your printer settings, choose /Define Configuration to display the Configuration settings sheet and select the *Save configuration settings permanently* option (see fig. 11.32). When you save print settings on the Configuration settings sheet, they are automatically saved to the JAV.CFG file.

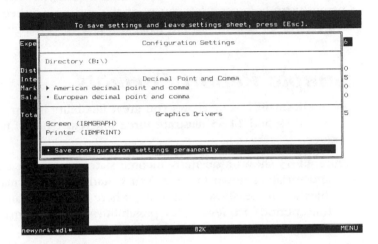

Fig. 11.32. Using the
Configuration settings sheet to
save printer settings.

Printer settings in Javelin are stored with Javelin's other configuration settings, not with your model. If you have several models with special printer settings for each, you have to modify the Printer settings sheet before printing from a model.

Special printer settings are a good application for Javelin macros. You can go through the process of adjusting settings once with the macro record mode turned on. Thereafter, you can use the macro to set the printer settings. Macros are stored with the models, so you can have one or more macros for printer settings per model.

Creating Custom Reports Using the WORKSHEET View

You have now seen the variety of ways that you can print reports from within Javelin along with the print commands and settings required to do the printing. We now turn to a more detailed discussion of printing reports from Javelin's

WORKSHEET view, with emphasis on how to format descriptive titles and headings for presentation-quality tabular reports.

The WORKSHEET view is Javelin's report generator. If you need a customized tabular report that looks as if it was typed manually rather than created by a word-processing program, the WORKSHEET view gives you that capability. You can use either the /Print Current view command or the /*Worksheet Range Print command to print presentation-quality tabular reports. The /Print Current view command lets you print the entire worksheet; the /*Worksheet Range Print command lets you print just a selected range.

Sample Report Formats

The WORKSHEET view allows you great flexibility in report format. Figures 11.33, 11.34, and 11.35 illustrate three different types of tabular reports you can produce.

Figure 11.33 shows a quarterly income statement report with dates across the top and variables down the side. You would use this format for reports where variables are to be shown over time, where you have many variables, and where the time periods are few. Other possibilities for this format include long-range plans, income statements, and sales reports.

```
                        Future Home Appliances, Inc.
                        New York Quarterly Income Statement
                        ------------------------------------

                           1 Q 1986     2 Q 1986     3 Q 1986     4 Q 1986        1986
New York Revenue
  Blender                   319,753      424,048      476,374      691,509    1,911,684
  Compactor               1,310,400    1,621,900    1,803,200    1,928,850    6,664,350
  Disposal                  505,125      652,860      710,730      755,010    2,623,725
                         -----------  -----------  -----------  -----------  -----------
  Total                  $2,135,278   $2,698,808   $2,990,304   $3,375,369  $11,199,759

New York Cost
  Blender                   282,499      305,663      279,744      325,617    1,193,524
  Compactor                 588,360      633,773      677,309      715,928    2,615,370
  Disposal                  267,712      326,367      315,708      310,690    1,220,477
                         -----------  -----------  -----------  -----------  -----------
  Total                  $1,138,571   $1,265,803   $1,272,761   $1,352,235   $5,029,371

New York Expense
  Distribution             202,289      254,715      282,615      318,012    1,057,631
  Interest                  31,856       26,474       16,267        2,958       77,555
  Marketing                  2,400        3,600        4,800        5,200       16,000
  Salary                   240,000      240,000      252,000      282,000    1,014,000
                         -----------  -----------  -----------  -----------  -----------
  Total Operating         $476,544     $524,789     $555,682     $608,170   $2,165,185

New York Income Before Taxes  520,162   908,216    1,161,861    1,414,964    4,005,203
New York Taxes              211,073      408,697      522,837      636,734    1,779,341
                         -----------  -----------  -----------  -----------  -----------
New York Net Income        $309,089     $499,519     $639,023     $778,230   $2,225,862
```

Fig. 11.33. Sample report with dates across the top and variables down the side.

For reports showing the behavior of variables over time, where here are few variables and many time periods, you would use the format shown in figure 11.34. This format places variables across the top and dates down the side.

Applications for this format include daily cash reports, ledger entry reports, or stock market data series.

```
-------------------New York Revenue---------------
              Blender    Disposal   Compactor      Total

Feb 1986     $113,271    $154,350    $396,725     $664,346
Mar 1986      $96,730    $157,275    $483,875     $737,880
Apr 1986     $163,778    $191,520    $446,950     $802,248
May 1986     $126,752    $221,670    $527,100     $875,522
Jun 1986     $133,518    $239,670    $647,850   $1,021,038
Jul 1986     $160,378    $260,865    $682,500   $1,103,743
Aug 1986     $184,144    $234,585    $586,250   $1,004,979
Sep 1986     $131,852    $215,280    $534,450     $881,582
Oct 1986     $158,457    $255,510    $616,175   $1,030,142
Nov 1986     $247,639    $265,500    $688,450   $1,201,589
Dec 1986     $285,413    $234,000    $624,225   $1,143,638
Jan 1987
Feb 1987
```

Fig. 11.34. Sample report with variables across the top and dates down the side.

For reports showing each variable broken down by company office and then further broken down by time period, you would use the format shown in figure 11.35. This format places variables and dates across the top and variables down the side. Common uses of this format might include budget-control reports, variance reports, production-cost reports, budget-consolidation reports, and consolidated income-statement reports.

```
                        Future Home Appliances, Inc.
                        Corporate Income Statement

                        -------------------1 U 1986---------------
                               NY            LA      Future Home
                        ---------------  ---------------  ---------------
Revenue
  Blender                   319,753.00      286,008.00       605,761.00
  Disposal                  505,125.00      552,915.00     1,058,040.00
  Compactor               1,310,400.00    1,268,575.00     2,578,975.00
                        ---------------  ---------------  ---------------
  Total                   2,135,278.00    2,107,498.00     4,242,776.00

Cost
  Blender                   282,499.30      252,396.46       534,895.76
  Compactor                 588,360.00      570,001.08     1,158,361.08
  Disposal                  267,712.15      293,020.73       560,732.88
                        ---------------  ---------------  ---------------
  Total                   1,138,571.45    1,115,418.27     2,253,989.72

Expense
  Distribution             202,288.50      207,105.75       409,394.25
  Interest                  31,958.43       33,737.59        65,696.03
  Marketing                  2,400.00        2,400.00         4,800.00
  Salary                   240,000.00      240,000.00       480,000.00
                        ---------------  ---------------  ---------------
  Total Operating          476,646.93      483,243.34       959,890.28

Income Before Taxes       520,059.62      508,836.39     1,028,896.00
Taxes                     211,026.83      205,976.37       417,003.20
                        ---------------  ---------------  ---------------
Net Income                309,032.79      302,860.01       611,892.80
```

Fig. 11.35. Sample report with variables and dates across the top and variables down the side.

Customizing the Titles and Format

We have already discussed the WORKSHEET view as a report generator. Keep in mind that data and calculations are stored in the model, not on the worksheet.

The worksheet merely provides a convenient way to specify how the data will be displayed on the screen or on paper.

A basic tabular report in the WORKSHEET view is easy to prepare. Figure 11.36 shows a simple balance-sheet report for two offices and the corporate consolidation for 1986. The report is set up by listing the line items and headings in the worksheet borders.

```
                       ----------------1986----------------
                            NY            LA      Future Home
                       --------------  --------------  --------------
   Assets:
Cash                       210,764.05      110,000.00      320,764.05
Accounts Receivable     12,862,096.70   12,011,244.70   24,873,341.40
Total Inventory            302,500.00      302,500.00      605,000.00
Plant and Equipment      9,600,000.00    9,600,000.00   19,200,000.00
------------------       --------------  --------------  --------------
Total Assets            22,975,360.75   22,023,744.70   44,999,105.45

   Liability
Accounts Payable            24,000.00       24,000.00       48,000.00
Loans                    9,740,425.00   10,580,611.11   20,321,036.11
Equity                  13,258,936.83   12,225,540.70   25,484,477.52
------------------       --------------  --------------  --------------
Total Liability and Equity  23,023,361.83   22,830,151.81   45,853,513.64
```

Fig. 11.36. Basic balance-sheet report for Future Home, Inc.

To display the numbers shown in the cells of the worksheet, Javelin combines the contents of the top and side borders into a complete variable name and time period to retrieve values from the Information Base. For example, the number in the first row, first column of the worksheet is Cash NY @ 1986. The number in the first row, second column, is Cash LA @ 1986. The dashes are labels entered into the worksheet borders and cells preceded by a label prefix (' , " , or ^).

Although the basic balance-sheet report presents all the necessary information, the report would probably not be suitable for presentation to a potential customer or a banker. Traditionally, a presentation report has multiline, descriptive titles and descriptive headings. Figure 11.37 shows the same figure after it has been "dressed up" for presentation.

```
                    Future Home Appliances, Inc.
                    Balance Sheet Consolidation
                       December 31, 1986
                    -------------------------------
                    ----------------1986----------------
                      New York     Los Angeles    Future Home
                    --------------  --------------  --------------
   Assets:
Cash and Equivalents      210,764.05      110,000.00      320,764.05
Accounts Receivable    12,862,096.70   12,011,244.70   24,873,341.40
Total Inventory           302,500.00      302,500.00      605,000.00
Plant and Equipment     9,600,000.00    9,600,000.00   19,200,000.00
-------------------     --------------  --------------  --------------
Total Assets           22,975,360.75   22,023,744.70   44,999,105.45

   Liability
Accounts Payable           24,000.00       24,000.00       48,000.00
Loans                   9,740,425.00   10,580,611.11   20,321,036.11
Equity                 13,258,936.83   12,225,540.70   25,484,477.53
-------------------     --------------  --------------  --------------
Total Liability and Equity  23,023,361.83   22,830,151.81   45,853,513.64
```

Fig. 11.37. Balance-sheet report with descriptive titles and headings.

Figure 11.38 shows the worksheet that produced the customized report. The multiline title is added by creating a second horizontal border three lines below the top border. The title is entered in the worksheet cells in the three rows above the new border. Using this technique, you can have any number of rows of titles at the top of a report.

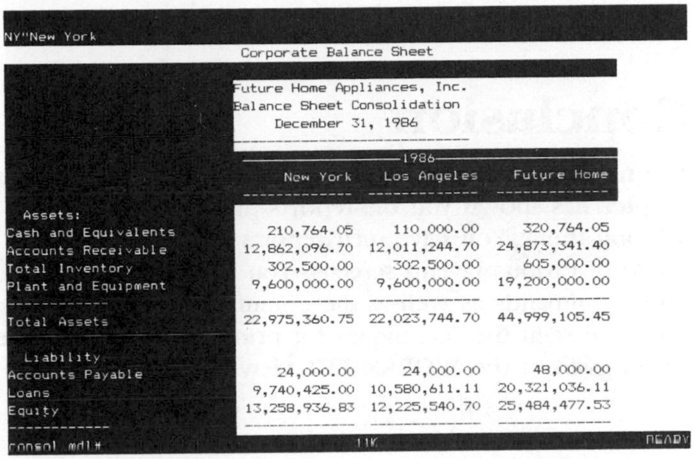

Fig. 11.38. Worksheet for balance-sheet report

The second horizontal border is expanded with the /*Worksheet Border Expand command to three rows before the date and headings are entered. Although the headings pull data from the Information Base like the basic budget report, the balance report's headings display descriptive names using labels following the variable names.

The *New York* heading is generated by the following statement:

NY"New York

This heading consists of *NY*, which as part of a variable name retrieves data from the Information Base, a label prefix ("), and a label. The Los Angeles heading is generated in a similar manner. When such a statement is entered in a header, the part before the label prefix retrieves data while the part after the label prefix is displayed in the border. The last row of the border holds labels consisting entirely of dashes. Labels do not affect the data-retrieval process that loads the numbers into the body of the worksheet.

You can supply descriptive labels for entries in the vertical border as well. For example, the *Cash and Equivalents* label in the first row of the report body is generated by the following information:

Cash'Cash and Equivalents

The portion before the label prefix (') is part of a variable name and is, therefore, used to retrieve data for the report. The portion after the label prefix is displayed as the row heading.

With these techniques for setting up descriptive titles and headings, you are well on your way to generating attractive, tabular reports with the WORKSHEET view.

Conclusion

The material in this chapter is some of the most important in the book. This chapter has shown you the reports that Javelin can print and how to go about printing them. You have seen reports from all of Javelin's views and from screen prints of various Javelin screens. You have learned the use of each of Javelin's print commands as well as the commands that define printer settings. Finally, you have seen the techniques for printing reports with descriptive titles and headings from the WORKSHEET view.

## Part V

Javelin Macros

12

Javelin Macros

Macro capability has become an expected feature of most spreadsheet programs and is now also a feature of many database and word-processing programs. Although the number and types of macro commands available vary from one program to another, most spreadsheet, database, and word-processing programs with macros provide two basic capabilities: (1) the ability to store a set of keystrokes and "play back" those keystrokes by pressing two or three keys, and (2) the ability to create simple programs using special macro commands.

Javelin offers both capabilities. You can record a series of keystrokes—a sequence, for example, required for completing certain command operations—and then play back these keystrokes automatically whenever you need them. You can also create your own simple programs in Javelin for automating many applications or for creating special menu and prompt systems for other users. This chapter describes Javelin macros, explains the steps and commands for creating macros, and presents sample macros you can copy.

Commands Emphasized in this Chapter

/View Macro
/Define Macro Begin
/Define Macro End
/Define Macro Rename
/File Import Macro

What Is a Macro?

Javelin macros, like macros in other business applications software, consist of two types: basic *typing alternative* macros and macros that use programming

357

commands. You will find it easy to begin using *typing alternative* macros because Javelin automatically records each command for you as you type keystrokes. Once you have created these simple macros, you can experiment with Javelin's set of programming commands to create more sophisticated macros.

Macros provide an alternative to typing data and commands from the keyboard. The basic *typing alternative* macro is simply a collection of keystrokes, such as keystrokes for entering commands, entering data, or moving the cursor. You can build keystroke combinations to perform data entry, report printing, model building, and many other activities. The following Javelin macro, for example, lists the series of keystrokes for changing a worksheet to comma format:

   @HOME @SLASH *f @DOWN @DOWN @DOWN @DOWN @ENTER @ESC

Keystroke-by-keystroke, the macro performs the following:

  1. Moves cursor on worksheet to Home   @HOME

  2. Selects Javelin command menu   @SLASH

  3. Selects *Worksheet command   *

  4. Selects Format   f

  5. Moves the cursor to the Commas format option   @DOWN @DOWN
                                                             @DOWN @DOWN

  6. Presses Enter to mark Commas format option   @ENTER

  7. Presses Esc to leave the settings sheet   @ESC

Typing alternative macros are particularly valuable for command operations that you repeat frequently such as entering settings into a settings sheet, printing Javelin views, saving models, or importing data.

Creating Javelin Macros

Depending on whether you are creating a *typing alternative* macro or a macro using program commands, you can create Javelin macros in two ways: letting Javelin copy your keystrokes or entering part or a complete macro manually by using Javelin's macro programming commands. Whether you create a macro automatically or manually, you must first give the macro a name. You can choose anything from a single alphabetic character to names that describe the function the macro performs.

Next, you must indicate what keystrokes are in the macro. You can either type commands in the MACRO view (see fig. 12.1) or have Javelin record your keystrokes by using the /Define Macro command.

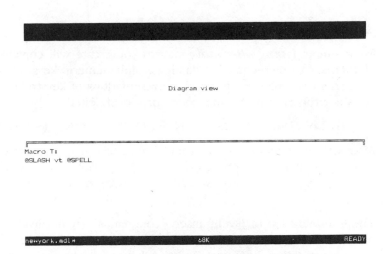

Fig. 12.1. A *typing alternative*
macro.

For example, the macro in figure 12.1 is a simple macro, created by recording keystrokes. The macro offers the user a selection of TABLE views (@SLASH vt @SPELL).

Typing alternative macros are easy to create because Javelin can record automatically all of the keystrokes required. The RECORD mode is activated by the /Define Macro command. Macros created by recording keystrokes can be viewed and changed through Javelin's MACRO view. However, if your macro requires one of the special macro programming commands, you will need to enter manually part or all of the macro using Javelin's MACRO view. If you enter a macro by typing the commands yourself, you must be careful to follow special spacing conventions. Be sure, for example, to provide spaces between all commands that begin with @ and between other elements. In the previous macro example, @SLASH and @SPELL are separated from the keystrokes vt by spaces.

After entering keystrokes, you run the macro first and then edit it to make sure the macro does exactly what you want. You may have to alter the macro several times as your needs change. When you become more adept at designing and using macros, you can fine tune your macros, removing unnecessary steps. See the following sections for more specific information on creating, naming, and using macros.

The Elements of Macros

Most simple *typing alternative* macros you create will contain two types of elements: (1) elements that duplicate alphanumeric keystrokes, and (2) elements that are special macro representations of keystrokes. For example, consider the comma format macro previously cited:

@HOME @SLASH *f @DOWN @DOWN @DOWN @DOWN @ENTER @ESC

Most of the elements in this macro are special macro commands. (Note: All macro commands are preceded by the @ symbol.) For example, @HOME means pressing the Home key. Notice, however, that * and *f* are actual keystrokes.

The complete list of Javelin macro commands may be divided into the seven categories of commands shown in figure 12.2. The first three sets, *Cursor movement*, *Other keys*, and *Function keys*, describe keys normally typed in a Javelin work session. The last four sets, *Prompt or pause*, *Flow of control*, *Conditional macros*, and *User-defined menus*, are commands that allow you to program in Javelin. These programming commands let you go beyond the simple keyboard alternatives and develop special applications such as custom menus and prompts, sophisticated print macros, and complex data input systems.

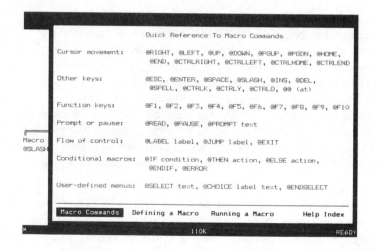

Fig. 12.2. The Macro help screen.

Using Cursor-Movement Commands

The cursor-movement commands mimic the keys that move the cursor on the screen. All of these keys are located on the numeric keypad, usually to the right of the typewriter keyboard. Each command moves the cursor as if the actual key were being pressed on the keyboard. The comma format macro presented previously, for example, uses the cursor-movement command @DOWN to move the cursor down four rows to select the comma format. Whenever you create a macro requiring cursor movement, it will contain one of the following commands:

@RIGHT	@HOME
@LEFT	@END
@UP	@CTRLRIGHT
@DOWN	@CTRLLEFT
@PGUP	@CTRLHOME
@PGDN	@CTRLEND

Note that the last four macro commands—those combining the Ctrl key with another cursor key—can be used only in certain views. @CTRLRIGHT and @CTRLLEFT represent cursor movement in the WORKSHEET view and on the edit line; @CTRLHOME and @CTRLEND are used only in the NOTES and MACRO views.

Using Macro Function-Key Commands

The macro function-key commands mimic the Javelin function keys. Suppose that you created a macro, for example, to change from a single-window screen to a two-window screen displaying and synchronizing a CHART view on top and a TABLE view on the bottom. Such a macro would consist of the following commands:

@SLASH w2 @SLASH vt @ENTER @F6 @SLASH vc @ENTER @F3

Two function-key commands are used in this macro. The @F6 command is used to move the cursor from one view to the other; the @F3 command is used to synchronize the two views. The complete list of function-key commands includes the following:

Command	Operation Performed by Command
@F1	Displays a Help screen
@F2	Begins Edit mode
@F3	Synchronizes two views or turns synchronization off
@F4	Displays on the edit line the variable highlighted by the cursor
@F5	Goes to a variable
@F6	Moves cursor from one window to the other

@F7	Begins running a macro
@F8	Displays a QUICK GRAPH view
@F9	Calculates a model
@F10	Displays a graph

Using Other Key Commands

There are also other macro commands for special keys, such as the slash key (/) or the SPELL key (Tab). A macro for selecting a Variable settings sheet, for example, would use the command for the SPELL key (Tab) as indicated in the following macro:

@SLASH dv @SPELL

The complete list of macro commands for keys other than cursor or function keys includes the following:

Command	Operation Performed by Command
@SLASH	Accesses Javelin's main menu
@SPELL	Accesses the POSSIBILITIES list
@ENTER	Enters information or completes a command
@ESC	Invokes escape
@BKSP	Moves cursor back a space
@INS	Invokes insert operation
@DEL	Invokes delete operation
@CTRLK	Deletes the text from the cue to the end of the exit line
@CTRLQ	Quotes the next character
@@	Types an at sign (@) when a macro is run

Using Programming Commands

Javelin has a set of special macro commands that can only be entered in the MACRO view. With these commands, you have a limited programming capability. These commands enable you to design macros that pause for user input, loop, contain subroutines, contain conditional statements for testing data, and produce custom menu systems and prompts.

Some macro commands, such as @READ, @PAUSE, and @EXIT, are used alone. Other macro programming commands, however, must be followed by other elements—a variable, date, text, or another macro command. The macro command and its adjoining elements make up a statement with a syntax similar to the verb-object syntax in English, demonstrated by the simple two-word imperative, "Do it." These commands must be followed by an "object," something for the command (verb) to act upon.

The macro commands @SELECT and @CHOICE, for example, must be completed with other elements. @SELECT and @CHOICE are commands used to create a custom menu system for users. @ENDSELECT follows the last @CHOICE statement to end the menu options. @SELECT begins the menu choices, and @CHOICE provides the menu options. If you wanted to create a custom menu enabling users to choose one of a series of model worksheets to print, you would use @SELECT and @CHOICE as follows:

@SELECT Choose a worksheet to print:
@CHOICE Inc Print Income Statement
@CHOICE Bal Print Balance Sheet
@CHOICE Sales Print Monthly Sales Report
@CHOICE Inven Print Inventory Report
@ENDSELECT

The command @CHOICE requires that two elements follow it: the label (*Inc*, *Bal*, *Sales*, *Inven*) indicating where the macro jumps if that device is selected and the prompt to appear in the menu.

Commands for User Input

When you want to create a macro that pauses to let a user enter data, you can use one of three commands: @READ, @PROMPT, or @PAUSE.

When you want the user data to complete an operation, use the @READ command. A macro, for example, that makes use of the SPELL key (Tab) would require the @READ command in order to allow the user to enter the necessary selection from the list. The @READ command would be used along with @SPELL as follows:

@SPELL @READ

After the @SPELL command activates the POSSIBILITIES menu, the user can move the cursor to the desired option. Pressing Enter ter the @SPELL command activates the POSSIBILITIES menu, the user can move the cursor to the desired option. Pressing Enter tells Javelin to read the chosen option. The @READ command can also ask for data from a user. The following macro requests an original value for a model:

Original @SPACE Value @SPACE =
@PROMPT What is the 'Original Value'? @READ @ENTER

This macro types the line *Original Value* = on the EDIT line, and then asks the user for a value. The @READ command waits for information from the user, who enters a value and presses Enter. Pressing Enter, the user indicates only that the @READ input is complete. To complete the macro and transmit the input data to the model, the macro contains a special @ENTER command.

Commands To Pause and Prompt

The @PAUSE command can be used to allow the user to input data. Like the @READ command, @PAUSE causes the macro to stop executing until certain conditions are met. The two commands are different, however, because @READ will let you access the Javelin menu while the macro has paused; the @PAUSE command will not allow you access the menu, nor use function keys other than the MACRO key (F7). In other words, @READ pauses for a line of input; @PAUSE pauses for changes within a view. The two commands differ also in the method used to continue macro execution. When the @READ command causes a macro to pause, you continue execution by pressing Enter. On the other hand, when the @PAUSE command is used, you press the MACRO key (F7) to tell Javelin to continue executing the macro.

The @PROMPT command causes Javelin to display a message indicating that the user can enter information or alter a screen. You can, for example, use @PROMPT in a macro for entering monthly sales. Suppose that you want to create a macro that will display automatically a TABLE view of the variables *Blender Units*, *Disposal Units*, and *Compactor Units*, move the cursor to the appropriate month, and prompt the user to enter sales data. Such a macro using @PROMPT would consist of the following:

@SLASH vtBlender @SPACE Units
@ENTER @END @DOWN
@PROMPT Enter this month's sales data for blenders, then press Enter.
@READ @ENTER
@SLASH vtDisposal @SPACE Units
@ENTER @END @DOWN
@PROMPT Enter this month's sales data for disposals, then press Enter.
@READ @ENTER
@SLASH vtCompactor @SPACE Units
@ENTER @END @DOWN

@PROMPT Enter this month's sales data for compactors, then press Enter.
@READ @ENTER
@SLASH fs @ENTER y
@SLASH qyy

Notice that each @PROMPT command asks the user to enter sales data for a particular product. The line that follows each of the lines beginning with @PROMPT uses the @READ and @ENTER commands to allow the macro to stop and enter the data provided for each TABLE view.

The use of the @PAUSE command is shown in the following macro:

@SLASH dg MODELS @ENTER
@PAUSE
@ESC
@F10

This macro first calls up the Graph settings sheet for the MODELS graph. The macro then uses the @PAUSE command to let the user define any or all of the settings for the MODELS graph. The user presses the MACRO key (F7) to indicate to Javelin that the input is over. Javelin then continues with the macro. @ESC saves the graph settings and returns to the previous screen. @F10 displays the MODELS graph.

Commands To Direct Macro Flow

Two command sets direct the flow of macros: the flow-of-control macros on the Macro command help screen and the commands that create user-defined menus. The flow control commands are usually used with the commands for conditional statements, which are discussed in the next section. Commands to create user-defined menus are discussed in "Commands to Create User-defined Menus."

There are three flow-of-control commands: @JUMP, @LABEL, and @EXIT. Flow control gives you the ability to bypass unnecessary steps in the macro. An example from nature would be placing a rock in a stream. You have bypassed the rock and redirected the flow of water rather than stopping it.

The @JUMP and @LABEL commands must be used together. The @JUMP command tells Javelin to skip any intervening steps between @JUMP and the @LABEL command. You can use @JUMP and @LABEL to move forward or go backwards. This pair often appears as it does in the following example:

```
@JUMP near
step1
step2
step3
    .
    .
    .
@LABEL near
step100
step101
step102
    .
    .
    .
```

As this example illustrates, the number of lines between @JUMP and @LABEL can be many (99 in this case). When the macro comes upon an @JUMP, it will search until it finds the correct @LABEL no matter how many lines intervene. @JUMP and @LABEL use the "verb-object" convention discussed previously so that these commands in tandem use the same object. You may use as many @JUMP-@LABEL pairs as you want in building your macros, but too many @JUMP-@LABEL pairs may prove confusing.

The @EXIT command also directs the flow of macros. By adding this command to your macro, you leave the macro mode and return to user mode. You use the @EXIT command to exit a macro before it would normally terminate.

Commands for Conditional Statements

The conditional commands are @IF-@THEN-@ELSE-@ENDIF and @ERROR. The first group is really one command with different parts. The four commands @IF, @THEN, @ELSE, and @ENDIF are used together. The last command, @ERROR, is unique because it is the only macro command that has a value. @ERROR is either true or false, depending on what happens in Javelin.

The syntax of the first group of commands is as follows:

@IF (a certain condition is met)
@THEN do some thing
@ELSE do some other thing
@ENDIF

To use these commands, it is necessary to know what constitutes a "condition." A condition is anything that Javelin can evaluate as either true or false. All of the following are valid Javelin conditions:

Sales @ Jan 87 20000
PMT(loan, interest rate, number of payments) < 700
Payment = TSUM(Monthpay) > 100000

The preceding examples show Javelin's capability to use both functions and data to determine valid conditions. Used with the commands for flow control, these conditional statement commands direct macro execution, based on the outcome of the @IF command set, as follows:

```
@IF Payment
@THEN @JUMP problem
@ELSE @JUMP response
@ENDIF
@LABEL problem
step1
step2
step3
.
.
.

@EXIT
@LABEL response
step101
step102
step103
.
.
.
```

The @ERROR command can be written into a macro when you suspect the user might encounter a problem, such as dividing by zero. This is the simplest and most common type of error, but remember that Javelin makes use of several types of error messages. You can have the @ERROR macro command alert the user to errors in the logic of the macro or errors in the model itself.

The @ERROR command is only used with the @IF command. The true value of the @ERROR command can be used to continue the macro at a certain point should problems occur while the macro is executing. Whenever you use a statement containing @IF @ERROR, you must follow these commands with @THEN and @ENDIF.

The @IF @ERROR combination will only work in Release 1 of Javelin with errors that do not produce an ERROR message in the status line. Consider, for example, the following section of a macro for printing a graph:

```
@SLASH pg @SPELL
@IF @ERROR
@THEN @JUMP problem
@ENDIF
@PROMPT Move cursor to graph name and press Enter.
@READ @ENTER
@LABEL problem
@ESC
@SELECT Create or import a graph:
    @CHOICE line Create a line graph
    @CHOICE bar Create a bar graph
    @CHOICE stack Create a stack-bar graph
    @CHOICE percent Create a percent bar graph
    @CHOICE horiz Create a horizontal bar graph
    @CHOICE pie Create a pie graph
    @CHOICE xy Create an xy scatter plot
    @CHOICE import Import a graph from another model
@ENDSELECT
```

The @ERROR command is used along with @IF in the second line in case no Graph settings sheets are available in the model containing the macro. If no Graph settings sheets exist, line 3 sends the macro to line 7. Line 7 begins the series of operations that lead to displaying menu selections enabling the user to create or import a graph before the macro loops to process the print command.

Commands To Create User-defined Menus

The commands to build user-defined menus, @SELECT, @CHOICE, and @ENDSELECT, also work together and can be used to create menus that allow the user several options. The command group directs the flow of the macro without using the @JUMP command. Note that these commands are the second set of flow-of-control commands mentioned previously in the chapter.

The commands are used as follows:

```
@SELECT prompt
@CHOICE (label to jump to) (first selection)
@CHOICE (label to jump to) (second selection)
    .
    .
    .
@ENDSELECT
```

The @CHOICE command works just like the @JUMP command. The only addition is the text to let the user know what label each @CHOICE jumps to. When you use @CHOICE, you must precede it with the @SELECT command and end it with @ENDSELECT. It is possible to include a maximum of 12 @CHOICE commands for each @SELECT. An example for this command set would be

```
@LABEL selector
@SELECT Please choose an option
@CHOICE graph Create a graph
@CHOICE worksheet Create a worksheet
@CHOICE printgraph Print a graph
@CHOICE printwks Print a worksheet
@CHOICE end Quit Javelin
@ENDSELECT
@LABEL graph
(steps to create a graph)
@JUMP selector
@LABEL worksheet
(steps to create a worksheet)
@JUMP selector
@LABEL printgraph
(steps to print a graph)
@JUMP selector
@LABEL printwks
(steps to print a worksheet)
@JUMP selector
@LABEL end
@SLASH qsy
```

This macro creates the menu in figure 12.3.

Defining and Naming a Macro

Use the /Define Macro command to record a sequence of keystrokes, to finish recording, or to rename an existing macro.

You can, for example, save a series of keystrokes for building a graph. In this case, the keystrokes you follow to build the graph will be recorded to form the macro. You can then move the macro into other models with the /File Import Macro command.

To create a keystroke-by-keystroke graphing macro, start with the command /Define Macro. Javelin shows you the /Define Macro submenu shown in figure

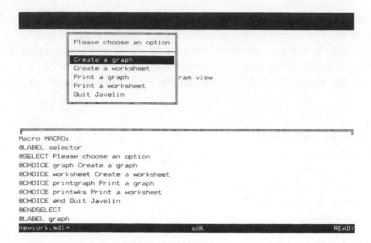

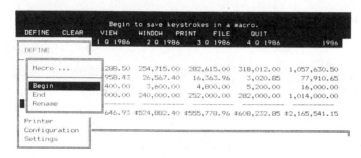

Fig. 12.3. Custom menu created
with the @CHOICE command.

12.4. To start defining the macro, you choose the Begin option and press Enter
to begin recording keystrokes.

Fig. 12.4. The /Define Macro
submenu.

Naming the Macro

Once you have selected /Define Macro, you must supply a macro name (see fig.
12.5). To complete the name you, can either use a single letter, such as *g*, or a
descriptive name, such as *Grapher*. Using a descriptive name helps you to
remember the function of the macro, particularly when you have many macros
in one file and are trying to recall their functions.

Using a single letter like *g*, on the other hand, requires fewer keystrokes when you want to run the macro. As explained more specifically in the following discussion, a descriptive macro name containing two or more characters must be invoked by using the MACRO key (F7), which requires that you enter a name when the prompt appears. Macros named with single letters, however, can be invoked by simply pressing and holding down the Alt key while you also press the single letter. Once these two keys are pressed, the macro begins running.

Macro name:					
		NY Operating Expense			
Expense	1 Q 1986	2 Q 1986	3 Q 1986	4 Q 1986	1986
Distribution	202,288.50	254,715.00	282,615.00	318,012.00	1,057,630.50
Interest	31,958.43	26,567.40	16,363.96	3,020.85	77,910.65
Marketing	2,400.00	3,600.00	4,800.00	5,200.00	16,000.00
Salary	240,000.00	240,000.00	252,000.00	282,000.00	1,014,000.00
Total Operating	$476,646.93	$524,882.40	$555,778.96	$608,232.85	$2,165,541.15

Macro MACRO:

newyork.mdl#   82K   READY

Fig. 12.5. Javelin prompts you to name the macro you are beginning to create.

Recording Your Keystrokes

You access the RECORD mode as soon as you have completed the two steps described previously: (1) selected /**Define Macro Begin** and pressed Enter and (2) supplied a name for the macro. Once these two steps are completed, you can return to the model to record your keystrokes. After you select /**Define Macro** and assign a macro name, Javelin reminds you that your keystrokes are being recorded by displaying RECORD in the status line and the prompt Beginning to define (name of the macro) in the edit line (see fig. 12.6).

Javelin places no limits on the number of keystrokes you can enter into a macro. You can, for example, use Javelin's RECORD mode to record most or all of the keystrokes required for building a certain model. You can then modify the macro so you can use it to automate creating models.

When you have entered the last keystroke you want recorded in the macro, you must end the RECORD mode by using the /**Define Macro End** command. This command can be entered during the RECORD mode without affecting the

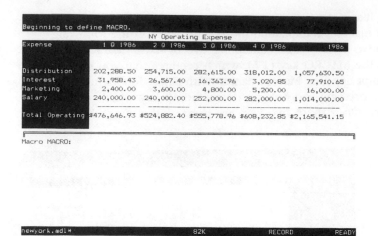

Fig. 12.6. Beginning to define a
macro in the prompt line.

macro being defined. When you give the command /Define Macro End, Javelin
responds by telling you that the macro is defined (see fig. 12.7).

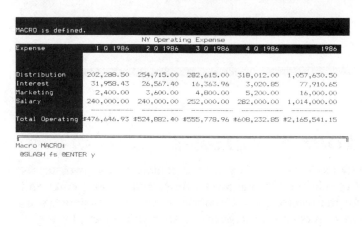

Fig. 12.7. Javelin indicates that
the macro is defined.

Renaming a Macro

You can rename an existing macro by using the /Define Macro Rename
command. When you select this command, Javelin asks you for the existing
macro's name. Type the current name and press Enter or use the SPELL key
(Tab) to select the macro name (see fig. 12.8). When Javelin prompts you for a
new name, type the name and press Enter.

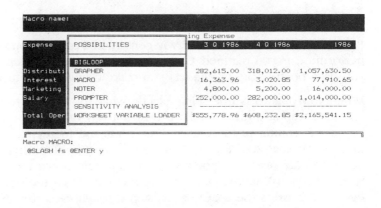

Fig. 12.8. Using the SPELL key (Tab) to retrieve an existing macro name when renaming.

Running a Javelin Macro

You can run any macro in the current model by pressing the MACRO key (F7), entering the macro name, and pressing Enter. If you wanted, for example, to use the macro named Grapher for creating a pie graph of your model's data, you would press the MACRO key (F7), enter Grapher, and press Enter. Remember that you can enter graph names either by using the SPELL key (Tab) alone or by typing a few characters and then pressing the SPELL key (Tab).

If a macro name is a single letter, you can run the command using the MACRO key (F7) or simply by pressing and holding down the Alt key while you also press and hold down the letter key. If you use the second method, you save one step by not having to enter the name at the prompt and then to press Enter. Give single letter names to those macros that you use most frequently and whose function you will be able to recall easily. You may want, for example, to create a macro that you can use frequently to save your model's file as you work on it. If you name this macro *s*, you can invoke it with the *Alt-s* key combination whenever you want to save new data.

Stopping a Macro during Execution

You can stop your macro's operation by pressing the key combination Ctrl-Break. The Ctrl key is at the left of the typewriter keyboard. The Break key can usually be found above the cursor/numeric keypad. Often the Break key is also identified as *Scroll Lock*.

Editing a Macro

Perhaps while running your newly constructed macro, you notice that it is not performing as you planned. Or, you may wish to add a step or two to a macro you have been using. Javelin lets you make changes to your macros several ways.

When your macro is not doing exactly what you want it to do, you can see it run, one step at a time. Javelin provides a way of taking you keystroke to keystroke, command to command, or command to keystroke through your macros. To analyze the macro's execution step-by-step, first press and hold down the Alt key while you also press and hold down the MACRO key (F7), type the macro's name, and then press Enter. When the prompt appears as in figure 12.9, press the space bar to step through each part of the macro. Use the Esc key to stop the macro and return to READY mode.

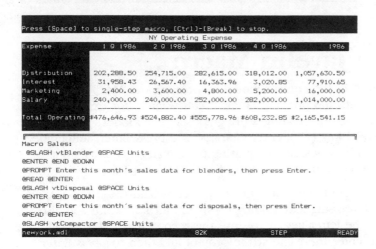

Fig. 12.9. Using Javelin's STEP mode to step through a macro.

Guidelines for Programming in the MACRO View

If the macro you are creating uses any of Javelin's special programming commands, you must use the MACRO view to create the whole macro or to enter those parts that involve programming commands. Because you will be entering part or all of the macro manually, the following guidelines will help ensure that the macro will run correctly the first time you use it. To use the MACRO view, select the /View Macro command, enter a macro name, and press Enter. When the macro view appears, write your macro, keeping the following guidelines in mind.

The first rule is to construct macros with only the commands necessary to achieve a goal. For instance, in the *Grapher* macro shown at the end of this chapter the @PGDN command is used to replace several @DOWN commands. The @END command can be used to replace several @DOWN and @LEFT commands. This reduces typing during the creation of the macro, memory needed to store the macro, and time required to execute the macro.

The second rule is to place user-defined menus only where needed. Do not put a menu in a macro that requires an IF-THEN-ELSE-ENDIF combination to work around the menu. Place the menu in a section where it will be used if (and only if) and when (and only when) it is needed. Remember that performing one step at a time is more efficient than having to jump all around your macro.

The third rule builds from the previous two rules and can be called "Using Top-Down Steps." This rule requests that you write your macro with a particular objective in mind, outlining the steps to reach the objectives before you start. Before you even start to write your macro, you will have a roadmap of what you want to do. Preplanning produces a clean and efficient set of commands that perform a specific task in Javelin.

Keeping these rules in mind as you develop your macros can be a great time saver, not only when you write the macros, but later when you must edit.

Using the SPELL Key (Tab) in the MACRO View

In the MACRO view, you can use the SPELL key (Tab) to edit macros (see fig. 12.8). The SPELL key lists Javelin's macro programming commands. In the MACRO view, however, the SPELL key shows available Javelin macro programming commands only. It does not show Javelin functions. Also, use the SPELL key to enter macro commands when you first create macro lines. The SPELL key will prevent typographical errors and thus prevent macro errors.

Sample Typing Alternative Macros

You can easily create *typing alternative* macros to automate your most frequently used command operations by using Javelin's /Define Macro command. Printing worksheets, creating backup files of models, creating graphs, and formatting worksheets are just a few of the many applications for *typing alternative* macros. This section describes two sample macros:

1. Macro for adjusting window size

2. Macro for printing

Creating any *typing alternative* macro requires the following steps:

1. Begin the macro RECORD mode by selecting /Define Macro **Begin**.

2. When the prompt appears asking for a macro name, type a name and press Enter. After you have entered a name, Javelin begins the RECORD mode.

3. Enter the keystrokes you want saved.

4. Select /Define Macro **End** to end the RECORD mode.

A Macro To Adjust Window Size

Even for operations requiring only a few keystrokes, *typing alternative* macros save you time. The *Macro to Adjust Window Size*, for example, will save nine keystrokes whenever you want to expand the size of the window in which you are working. The *Macro to Adjust Window Size* will enable you to change a screen like that in figure 12.10 (with windows of equal size) to a screen like that in figure 12.11.

The *Macro to Adjust Window Size* is created by following the five steps listed previously for *typing alternative* macros. After beginning the RECORD mode, enter the following keystrokes:

1. Slash (/) to access the Javelin menu.

2. *wa* to select the /**W**indow **A**djust command.

3. Up-arrow key (↑) five times.

4. Enter

Once you finish recording keystrokes, your macro is ready to use. Notice that if you view the macro through Javelin's MACRO view, as shown in figure 12.12, all of the keystrokes listed previously have been recorded.

To run the macro, press the MACRO key (F7), enter the macro name *Up 5* when the prompt appears, and press Enter. The macro expands the size of the window you are working in and returns the program to READY mode.

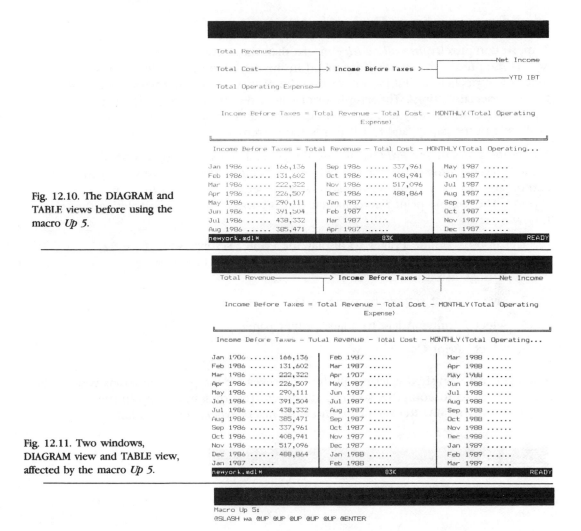

Fig. 12.10. The DIAGRAM and TABLE views before using the macro *Up 5*.

Fig. 12.11. Two windows, DIAGRAM view and TABLE view, affected by the macro *Up 5*.

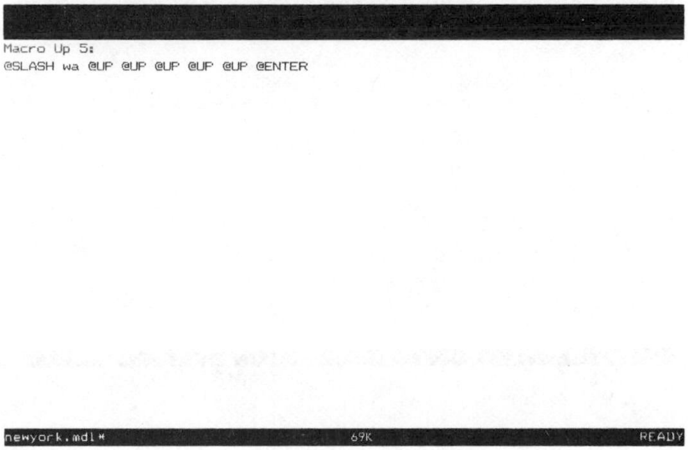

Fig. 12.12. The macro *Up 5*.

A Macro for Printing

A more complex *typing alternative* macro than the *Macro to Adjust Window Size* is the *Macro for Printing* described in the discussion that follows. This macro is especially useful for automating the process of printing worksheets that require special settings. The sample print macro described here performs three types of operations: (1) it enters settings in Javelin's Printer settings sheet, (2) it aligns printer paper, and (3) it prints the current view.

To create a *Macro for Printing*, follow the general steps listed previously for creating *typing alternative* macros. When you begin to record keystrokes, you can create the macro with all the special print settings you need to print reports. The sample print macro in figure 12.13 was created by completing the following steps:

1. Choose /**Define Printer** to display the Printer settings sheet (see fig. 12.14) and enter all the margin, setup string, and header string settings listed.

2. Save all print settings by pressing Esc.

3. Select /**Printer Adjust** to adjust printer paper.

4. Select /**Print Current** view.

When you have finished entering all the keystrokes for the print operations you want the macro to complete, you end the macro record session. To run the macro, press the MACRO key (F7), enter the macro name, and press Enter.

```
Macro Print:
 @SLASH dp @RIGHT 240 @ENTER @DOWN 66 @ENTER @DOWN 2 @ENTER @DOWN 2 @ENTER
@DOWN 2 @ENTER @DOWN 2 @ENTER @DOWN @DOWN @DOWN @LEFT @DOWN @DOWN \015 @ENTER
@RIGHT Future @SPACE Home, @SPACE Inc. @SPACE @@ date @ENTER @ESC @SLASH pa
@SLASH pc
```

newyork.mdl#   68K   READY   Fig. 12.13. Macro for printing.

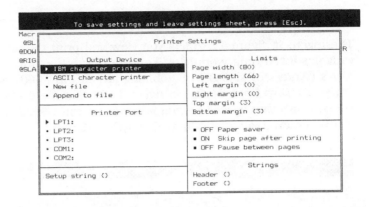

Fig. 12.14. Javelin's Printer settings sheet.

Macros Using Special Programming Commands

Javelin's macro programming commands extend the applications for macros far beyond *typing alternative* macros. As described previously in the discussion of macro programming commands, you can create complex input systems, customized menus and prompts, or error-checking systems, for example.

The following sample macros will help you get started creating macros with programming commands. The following sections describe:

1. A macro for viewing and printing notes

2. A macro for creating graphs

Macros using programming commands can be created in one of two ways: (1) you can enter the whole macro manually by typing each macro command, checking the macro for errors, and then testing it; or (2) you can create parts of the macro by using Javelin's RECORD mode, editing the macro by adding the programming commands you need, checking the macro for errors, and then testing it. The method you choose should depend on the complexity of the macro and the number of programming commands the macro uses. The *Macro to View and Print Notes,* can be created by combining the RECORD mode with manually entered macro lines. The *Macro for Creating Graphs*, on the other hand, is most easily created by entering the complete macro manually.

A Macro To View and Print Notes

The macro in figure 12.15 lets you view and print the notes associated with variables listed on a worksheet. You can create the *Macro to View and Print Notes* (*Noter,* for short) by combining Javelin's RECORD mode with manual entry of macro lines. Notice in figure 12.15 that the first four lines of the macro contain only one special programming command (**@READ**); all other commands can be entered automatically with **/Define Macro.**

```
Macro Noter:
@SLASH w2
@F6 @SLASH vw @SPELL @READ @ENTER
@F6 @SLASH vn @ENTER
@F6 @F3
@JUMP selection
@LABEL y
@PROMPT Move the cursor to the variable whose note you wish to print and press
Enter @READ @ENTER
@F6 @SLASH pc @F6
@LABEL selection
@SELECT Print a note?
@CHOICE y Yes
@CHOICE n No
@ENDSELECT
@LABEL n
```

```
newyork.mdl H                    95K                              READY
```

Fig. 12.15. Macro for viewing and printing notes.

To create this macro, begin by selecting **/Define Macro Begin,** naming the macro, and pressing Enter. When Javelin indicates that the RECORD mode is active, complete the following:

1. Select **/Window 2 windows.**

2. Press the WINDOW key (F6).

3. Select **/View Worksheet.**

4. Press the SPELL key (Tab),then press Enter.

5. Press the WINDOW key (F6).

6. Select **/View Notes** and press Enter.

7. Press the WINDOW key (F6), then press the SYNC key (F3).

Stop the RECORD mode at this point by selecting **/Define Macro End.** You can now complete the macro by adding special programming commands. To complete the macro, display the macro just created through RECORD mode by choosing **/View Macro.** With the partial macro displayed, enter the @READ command in line 3 and then type the other macro lines from line 5 to the end, as shown in figure 12.15.

Each line of the *Noter* macro operates as follows. The first line of the macro puts Javelin into two-window mode. (This command has no effect if Javelin is already in two-window mode.) If you run the macro and the screen is already divided into two windows, your computer will beep when the macro processes the first line, but will continue running.

The first command in the second line, @F6, moves the cursor from the window where it is currently located to the second window. The commands following the @F6 command, @SLASH vw @SPELL @READ @ENTER, allow the user to display an existing WORKSHEET view. The third and fourth lines place the cursor back in the previous window (@F6), display a NOTES view in this window, and synchronize the NOTES and WORKSHEET views (@F3).

The macro's fifth line then moves macro execution to the *selection* place marker (line 10). The combination of the @JUMP command in line 5 and the @LABEL command in line 10 causes the macro to begin processing on line 11. Lines 11, 12, and 13 display a custom menu, giving the user the option of exiting the macro or of selecting the NOTES view for a particular variable and printing the NOTES view currently displayed.

If the user chooses to print a NOTES view, the macro moves back to line 7, which displays the following prompt:

```
Move the cursor to the variable whose note you
wish to print and press Enter
```

The easiest way to see a note is to ask for the variable the note is linked to. The user can move the cursor to the desired variable and press Enter. *Noter* reads and enters that information into Javelin. Once a variable is selected, the macro switches windows (@F6). Remember that the views are synchronized at this point, so positioning the cursor on a variable in the WORKSHEET view causes that variable's note to appear in the NOTES view, assuming that you have displayed a worksheet containing variables. The note is then printed (@SLASH pc), and the cursor is returned to the WORKSHEET view (@F6).

A Macro To Create Graphs

One of the benefits of using Javelin's macro programming commands is that they enable you to create custom menu systems. These menu systems can simplify Javelin's regular command operations and save you the trouble of having to select from many different commands or move through many command levels. The *Grapher* macro in figure 12.16 is one example of how you can simplify the process of entering settings into the Graph settings sheet and of displaying graphs you have created.

```
    Macro Grapher:

 1. @SLASH dg
 2. @PROMPT What is the name of this new graph? @READ @ENTER
 3. @PGDN @PGDN @PGDN @SPELL @READ @ENTER @RIGHT
 4. @JUMP prompter

 5. @LABEL y0
 6. @DOWN @LEFT @SPELL @READ @ENTER @RIGHT

 7. @LABEL prompter
 8. @PROMPT Please type in a label for this variable @READ @ENTER
 9. @SELECT Is there another variable to include in the graph?
10. @CHOICE y0 Yes
11. @CHOICE n0 No
12. @ENDSELECT

13. @LABEL n0
14. @SELECT Do you want to change the type of graph?
15. @CHOICE y1 Yes
16. @CHOICE n1 No
17. @ENDSELECT

18. @LABEL y1
19. @HOME @RIGHT @RIGHT
20. @PROMPT Please select the type of graph you want to see. @READ @ENTER
21. @LABEL n1
22. @F10
```

Fig. 12.16. The macro *Grapher* in the MACRO view.

The *Grapher* macro is designed to help the user create graphs from any variables in a model since no specific settings are included in the macro.

You begin the *Grapher* macro by selecting the MACRO view (/View Macro), entering the name *Grapher*, and pressing Enter. When the blank MACRO view appears, enter each macro line as shown in figure 12.16.

The first line of the macro accesses the Graph settings sheet with the /Define Graph command. Because this command moves the cursor to the *Name* box of the Graph settings sheet, the second line prompts the user, What is the name of this new graph? The macro reads (READ) then enters (@ENTER) the user's response.

Once the graph is named, the macro moves the cursor down (@PGDN) three boxes to the *Variables* box on the Graph settings sheet. Here the SPELL key (@SPELL) is used to list the first variable available for graphing. The macro reads the user's selection, enters it, then moves right (@RIGHT) on the settings sheet to the *Labels* box.

At line 4, the macro goes (@JUMP) to line 7, which begins the process for entering labels and additional variables. @PROMPT in line 8 prompts the user to enter a label for the variable entered in line 3. After the user responds to this prompt, the last two commands in line 8 accept (@READ) and enter (@ENTER) the label. Lines 9, 10, and 11 create a menu box that allows the user to enter another variable or change the type of graph.

Lines 10 and 11 display the Yes and No prompts, and send the macro to the appropriate macro line, depending on the user's choice. The @ENDSELECT command in line 12 ends the menu choices of the previous two lines. Notice that creating a menu system requires using @SELECT at the beginning, @CHOICE for each menu item, and @ENDSELECT to close the menu selections. If the user chooses Yes in response to the question, Is there another variable to include in the graph?, the macro moves to line 5. (The label y0 in line 5 indicates where the macro continues based on the y0 label after @CHOICE in line 10.) When the user selects No, as displayed by the @CHOICE command in line 11, the macro moves to line 13.

Lines 14, 15, 16, and 17 enable the user to change the type of graph. Line 14 displays the prompt, Do you want to change the type of graph?; the @CHOICE commands in lines 15 and 16 provide the Yes and No selections, respectively. If the user selects Yes to change the type of graph, the macro moves to line 18 and then executes the cursor-movement commands in line 19 for changing graph type. Line 20 prompts the user to select a type of graph. If the user chooses No, as displayed in line 16, the macro proceeds to line 21 and ends by displaying the graph through the @F10 command in line 22.

Conclusion

If you make creating and using macros a regular part of your use of Javelin, you will find that this can save you much time. Macros can significantly speed up printing reports and creating models, graphs, and worksheets. Javelin macros are also valuable when you need to support inexperienced users who must input, display, or print data. This chapter helps you get started creating and using both simple typing alternative macros and macros that use Javelin's programming language.

## Part VI

A Comprehensive Javelin Model

13

A Comprehensive
Javelin Model

This chapter integrates all of Javelin's main elements, which were introduced in the preceding chapters. In particular, you will see how one corporate model is developed, using all of Javelin's sophisticated capabilities for model building, analysis, and presentation. This chapter shows how all the elements—Javelin views, building blocks, and macro capability—work together to produce a unified model.

The comprehensive model is designed by Art Abacus for his boss, Busby T. Numbacrunch, the corporate controller of Future Home Appliances, Inc. Numbacrunch must ensure that an accurate reporting system exists between the company's two divisions (New York and Los Angeles) and the corporate headquarters. For example, reports on revenue, operating expenses, and manufacturing costs must all funnel to Numbacrunch's office so that data can be consolidated into a single corporate Income Statement and Balance Sheet.

Numbacrunch uses the corporate Income Statement and Balance Sheet when he reports to the company president, J. D. Pocketful. Because the president is particularly concerned about planning for the company's growth, he depends heavily on Numbacrunch to have accurate, reliable, and easily understood information. Pocketful expects to see complete reports and to get answers to his questions about monthly net income over the course of the year.

A General Description of the Model

Using Javelin, Abacus designs a single model for the analysis and reporting needs of each division and for the corporation. Abacus saves the original model under two different file names: NY.MDL and LA.MDL. He sends the NY.MDL file to the New York division, and the LA.MDL file to the Los Angeles division. Both files contain the same variables and formulas; the files differ only in their names. Each office is directed to provide data for the model. Then Abacus uses Javelin's Rollup building block to consolidate data supplied by the divisions.

After Abacus sends the model to the New York and Los Angeles divisions, each divisional office uses the model for internal analysis and reporting as well as for reporting to the corporate headquarters. The New York and Los Angeles offices import variables from the corporate model into other files, thus creating separate models for divisional sales, marketing, and manufacturing needs.

All the models maintain the variables from Abacus' original corporate model. This model contains formulas and variables for analyzing and reporting the following:

- Total sales for the products manufactured by each division: blenders, compactors, and disposals

- Manufacturing costs for the products manufactured by each division

- Marketing, distribution, salary, and interest expenses

Using the variables for reporting revenue, cost of goods, and operating expenses, each department can then keep its own files for inputting data, analyzing this data by using various Javelin views, and presenting data to managers in various departments. Each month new data from departments can be imported into the consolidated corporate model. Javelin makes the consolidation of data easy and reliable.

The Original Corporate Model

The complete original model contains all the variables necessary to prepare the final corporate Income Statement and Balance Sheet shown in figures 13.1 and 13.2. These two figures illustrate how both the Income Statement and the Balance Sheet can be summarized and printed in report form, using information in Javelin's WORKSHEET view.

This view of the Income Statement and Balance Sheet, though, fails to show Javelin's power and tells us little of the model's sophistication. A much better picture of the model's sophistication is seen through Javelin's FORMULAS view,

Future Home Appliances, Inc. Income Statement 10 Apr 1986

| | | 1 Q 1986 | |
	NY	LA	Future Home
Revenue			
Blender	319,753.00	286,008.00	605,761.00
Disposal	505,125.00	552,915.00	1,058,040.00
Compactor	1,310,400.00	1,268,575.00	2,578,975.00
Total	2,135,278.00	2,107,498.00	4,242,776.00
Cost			
Blender	282,499.30	252,396.46	534,895.76
Compactor	588,360.00	570,001.08	1,158,361.08
Disposal	267,712.15	293,020.73	560,732.88
Total	1,138,571.45	1,115,418.27	2,253,989.72
Expense			
Distribution	202,288.50	207,105.75	409,394.25
Interest	31,958.43	33,737.59	65,696.03
Marketing	2,400.00	2,400.00	4,800.00
Salary	240,000.00	240,000.00	480,000.00
Total Operating	476,646.93	483,243.34	959,890.28
Income Before Taxes	520,059.62	508,836.39	1,028,896.00
Taxes	211,026.83	205,976.37	417,003.20
Net Income	309,032.79	302,860.01	611,892.80

Fig. 13.1. Income Statement for Future Home Appliances, Inc.

Future Home Appliances, Inc. Balance Sheet 10 Apr 1986

| | | 1986 | |
	NY	LA	Future Home
Assets:			
Cash	210,764.05	110,000.00	320,764.05
Accounts Receivable	12,862,096.70	12,011,244.70	24,873,341.40
Total Inventory	302,500.00	302,500.00	605,000.00
Plant and Equipment	9,600,000.00	9,600,000.00	19,200,000.00
Total Assets	22,975,360.75	22,023,744.70	44,999,105.45
Liability			
Accounts Payable	24,000.00	24,000.00	48,000.00
Loans	9,740,425.00	10,580,611.11	20,321,036.11
Equity	13,258,936.83	12,225,540.70	25,484,477.52
Total Liability and Equity	23,023,361.83	22,830,151.81	45,853,513.64

Fig. 13.2. Balance Sheet for Future Home Appliances, Inc.

which displays each original formula and variable. Printing the FORMULAS view for the original model provides the complete list of formulas and variables shown in figure 13.3. In addition to obtaining a list of all formulas, Abacus uses /View Formulas Roots to focus on specific variables and their roots. See, for example, the roots of *Net Income* in figure 13.4.

Indentation in the FORMULAS Roots view conveys an overall picture of the relationship of all variables connected to *Net Income*. The variables that directly affect *Net Income* (*Income Before Taxes* and *Taxes*) are indented once; variables that directly affect *Income Before Taxes* and *Taxes* are indented twice, and so on.

```
Accounts Payable = < Monthly data: December 1985 - December 1987 >
Accounts Receivable = Accounts Receivable from Revenue ; Beginning Accounts
    Receivable
Accounts Receivable from Revenue = < Accounts Receivable Time Delay > Total
    Revenue
Beginning Accounts Receivable = 0
Beginning Cash = 5000
Beginning Equity = 100000
Beginning Loans = 705000
Blender Cost = Blender Unit Cost * Blender Units
Blender Inventory = < Monthly data: December 1985 - December 1986 >
Blender Price = 17
Blender Revenue = Blender Price * Blender Units
Blender Shipping Rate = 1.5
Blender Unit Cost = < Monthly data: January 1986 - December 1987 >
Blender Units = < Monthly data: January 1986 - December 1986 >
Cash = IF(AND(Cash Unadjusted>Cash min, Cash Unadjusted<Cash max), Cash
    Unadjusted, IF(Cash Unadjusted<Cash min, Cash min, IF(PREVIOUS(Loans) +
    Cash max - Cash Unadjusted >=0, Cash max, Cash Unadjusted - PREVIOUS(Loans)
    ))) ; Beginning Cash
Cash max = 10000
Cash min = 5000
Cash Unadjusted=PREVIOUS(Cash)-CHANGE(Accounts Receivable)-CHANGE(Total
    Inventory)-CHANGE(Plant and Equipment)-CHANGE(Accounts Payable)+Net Income;
    Beginning Cash
Compactor Cost = Compactor Unit Cost * Compactor Units
Compactor Inventory = < Monthly data: December 1985 - December 1986 >
Compactor Price = 175
Compactor Revenue = Compactor Price * Compactor Units
Compactor Shipping Rate = 18.75
Compactor Unit Cost = < Monthly data: January 1986 - February 1988 >
Compactor Units = < Monthly data: January 1986 - December 1986 >
Cost Increase = CHANGE(Total Cost Per Unit)
Disposal Cost = Disposal Unit Cost * Disposal Units
Disposal Inventory = < Monthly data: December 1985 - December 1986 >
Disposal Price = 45
Disposal Revenue = Disposal Price * Disposal Units
Disposal Shipping Rate = 3
Disposal Unit Cost = < Monthly data: January 1986 - October 1987 >
Disposal Units = < Monthly data: January 1986 - December 1986 >
Distribution Expense = (Blender Shipping Rate * Blender Units) + (Compactor
    Shipping Rate * Compactor Units) + (Disposal Shipping Rate * Disposal
    Units)
Equity = PREVIOUS(Equity) + Net Income ; Beginning Equity
Income Before Taxes = Total Revenue - Total Cost - MONTHLY(Total Operating
    Expense)
Interest Expense = Loans * ((Interest Rate/100)/12)
Interest Rate = < Monthly data: January 1986 - December 1987 >
Loans = IF(PREVIOUS(Loans) + Cash - Cash Unadjusted <0, 0, PREVIOUS(Loans) +
    Cash - Cash Unadjusted) ; Beginning Loans
Marketing Expense = < Quarterly data: 1 Quarter 1986 - 4 Quarter 1986 >
Month = < Monthly data: January 1986 - January 1989 >
Net Income = Income Before Taxes - Taxes
Plant and Equipment = < Monthly data: December 1985 - January 1988 >
Predicted Blender Sales = TREND(Blender Units,Jan 1987,Dec 1987)
Salary Expense = < Quarterly data: 4 Quarter 1985 - 4 Quarter 1987 >
Taxes = IF(Month = 1, YTD Taxes, YTD Taxes - PREVIOUS(YTD Taxes))
Total Assets = Cash + Accounts Receivable + Total Inventory + Plant and
    Equipment
Total Cost = Blender Cost + Disposal Cost + Compactor Cost
Total Cost Per Unit = < UNDEFINED >
Total Inventory = Blender Inventory + Compactor Inventory + Disposal Inventory
Total Liability and Equity = Accounts Payable + Loans + Equity
Total Operating Expense = Marketing Expense + QUARTERLY(Distribution Expense) +
    Salary Expense + QUARTERLY(Interest Expense)
Total Revenue = Blender Revenue + Disposal Revenue + Compactor Revenue
Total Units = Blender Units + Disposal Units + Compactor Units
YTD IBT = YTD(Income Before Taxes)
YTD Taxes = < Taxes Lookup Table > YTD IBT
```

Fig. 13.3. All variables in the model.

```
Formulas for all variables that affect Net Income:
Net Income = Income Before Taxes - Taxes
• Income Before Taxes = Total Revenue - Total Cost - MONTHLY(Total Operating
  Expense)
• • Total Revenue = Blender Revenue + Disposal Revenue + Compactor Revenue
• • • Blender Revenue = Blender Price * Blender Units
• • • • Blender Price = 17
• • • • Blender Units = ◄ Monthly data: January 1986 - December 1986 ►
• • • Disposal Revenue = Disposal Price * Disposal Units
• • • • Disposal Price = 45
• • • • Disposal Units = ◄ Monthly data: January 1986 - December 1986 ►
• • • Compactor Revenue = Compactor Price * Compactor Units
• • • • Compactor Price = 175
• • • • Compactor Units = ◄ Monthly data: January 1986 - December 1986 ►
• • Total Cost = Blender Cost + Disposal Cost + Compactor Cost
• • • Blender Cost = Blender Unit Cost * Blender Units
• • • • Blender Unit Cost = ◄ Monthly data: January 1986 - December 1987 ►
• • • • Blender Units = ◄ Monthly data: January 1986 - December 1986 ►
• • • Disposal Cost = Disposal Unit Cost * Disposal Units
• • • • Disposal Unit Cost = ◄ Monthly data: January 1986 - October 1987 ►
• • • • Disposal Units = ◄ Monthly data: January 1986 - December 1986 ►
• • • Compactor Cost = Compactor Unit Cost * Compactor Units
newyork.mdl                                  69k                        CALC READY
```

Fig. 13.4. Variables that affect *Net Income*. (Note: The variable *Taxes* doesn't fit on the screen.)

> Directions for Re-creating the Balance Sheet–Income Statement Model:
>
> You can create the Balance Sheet–Income Statement model by entering the variables listed in figure 13.3. In addition to entering variables, however, you need to set the *Combine Periods By* setting on each Variable settings sheet to *Last Period* for the following variables:
>
> | Cash | Accounts Receivable | Total Inventory |
> |------|---------------------|-----------------|
> | Loans | Accounts Payable | Total Liability |
> | Equity | Plant and Equipment | Total Assets |
>
> You will also need to create the building blocks shown in figures 13.19 and 13.20.

Using Javelin Views

Each divisional office of Future Home Appliances uses Javelin not only for supplying Abacus with data for corporate consolidation, but also for developing specific models for analysis and planning. The New York and Los Angeles offices use the FORMULAS and ERRORS views, for example, to check the accuracy of the models and to check the relationships among variables. As discussed in Chapters 3 and 8, the FORMULAS view can be used by itself to check model assumptions and logic. Through the FORMULAS view, users in the New York office can check for circular references (see fig. 13.5), for a list of all roots (see fig. 13.6), or for a list of all undefined variables (see fig. 13.7).

```
Formulas for variables involved with circular references:
Cash = IF(AND(Cash Unadjusted>Cash min, Cash Unadjusted<Cash max), Cash
     Unadjusted, IF(Cash Unadjusted<Cash min, Cash min, IF(PREVIOUS(Loans) +
     Cash max - Cash Unadjusted >=0, Cash max, Cash Unadjusted - PREVIOUS(Loans)
     ))) ; Beginning Cash
Cash Unadjusted=PREVIOUS(Cash)-CHANGE(Accounts Receivable)-CHANGE (Total
     Inventory)-CHANGE(Plant and Equipment)-CHANGE(Accounts Payable)+Net Income;
     Beginning Cash
Equity = PREVIOUS(Equity) + Net Income ; Beginning Equity
Income Before Taxes = Total Revenue - Total Cost - MONTHLY(Total Operating
     Expense)
Interest Expense = Loans * ((Interest Rate/100)/12)
Loans = IF(PREVIOUS(Loans) + Cash - Cash Unadjusted <0, 0, PREVIOUS(Loans) +
     Cash - Cash Unadjusted) ; Beginning Loans
Net Income = Income Before Taxes - Taxes
Taxes = IF(Month = 1, YTD Taxes, YTD Taxes - PREVIOUS(YTD Taxes))
Total Operating Expense = Marketing Expense + QUARTERLY(Distribution Expense) +
     Salary Expense + QUARTERLY(Interest Expense)
YTD IBT = YTD(Income Before Taxes)
YTD Taxes = ◀ Taxes Lookup Table ▶ YTD IBT
```
```
newyork.mdl                          69K                              CALC READY
```

Fig. 13.5. Formulas for variables with circular references.

```
Formulas for all variables that affect Cash:
Cash = IF(AND(Cash Unadjusted>Cash min, Cash Unadjusted<Cash max), Cash
Unadjusted, IF(Cash Unadjusted<Cash min, Cash min, IF(PREVIOUS(Loans) + Cash
max - Cash Unadjusted >=0, Cash max, Cash Unadjusted - PREVIOUS(Loans)))) ;
Beginning Cash
• Cash Unadjusted=PREVIOUS(Cash)-CHANGE(Accounts Receivable)-CHANGE (Total
     Inventory)-CHANGE(Plant and Equipment)-CHANGE(Accounts Payable)+Net Income;
     Beginning Cash
• • Cash = ◀ CIRCULAR DEFINITION ▶
• • Accounts Receivable = Accounts Receivable from Revenue ; Beginning Accounts
     Receivable
• • • Accounts Receivable from Revenue = ◀ Accounts Receivable Time Delay ▶
     Total Revenue
• • • • Total Revenue = Blender Revenue + Disposal Revenue + Compactor Revenue
• • • • • Blender Revenue = Blender Price * Blender Units
• • • • • • Blender Price = 17
• • • • • • Blender Units = ◀ Monthly data: January 1986 - December 1986 ▶
• • • • • Disposal Revenue = Disposal Price * Disposal Units
• • • • • • Disposal Price = 45
• • • • • • Disposal Units = ◀ Monthly data: January 1986 - December 1986 ▶
• • • • • Compactor Revenue = Compactor Price * Compactor Units
• • • • • • Compactor Price = 175
```
```
newyork.mdl *                        69K                                  READY
```

Fig. 13.6. Formulas for all variables that affect *Cash*.

```
Undefined variables:
Total Cost Per Unit = ◀ UNDEFINED ▶
```
```
newyork.mdl *                        69K                                  READY
```

Fig. 13.7. All undefined variables.

As figure 13.5 indicates, there are a number of circular references in formulas in the model. Javelin handles circular formulas like ***Cash***, ***Interest Expense***, or ***Loans*** through multiple recalculation. You need, therefore, to recalculate such a model a number of times until values converge.

Using Javelin Functions

For the analysts in the New York division, planning and analysis are much easier with Javelin functions than with conventional spreadsheet software. For example, when the New York office wants to estimate 1987 sales based on the trend of 1986 sales, Javelin's TREND function gives the estimate (see fig. 13.8). The table of estimated blender sales results from this formula:

Predicted Blender Sales = TREND(Blender Units,Jan 1987,Dec 1987)

In the formula, the TREND function estimates 1987 sales based on the series ***Blender Units***. Notice also in figure 13.8 that combining a TABLE view of ***Predicted Blender Sales*** with a TABLE view of ***Blender Units*** gives a numeric comparison of actual and estimated values. Combining CHART views of the same two variables provides a graphic comparison (see fig. 13.9). Other special functions, such as PCT and CHANGE, help the New York office analysts easily calculate percent and the amount of change in product costs from one month to the next (see figs. 13.10 and 13.11). By combining the TABLE and CHART views of the same variables, you can see both values and graphs of the changes in product cost.

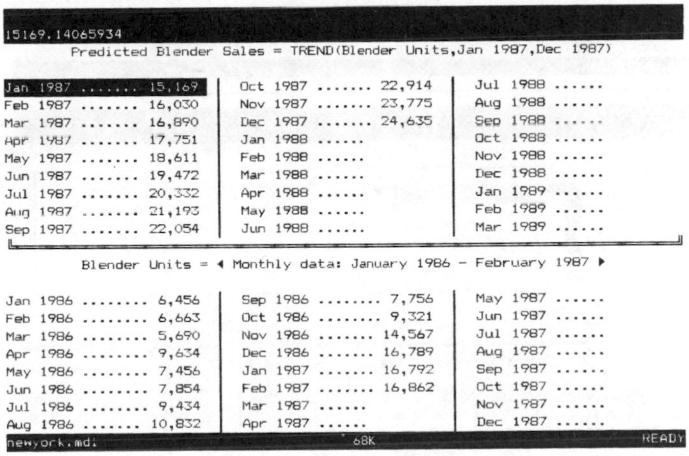
15169.14065934

Predicted Blender Sales = TREND(Blender Units,Jan 1987,Dec 1987)

Jan 1987 15,169	Oct 1987 22,914	Jul 1988 ......
Feb 1987 16,030	Nov 1987 23,775	Aug 1988 ......
Mar 1987 16,890	Dec 1987 24,635	Sep 1988 ......
Apr 1987 17,751	Jan 1988	Oct 1988 ......
May 1987 18,611	Feb 1988	Nov 1988 ......
Jun 1987 19,472	Mar 1988	Dec 1988 ......
Jul 1987 20,332	Apr 1988	Jan 1989 ......
Aug 1987 21,193	May 1988	Feb 1989 ......
Sep 1987 22,054	Jun 1988	Mar 1989 ......

Blender Units = ◀ Monthly data: January 1986 - February 1987 ▶

Jan 1986 6,456	Sep 1986 7,756	May 1987 ......
Feb 1986 6,663	Oct 1986 9,321	Jun 1987 ......
Mar 1986 5,690	Nov 1986 14,567	Jul 1987 ......
Apr 1986 9,634	Dec 1986 16,789	Aug 1987 ......
May 1986 7,456	Jan 1987 16,792	Sep 1987 ......
Jun 1986 7,854	Feb 1987 16,862	Oct 1987 ......
Jul 1986 9,434	Mar 1987	Nov 1987 ......
Aug 1986 10,832	Apr 1987	Dec 1987 ......

newyork.mdl 68K READY

Fig. 13.8. Using the TREND function to estimate 1987 sales.

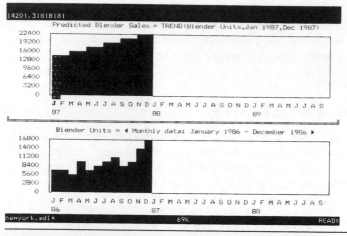

Fig. 13.9. Combining CHART views to compare two variables.

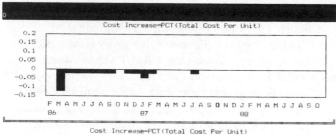

Feb 1986 .... (0.00)	Oct 1986 .... 0.00	Jun 1987 .... 0.01
Mar 1986 .... (0.13)	Nov 1986 .... (0.01)	Jul 1987 .... (0.01)
Apr 1986 .... (0.02)	Dec 1986 .... (0.03)	Aug 1987 .... 0.00
May 1986 .... (0.01)	Jan 1987 .... (0.05)	Sep 1987 .... 0.00
Jun 1986 .... (0.03)	Feb 1987 .... (0.01)	Oct 1987 .... 0.00
Jul 1986 .... (0.03)	Mar 1987 .... 0.00	Nov 1987 ......
Aug 1986 .... (0.02)	Apr 1987 .... 0.00	Dec 1987 ......
Sep 1986 .... (0.03)	May 1987 .... 0.00	Jan 1988 ......

Fig. 13.10. Using the PCT function to calculate percent change in product costs.

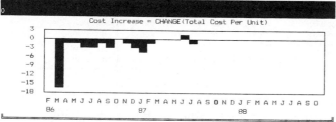

Feb 1986 .... (0.10)	Oct 1986 .... (0.21)	Jun 1987 .... 0.75
Mar 1986 .... (16.38)	Nov 1986 .... (1.28)	Jul 1987 .... (1.25)
Apr 1986 .... (1.73)	Dec 1986 .... (2.34)	Aug 1987 .... 0.00
May 1986 .... (1.53)	Jan 1987 .... (4.10)	Sep 1987 .... 0.00
Jun 1986 .... (3.29)	Feb 1987 .... (1.25)	Oct 1987 .... 0.00
Jul 1986 .... (3.10)	Mar 1987 .... 0.00	Nov 1987 ......
Aug 1986 .... (1.49)	Apr 1987 .... 0.00	Dec 1987 ......
Sep 1986 .... (2.59)	May 1987 .... 0.00	Jan 1988 ......

Fig. 13.11. Using the CHANGE function to calculate the amount of change in product costs.

Figure 13.10, for example, suggests that except for March, 1986, and January, 1987, the percent change in total costs has not fluctuated much. The actual dollar differences in the change of costs from one month to the next, as displayed in figure 13.11, however, shows the fluctuation in costs more clearly.

Entering, Analyzing, and Reporting Data with Javelin

Each division is responsible for maintaining its own Javelin files for reporting revenue from the three products manufactured by Future Home Appliances. Through the TABLE view, for example, the New York sales department has a tool for entering the number of blenders, compactors, and disposals sold each month. The WORKSHEET view provides the same department with numerous options for displaying and reporting revenue data. In figure 13.12, for instance, blender, disposal, and compactor revenues are displayed by month. This worksheet was created by entering variable names in the left border and dates in the top border. Data was then automatically displayed from Javelin's Information Base.

	NY Total Revenue				
	Feb 1986	Mar 1986	Apr 1986	May 1986	Jun 1986
Blender					
Units	6,663	5,690	9,634	7,456	7,854
Price	17.00	17.00	17.00	17.00	17.00
Revenue	$113,271.00	$96,730.00	$163,778.00	$126,752.00	$133,518.00
Disposal					
Units	3,430	3,495	4,256	4,926	5,326
Price	45.00	45.00	45.00	45.00	45.00
Revenue	$154,350.00	$157,275.00	$191,520.00	$221,670.00	$239,670.00
Compactor					
Units	2,267	2,765	2,554	3,012	3,702
Price	175.00	175.00	175.00	175.00	175.00
Revenue	$396,725.00	$483,875.00	$446,950.00	$527,100.00	$647,850.00
Total Revenu	$664,346.00	$737,880.00	$802,248.00	$875,522.00	$1,021,038.00

newyork.mdl*   68K   READY

Fig. 13.12. Monthly NY revenues for blenders, disposals, and compactors.

Figure 13.13 shows the flexibility of reporting data through Javelin's WORKSHEET view. Variable names are placed in the top border, and dates are placed in the left border. Notice also that the top border in figure 13.13 contains two rows of headings: *Revenue* extends across the top row; and *Blender*, *Disposal*, *Compactor*, and *Total* are each entered in a column in the second row. Combining each of these headings with *Revenue* provides the exact variable names originally entered in Javelin's Information Base: *Blender Revenue*, *Disposal Revenue*, *Compactor Revenue*, and *Total Revenue*.

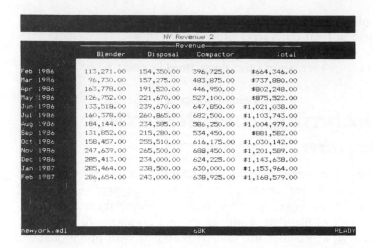

| | | NY Revenue 2 | | |
| | | —Revenue— | | |
	Blender	Disposal	Compactor	Total
Feb 1986	113,271.00	154,350.00	396,725.00	$664,346.00
Mar 1986	96,730.00	157,275.00	483,875.00	$737,880.00
Apr 1986	163,778.00	191,520.00	446,950.00	$802,248.00
May 1986	126,752.00	221,670.00	527,100.00	$875,522.00
Jun 1986	133,518.00	239,670.00	647,850.00	$1,021,038.00
Jul 1986	160,378.00	260,865.00	682,500.00	$1,103,743.00
Aug 1986	184,144.00	234,585.00	586,250.00	$1,004,979.00
Sep 1986	131,852.00	215,280.00	534,450.00	$881,582.00
Oct 1986	158,457.00	255,510.00	616,175.00	$1,030,142.00
Nov 1986	247,639.00	265,500.00	688,450.00	$1,201,589.00
Dec 1986	285,413.00	234,000.00	624,225.00	$1,143,638.00
Jan 1987	285,464.00	238,500.00	630,000.00	$1,153,964.00
Feb 1987	286,654.00	243,000.00	638,925.00	$1,168,579.00

newyork.mdl   68K   READY

Fig. 13.13. Using the WORKSHEET view to report revenue data.

Fig. 13.13. Using the WORKSHEET view to report revenue data.

The expanded top border in the worksheet in figure 13.13 is created by moving the cursor to the top border and selecting the /*Worksheet **B**order Expand command. After the border is expanded to two rows, *Blender*, *Disposal*, *Compactor*, and *Total* can be entered into the bottom row. Finally, to produce the *Revenue* heading, enter *Revenue* in the column above *Blender*, move the cursor to the column above Total, and press Enter.

The New York office uses Javelin's WORKSHEET view also to display different reports on the same worksheet. Figure 13.14, for instance, uses the /*Worksheet **B**order Insert command to create a second set of worksheet borders. With this set, New York managers can display product cost along with product revenue.

| | | NY Revenue 3 | | |
| | | —Mar 1986— | | |
	Blender	Disposal	Compactor	Total
Units	5,690	3495	2765	11950
Price	17	45	175	
Revenue	96,730	157,275	483,875	$737,880
		—Mar 1986—		
	Blender	Disposal	Compactor	Total
Units	5,690	3495	2765	11950
Unit Cost	14.72	24.07	68.28	
Cost	83,757	84,125	188,794	356,676

newyork.mdl   68K   READY

Fig. 13.14. Using the /*Worksheet Border Insert command to create a second set of worksheet borders.

The chief controller of the New York office uses the WORKSHEET view to prepare a report on that division's operating expenses (see fig. 13.15). This worksheet illustrates more WORKSHEET view capabilities. The variable names in the left border were entered with the /*Worksheet Border Variable Names command. The user simply enters *Expense* and selects the command; Javelin then lists all variable names containing *Expense*. Notice also that figure 13.15 shows both months and quarters.

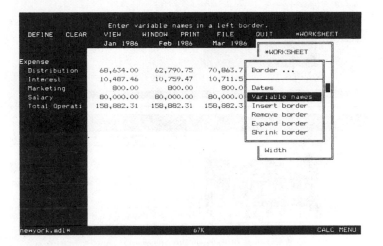

Fig. 13.15. Using the /*Worksheet Border Variable Names command to enter variable names.

Although various departments in the New York office rely on Javelin's WORKSHEET view, the sales and marketing departments depend also on other views and analyze sales data by combining views. Showing a CHART view of *Total Cost* in the top window and a CHART view of *Total Revenue* in the bottom window gives management a quick comparison of the two variables over time (see fig. 13.16). And when managers ask to see numbers instead of only a graph of sales, synchronizing the CHART and TABLE views provides the necessary information (see fig. 13.17). The controller in the New York office finds using the full-screen QUICK GRAPH view particularly effective for responding to "what if" questions in presentations at management meetings. A single screen display of the QUICK GRAPH view of *Net Income* for the New York office gives a clear picture of the office's continual success (see fig. 13.18).

Using Javelin Building Blocks

Future Home Appliances uses Javelin building blocks for many applications at divisional and corporate levels. The Time delay building block, for example, is

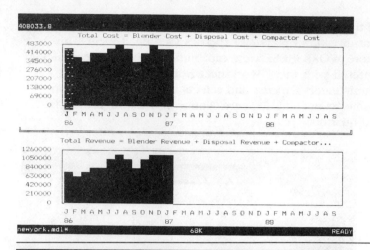

Fig. 13.16. Using two charts to compare two variables.

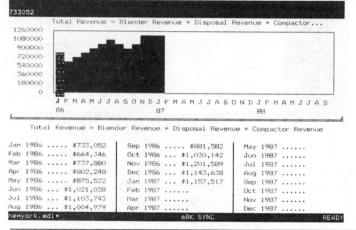

Total Revenue = Blender Revenue + Disposal Revenue + Compactor Revenue

Jan 1986 ..... $733,052	Sep 1986 ..... $881,582	May 1987 ......
Feb 1986 ..... $664,346	Oct 1986 ... $1,030,142	Jun 1987 ......
Mar 1986 ..... $737,880	Nov 1986 ... $1,201,589	Jul 1987 ......
Apr 1986 ..... $802,248	Dec 1986 ... $1,143,638	Aug 1987 ......
May 1986 ..... $875,522	Jan 1987 ... $1,157,517	Sep 1987 ......
Jun 1986 ... $1,021,038	Feb 1987	Oct 1987 ......
Jul 1986 ... $1,103,743	Mar 1987	Nov 1987 ......
Aug 1986 ... $1,004,979	Apr 1987	Dec 1987 ......

Fig. 13.17. Synchronizing the CHART and TABLE views.

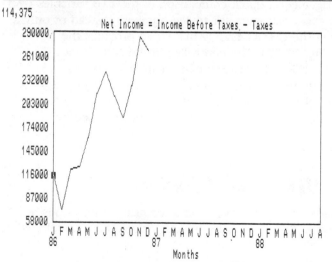

Fig. 13.18. A QUICK GRAPH view of *Net Income* for the New York office.

used to calculate *Accounts Receivable* for the New York and Los Angeles offices. Figure 13.19 displays the Time delay building block used by the New York office. This building block shows that 80 percent of current revenues are uncollected at the end of the first period, 30 percent are uncollected at the end of the second period, and 10 percent are uncollected after the third period.

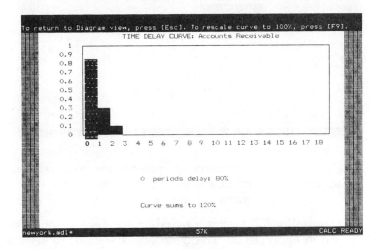

Fig. 13.19. Using the Time delay building block to calculate *Accounts Receivable.*

To create the Time delay building block, the New York office analyst entered the input variable, *Total Revenue*, and the output variable, *Accounts Receivable from Revenue*, and indicated the time period for time delay. In this application the time delay period is months. Notice that the sum of the time delay curve equals 120 percent. Cash flow from revenues must always equal 100 percent, but accounts receivable may be more or less than revenues from one period. This accounts receivable pattern shows that cash from current sales is received in the following pattern:

20 percent	Current month
50	1 month later
20	2 months later
10	3 months later

Another building block used in the Future Home Appliances model is the Lookup table building block shown in figure 13.20. This building block calculates taxes for the Income Statement. The model contains the following formula:

Taxes = IF(MONTH = 1, YTD Taxes, YTD Taxes - PREVIOUS(YTD Taxes)); YTD Taxes

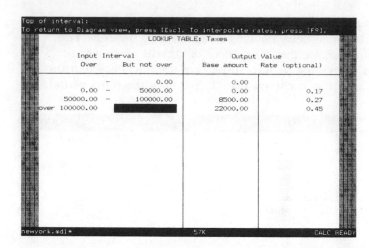

Fig. 13.20. Using the Lookup table building block to calculate base amounts.

The Lookup table calculates the year-to-date taxes, whereas the *Taxes* formula either adds the current month's taxes to the year-to-date or simply provides taxes for the first month of the period if such is the case.

The values for YTD taxes is based on the Lookup table building block for taxes shown in figure 13.20. This table was developed by selecting /**D**efine **B**uilding block **L**ookup table and entering input ranges and tax rates: 17% for amounts between 0 and 50,000; 27% for amounts between 50,000 and 100,000; and 45% for amounts over 100,000.

Consolidating with Javelin

The most important building block for Future Home Appliances is the Rollup building block. This building block imports variables and data from each division's files and consolidates them into a set of corporate variables. Using Javelin's /**D**efine **B**uilding block **R**ollup command, Abacus can easily choose from the two divisions the variables he wants to import and consolidate into corporate totals.

After completing the Rollup building block operation, Abacus uses the FORMULAS view to check whether all variables needed for the corporate model have been rolled up. Figure 13.21 shows the list of variables from the rollup of variables in the New York and Los Angeles models. Notice that variable names from the original New York and Los Angeles models are preceded by identifying labels. The original *Accounts Receivable* variable from the New York model is named *NY Accounts Receivable*, and the original *Accounts Receivable* variable from the Los Angeles model is named *LA Accounts Receivable*. The consolidated variable is identified as *Future Home Accounts Receivable*.

```
Formulas for all variables:

Future Home Accounts Payable = < Corp Rollup >
Future Home Accounts Receivable = < Corp Rollup >
Future Home Blender Cost = < Corp Rollup >
Future Home Blender Inventory = < Corp Rollup >
Future Home Blender Price = < Corp Rollup >
Future Home Blender Revenue = < Corp Rollup >
Future Home Blender Unit Cost = < Corp Rollup >
Future Home Blender Units = < Corp Rollup >
Future Home Cash = < Corp Rollup >
Future Home Compactor Cost = < Corp Rollup >
Future Home Compactor Inventory = < Corp Rollup >
Future Home Compactor Price = < Corp Rollup >
Future Home Compactor Revenue = < Corp Rollup >
Future Home Compactor Unit Cost = < Corp Rollup >
Future Home Cost Increase = < Corp Rollup >
Future Home Disposal Cost = < Corp Rollup >
Future Home Disposal Inventory = < Corp Rollup >
Future Home Disposal Price = < Corp Rollup >
Future Home Disposal Revenue = < Corp Rollup >
Future Home Disposal Unit Cost = < Corp Rollup >
Future Home Distribution Expense = < Corp Rollup >
Future Home Equity = < Corp Rollup >
Future Home Interest Expense = < Corp Rollup >
Future Home Interest Rate = < Corp Rollup >
Future Home Loans = < Corp Rollup >
Future Home Marketing Expense = < Corp Rollup >
Future Home Month = < Corp Rollup >
Future Home Net Income = < Corp Rollup >
Future Home Plant and Equipment = < Corp Rollup >
Future Home Salary Expense = < Corp Rollup >
Future Home Taxes = < Corp Rollup >
Future Home Total Assets = < Corp Rollup >
Future Home Total Cost = < Corp Rollup >
Future Home Total Inventory = < Corp Rollup >
Future Home Total Liability and Equity = < Corp Rollup >
Future Home Total Operating Expense = < Corp Rollup >
Future Home Total Revenue = < Corp Rollup >
Future Home Total Units = < Corp Rollup >
Future Home YTD IBT = < Corp Rollup >
Future Home YTD Taxes = < Corp Rollup >
LA Accounts Payable = < Corp Rollup >
LA Accounts Receivable = < Corp Rollup >
LA Blender Cost = < Corp Rollup >
LA Blender Inventory = < Corp Rollup >
LA Blender Price = < Corp Rollup >
LA Blender Revenue = < Corp Rollup >
LA Blender Unit Cost = < Corp Rollup >
LA Blender Units = < Corp Rollup >
LA Cash = < Corp Rollup >
LA Compactor Cost = < Corp Rollup >
LA Compactor Inventory = < Corp Rollup >
LA Compactor Price = < Corp Rollup >
LA Compactor Revenue = < Corp Rollup >
LA Compactor Unit Cost = < Corp Rollup >
LA Cost Increase = < Corp Rollup >
LA Disposal Cost = < Corp Rollup >
LA Disposal Inventory = < Corp Rollup >
LA Disposal Price = < Corp Rollup >
LA Disposal Revenue = < Corp Rollup >
LA Disposal Unit Cost = < Corp Rollup >
LA Distribution Expense = < Corp Rollup >
LA Equity = < Corp Rollup >
LA Interest Expense = < Corp Rollup >
LA Interest Rate = < Corp Rollup >
LA Loans = < Corp Rollup >
LA Marketing Expense = < Corp Rollup >
LA Month = < Corp Rollup >
LA Net Income = < Corp Rollup >
LA Plant and Equipment = < Corp Rollup >
LA Salary Expense = < Corp Rollup >
LA Taxes = < Corp Rollup >
LA Total Assets = < Corp Rollup >
LA Total Cost = < Corp Rollup >
LA Total Inventory = < Corp Rollup >
LA Total Liability and Equity = < Corp Rollup >
LA Total Operating Expense = < Corp Rollup >
LA Total Revenue = < Corp Rollup >
LA Total Units = < Corp Rollup >
LA YTD IBT = < Corp Rollup >
LA YTD Taxes = < Corp Rollup >
NY Accounts Payable = < Corp Rollup >
NY Accounts Receivable = < Corp Rollup >
NY Blender Cost = < Corp Rollup >
NY Blender Inventory = < Corp Rollup >
NY Blender Price = < Corp Rollup >
NY Blender Revenue = < Corp Rollup >
NY Blender Unit Cost = < Corp Rollup >
NY Blender Units = < Corp Rollup >
NY Cash = < Corp Rollup >
NY Compactor Cost = < Corp Rollup >
NY Compactor Inventory = < Corp Rollup >
NY Compactor Price = < Corp Rollup >
NY Compactor Revenue = < Corp Rollup >
NY Compactor Unit Cost = < Corp Rollup >
NY Cost Increase = < Corp Rollup >
NY Disposal Cost = < Corp Rollup >
NY Disposal Inventory = < Corp Rollup >
NY Disposal Price = < Corp Rollup >
NY Disposal Revenue = < Corp Rollup >
NY Disposal Unit Cost = < Corp Rollup >
NY Distribution Expense = < Corp Rollup >
NY Equity = < Corp Rollup >
NY Interest Expense = < Corp Rollup >
NY Interest Rate = < Corp Rollup >
NY Loans = < Corp Rollup >
NY Marketing Expense = < Corp Rollup >
NY Month = < Corp Rollup >
NY Net Income = < Corp Rollup >
NY Plant and Equipment = < Corp Rollup >
NY Salary Expense = < Corp Rollup >
NY Taxes = < Corp Rollup >
NY Total Assets = < Corp Rollup >
NY Total Cost = < Corp Rollup >
NY Total Inventory = < Corp Rollup >
NY Total Liability and Equity = < Corp Rollup >
NY Total Operating Expense = < Corp Rollup >
NY Total Revenue = < Corp Rollup >
NY Total Units = < Corp Rollup >
NY YTD IBT = < Corp Rollup >
NY YTD Taxes = < Corp Rollup >
```

Fig. 13.21. A list of all variables in the Rollup building block.

The process for creating the consolidated model consists of three steps. First, beginning in a new file, Abacus selects the /Define Building block Rollup command. When the Rollup building block appears (see fig. 13.22), Abacus selects Edit org chart (edit organizational chart) in order to define how the consolidated variables should be rolled up and which models should be consolidated. The organizational chart for the consolidated Income Statement and Balance Sheet for Future Home Appliances is shown in figure 13.23. The names entered in the top row of each box indicate how Javelin should distinguish between the variables from the original models and the variables consolidating the two models. In the second row of each box are the file names (shown in braces) of the original files.

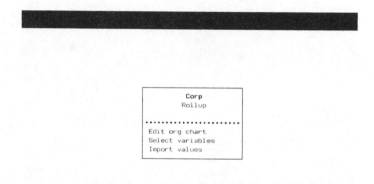

Fig. 13.22. The Rollup building block.

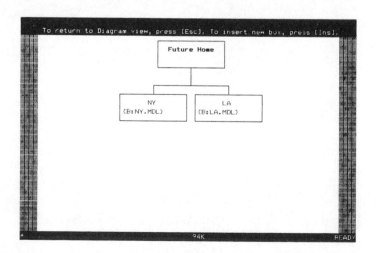

Fig. 13.23. The organizational chart for the consolidated reports.

Second, once the organizational chart has been created, Abacus selects the
variables to be imported and consolidated. The screen shown in figure 13.24 is
the input screen for variables to be consolidated. Because the original variable
names are the same in the models to be consolidated, Abacus uses the SPELL
key (Tab) to access a list of variable names from the New York model and then
enters the variable names he needs. When Abacus finishes selecting variable
names and presses the Esc key, Javelin displays a DIAGRAM view of all variable
names involved in the Rollup: variable names for the New York, Los Angeles,
and consolidated models (see fig. 13.25).

Fig. 13.24. The screen for
variables to be consolidated.

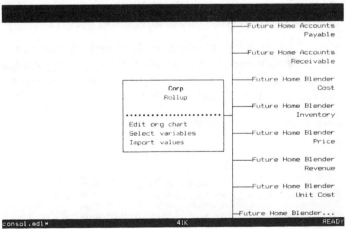

Fig. 13.25. Variable names for the
New York, Los Angeles, and
consolidated models.

After Abacus selects the variable names to be consolidated, his final step is to
import values. Selecting the Import values option from the Rollup building
block transfers and consolidates the specific variables from the input models.

Having completed the rollup, Abacus can now view variables, create worksheets, make graphs, and produce final reports.

Preparing Reports and Using Javelin Views for Presentation

From past experience, Abacus' boss, Busby T. Numbacrunch, knows that the company president, J. D. Pocketful, appreciates having summary reports and graphs depicting data he needs in order to make important decisions. But Numbacrunch knows also that Pocketful, an experienced business analyst, likes to analyze data in many ways and be assured of its soundness before making a decision. Numbacrunch therefore prepares printed reports and graphs and, with the help of a macro, develops an electronic presentation of Javelin views displaying information from the consolidated model.

First, the final printed reports displayed in figures 13.26 and 13.27 are produced by the following settings entered in Javelin's /Define Printer settings:

Page width	80
Page length	66
Left margin	4
Right margin	4
Top margin	3
Bottom margin	3
Setup string	\015
Header: Future Home Appliances, Inc. @DATE	

Second, along with the Balance Sheet and Income Statement reports, Numbacrunch creates and prints a bar graph reporting total product revenues (see fig. 13.28) and a pie graph reporting Future Home Appliances' Revenue, Operating Expense, and Costs for 1986 (see fig. 13.29). To create the bar

```
Future Home Appliances, Inc. 10 Apr 1986

                         --------------------1986--------------------
                              NY            LA        Future Home

    Assets:
Cash                     210,764.05    110,000.00      320,764.05
Accounts Receivable   12,862,096.70 12,011,244.70   24,873,341.40
Total Inventory          302,500.00    302,500.00      605,000.00
Plant and Equipment    9,600,000.00  9,600,000.00   19,200,000.00
------------          ------------- -------------   -------------
Total Assets          22,975,360.75 22,023,744.70   44,999,105.45

    Liability
Accounts Payable          24,000.00     24,000.00       48,000.00
Loans                  9,740,425.00 10,580,611.11   20,321,036.11
Equity                13,258,936.83 12,225,540.70   25,484,477.52
------------          ------------- -------------   -------------
Total Liability and Equity 23,023,361.83 22,830,151.81 45,853,513.64
```

Fig. 13.26. The final Balance Sheet for Future Home Appliances, Inc.

graph, Numbacrunch enters the settings indicated in figure 13.30. To create the pie graph, he enters the settings indicated in figure 13.31. Numbacrunch then uses the **/Print Graph** command to print the graphs.

Future Home Appliances, Inc. 10 Apr 1986

```
                       ------------------1 Q 1986------------------
                              NY            LA         Future Home

Revenue
  Blender               319,753.00    286,008.00       605,761.00
  Disposal              505,125.00    552,915.00     1,058,040.00
  Compactor           1,310,400.00  1,268,575.00     2,578,975.00
                      ------------  ------------     ------------
  Total               2,135,278.00  2,107,498.00     4,242,776.00

Cost
  Blender               282,499.30    252,396.46       534,895.76
  Compactor             588,360.00    570,001.08     1,158,361.08
  Disposal              267,712.15    293,020.73       560,732.88
                      ------------  ------------     ------------
  Total               1,138,571.45   1,115,418.27     2,253,989.72

Expense
  Distribution          202,288.50    207,105.75       409,394.25
  Interest               31,958.43     33,737.59        65,696.03
  Marketing               2,400.00      2,400.00         4,800.00
  Salary                240,000.00    240,000.00       480,000.00
                      ------------  ------------     ------------
  Total Operating       476,646.93    483,243.34       959,890.28

Income Before Taxes     520,059.62    508,836.39     1,028,896.00
Taxes                   211,026.83    205,976.37       417,003.20
                      ------------  ------------     ------------
Net Income              309,032.79    302,860.01       611,892.80
```

Fig. 13.27. The final Income Statement for Future Home Appliances, Inc.

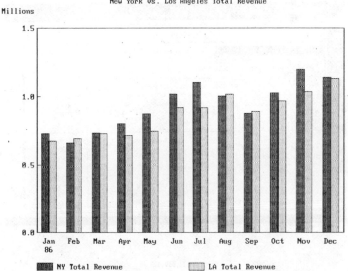

Fig. 13.28. Product revenues for the divisional offices.

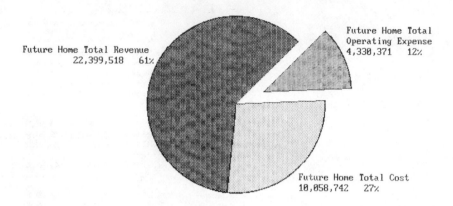

FUTURE HOME APPLIANCES, INC.
Income before Taxes

Future Home Total Revenue
22,399,518   61%

Future Home Total
Operating Expense
4,330,371   12%

Future Home Total Cost
10,058,742   27%

1986

Fig. 13.29. Future Home Appliances' 1986 revenue, operating expense, and costs.

```
 To save settings and leave settings sheet, press [Esc].

                         Graph Settings

     Name (Total Revenue)         Time Axis Limits          Graph
Reve                          Begin date ()                  Type
 Bl                           End date ()                  • Line
 Di        Left Axis                                       ▶ Bar
 Co  Max ()                         Labels                 • Stack bar
---  Min ()                   Title (FUTURE HOME APPLI...)  • % bar
 To                           Subtitle (New York vs. L...) • Horiz. bar
           Right Axis         X-axis ()                    • Pie
Cost Max ()                   Y-axis ()                    • XY plot
 Bl  Min ()
 Co        Variables                Legends                  Axis
 Di  (NY Total Revenue)       ()                           ■ Left
---  (LA Total Revenue)       ()                           ■ Left
 To  ()                       ()                           ■ Left
     ()                       ()                           ■ Left
Expe ()                       ()                           ■ Left
 Di  ()                       ()                           ■ Left
 In  ()                       ()                           ■ Left
 Ma
consol.mdl *              29K                       MENU
```

Fig. 13.30. Graph settings for creating the bar graph.

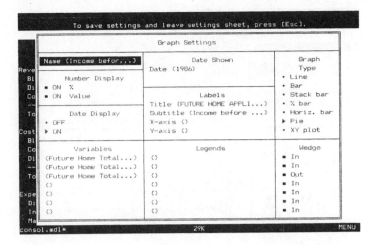

Fig. 13.31. Graph settings for
creating the pie graph.

It's not unusual for President Pocketful to query Numbacrunch about his data. Typically, the president may ask, "Are you sure all the data from all Future Home Appliances divisions has been consolidated? These corporate operating expenses for March are much lower than I expected. Surely you forgot to consolidate LA's expenses with New York's!" With Javelin, however, Numbacrunch can show Pocketful that the values are correct. Numbacrunch can instantly display the TABLE views showing the totals for each division, with the corporate totals displayed in the bottom window. Afterward, Pocketful is convinced that both operating expenses have been consolidated (see figs. 13.32 and 13.33).

Fig. 13.32. TABLE views showing New York and corporate expenses.

```
158848.1064758
        LA Operating Expense = MONTHLY(LA Total Operating Expense)

Jan 1986 ...... 158,848    Oct 1986 ...... 202,723    Jul 1987 ......
Feb 1986 ...... 158,848    Nov 1986 ...... 202,723    Aug 1987 ......
Mar 1986 ...... 158,848    Dec 1986 ...... 202,723    Sep 1987 ......
Apr 1986 ...... 174,930    Jan 1987 ......            Oct 1987 ......
May 1986 ...... 174,930    Feb 1987 ......            Nov 1987 ......
Jun 1986 ...... 174,930    Mar 1987 ......            Dec 1987 ......
Jul 1986 ...... 185,227    Apr 1987 ......            Jan 1988 ......
Aug 1986 ...... 185,227    May 1987 ......            Feb 1988 ......
Sep 1986 ...... 185,227    Jun 1987 ......            Mar 1988 ......

    Corporate Operating Expense = MONTHLY(Future Home Total Operating Expense)

Jan 1986 ...... 317,696    Sep 1986 ...... 370,455    May 1987 ......
Feb 1986 ...... 317,696    Oct 1986 ...... 405,447    Jun 1987 ......
Mar 1986 ...... 317,696    Nov 1986 ...... 405,447    Jul 1987 ......
Apr 1986 ...... 349,859    Dec 1986 ...... 405,447    Aug 1987 ......
May 1986 ...... 349,859    Jan 1987 ......            Sep 1987 ......
Jun 1986 ...... 349,859    Feb 1987 ......            Oct 1987 ......
Jul 1986 ...... 370,455    Mar 1987 ......            Nov 1987 ......
Aug 1986 ...... 370,455    Apr 1987 ......            Dec 1987 ......
consol.mdl*                      29K                          READY
```

Fig. 13.33. TABLE views showing Los Angeles and corporate expenses.

Using Javelin Macros

To make his job easier, Abacus has learned to use Javelin's macro capability for automating operations he frequently has to perform for Busby Numbacrunch. Abacus uses two particular macros for the corporate model. One macro is a simple macro automating the creation of a Rollup building block (see fig. 13.34). Notice in figure 13.34 that the macro contains two types of command lines: lines that direct Javelin to execute keystrokes for creating a Rollup building block, and lines that provide prompts directing users through each step of creating a Rollup building block.

```
Macro Build box:
@SLASH dbr
@PROMPT What is the name of this Rollup building block?
@READ @ENTER
@DOWN @ENTER
@PROMPT Create the organization chart here. Type F7 when ready to continue
@READ @ENTER
@PAUSE
@ESC @DOWN @DOWN @ENTER
@PROMPT Enter the variables you want to use here. Type F7 to continue.
@READ @ENTER
@PAUSE
@ESC @DOWN @DOWN @DOWN @ENTER
```

Fig. 13.34. A macro that automates the creation of a Rollup building block.

To create the macro, Abacus uses the MACRO view. After selecting /View Macro and naming the macro, he enters each macro line as shown in figure 13.34. All macro commands, cursor keys, and functions (items preceded by the @) are entered by using Javelin's SPELL key (Tab). To enter the first line, for example, Abacus types @S and presses the SPELL key (Tab). Javelin responds with the POSSIBILITIES menu (see fig. 13.35). After selecting @SLASH, Abacus types *dbr* and presses Enter to complete the first line of the macro. Abacus continues to create the macro by entering each line, using the SPELL key (Tab) when possible and also typing text. The last step is for Abacus to proofread the macro, making sure that he hasn't accidentally entered a wrong character. Better yet, he can step through the macro by using the Alt-F7 key combination (see Chapter 12 for information on editing a macro.)

Fig. 13.35. The POSSIBILITIES menu.

Having saved the file containing the new macro, Abacus can use it from any view by pressing the MACRO key (F7), entering the macro name, and pressing Enter.

Another timesaving macro is the graph macro shown in figure 13.36. With this macro, Abacus automates the process of creating graphs. The macro displays prompts asking the user to name the graph, enter variables, and change the graph type. To create a graph with this macro, Abacus presses the MACRO key (F7), enters the macro name—*Grapher*, and responds to each prompt. Abacus created the graph shown in figure 13.28 by entering *Future Home Division Revenues* as the name. He entered the variables *NY Total Revenue* and *LA Total Revenue*.

Because of the options provided, the macro for creating graphs is more complex than the one for creating a Rollup building block. Let's consider the operation of each line. The first line of the macro selects the /**Define Graph** command. Line 2 displays the prompt What is the name of this new graph?·After the user types the name, the macro then enters the name. The macro's third line moves the cursor to the *Variables* box in the Graph settings sheet, displays the POSSIBILITIES list, and waits for the user to choose a variable. The third line then moves the cursor to the *Legends* box for entering graph legends. The fourth line jumps the macro to line 7, which begins the process for entering labels (line 8). Line 9 gives the user the chance to enter another variable.

```
     Macro Grapher:

 1. @SLASH dg
 2. @PROMPT What is the name of this new graph? @READ @ENTER
 3. @PGDN @PGDN @PGDN @SPELL @READ @ENTER @RIGHT
 4. @JUMP prompter

 5. @LABEL y0
 6. @DOWN @LEFT @SPELL @READ @ENTER @RIGHT

 7. @LABEL prompter
 8. @PROMPT Please type a label for this variable. @READ @ENTER
 9. @SELECT Is there another variable to include in the graph?
10. @CHOICE y0 Yes
11. @CHOICE n0 No
12. @ENDSELECT

13. @LABEL n0
14. @SELECT Do you want to change the type of graph?
15. @CHOICE y1 Yes
16. @CHOICE n1 No
17. @ENDSELECT

18. @LABEL y1
19. @HOME @RIGHT @RIGHT
20. @PROMPT Please select the type of graph you want to see. @READ @ENTER
21. @LABEL n1
22. @F10
```

Fig. 13.36. The macro *Grapher* for automating the creation of graphs.

Lines 10 and 11 display the Yes and No prompts and send the macro to the appropriate macro line, depending on the user's choice. The @ENDSELECT command in line 12 ends the menu choices of the previous two lines. If the user answers Yes to the question Is there another variable to include in the graph?, the macro moves back to line 5. The @label y0 command in line 5 indicates where the macro continues based on the y0 label after @CHOICE in line 10. When the user selects No, the macro moves to line 13. Line 14 asks whether the user wants to change the type of graph. Lines 15 and 16 present the Yes/No menu. The macro continues at line 18 if the choice is Yes and continues at line 20 if the choice is No. Line 19 moves the cursor for changing the graph type, and line 21 displays the prompt asking the user to move the cursor to change the graph type. Finally, line 22 displays the graph.

Conclusion

The comprehensive model described in this chapter illustrates the powerful capabilities of Javelin for serving the complete business analysis needs of one company. This model shows that Javelin provides all the capabilities needed for model building, analysis, and presentation throughout all divisions of a company. Javelin is also powerful enough to serve the needs of many departments.

With one original model, importing information between departments and corporate offices is easy. Variables from the single model can be imported to other models and used by different departments. Each department can then use Javelin to enter data, analyze it, and report the results. Data entered at department levels can be imported to a final corporate consolidated model.

The application described in this chapter is only one example of the power of Javelin. Its capabilities go much further than those described here. You'll discover these capabilities when you begin to apply Javelin to the model-building, analysis, and reporting needs of your company.

As you continue learning, depend on Que publications to help you get the most from your software and computer. From beginning tutorial help to intermediate tips to advanced applications, the Que publications listed in the back of this book give you the support you need to make your software, computer, and time investment pay off!

## Part VII

Javelin Reference Guide

A

Javelin Function Summary

Javelin offers most of the functions found in spreadsheet packages, plus others that are unique to Javelin. These functions should not be confused with commands. Commands are used to get Javelin to produce reports, print graphs and worksheets, change views, define models, printers, building blocks, and so on. Functions are the mathematical and financial "verbs" that act upon the data in the model to produce results.

To understand how functions work with Javelin, you need to know how the program handles time and interprets variables. There are two types of variables in Javelin: constant and time-series. A constant variable is a variable that you have defined as having one and only one value for the entire time span of your model. An example is the interest rate for a fixed-rate loan. You can change the value at any time, but Javelin will still interpret the constant as a single value in the model. Javelin will not alter the value of the constant throughout time unless you elect to change the value yourself.

The other type of variable is a time-series variable, one that has a specified periodicity and can have a distinct value in each period within the time span of the model. A good example of a time-series variable is the interest rate for a variable rate mortgage. There are formulas that determine when the mortgage rate changes and the rate at which the changes can take place. The variable's value is tied to some formula or data that allows the variable to have different values over time.

Some functions only work with time-series variables, whereas others only work with constants. This appendix notes which functions use constants, time-series variables, or both. For a complete discussion of Javelin variables, see Chapter 3, "Using the DIAGRAM, FORMULAS, TABLE, and NOTES Views."

To hasten the process of finding the right function for your purpose, this appendix

- names the function using the same name that is used in Javelin
- gives a description of the function, using the same terms you might use, and shows the use of the function in an example
- shows the function's syntax
- shows the type of variable, constant or time-series, that the function takes

To help you locate the function you want, this appendix is divided into ten categories of functions:

1. Arithmetic
2. Time
3. Calendar
4. Period Conversion
5. Logical
6. Statistical
7. Prediction
8. Mathematical
9. Financial
10. Extra

Arithmetic Functions

These are the functions that most people are familiar with, whether or not they have used financial and business modeling software. They include SUM, AVG, MAX, and MIN.

[SUM]

USE: The SUM function is used to add the values of several different variables in each time period. For instance, if you wanted to add the values of variables *Blender Units, Compactor Units* and *Disposal Units* for each time period, you would use the SUM function as follows:

Z = SUM(Blender Units, Compactor Units,
    Disposal Units)

The time-series variable Z is defined for each time period as the sum of the values of *Blender Units*, *Compactor Units*, and *Disposal Units* in that period.

SYNTAX: Result = SUM(argument 1, argument 2, argument 2,
                argument 3, . . .argument n)

There can be as many arguments to the SUM function as you wish.

Do not confuse the SUM function with the /*Worksheet **Range Sum** command. That command is linked to the WORKSHEET view and produces a summation only as long as the worksheet is kept in the model. Deleting the worksheet also deletes the summation. The SUM function produces a result that can only be deleted by using the /Clear **Variable** command.

CONDITION: The arguments can be all time-series variables or a mixture of time-series variables and constants, in which case the result is a time series; or the arguments can be all constants, in which case the result is a constant.

[AVG]

USE: The AVG function is used to determine the mean or average value of a group of variables. If you wanted to find the average value of variables *Blender Units*, *Compactor Units*, and *Disposal Units* for each time period, you would use the AVG function as follows:

Z = AVG(Blender Units, Compactor Units, Disposal Units)

The time-series variable Z is defined for each time period as the average of the values of *Blender Units*, *Compactor Units*, and *Disposal Units* in that period.

SYNTAX: Result = AVG(argument 1, argument 2, argument 3,
              . . . argument n)

There can be as many arguments to the AVG function as you wish. Do not confuse the AVG function with the /*Worksheet **Range Average** command. That command is linked to the WORKSHEET view and produces an average only as long as the worksheet is kept in the model. Deleting the worksheet also deletes the average. The AVG function produces a result that can only be deleted by using the /Clear **Variable** command.

CONDITION: The arguments can be all time-series variables or a mixture of time-series variables and constants, in which case the result is a time series; or the arguments can be all constants, in which case the result is a constant.

[MAX]

USE: The MAX function is used to find the highest, greatest, or maximum value in a series of variables. Assume you have three variables, *Blender Units*, *Compactor Units*, and *Disposal Units*, and want to find which of the three variables had the greatest value in each time period. The MAX function would be used as follows:

Z = MAX(Blender Units, Compactor Units, Disposal Units)

The time-series variable Z is defined for each period as the maximum of the values of *Blender Units*, *Compactor Units*, and *Disposal Units* in that period.

SYNTAX: Result = MAX(argument 1, argument 2, argument 3,
. . . argument n)

There can be as many arguments to the MAX function as you wish. Do not confuse the MAX function with the /*Worksheet **Range High**/Max command. That command is linked to the WORKSHEET view and produces a maximum value only as long as the worksheet is kept in the model. Deleting the worksheet also deletes the maximum value. The MAX function produces a result that can only be deleted by using the /Clear Variable command.

CONDITION: The arguments can be all time-series variables or a mixture of time-series variables and constants, in which case the result is a time series; or the arguments can be all constants, in which case the result is a constant.

[MIN]

USE: The MIN function is used to find the lowest, least, or minimum value in a series of variables. Assume you have three variables, *Blender Units*, *Compactor Units*, and *Disposal Units*, and want to find which of the three variables had the lowest value in September, 1986. The MIN function would be used as follows:

Z = MIN(Blender Units, Compactor Units, Disposal Units)

The time-series variable Z is defined for each period as the minimum of the values of *Blender Units*, *Compactor Units*, and *Disposal Units* in that period.

SYNTAX: Result = MIN(argument 1, argument 2, argument
3, . . . argument n)

There can be as many arguments to the MIN function as you wish. Do not confuse the MIN function with the /*Worksheet **Range Low**/Min command. That command is linked to the WORKSHEET view and produces a minimum value only as long as the worksheet is kept in the model. Deleting the worksheet also deletes the minimum value. The MIN function produces a result that can only be deleted by using the /Clear Variable command.

CONDITION: The arguments can be all time-series variables or a mixture of time-series variables and constants, in which case the result is a time series; or the arguments can be all constants, in which case the result is a constant.

Rolling Arithmetic Functions

These functions are very similar to the arithmetic functions. The major difference is that their values accumulate over time, with the smallest value being at the beginning of the time series and the largest values being at the end of the time series (see fig. A.1).

Fig. A.1. *Salaries* is a constant variable, with a value throughout the time span of the model of $118,000. *Cost of Goods* is a time-series variable with a changing value throughout the time span of the model.

```
Salaries CUM: CUM(Salaries)
                      Rolling Arithmetic Functions
                 Jan 1986    Feb 1986    Mar 1986    Apr 1986    May 1986

Salaries         $118,000    $118,000    $118,000    $118,000    $118,000
Cost of Goods     $48,000     $52,000     $49,567     $51,325     $49,700


Salaries
   CUM           $118,000    $236,000    $354,000    $472,000    $590,000
   RSUM          $118,000    $236,000    $354,000    $472,000    $590,000
   RAVG          $118,000    $118,000    $118,000    $118,000    $118,000
   RMAX          $118,000    $118,000    $118,000    $118,000    $118,000
   RMIN          $118,000    $118,000    $118,000    $118,000    $118,000

Cost of Goods
   CUM            $48,000    $100,000    $149,567    $200,892    $250,592
   RAVG           $48,000     $50,000     $49,856     $50,223     $50,118
   RMAX           $48,000     $52,000     $52,000     $52,000     $52,000
   RMIN           $48,000     $48,000     $48,000     $48,000     $48,000
   RSUM           $48,000    $100,000    $149,567    $200,892    $250,592

                                         90K                        READY
```

[CUM]

USE: The CUM function is used to determine the total value of a time-series variable in all periods from the earliest time period for the variable to the current time period. It is equivalent to taking the SUM of a single variable for all dates the variable is active. For instance, if the variable *Blender Cost* has values for January through December of 1986, you can find the sum of *Blender Cost* for that entire period with either of the following equations:

```
Total
Blender
Costs    = SUM(Blender Costs @ Jan 86,
              Blender Costs @ Feb 86, Blender
              Costs @ Mar 86, Blender Costs @
              Apr 86, Blender Costs @ May 86,
              Blender Costs @ Jun 86, Blender
              Costs @ Jul 86, Blender Costs @
              Aug 86, Blender Costs @ Sept 86,
              Blender Costs @ Oct 86, Blender
              Costs @ Nov 86, Blender Costs @
              Dec 86)
```

Total Blender Costs = CUM(Blender Costs)

When the CUM function is used, *Total Blender Costs* is defined in each period to be the sum of blender costs from January, 1986, to the current period. *Total Blender Cost* for February, 1986, is the sum of *Blender Costs* for January, 1986, plus *Blender Costs* for February, 1986. *Total Blender Costs* for December, 1986, is the sum of blender costs in each month from January, 1986, through December, 1986.

SYNTAX: Result = CUM(argument)

CONDITION: The CUM function is best used with a time-series argument, but you are not limited to that variable type. Using a constant variable as the CUM argument merely returns the constant value.

[RSUM]

USE: The RSUM function is used to determine the SUM of a variable over a specified number of periods back from the current period of the function.

Rolling Cost of Goods = RSUM(Cost of Goods, 5)

This formula returns the summation of the last five periods that *Cost of Goods* is defined for. For example, in January, 1986, *Rolling Cost of Goods* is equal to the sum of the monthly values of *Cost of Goods* from September, 1985, through January, 1986.

SYNTAX: Result = RSUM(time-series variable, [number of
                       previous periods to sum over])

Note that the last argument to RSUM, number of previous periods to sum over, is an optional argument. Not using the "number of periods to sum over" argument causes the RSUM function to behave like the CUM function.

CONDITION: The RSUM function uses only time-series variables. Using constant variables will cause an error condition, such as NA. This is not an error that will hinder your model from producing correct results; it is merely Javelin's indication that data is not available for this function.

[RAVG]

USE: The RAVG function is used to determine the AVG of a variable, but for a specified number of periods back from the current period of the function.

   Rolling Avg Cost of Goods = RAVG(Cost of Goods, 5)

This formula returns the average value of the last five periods that *Cost of Goods* is defined for. For example, in January, 1986, *Rolling Avg Cost of Goods* is the average of *Cost of Goods* in September, 1985, October, 1985, November, 1985, December, 1985, and January, 1986.

SYNTAX: Result = RAVG(time-series variable, [number of previous periods to average over])

Note that the last argument to RAVG, number of periods to average over, is an optional argument. If the number of periods is left off, RAVG returns the average of all values of the argument variable in the current period and all previous periods.

CONDITION: The RAVG function uses only time-series variables. Using constant variables will cause an error condition, such as NA. This is not an error that will hinder your model from producing correct results, it is merely Javelin's indication that data is not available for this function.

[RMAX]

USE: The RMAX function is used to determine the maximum value of a variable over a specified number of periods back from the current period of the function.

   Rolling Max Cost of Goods = RMAX(Cost of Goods, 5)

This formula returns the highest/greatest/maximum value of the last five periods that *Cost of Goods* is defined for. For example, in January, 1986, *Rolling Max Cost of Goods* is the maximum value of *Cost of Goods* for September, 1985, October, 1985, November, 1985, December, 1985, and January 1986.

SYNTAX: Result = RMAX(time-series variable, [number of
                         previous periods to find a maximum over])

Note that the last argument to RMAX, number of periods to determine the
maximum for, is an optional argument. If this argument is left off, RMAX finds
the maximum value over the current period and all previous periods of the
variable.

CONDITION: The RMAX function uses only time-series variables. Using
constant variables will cause an error condition, such as NA. This is not an error
that will hinder your model from producing correct results, it is merely Javelin's
indication that data is not available for this function.

[RMIN]

USE: The RMIN function is used to determine the minimum value of a variable,
but for a specified number of periods back from the current period of the
function.

> Rolling Min Cost of Goods = RMIN(Cost of Goods, 5)

This formula returns the least/lowest/minimum value of the last five periods
that *Cost of Goods* is defined for. For example, in January, 1986, Rolling Min
Cost of Goods is the minimum value of *Cost of Goods* for September, 1985,
October, 1985, November, 1985, December, 1985, and January, 1986.

SYNTAX: Result = RMIN(time-series variable, [number of
                         previous periods to find a minimum over])

Note that the last argument to RMIN, number of periods to determine the
minimum for, is an optional argument. If this argument is left off, RMIN finds
the minimum value over the current period and all previous periods of the
variable.

CONDITION: The RMIN function uses only time-series variables. Using
constant variables will cause an error condition, such as NA. This is not an error
that will hinder your model from producing correct results, it is merely Javelin's
indication that data is not available for this function.

Time-Series Arithmetic Functions

The time-series arithmetic functions are similar to the rolling arithmetic
functions in one way: they can use only time-series variables (the exception in
the rolling arithmetic functions is the CUM function).

Unlike the rolling arithmetic functions, they do not allow for a second argument. They only allow one argument, and that argument must be a time-series variable. The result of a time-series arithmetic function is a constant. Notice, for example, in figure A.2 that each of the time-series functions remains constant over the period from January to May, 1986.

Fig. A.2. *Salaries* is a constant variable, with a value throughout the time span of the model of $118,000. *Cost of Goods* is a time-series variable with a changing value throughout the time span of the model.

Salaries TSUM: TSUM(Salaries)					
Time Series Arithmetic Functions					
	Jan 1986	Feb 1986	Mar 1986	Apr 1986	May 1986
Salaries	$118,000	$118,000	$118,000	$118,000	$118,000
Cost of Goods	$48,000	$52,000	$49,567	$51,325	$49,700
Salaries					
TSUM	$590,000	$590,000	$590,000	$590,000	$590,000
TAVG	$118,000	$118,000	$118,000	$118,000	$118,000
TMAX	$118,000	$118,000	$118,000	$118,000	$118,000
TMIN	$118,000	$118,000	$118,000	$118,000	$118,000
COUNT	5	5	5	5	5
Cost of Goods					
TSUM	$250,592	$250,592	$250,592	$250,592	$250,592
TAVG	$50,118	$50,118	$50,118	$50,118	$50,118
TMAX	$52,000	$52,000	$52,000	$52,000	$52,000
TMIN	$48,000	$48,000	$48,000	$48,000	$48,000
COUNT	5	5	5	5	5
			90K		READY

[TSUM]

USE: The TSUM function is used to determine the sum of a variable over the entire time span that variable is active. The TSUM of a variable is a constant value, the sum of the variable for the entire time span.

TSUM Cost of Goods = TSUM(Cost of Goods)

This formula will return the sum over time of the *Cost of Goods* variable.

SYNTAX: Result = TSUM(time-series variable)

CONDITION: The TSUM function uses only time-series variables. Using constant variables causes an error condition, such as #UNDEF. This error prevents your model from producing correct results. Javelin is telling you that the function is undefined for this type of variable.

[TAVG]

USE: The TAVG function is used to determine the average of a variable over the entire time span that variable is active. The TAVG of a monthly variable in January, 1986, and December, 1986, is the same value, the average of the variable for the entire time span.

TAVG Cost of Goods = TAVG(Cost of Goods)

This formula returns the average over time of the *Cost of Goods* variable.

SYNTAX: Result TAVG(time-series variable)

CONDITION: The TAVG function uses only time-series variables. Using constant variables causes an error condition, such as #UNDEF. This is an error that prevents your model from producing correct results. Javelin is telling you that the function is undefined for this type of variable.

[TMAX]

USE: The TMAX function is used to determine the highest/greatest/maximum value of a variable over the entire time span that variable is active. The TMAX of a variable is a constant value, the highest/greatest/maximum value of the variable for the entire time span.

   TMAX Cost of Goods = TMAX(Cost of Goods)

This formula returns the highest/greatest/maximum value over time of the *Cost of Goods* variable.

SYNTAX: Result = TMAX(time-series variable)

CONDITION: The TMAX function uses only time-series variables. Using constant variables causes an error condition, such as #UNDEF. This is an error that prevents your model from producing correct results. Javelin is telling you that the function is undefined for this type of variable.

[TMIN]

USE: The TMIN function is used to determine the lowest/least/minimum value of a variable over the entire time span that variable is active. The TMIN of a variable is a constant value, the lowest/least/minimum value of the variable for the entire time span.

   TMIN Cost of Goods = TMIN(Cost of Goods)

This formula returns the lowest/least/minimum value over time of the *Cost of Goods* variable.

SYNTAX: Result = TMIN(time-series variable)

CONDITION: The TMIN function uses only time-series variables. Using constant variables causes an error condition, such as #UNDEF. This error prevents your model from producing correct results. Javelin is telling you that the function is undefined for this type of variable.

[COUNT]

USE: The COUNT function is used to determine the number of periods during the time span of a variable in which a variable has data. The COUNT of a variable is a constant value, the number of periods in which the variable has valid data.

    COUNT Cost of Goods = COUNT(Cost of Goods)

This formula returns the number of periods that *Cost of Goods* has data. It will not count NA as data, but will count 0 as data.

SYNTAX: Result = COUNT(time-series variable)

CONDITION: The COUNT function uses only time-series variables. Using constant variables causes an error condition, such as #UNDEF. This is an error that prevents your model from producing correct results. Javelin is telling you that the function is undefined for this type of variable.

Series-to-Date Functions

Javelin has three functions that allow you to sum over specific periods, much like the RSUM and TSUM functions. The difference with the series-to-date functions is in their period specificity. These functions are linked to particular time periods: month, quarter, and year.

An important aspect of the series-to-date functions has to do with how time-series variables are defined. Each variable's settings sheet includes a box labeled *Combine Periods By* (see fig. A.3).

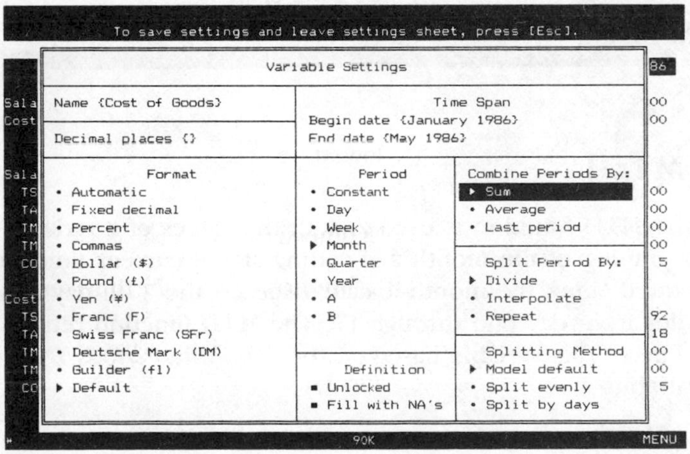

Fig. A.3. Variable settings sheet with the *Combine Periods By* box highlighted.

All series-to-date functions are governed by the parameter set in the *Combine Periods By* box on the Variable settings sheet. A variable that has *Sum* marked will be summed. Each time period is added to the next and the result placed in the series-to-date function. Summing a series-to-date function has the same effect as a rolling sum with each summation starting at the first of each new time span (the first of the month, the first of the quarter, or the first of the year). A variable with *Average* marked will be averaged. Each time period is added to the next for the particular time span, then the total is divided by the number of time periods in that time span. The result is placed in the series-to-date function. This has the same effect as a rolling average with each average starting at the first of each new time span. A variable with *Last period* marked will have a series-to-date result equal to the value of the variable in the last period in the time span. Figure A.4 illustrates the MTD, QTD, and YTD functions used with the same variable over a period varying from the first to the nineteenth week of 1986.

```
                     Series-to-Date Functions
                  ------------Compactor------------
                     Units   MTD Units   QTD Units   YTD Units
 1  W  1986           614        614        614         614
 2  W  1986           614      1,228      1,228       1,228
 3  W  1986           614      1,842      1,842       1,842
 4  W  1986           614      2,456      2,456       2,456
 5  W  1986           567        567      3,023       3,023
 6  W  1986           567      1,134      3,590       3,590
 7  W  1986           567      1,700      4,156       4,156
 8  W  1986           567      2,267      4,723       4,723
 9  W  1986           553        553      5,276       5,276
10  W  1986           553      1,106      5,829       5,829
11  W  1986           553      1,659      6,382       6,382
12  W  1986           553      2,212      6,935       6,935
13  W  1986           553      2,765      7,488       7,488
14  W  1986           639        639        639       8,127
15  W  1986           639      1,277      1,277       8,765
16  W  1986           639      1,916      1,916       9,404
17  W  1986           639      2,554      2,554      10,042
18  W  1986           602        602      3,156      10,644
19  W  1986           602      1,205      3,759      11,247
*                                          63K                         READY
```

Fig. A.4. MTD, QTD, and YTD functions. Notice that the time period for the variable *Compactor Units* is defined as bimonthly.

[MTD]

The MTD function is used to sum the values of a variable starting at the beginning of the month and ending at the current time. For the daily variable named *Sales*, the month-to-date value on the 17th day in a month is the sum of sales from day one through 17. The MTD function returns the month-to date-value of this variable based on the *Combine Periods By* setting for the input variable.

Month-to-Date Compactor Units = MTD(Compactor Units)

SYNTAX: Result = MTD(argument)

CONDITION: The MTD function requires time-series variables. Using a constant variable causes a #NODATE error. Javelin will not stop the model from calculating because of this error, but the result of the calculations will probably be wrong.

[QTD]

USE: The QTD function is used to sum the values of a variable starting at the beginning of the quarter and ending at the current time. For the monthly variable named *Sales*, the quarter-to-date value for August is the sum of sales for July and August. The QTD function returns the quarter-to-date value of this variable based on the *Combine Periods By* setting for the input variable.

Quarter-to-Date Compactor Units = QTD(Compactor Units)

SYNTAX: Result = QTD(argument)

CONDITION: The QTD function requires time-series variables. Using a constant variable causes a #NODATE error. Javelin will not stop the model from calculating because of this error, but the result of the calculations will probably be wrong.

[YTD]

USE: The YTD function is used to sum the values of a variable starting at the beginning of the year and ending at the current time. For the variable named *Sales*, the August year-to-date value is the sum of January-August sales. The YTD function returns the year-to-date value of this variable based on the *Combine Periods By* setting for the input variable.

Year-to-Date Compactor Units = YTD(Compactor Units)

SYNTAX: Result = YTD(argument)

CONDITION: The YTD function requires time-series variables. Using a constant variable causes a #NODATE error. Javelin will not stop the model from calculating because of this error, but the result of the calculations will probably be wrong.

Time Functions

These functions are listed by Javelin as LEAD, LAG, etc (see fig. A.5). Actually, these functions are used to find out what happened before and after a specific date, and how that change occurred. The basis of these functions is the need to know information about past and future events. The PREVIOUS function, for example, lets you calculate this month's data based on last month's data.

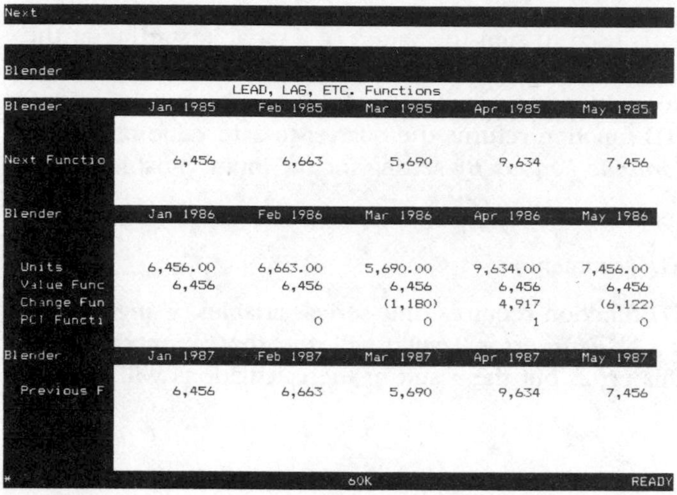

```
Next

Blender
                        LEAD, LAG, ETC. Functions
Blender         Jan 1985   Feb 1985   Mar 1985   Apr 1985   May 1985

Next Functio      6,456      6,663      5,690      9,634      7,456

Blender         Jan 1986   Feb 1986   Mar 1986   Apr 1986   May 1986

Units           6,456.00   6,663.00   5,690.00   9,634.00   7,456.00
Value Func         6,456      6,456      6,456      6,456      6,456
Change Fun                             (1,180)    4,917     (6,122)
PCT Functi                     0          0          1          0

Blender         Jan 1987   Feb 1987   Mar 1987   Apr 1987   May 1987

Previous F        6,456      6,663      5,690      9,634      7,456

*                                 60K                          READY
```

Fig. A.5. An example of the PREVIOUS, NEXT, VALUE, CHANGE, and PCT functions.

Each of these functions can use any of Javelin's time periods, including the custom time periods A and B.

Javelin's concept of variables is strongly tied to its knowledge of time. Because there is such a strong link, Javelin incorporates special functions that make use of the time-spans of variables. These functions allow you to restrict the span of a previously defined time-series variable in the definition of another. They also allow you to convert a constant to a time series over a specified time span. The WORKSHEET and FORMULAS views in figure A.6 show the BEGIN, END, and RANGE functions used with the variable *Blender Units*.

[PREVIOUS]

USE: The PREVIOUS function is used to refer to values in a period prior to a given time period. You would use the PREVIOUS function to calculate a value in the current period based on a variable's value yesterday, last week, last month,

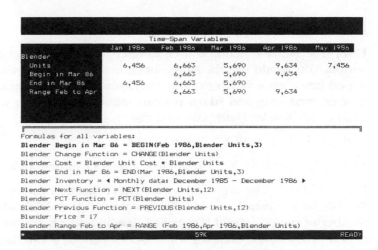

Fig. A.6. An example of the BEGIN, END, and RANGE functions.

last quarter, last year, and so on. For example, to determine a value today for the number of *Blender Units* produced this month last year:

Blender Units Last Year = PREVIOUS(Blender Units, 12)

Or, to calculate the difference between this month's interest rate and last month's interest rate we could write:

Interest Rate Change = Interest Rate – PREVIOUS(Interest Rate)

In this case, PREVIOUS refers to only one period back. To go back further, we would specify:

Interest Rate Change = Interest - PREVIOUS(Interest,2)

SYNTAX: Result = PREVIOUS(argument, [number of periods back])

CONDITION: The argument to the PREVIOUS function can be either a time-series variable or a constant variable. The number of periods back is optional. If no number of periods back is specified, Javelin assumes you want the value for the period just before. Choosing a number of periods back that calls for data before the time span of the argument produces no result. This choice will not affect your model, nor will there be any error messages. However, if you use the PREVIOUS function as part of a formula, note that no values will be computed where no argument values exist.

[NEXT]

USE: The NEXT function is used to refer to values following a given time period. You would use the NEXT function to calculate a value in the current period based on a variable's value tomorrow, next week, next month, next quarter, next year, and so on. For example, to determine a value today for the number of *Blender Units* produced this month next year:

Blender Next = NEXT(Blender Units, 12)

SYNTAX: Result = NEXT(argument, [number of periods ahead])

CONDITION: The argument to the NEXT function can be either a time-series variable or a constant variable. The number of periods ahead is optional. If no number of periods ahead is specified, Javelin assumes you want the value for the period that follows. Choosing a number of periods ahead that calls for data after the time span of the argument produces no result. This will not affect your model, nor will there be any error messages. However, if you use the NEXT function as part of a formula, note that no values will be computed where no argument values exist.

[VALUE]

USE: The VALUE function is used to refer to the value of a variable at a specific time period. You would use the VALUE function to calculate a value in the current period based on a variable's value on a certain day, during a certain week, month, quarter, year, and so on. The VALUE command returns a constant value. For example, to determine a value today for the number of *Blender Units* produced in January, 1986:

Blender Value = VALUE(Blender Units, Jan 86)

SYNTAX: Result = VALUE(argument, time period)

CONDITION: The argument to the VALUE function can be either a time-series variable or a constant variable. The time period must be a valid time period for the argument. In other words, you can't ask for a weekly value of a monthly variable. You must must include the time period as part of the function. Using either no time period or an invalid time period will produce an error that can stop Javelin from correctly computing values in your model.

[CHANGE]

USE: The CHANGE function is used to determine the difference in a variable from one period to the next. This is usually called determining the first difference of a variable. The change is calculated using the time period of the variable; it can be month, day, week, year, or custom time period. You would use the CHANGE function to calculate how much growth or decline a variable has from one month to the next, one year to the next, and so on. For example, to determine the change in the number of *Blender Units* produced from one month to the next, you would use this formula:

Blender Change = CHANGE(Blender Units)

SYNTAX: Result = CHANGE(argument)

CONDITION: The argument to the CHANGE function must be a time-series variable.

[PCT]

USE: The PCT function is used like the CHANGE function; the difference is that PCT determines the percent difference in a variable from one period to the next. The percent difference is calculated using the time period of the variable; it can be month, day, week, year, or custom time period. You would use the PCT function to calculate the percent growth or decline a variable experiences from one month to the next, one year to the next, and so on. For example, to determine the percent change in the number of *Blender Units* produced from one month to the next:

Blender PCT = PCT(Blender Units)

SYNTAX: Result = PCT(argument)

CONDITION: The argument to the PCT function must be a time-series variable.

[BEGIN]

USE: Javelin's BEGIN function is used to return the values of a variable starting on a specified date and for some or all subsequent periods. You can be selective or not in how far beyond the specific date Javelin looks.

To find the number of *Blender Units* that were produced beginning in February, 1986, and for the three months after (March, April, and May):

Blender Begin = BEGIN(Feb 86 Blender Units, 3)

SYNTAX: Result = BEGIN(starting date, argument, [number of
                          periods ahead of the starting date to
                          evaluate])

CONDITION: The starting date of the BEGIN function must be a valid date for the argument. You can only specify a starting date that is a month for a monthly variable, and so on. The argument can be either a time-series variable or a constant variable. The number of periods ahead of the starting date to evaluate is optional. Specifying no number of periods ahead tells Javelin to find values as long as the argument has data.

[END]

USE: Javelin's END function is used to find the values of a variable in time periods up to a specified date. You can be selective or not in how far before the specific date Javelin looks.

To find the number of *Blender Units* that were produced in March, 1986, and for the two months preceding March, 1986 (January, February and March), you would use this formula:

    Blender End = END(March 86, Blender Units, 3)

SYNTAX: Result = END(stop date, argument, [number of periods prior
                        to the stop date to evaluate])

CONDITION: The stop date of the END function must be a valid date for the argument. You can only specify a stop date that is a month for a monthly variable, and so on. The argument can be either a time-series variable or a constant variable. The number of periods prior to the stop date to evaluate is optional. Specifying no number of periods prior tells Javelin to find values from the first period for which the argument has data.

[RANGE]

USE: Javelin's RANGE function is used to find the values of a variable between two specified dates. To find the number of *Blender Units* that were produced between February, 1986, and April, 1986, you would use this formula:

    Blender Range = RANGE(Feb 86, Apr 86, Blender Units)

SYNTAX: Result = RANGE(start date, stop date, argument)

CONDITION: Both the start and stop dates of the RANGE function must be valid dates for the argument. You can only specify start or stop dates that are months for monthly variables, and so on. The argument can be either a time-series variable or a constant variable. If the latter, you can specify any time period as long as the start date and end date are the same type (that is, monthly).

[INTERP]

USE: There are times when the value of a variable at specific times is known, but nothing about what happens between those times. If you have to make an intelligent guess as to what happens in the in-between times, you can use the INTERP function. The INTERP function is used to fill in the blank values in a variable's time span.

For example, if we know that *Blender* Cost @ Jan 86 = $75 and *Blender Cost* @ Dec 87 = $13, we can find the relative costs in the months between using this formula:

Blender Cost = INTERP(75 @ Jan 86, 13 @ Dec 87)

Javelin returns a time series based on a straight- line projection between 75 and 13.

SYNTAX: Result = INTERP(value on starting date, value on stopping date)

CONDITION: Both arguments to the INTERP function must be values on a specific date. You cannot use any variable forms for either argument.

Calendar Functions

[YDAYS], [QDAYS], [MDAYS]

USE: Javelin knows what days are, and that it is important to know how many days fall in a certain period. There are three functions that can be used to determine the number of days: YDAYS, QDAYS, and MDAYS. The three functions are so similar that they are covered here as a group.

You can determine the number of days in any given month with MDAYS:

Days in December 86 = MDAYS( ) @ Dec 86;

Or you can determine the number of days in a given quarter with QDAYS:

Days in 2 Q 86 = QDAYS( ) @ 2 Q 86;

Finally, you can determine the number of days in a given year with YDAYS:

Days in 1986 = YDAYS( ) @ 1986

Notice that these three functions are unlike the other Javelin functions in that they take no argument.

SYNTAX: Result = Function( )

Use this syntax where *Function* is either MDAYS, QDAYS, or YDAYS. *Result* is a time series whose period is determined by which function you are using: monthly for MDAYS, quarterly for QDAYS, and yearly for YDAYS. You can generate a constant value giving the number of days in a specific month, quarter, or year by using:

Result = Function( ) @ argument

Use this syntax where *argument* is a specific month for MDAYS, quarter for QDAYS, or year for YDAYS.

Further note that QDAYS and YDAYS are linked to the fiscal year setting on the Define settings sheet. A month is always a month, but quarters and fiscal years are determined by the fiscal year setting.

Javelin has the ability to tell you the number of periods between two dates. This can be the number of years a variable is active, the number of days in a several-year model, or the number of quarters in a seven-and-a-half year period. All of these functions are based on Javelin's ability to understand time.

[BETWEEN]

USE: This function is best used as an argument to other functions that require a "number of periods" argument. For example:

Result = NEXT(argument, BETWEEN(Dec 86, Jan 89))

This example shows the use of the BETWEEN function as an argument to the NEXT function. The BETWEEN function is used to determine the number of periods forward the NEXT function looks for information.

How many months are there between August, 1985, and June, 1999? How many days are there between 27 February 1986 and 3 Dec 1990? Javelin has the ability to compute the number of periods between two dates. The dates can be days, weeks, months, quarters, years, or custom time periods. Finding the number of days between 27 Feb 86 and 3 Dec 90 is done by:

Total Days = BETWEEN(27 Feb 86, 3 Dec 90)

The number of years between two dates is found by:

Total Years = BETWEEN(1985, 2007)

SYNTAX: Result = BETWEEN(argument 1, argument 2)

Use this syntax where arguments 1 and 2 are two dates. Argument 2 must be chronologically greater than argument 1. Javelin determines which time period you want evaluated by the arguments themselves. To determine the number of days between two dates, you'd use day arguments (such as 27 Feb 86). To determine the number of quarters between two dates you'd use quarter arguments (such as 3 Q 87). Note that the BETWEEN function returns a constant value, not a variable.

CONDITION: The BETWEEN function uses neither constant nor time-series variables. Both arguments must be dates.

[UNTIL]

USE: How many months are there between the current month and June, 1999? How many days are there between today and 3 Dec 1990?

Javelin has the ability to compute the number of periods between the present time period and a future time period. The future time period can be a specific day, week, month, quarter, year, or custom time period. To find the number of days from today to 3 Dec 90, you would use this formula:

    Total Days = UNTIL(3 Dec 90)

To find the number of years from now until 2007, you would use this formula:

    Total Years = UNTIL(2007)

SYNTAX: Result = UNTIL(argument)

Use this syntax where the argument is a date. Javelin determines which time period you want evaluated by the argument itself. To determine the number of days until a date, you'd use day arguments (such as 27 Feb 86). To determine the number of quarters until a date you'd use quarter arguments (such as 3 Q 87). Note that the UNTIL function returns a time-series variable, not a constant.

CONDITION: The UNTIL function uses neither constant nor time-series variables. The argument must be a date, not a variable.

[SINCE]

USE: How many months has it been since June, 1985? How many days has it been since 3 Dec 1975?

Javelin can compute the number of periods between a past time period and today. The past time period can be a specific day, week, month, quarter, year, or custom time period. Finding the number of days between 3 Dec 85 and today is done as follows:

    Total Days = SINCE(3 Dec 85)

The number of years since 1977 is found with this formula:

Total Years = SINCE(1977)

SYNTAX: Result = SINCE(argument)

The argument, which is a date, determines which time period you want Javelin to evaluate. To determine the number of days since a date, you'd use day arguments (such as 27 Feb 86). To determine the number of quarters since a date you'd use quarter arguments (such as 3 Q 87). Note that the SINCE function returns a time-series variable, not a constant.

CONDITION: The SINCE function uses neither constant nor time-series variables. The argument must be a date.

[LENGTH]

USE: Suppose that you are determining cash flow for Future Home Appliances, Inc., and want to know how many time periods you have data for *Blender Units*. Basically, you want to know how many time periods of useful data for a specific variable exist in a specific model. Javelin takes care of this with the LENGTH function.

As mentioned previously, you would determine the total number of time periods that *Blender Units* is active with this formula:

Time = LENGTH(Blender Units)

Javelin would return the number of time periods for which valid data exist. Note that valid data includes #NA if there is no data between two data points.

SYNTAX: Result = LENGTH(argument)

The argument is a time-series variable. Javelin determines which time period you are interested in by the argument itself. A variable that is defined in days returns the number of days of valid data. A variable defined in years returns the number of years of valid data.

CONDITION: The LENGTH function uses only time-series variables and returns a constant value.

Period Conversion Functions

Any attempt to mix different time periods in a formula causes Javelin to stop calculating your model and produce error messages. These errors can be avoided by remembering that Javelin knows the difference between months, days, years, and so on, and that it will not mix monthly data with yearly data, and similarly with the other time periods.

[WEEKLY], [MONTHLY], [QUARTERLY], [YEARLY], [A], [B]

USE: An example of how these functions are used can be seen with the DAILY function and the *Blender Sales* variable.

The DAILY function is used to convert the values of one variable, not defined with a daily time period, to another variable that needs daily input. Converting the monthly *Blender Sales* values to daily values is done with:

    Blender Daily = DAILY(Blender Sales)

SYNTAX: Result = DAILY(argument)

This same syntax follows for all the other time period conversion functions:

    Result = WEEKLY(argument)
    Result = MONTHLY(argument)
    Result = QUARTERLY(argument)
    Result = YEARLY(argument)
    Result = A(argument)
    Result = B(argument)

Note that you can use both custom time periods A and B for time period conversion functions. The conversions that take place when you use either A or B depend on how you defined the custom time periods (whether you based them on weeks, months, hours, and so on).

These functions can convert from smaller time periods to larger time periods and vice versa. The method of conversion is determined on the Model settings sheet. Each of the functions listed in this section is dependent on three boxes found to the right on the Variable settings sheet (see fig. A.4): *Combine Periods By*, *Split Period by*, and *Splitting Method*.

CONDITION: The time period conversion functions can take either time-series or constant variable data. The result is a time series with the specified period.

Logical Functions

There will be times in the building of your Javelin model that complex relationships will have to be evaluated. These relationships can take many forms.

One relationship may call for the evaluation of two separate conditions, whereas another may call for an action based on a condition (If-Then-Else statements).

Javelin incorporates special functions to handle such needs. These functions are sometimes called conditional functions, and other times logical functions. Javelin chooses the latter definition.

[IF]

USE: The IF statement allows you to do one of two things based on whether a condition is true or false. Note: Don't confuse the IF function with the macro @IF command.

The IF function is used to choose between two actions based on one condition. The condition must be either true or false. The IF function uses such conditions in the following way:

   Royalties = IF(Sales @ March 86 < 50000, .08*Sales, .1*Sales)

SYNTAX: Result = IF(conditional argument, action if true, action if false)

The conditional argument in our example is *Sales @ March 86 < 50000*. The action if sales in March of 86 are less than 50000 is *Royalties = .08*Sales*. The action if sales are more than 50000 in March of 86 is *Royalties = .1*Sales*.

CONDITION: The conditional argument to the IF function can be any valid Javelin condition. Either constant or time-series variables can be used.

[AND]

USE: Javelin allows you to determine the combined truth or falsehood of several conditions with the AND function. Note: Don't confuse the AND function with the macro @AND command.

This function is used to determine the combined truth or falsehood of several conditions. All these conditions must be true for the entire expression to be evaluated as true. A single false expression in several true expressions will evaluate the AND function as false. An example of true and false conditions would be

   Sales @ March 86 < 50000, Tax Rate = .20

This and similar expressions are conditions that can be evaluated as either true or false.

An application of the AND function can be seen here in the IF function:

Bonus = IF(AND(Sales > Plan, Expenses < Budget),
            High Bonus, Low Bonus)

This equation reads: "If *Sales* is greater than *Plan*, and *Expenses* is less than *Budget*, then *Bonus* = *High Bonus*. If either equation (*Sales* > *Plan* and *Expenses* < *Budget*) is *not* true, then *Bonus* = *Low Bonus*."

SYNTAX: Result = AND(conditional argument 1, conditional
                      argument 2, conditional argument 3, . . .
                      conditional argument n)

The first conditional arguments in our example are *Sales @ March 86 < 50000*, *Tax Rate = .20*, and *Overhead > .15 * Sales*. There are some interesting things to note about the AND function. First, you can have as many arguments to the AND function as you wish. Second, the AND function allows for calculated conditions (*Overhead > .15 * Sales*). Third, the AND function returns only one of two values, either 1 or 0.

A returned value of 1 indicates that all the arguments to AND were true. A returned value of 0 indicates that at least one of the arguments to AND was false.

CONDITION: The conditional arguments to the AND function can be any valid Javelin condition. Either constant or time-series variables can be used, as well as calculated variables. AND returns a time series of 0 and 1 values unless all its arguments are constants, in which case it returns a 0 or 1 constant.

[OR]

USE: Javelin allows you to determine the truth or falsehood of one or several conditions with the OR function.

This function is used to determine whether any of several conditions is true. Any one of these conditions can be true for the entire expression to be evaluated as true. All the expressions must be false to evaluate the OR function as false. An example of true and false conditions would be

Sales @ March 86 < 50000, Tax Rate = .20

This and similar expressions are conditions that can be evaluated as either true or false. The OR function uses such conditions in the following way:

Sales Index = OR(Sales @ March 86 < 50000,
                  Tax Rate = .20, Overhead > .15
                  * Sales)

The OR function is typically used with the IF function to allow an action to be taken based on the combined truth or falsehood of several conditions.

SYNTAX: Result = OR(conditional argument 1, conditional argument 2, conditional argument 3, . . . conditional argument n)

The conditional arguments in our example are *Sales @ March 86 < 50000*, *Tax Rate = .20*, and *Overhead > .15 * Sales*. There are some interesting things to note about the OR function. First, you can have as many arguments to the OR function as you wish. Second, the OR function allows for calculated conditions (*Overhead > .15 * Sales*). Third, the OR function returns only one of two values, either 1 or 0.

A returned value of 1 indicates that at least one of the arguments to OR was true. A returned value of 0 indicates that all of the arguments to OR were false.

CONDITION: The conditional arguments to the OR function can be any valid Javelin condition. Either constant or time-series variables can be used, as well as calculated variables. OR returns a time series of 0 and 1 values unless all its arguments are constants, in which case it returns a 0 or 1 constant value.

[NOT]

USE: Javelin allows you to negate the truth or falsehood of a condition with the NOT function. An example of true or false conditions would be

Sales @ March 86 < 50000, Tax Rate = .20

This and similar expressions can be evaluated as either true or false. The NOT function uses such conditions in the following way:

Sales Index = NOT(Sales @ March 86 < 50000)

In this example, *Sales Index* is true if the expression *Sales @ March 86 < 50000* is *NOT* true, that is, if *Sales @ March 86 > = 50000*.

SYNTAX: Result = NOT(conditional argument)

The conditional argument in our example is *Sales @ March 86 < 5000*. There are some interesting things to note about the NOT function. First, the NOT function allows for calculated conditions (*Overhead > .15 * Sales* would be an example). Second, the NOT function returns only one of two values, either 1 or 0.

Note that a returned value of 1 indicates that the argument to NOT was false. A returned value of 0 indicates that the argument to NOT was true. If something is not true, then it is false. The NOT function evaluates this as:

If the condition is true, then NOT(condition) is false. (Hence, 0.)

If the condition is false, then NOT(condition) is true. (Hence, 1.)

CONDITION: The conditional argument to the NOT function can be any valid Javelin condition. Either constant or time-series variables can be used, as well as calculated variables.

Statistical Functions

When we need to know the change in a variable over time, the amount of change in a variable over time, or the correlation one variable has to another, for example, we are seeking statistical information.

[VAR]

USE: The VAR function computes the variance, or the amount that a population varies from the "norm" in a time-series variable.

An example of the VAR function:

Blender Revenue Variance = VAR(Blender Revenue)

This formula equates *Blender Revenue Variance* to the variance in the time-series variable *Blender Revenue*.

SYNTAX: Result VAR(argument)

CONDITION: The VAR function's argument must be a time-series variable. VAR returns a constant value.

[STDEV]

USE: The STDEV function calculates the standard deviation, which is the square root of the variance. For the variable *Blender Units*, the AVG function will tell us the average value over time. Although the individual values of *Blender Units* may range from high to low, 67% of the values will fall less than the value of STDEV away from the average value. In the same mode, 95% of all values will fall between 2 x STDEV away from the average.

An example of the STDEV function:

Blender Revenue Standard Deviation = STDEV(Blender Revenue)

This formula equates *Blender Revenue Standard Deviation* to the standard deviation in the time-series variable *Blender Revenue*.

SYNTAX: Result = STDEV(argument)

CONDITION: The STDEV function's argument must be a time-series variable. STDEV returns a constant value.

[CORR]

USE: The CORR function is Javelin's correlation coefficient function. It allows you to determine how closely two variables' values are related to each other. Correlation can be determined graphically by plotting the two variables in question on an x-y graph. If all the points in the graph are in a line, the two variables are highly correlated ($r = 1$ or $r = -1$). If the points are uniformly dispersed over all areas of the x-y graph, the correlation is low ($r = 0$). The closeness of fit is determined by Pearson's r method and has a range of -1 to 1. The best fits are those with a CORR closest to either -1 or 1.

An example of the CORR function:

Accuracy = CORR(Projected Blender Revenue, Blender Revenue)

This formula determines how accurate the predicted *Blender Revenue* figures were by comparing them to actual *Blender Revenue* in the same period.

SYNTAX: Result = CORR(argument 1, argument 2)

CONDITION: The CORR function's arguments can be either time-series or constant variables. CORR returns a constant value.

Prediction Functions

There are times in our modeling when we must estimate certain values. These estimates are often eyeball predictions based on trends we see in the variables we work with. Javelin takes the guesses out of the estimates with three prediction functions.

[SLOPE]

USE: The slope of a line is also called "the rise over the run." It is the measure of how much change is on the y-axis divided by the change on the x-axis. Javelin will evaluate a series of points and "draw" a straight line through the points that best describe the series of points. The equation for the line will be in the form:

y = mx + b

SLOPE returns the value of m.

You can determine the slope of *Blender Revenue* and *Blender Sales* by the following formula:

Blender Slope = SLOPE(Blender Sales, Blender Revenue)

SYNTAX: Result SLOPE(x-axis argument, y-axis argument)

CONDITION: The arguments to the SLOPE function can be either time-series or constant variables. SLOPE always returns a constant value.

[INTERCEPT]

USE: The intercept of a line is also called "x=0 point." It is the point on the y-axis that the line crosses. The INTERCEPT function returns the intercept of the "best fit" line between x and y. The intercept is the *b* factor in the following formula:

y = mx + b

You can determine the intercept of the line formed by matching *Blender Revenue* on the y-axis and *Blender Sales* on the x-axis by the following formula:

Blender Intercept = INTERCEPT(Blender Sales, Blender Revenue)

SYNTAX: Result = INTERCEPT(x-axis argument, y-axis argument)

CONDITION: The arguments to the INTERCEPT function can be either time-series or constant variables. INTERCEPT always returns a constant value.

[PREDICT]

USE: The PREDICT function is used to determine the value of the y-axis variable based on a known x-axis variable. For instance, if several values of both x and y are known, both m and b can be calculated using the SLOPE and INTERCEPT functions listed above. What would you do if you wanted to know the value of y for an unknown value of x, as in "If x, then this y"? Javelin uses the PREDICT function for this type of evaluation.

You can predict a *Blender Revenue* value for an undetermined *Blender Sales* value by assuming a *Blender Sales* value:

> Blender Prediction = PREDICT(Blender Sales, Blender Revenue, Blender Sales
> @ Aug 88)

SYNTAX: Result = PREDICT(x-axis argument, y-axis
argument, x-axis value)

CONDITION: The arguments to the PREDICT function can be either time-series or constant variables. The x-axis value to the PREDICT function must be a constant or a time-series variable on a specified date. PREDICT returns a constant value.

Determining Trends

Trend analysis is a tool used to determine how variables change over time. Javelin has four trend analysis functions: TREND, TRENDCORR, TRENDSLOPE, and TRENDSTART.

[TREND]

Javelin allows you to determine a trend line reflecting the growth or decline of a variable over time with the TREND function.

USE: You would use the TREND function to determine the overall trend in *Blender Sales* over time with the formula:

> Blender Sales Trends = TREND(Blender Sales)

You could also be more specific and limit the time span of the trend analysis to a specific time period by modifying the formula slightly:

> Blender Sales
> Trends in 1st Quarter 87 = TREND(Blender Sales, 1 Q 87)

SYNTAX: Result = TREND(argument, (starting date), (stopping date))

CONDITION: The argument to the TREND function must be a time-series variable. The TREND function returns either a time-series or constant variable depending on how the function is used.

Using the TREND(argument) form returns time-series variable for the entire time span of the argument variable. Using the TREND(argument, starting date) form returns a constant variable. Using the TREND(argument, starting date, stopping date) form returns a time-series variable for the time period between the start and stop dates.

[TRENDCORR]

USE: The TRENDCORR function is Javelin's trend analysis correlation coefficient function. It allows you to determine how closely a trend line projection fits the actual values of a variable. An example of this would be to plot a variable's values over time, then run a line from point to point. The TRENDCORR function would tell you how much deviation from a straight line exists in the data points. The closeness of fit between the variable's values and a straight line is determined by Pearson's r method and has a range of -1 to 1. The best fits are those with a TRENDCORR closest to either -1 or 1.

An example of the TRENDCORR function:

Linearity = TRENDCORR(Blender Revenue)

This formula determines how well the *Blender Revenue* figures approximate a straight line.

SYNTAX: Result TRENDCORR(argument)

CONDITION: The TRENDCORR function's argument must be a time-series variable. TRENDCORR returns a constant value.

[TRENDSLOPE]

USE: The TRENDSLOPE function is used to determine the slope of a trend line for a time-series variable. This method assumes the values of the variable are on the y-axis and uses time as the x-axis. To determining the slope of *Blender Sales* over time, you would use this formula:

Blender Trend Slope = TRENDSLOPE(Blender Sales)

The trend slope can be interpreted as the average growth rate from period to period of the variable over its time span. (This is different from the compound growth rate over the time span.)

SYNTAX: Result = TRENDSLOPE(argument)

CONDITION: The argument to the TRENDSLOPE function must be a time-series variable. TRENDSLOPE returns a constant value.

[TRENDSTART]

USE: The TRENDSTART function is used to determine the value of the trend line for a variable in the first period of the variable's time span. If the model assumes a starting time of 0 (as in custom time periods) the TRENDSTART function determines the intercept of the trend line.

To determine the starting point of the trend line for *Blender Sales*, you would use this formula:

    Blender Trend Start = TRENDSTART(Blender Sales)

SYNTAX: Result = TRENDSTART(argument)

CONDITION: The argument to the TRENDSTART function must be a time-series variable. TRENDSTART returns a constant value.

Mathematical Functions

Javelin has five basic mathematical functions that can be used in formulas: LN, EXP, SQRT, ABS, MOD, INT, and ROUND.

[LN]

USE: The LN function is Javelin's natural log function. An example of the LN function:

    Log Blender Revenue = LN(Blender Revenue)

This formula determines the natural log of *Blender Revenue* over time.

SYNTAX: Result = LN(argument)

CONDITION: The LN function's arguments can be either time-series or constant variables. LN returns a time series unless its argument is a constant, in which case it returns a constant value.

[EXP]

USE: The EXP function is Javelin's exponential function. An example of the EXP function:

Log Blender Revenue = EXP(Blender Revenue)

This formula determines the exponent of *Blender Revenue* over time.

SYNTAX: Result = EXP(argument)

CONDITION: The EXP function's arguments can be either time-series or constant variables. EXP returns a time series unless its argument is a constant, in which case it returns a constant value.

[SQRT]

USE: The SQRT function is Javelin's square root function. You use it to find the square root of any variable.

SYNTAX: Result SQRT(argument)

CONDITION: The SQRT function can use either constant or time-series variables as arguments, and returns a result of the same type as its argument. The SQRT function applied to a time-series variable returns a time series of square root values.

[ABS]

USE: The ABS function is Javelin's absolute value function. A variable's absolute value is the positive value of the whole number. The absolute value of -7.5 is 7.5. The absolute value of 7.5 is also 7.5. The absolute value of any variable can be found with the formula:

SYNTAX: Result = ABS(argument)

CONDITION: The ABS function can use either constant or time-series variables as arguments. The ABS function of a time-series variable returns a time series.

[MOD]

USE: The MOD function is Javelin's modulo arithmetic function. The modulo of two numbers is determined by finding the remainder of one number when divided by a second number. The modulo of 7/2 is 1. The modulo of 6/3 is 0. The modulo of any two numbers can be found with the formula:

SYNTAX: Result = MOD(dividend, divisor)

CONDITION: The MOD function can use either constant or time-series variables as arguments. The arguments do not have to have integer values. The MOD function returns a time series if the argument is a time series.

[INT]

USE: The INT function is Javelin's integer value function. It determines the greatest integer contained in a number. The integer value of 7.2 is 7. The integer value of 7.0 is 7.

SYNTAX: Result = INT(argument)

CONDITION: The INT function can use either constant or time-series variables as arguments. The INT function returns a time series if the argument is a time series.

[ROUND]

USE: The ROUND function is Javelin's round off function. It truncates a value to the specified number of decimal places. The value of 7.25660785 rounded off to two places is 7.26. That same number rounded off to zero places is 7.

SYNTAX: Result = ROUND(argument, decimal places)

CONDITION: The ROUND function can use either constant or time-series variables as arguments. The ROUND function returns a time series if the argument is a time series.

Financial Functions

Javelin takes care of such intricacies as net present value determination, internal rate of return calculation, and payment calculation with its financial functions.

Investment and Loan Functions

[NPV]

USE: The NPV function is used to determine the net present value of a given time-series variable. Assume you are considering a building purchase with the following five year income table:

100,000 @1987
120,000 @1988
130,000 @1989
140,000 @1990
 50,000 @1991

The problem is to determine what purchase price is a reasonable investment for the above income. You also know the initial investment in addition to the purchase price will be 20,000 and that you require your investment to earn the equivalent of a 15 percent per year interest rate to be attractive. You would use this formula:

Purchase = NPV(20000,income table,.15)

Javelin would calculate *Purchase* = 348,075. If the purchase price is less than or equal to this amount, you would know that the investment was a good one.

SYNTAX: Result = NPV(initial investment, cash flow series, rate per period)

CONDITION: The initial investment and rate per period arguments in the NPV function can be either entered data or variable names. The initial investment and rate per period arguments must be constants. The rate per period argument must be in decimal form. NPV returns a constant value.

[PV]

USE: The PV function is used to determine the present value of a given time-series variable. The present value function allows you to calculate the present value of an ordinary annuity.

An ordinary annuity is a series of payments to be made at equally spaced intervals. The present value is the value in today's dollars of the payments to be made or received later. This method also assumes a given discount rate or interest rate per period.

SYNTAX: Result = PV(cash flow, rate per period, number of periods)

The rate per period and number of periods in the PV function can be either entered data or variable names. The cash flow argument can be either a constant or time-series variable. The number of periods and rate per period arguments must be constants. The rate per period argument must be in decimal form. PV returns a constant value.

[FV]

USE: The FV function is used to determine the future value of a given time-series variable. The future value function allows you to calculate the future value of an ordinary annuity.

An ordinary annuity is a series of payments to be made at equally spaced intervals. The future value is the value in dollars of the payments to be made or received on that future date. This method also assumes a given discount rate or interest rate per period.

SYNTAX: Result = FV(cash flow, rate per period, number or periods)

The rate per period and number of periods in the FV function can be either entered data or variable names. The cash flow argument can be either a constant or time-series variable. The number of periods and rate per period arguments must be constants. The rate per period argument must be in decimal form. The FV function returns a constant value.

[IRR]

USE: The IRR function is used to determine the internal rate of return of a given time-series variable. The IRR function is an alternative to the NPV function for calculating the attractiveness of an investment.

SYNTAX: Result = IRR(cash flow, [rate per period])

CONDITION: The rate per period in the IRR function can be either entered data or a variable name. The cash flow argument can be either a constant or time-series variable. The rate per period argument is optional. However, if one is given it must be a constant and must be in decimal form. Javelin assumes a 10 percent rate per period if you do not provide one.

[PMT]

USE: The PMT function is used to determine the installment payments for a given principal amount of a fixed rate loan. (Do not try to use this function for add-on interest loans.) A common use for such a function would be in mortgage calculations.

SYNTAX: Result = PMT(principal, rate per period, number of periods)

CONDITION: All arguments to the PMT function must be constants, but can be either entered data or variable names. The rate per period argument must be constant data and must be in decimal form.

Depreciation Functions

Javelin has three functions that are used to determine depreciation. Each uses a different method to determine depreciation values over time. Each of the separate functions makes the same standard assumptions, however. Each uses a standard depreciation method, each returns values for a specified time span, and each assumes a constant initial value, final value, and number of periods to depreciate.

[DEPRDECL]

USE: This function uses the declining balance method to determine the depreciation values over the specified time span. This function might be used to determine the depreciation in a piece of equipment over a five year depreciable life. Given a $20,000 initial value, $0 final value, a depreciable life of 5 years starting in 1986, and a declining balance factor of 1.5, the DEPRDECL function becomes:

Depreciation DEPRDECL(20000,0,5,1986,1.5)

SYNTAX: Result = DEPRDECL(initial value, final value,
     number of periods to depreciate, starting date of
     depreciation, [depreciation factor])

CONDITION: The initial value, final value, and number of periods to depreciate must be constant variables. You can enter either data or variable names. The depreciation factor argument is optional. Javelin assumes a depreciation factor of 2 if none is given. The result of DEPRDECL is a time series of depreciation amounts by period. The period of the result is specified by the date entered for begin date.

[DEPRSL]

USE: This function uses the straight line method to determine the depreciation values over the specified time span. This function might be useful to determine the depreciation in a piece of equipment over a five year depreciable life. Given a $20,000 initial value, $0 final value, and a depreciable life of 5 years starting in 1986, the DEPRSL function becomes:

Depreciation DEPRSL(20000,0,5,1986)

SYNTAX: Result = DEPRSL(initial value, final value, number
     of periods to depreciate, starting date
     of depreciation)

CONDITION: The initial value, final value and number of periods to depreciate must be constant variables. You can enter either data or variable names. DEPRSL returns a time series of depreciation amounts by period.

[DEPRSOYD]

USE: This function uses the sum-of-years'-digits method to determine the depreciation values over the specified time span. This function might be useful to determine the depreciation in a piece of equipment over a five year depreciable life. Given a $20,000 initial value, $0 final value, and a depreciable life of 5 years starting in 1986, the DEPRSOYD function becomes

Depreciation = DEPRSOYD(20000,0,5,1986)

SYNTAX: Result = DEPRSOYD(initial value, final value, number of periods to depreciate, starting date of depreciation)

CONDITION: The initial value, final value and number of periods to depreciate must be constant variables. You can enter either data or variable names. DEPRSOYD returns a time series of depreciation amounts by period.

Functions that deal with Bond issues

Bonds, bond prices, and bond yields are an important part of business analysis, yet very few business software packages include functions to deal effectively with these topics.

Javelin recognizes the importance of bonds and has two functions to deal with them.

[BONDPRICE]

USE: Javelin's BONDPRICE function allows you to determine the fair market price of a bond. There are certain things that Javelin has to know first. These include the yield, face value, coupon rate, years to maturity, and payments per year.

SYNTAX: Result = BONDPRICE(yield, face value, coupon rate, years to maturity, number of payments per year)

CONDITION: All of the arguments to the BONDPRICE function must be constants, although they can be either entered data or constant variable names. BONDPRICE returns a constant value.

[BONDYTM]

USE: Javelin's BONDYTM function allows you to determine the yearly yield to maturity of a bond. This function is the anti-function to the BONDPRICE function listed previously.

There are certain things that Javelin has to know about the bond before calculating the yield to maturity. These include the bond price, face value, coupon rate, years to maturity, and payments per year.

SYNTAX: Result = BONDYTM(bond price, face value, coupon rate, years to maturity, number of payments per year)

CONDITION: All of the arguments to the BONDYTM function must be constants, although they can be either entered data or constant variable names. BONDYTM returns a constant value.

[GROW]

USE: There will be times when we know the first of several data points of a variable, but nothing about the values at the end of the variable's time span. The problem is that we may have to know or at least make an intelligent guess on values for future dates. Javelin does this with the GROW function.

For example, if we know that *Blender Cost* for January, 1986, is $75, we can find the relative costs from March, 1986, to December, 1987, by using the following formula:

    Blender Cost = GROW(Blender Cost, -.02)

Javelin returns the first value for *Blender Cost*, then calculates the remaining values for the rest of the time span based on a 2 per cent decline in each period.

SYNTAX: Result = GROW(argument, rate of change per period)

CONDITION: The argument to the GROW function can be either a time-series or constant variable. The rate of change per period must be a constant variable. GROW returns a time series containing the value or values of the input argument followed by growing numbers to the end of the resulting time span.

[GROWRATE]

USE: There will be times when we need to know the rate of change a variable goes through during its time span. Javelin does this with the GROWRATE function. The GROWRATE function is used to find how fast a time-series variable is changing (ompound growth rate).

If we know the values for *Blender Cost* for the entire time span of the model, we can find the rate of change from period to period using:

Blender Cost = GROWRATE(Blender Cost)

Javelin returns a constant that is equal to the period-by-period change in *Blender Cost.*

SYNTAX: Result = GROWRATE(argument)

CONDITION: The argument to the GROWRATE function must be a time-series variable.

Extra Functions

Javelin has two other functions that don't fit comfortably in any of the previously defined sections. One of the functions, SELECT, allows selection criteria to be established. The other, F, serves as a place holder.

[SELECT]

USE: The SELECT function enables users to supply a number of choices (one of which is returned, depending on whether the condition is met) specified at the beginning of the SELECT argument.

To determine which of two discount rates to allow based on a purchase order you could use the SELECT function:

Discount = SELECT(Purchase Order > 5000,.10,0)

This formula results in a discount of 10 percent if the purchase order is greater than 5000. If the purchase order is less than 5000 the discount is 0 percent.

SYNTAX: Result = SELECT(condition, result 1, result 2, result 3, . . . result n)

CONDITION: The condition to the SELECT function can be any valid Javelin variable or calculation. Result 1 is returned if the value of the condition is 1. Result 2 is returned if the value of the condition is 2, and so on. Javelin returns the last value in the series of results if the value of the condition is negative, not a whole number, or greater than the number of results.

The previous example used a logical expression, *Purchase Order > 5000*. This condition can return only one of two values, 0 or 1. A condition of 1 corresponds to a purchase order greater than 5000 units. This condition tells the SELECT function to return the first result, corresponding to a discount of 10 percent. A condition of 0 corresponds to a purchase order less than 5000 units. This condition tells the SELECT function to return the last result, as 0 is not a valid condition for the SELECT function. Hence, the discount is 0 percent.

[F]

USE: There are times when we aren't sure what relationship exists between variables, but do know that one does exist. This can pose a problem in designing our model, as we need to specify something in the calculations but don't know what to specify exactly.

Javelin allows us a place marker in our calculations with the F function.

SYNTAX: Result = F(argument 1, argument 2,...argument 3)

CONDITION: This function is not calculated. The arguments can be any valid Javelin variable, time series or constant, or calculated result. The result is undefined.

B

Javelin Command Summary

This appendix describes all the Javelin commands. Each description explains how the command functions and is used, including tips on how to use commands efficiently and how to avoid problems. Commands are divided into two major sections: (1) commands accessed through Javelin's main menu and (2) view-sensitive commands, which are active only within the WORKSHEET, FORMULAS, and ERRORS views.

Commands from Main Menu Options

You can display Javelin's main menu by pressing the slash key (/). The following main menu options appear at the top of the screen:

```
DEFINE  CLEAR  VIEW  WINDOW  PRINT  FILE  QUIT
```

Define Commands

/Define Variable

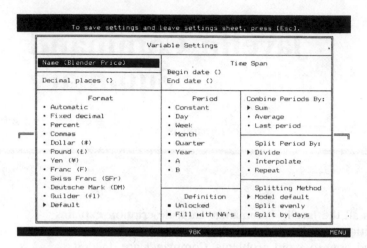

```
          To save settings and leave settings sheet, press [Esc].

                           Variable Settings                           .

  Name (Blender Price)                      Time Span
                                  Begin date ()
  Decimal places ()               End date ()

         Format                Period         Combine Periods By:
   • Automatic            • Constant         ▶ Sum
   • Fixed decimal        • Day              • Average
   • Percent              • Week             • Last period
   • Commas               • Month
   • Dollar ($)           • Quarter            Split Period By:
   • Pound (£)            • Year             ▶ Divide
   • Yen (¥)              • A                • Interpolate
   • Franc (F)            • B                • Repeat
   • Swiss Franc (SFr)
   • Deutsche Mark (DM)                        Splitting Method
   • Guilder (fl)            Definition      ▶ Model default
   ▶ Default              ■ Unlocked         • Split evenly
                          ■ Fill with NA's   • Split by days

                          98K                         MENU
```

PURPOSE: The /Define Variable command lets you change the characteristics of any variable in the model, regardless of where you are in the model. The characteristics of each variable are displayed on the Variable settings sheet.

Each variable has its own settings sheet. You select the variable by typing its name at the DEFINE VARIABLES prompt. The variable characteristics that you can change with /Define Variable are

> Name
> Decimal places
> Format
> Time span
> Period
> Definition

USE: The /Define Variable command is activated by typing

> /DV

Javelin then prompts you to enter the variable name. You can enter a variable name in one of four ways:

> 1. If the variable has not been defined elsewhere in the model, type the variable name and then press Enter.

2. If the cursor is highlighting the variable you want to define, simply press Enter.

3. If the variable you want to define is in the active view, use the POINT key (F4) to highlight the variable and then press press Enter. This method will work in any view.

4. If the variable has already been defined elsewhere in the model, you can use the SPELL key (Tab) to select the variable, and then press Enter.

/Define Building Block

PURPOSE: The /Define Building block command is used to define any of Javelin's five building blocks, and lets you change the name of an existing building block. The command activates a submenu listing different building-block options.

The /Define Building block submenu lets you create the following Javelin building blocks:

Time delay
Rollup
Import data
Lookup table
Curve
Name change

USE: The /Define Building block command is activated by typing

/DB

The submenu options can be selected in either of two ways:

1. Type the first letter of the desired building block. Type a *T* to select a Time delay building block, an *R* to select a Rollup building block, and so on.

2. Use the cursor keys to highlight the desired building block and press Enter.

After you have selected a building block, Javelin prompts you to name it. Enter the name at the prompt and then press Enter. Javelin tells you if another building block exists with the same name.

/Define Worksheet

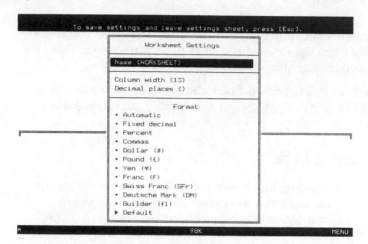

PURPOSE: The /Define Worksheet command is used to set or change various default settings of a Javelin worksheet. Javelin activates the Worksheet settings sheet as soon as a worksheet name is supplied.

The worksheet settings that can be set or defined with the /Define Worksheet command are

> Name
> Column width
> Decimal places
> Format

USE: The /Define Worksheet commands are activated by typing

> /DW

Javelin responds by asking for a worksheet name. You can supply worksheet names in three different ways.

1. If the cursor is in an active WORKSHEET view, press Enter to use the worksheet. Javelin assumes a default worksheet name of *WORKSHEET* if no other name is given and the cursor is not in an active WORKSHEET view.

2. Type the name of the worksheet and press Enter. This method also creates a worksheet if none exists with the name you supply.

3. If the worksheet you want has already been defined elsewhere in the model, you can use the SPELL key (Tab) to make your selection from the list of worksheets available.

/Define Graph

```
To save settings and leave settings sheet, press [Esc].

                          Graph Settings

Name (GRAPH)                 Time Axis Limits            Graph
                          Begin date ()                  Type
          Left Axis       End date ()                 • Line
Max ()                                                ▶ Bar
Min ()                             Labels             • Stack bar
                          Title ()                    • % bar
          Right Axis      Subtitle ()                 • Horiz. bar
Max ()                    X-axis ()                   • Pie
Min ()                    Y-axis ()                   • XY plot

          Variables              Legends                  Axis
()                        ()                          ■ Left
()                        ()                          ■ Left
()                        ()                          ■ Left
()                        ()                          ■ Left
()                        ()                          ■ Left
()                        ()                          ■ Left
()                        ()                          ■ Left

                               98K                             MENU
```

PURPOSE: The /Define Graph command is used to create and modify graphs. This command must be used to create graph definitions for the GRAPH view and the /Print Graph command. After you enter the /Define Graph command, Javelin prompts you for a graph name and assigns the default name *GRAPH* if no name is given. The command lets you create the following graphs:

Line
Bar
Stack bar
% bar
Horiz. bar
Pie
XY plot

Select the graph and its options on the /Define Graph settings sheet. The graph options, some active only in specific graphs, include:

Time axis limits
Left axis
Variables
Labels
Legends
Axis
Horizontal axis
Date display
Date shown

USE: The /Define Graph settings sheet is activated by typing

/DG

Javelin then asks for a graph name, which you can enter in any of three ways:

1. If you want to change settings for the last graph defined, press Enter. Then Javelin pulls up the settings sheet for the last active graph. Javelin assumes a default graph name of *GRAPH* if no other name is given and there are no graphs defined in the model.

2. Type the desired graph name and press Enter. This method also creates a graph if none exists with the name you supply.

3. If the graph you want has already been defined elsewhere in the model, you can use the SPELL key (Tab) to select the graph.

/Define Macro

PURPOSE: The /Define Macro command is used to record a new macro or rename an existing one. (This command does not let you edit existing macros.) The three options are

Begin
End
Rename

USE: The /Define Macro command is selected by typing

/DM

Javelin then prompts you to enter a macro name. You can enter the macro name in either of two ways:

1. Press Enter; Javelin then uses *MACRO* as the default name.

2. Create a new name by typing it at the prompt and then pressing Enter. Note that Javelin allows one-character macro names, executed with an Alt-(key) combination. (If you type the name of an existing macro, Javelin indicates that the name is already in use.)

If you want to rename an existing macro, you can use the SPELL key (Tab) to select the macro name.

/Define Time Period

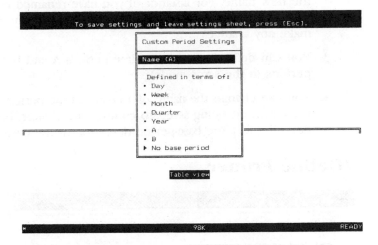

PURPOSE: The /Define Time period command is used to create and modify Javelin's two custom time periods, A and B. These custom time periods can be given new names, defined as functions of real time periods, or defined as periods based on no real time period.

Custom time periods can be defined in terms of a base time period or no base time period. Allowable base periods are

Days
Weeks
Months
Quarters
Years
A
B
No base period

USE: The /Define Time period command is activated by typing

/DT

Javelin responds by asking which custom time period you wish to define. If you don't remember the current name of the time period you want to define, use the SPELL key (Tab). When defining custom time periods, keep the following in mind:

1. After a custom time period has been named, the new name appears in all the *Period* boxes on all settings sheets.

2. Javelin will access a renamed custom time period only by reference to the new name. For instance, if you have renamed custom time period B as *bimonthly*, you must type */DT bimonthly* and then press Enter to make any changes.

3. You can define two custom time periods A and B as different time periods in the same model.

4. You can change the name of a custom time period as often as you wish without being asked to confirm the change, because a new name doesn't affect the base-period definition of the custom time period.

/Define Printer

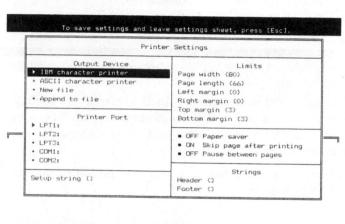

PURPOSE: The /Define Printer command provides all the necessary print settings for a Javelin session, including a setting for printer port. The /Define Printer command allows you to change:

Output device
Printer port
Setup string
Page limits
Miscellaneous printer settings
Header and footer strings

USE: The /Define Printer command is invoked by typing

/DP

You need not press Enter or type a name to display the settings sheet.

/Define Configuration

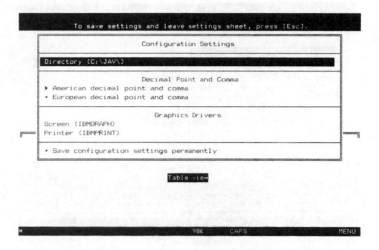

PURPOSE: The /Define Configuration command is used to change existing system settings. You need this command to reconfigure Javelin for a new monitor or printer requiring a different device driver, to change the directory that saves and read files, and to switch between U.S. and European-style numeric formats. The changes made on this menu do not make permanent changes to the Javelin system. The /Define Configuration settings sheet allows changes to:

Directory
Numeric notation
Screen drivers
Printer drivers
Making changes permanent

USE: The /Define Configuration command is invoked by typing

/DC

Remember that changes made on this settings sheet always affect the current modeling session and are not permanent unless you move the cursor to Save configuration settings permanently and press Enter. Javelin will not ask you if you are sure you want to make the changes permanent, so be sure to check your changes before telling Javelin to make them permanent.

/Define Settings

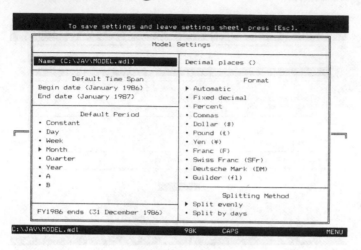

PURPOSE: The **/Define Settings** command is used to change existing model settings. Settings that can be changed include:

>   Name
>   Time span
>   Time periods
>   Fiscal year
>   Decimal places
>   Format
>   Splitting method

USE: The **/Define Settings** command is invoked by typing

>   /DS

You need not type a name or press Enter. Note that changes made on this settings sheet affect only the model you are working on. Clearing the current model or loading a new model erases any changes made to the **/Define Settings** settings sheet.

Note that Javelin uses the following hierarchy for format settings:

1. Model

2. Variable

3. Worksheet

4. Row or column

5. Worksheet cell

Each type of format overrides the format lower on the hierarchy. For example, worksheet cell formats override all other format specifications.

Clear Commands

/Clear Variable

PURPOSE: The /Clear Variable command is used to eliminate a variable from the model. Note that you can remove the variable's data and logic, but you cannot always remove the variable itself. Javelin warns you if the variable you want to remove is used in a formula defining another variable in the model. If this is the case, the data and logic associated with the variable are deleted but the variable remains in the model as an undefined variable—a variable without value.

USE: The /Clear Variable command is activated by typing

/CV

Javelin then asks you for the name of the variable to be cleared. There are four ways to select a variable for clearing:

1. If the variable you want to clear is the one highlighted in the current view, simply press Enter.

2. Type the name of the variable to be cleared, then press Enter.

3. Use the POINT key (F4) to move the cursor to the variable you want to clear, then press Enter.

4. Use the SPELL key (Tab) to highlight the variable you want to clear, then press Enter.

/Clear Building Block

PURPOSE: The /Clear Building Block command is used to eliminate a building block from the model.

USE: The Clear Building Block command is activated by typing

/CB

Javelin then prompts you to enter the name of the building block name to be cleared. You can choose the building block in four ways:

1. To clear the building block that is highlighted in the current view, press Enter.

2. Type the name of the building block to be cleared, then press Enter.

3. Use the POINT key (F4) to move the cursor to the building block you want to clear, then press Enter.

4. Use the SPELL key (Tab) and cursor keys to highlight the building block you want to clear, then press Enter.

/Clear Worksheet

PURPOSE: The /Clear Worksheet command is used to eliminate a worksheet from the model. Note that the /Clear Worksheet command will affect any variables that have been defined through the /*Worksheet Range commands (Sum, Average, High/Max, Low/Min) for the worksheet being cleared.

USE: The /Clear Worksheet command is activated by typing

/CW

Javelin then asks you for the name of the worksheet to be cleared. You can use this command in three ways:

1. If the worksheet on the screen is the one you want to clear, simply type Enter.

2. Type the name of the worksheet to be cleared, then press Enter.

3. Use the SPELL key (Tab) to highlight the name of the worksheet you want to clear, then press Enter.

/Clear Graph

PURPOSE: The /Clear Graph command is used to eliminate a graph from the model.

USE: The /Clear Graph command is called by typing

/CG

Javelin then asks you for the name of the graph to be cleared. You can select a graph in three different ways:

1. To clear the graph on the screen, simply press Enter.

2. Type the name of the graph to be cleared, then press Enter.

3. Use the SPELL key (Tab) to highlight the name of the graph you want to clear, then press Enter.

/Clear Macro

PURPOSE: The /Clear Macro command is used to eliminate a macro from the model.

USE: The /Clear Macro command is activated by typing

/CM

Javelin then prompts for a macro name. There are three ways to select a macro for clearing:

1. If the macro you want to clear is in the present MACRO view, simply press Enter.

2. Type the name of the macro to be cleared, then press Enter.

3. Use the SPELL key (Tab) to highlight the name of the macro you want to clear, then press Enter.

/Clear Data

PURPOSE: The /Clear Data command is used to eliminate data for specified periods from the model. Javelin asks you for a beginning and an ending date, and then requests confirmation before clearing any data. After confirmation, Javelin clears all data before the beginning date and after the ending date.

USE: The /Clear Data command is activated by typing

/CD

Javelin prompts you for a Begin Date, supplying (in parentheses) either the default *Begin date* of the model or the *Begin date* you supplied on the /Define Settings settings sheet. If you want to accept the default date offered by Javelin, press Enter. If you want to change the default date, type the appropriate *Begin date* and press Enter.

Javelin then prompts you for an End Date, supplying (in parentheses) either the default *End date* of the model or the *End date* you supplied on the /Define Settings settings sheet. Again, you can either press Enter to accept the date offered, or type a new date and press Enter.

Javelin asks for confirmation before clearing the data from the model (see fig. B.1). Press *Y* (for Yes) to clear the data or *N* (for No) to stop the operation.

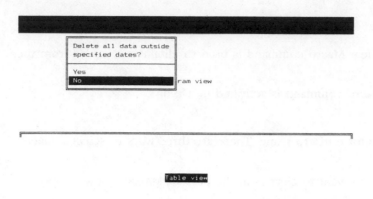

Fig. B.1. Javelin asks you for confirmation before clearing any data from the model.

/Clear Note

PURPOSE: The /Clear Note command is used to eliminate a note from the model. Javelin doesn't give you a warning when you clear a note.

USE: The /Clear Note command is invoked by typing

/CN

Javelin then prompts you for the name of the variable to which the note is attached. You can clear a note in three ways:

1. To clear the note in the active view, simply press Enter.

2. Type the name of the variable whose note is to be cleared, then press Enter.

3. Use the SPELL key (Tab) to highlight the name of the variable whose note you want to clear, then press Enter.

/Clear All

PURPOSE: The /Clear All command is used to remove all existing work from the current Javelin session. This command has the same effect as starting a new Javelin work session without calling in a model from disk. When you use /Clear All, any work not saved previously to the disk will be lost.

USE: The /Clear All command is activated by typing

/CA

Javelin asks for confirmation before clearing everything from the model (see fig. B.2).

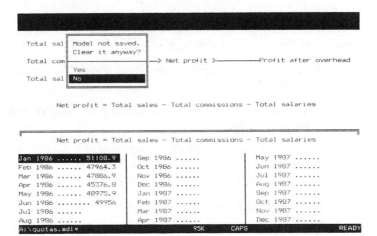

Fig. B.2. Javelin asks for
confirmation before clearing the
entire model.

View Commands

/View Diagram

PURPOSE: The /View Diagram command is used to select a variable or
building block for highlighting in the DIAGRAM view (see fig. B.3).

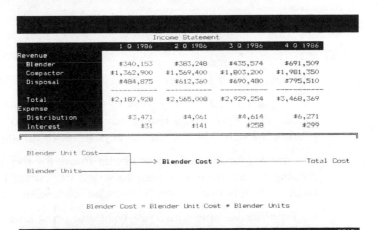

Fig. B.3. The bottom window
displays Javelin's DIAGRAM view
with the variable *Blender Cost*
highlighted.

USE: The /View Diagram command is activated by typing

/VD

Javelin asks you for the name of either a building block or a variable to display in the DIAGRAM view. You can select a variable or building block for the DIAGRAM view in four different ways:

1. If the cursor is highlighting either a variable or building block in the current view, simply press Enter.

2. Type the name of the building block or variable you want to view, then press Enter.

3. Use the POINT key (F4) to highlight the desired variable or building block, then press Enter. This method only works if the desired building block or variable is in the active view.

4. Use the SPELL key (Tab) to highlight the desired building block or variable, then press Enter.

/View Formulas

PURPOSE: The /View Formulas command is used to select a set of formulas for viewing. You can choose to see all the formulas in the model or only the roots or branches of a particular variable. The three options of the /View Formulas command are

All
Roots
Branches

USE: The /View Formulas command is activated by typing

/VF

Javelin responds with a submenu of three options:

1. Pressing *A* (for *All*) tells Javelin to list all the formulas in the current model. This alphabetical listing may be too large to fit on one screen in some models. Use the cursor keys to move through the view.

2. Pressing *R* (for *Roots*) causes Javelin to ask for the name of the variable whose roots you want to see. If the cursor is on the desired variable, simply press Enter. Otherwise, choose one of the following:

   a. Type the variable name you want and press Enter.

   b. Use the POINT key (F4) to highlight the variable and press Enter.

   c. Use the SPELL key (Tab) to highlight the name and then press Enter.

3. Pressing *B* (for *Branches*) causes Javelin to ask for the name of the variable name whose branches you want to see. If the cursor is on that variable, simply press Enter. Otherwise, choose one of the following:

    a. Type the name of the variable and press Enter.

    b. Use the POINT key (F4) to highlight the variable and press Enter.

    c. Use the SPELL key (Tab) to highlight the name of the variable and press Enter.

/View Table

PURPOSE: The /View Table command is used to select a variable for viewing in the TABLE view. This view provides a list of times in whatever period has been assigned to a variable (daily, weekly, monthly, quarterly, yearly, or custom periods).

USE: The /View Table command is invoked by typing

/VT

Javelin then prompts you for the name of the variable to use in the TABLE view. You can select such a variable in four different ways:

1. If the cursor is on the variable you want, simply press Enter.

2. Type the name of the variable to be viewed, and then press Enter.

3. Use the POINT key (F4) to highlight the desired variable, then press Enter. This method only works if the desired variable is in the active view.

4. Use the SPELL key (Tab) to highlight the desired variable, then press Enter.

/View Chart

PURPOSE: The /View Chart command selects a variable for viewing in the CHART view. The CHART view provides a bar graph for the variable selected.

USE: The /View Chart command is activated by typing

/VC

Javelin then asks you for the name of the variable to use in the CHART view. You can select this variable in four different ways:

1. If the variable you want is in another view and the cursor is on the variable, simply press Enter.

2. Type the name of the variable you want and then press Enter.

3. Use the POINT key (F4) to highlight the desired variable and press Enter. (This method works only if the desired variable is in the current view.)

4. Use the SPELL key (Tab) to highlight the desired variable and then press Enter.

/View Quick Graph

PURPOSE: The /View Quick graph command is used to select a variable for the QUICK GRAPH view. The QUICK GRAPH view provides a graph of the selected variable over time.

USE: The /View Quick graph command is activated by typing

/VQ

Javelin prompts you for the name of the variable you want to use in the QUICK GRAPH view. You can select the variable in four ways:

1. If the cursor is on the variable in another view, press Enter.

2. Type the name of the variable you want to view and then press Enter.

3. Use the POINT key (F4) to highlight the desired variable and then press Enter. This method only works if the desired variable is in the current view.

4. Use the SPELL key (Tab) to highlight the desired variable, then press Enter.

/View Worksheet

PURPOSE: The /View Worksheet command is used to display a specific worksheet for the current model. The WORKSHEET view provides a spreadsheet for displaying portions of the model and for entering data and model logic. You can create as many worksheets in the current file as available memory allows.

USE: The /View Worksheet command is activated by typing

/VW

Javelin asks you for the name of the worksheet you want to use in the WORKSHEET view. You can choose the view in either of two ways:

1. Type the name of the worksheet to view and then press Enter. Javelin assumes the worksheet name *WORKSHEET* if no other name is given.

2. Use the SPELL key (Tab) to highlight the desired variable and then press Enter.

/View Notes

PURPOSE: The /View Notes command is used to select a specific variable's or building block's notes for viewing in the NOTES view. The NOTES view lets you associate notes with particular variables or building blocks to document the logic and assumptions that go into the variable or building block.

USE: The /View Notes command is activated by typing

/VN

Javelin prompts you for the name of the variable or building block to use in the NOTES view. There are four ways to select a variable or building block for the NOTES view:

1. If the variable or building block you want is displayed in another view and the cursor is on that variable, simply press Enter.

2. Type the name of the variable or building block to view and then press Enter.

3. Use the POINT key (F4) to highlight the variable or building block you want and then press Enter. This method only works if the desired variable or building block is in the current view.

4. Use the SPELL key (Tab) to highlight the desired variable or building block and then press Enter.

/View Errors

PURPOSE: The /View Errors command is used to show all the errors in the current model. This command shows time-period errors and undefined variable errors.

USE: The /View Errors command is invoked by typing

/VE

Javelin responds with a list of all errors in the active model.

/View Macro

PURPOSE: The /View Macro command is used to select a macro for viewing or editing. The macro you select can be one you have created with the /Define Macro command or created in the MACRO view.

USE: The /View Macro command is activated by typing

/VM

Javelin asks you for the name of the macro to use in the view. You can select a variable or building block in the MACRO view two different ways:

1. Type the name of the variable or building block to view, then press Enter. Javelin assumes a macro name of *MACRO* if no other macro names are given.

2. Use the SPELL key (Tab) to highlight the desired macro and press Enter.

/View Graph

PURPOSE: The /View Graph command is used to select a graph for viewing in the GRAPH view. The GRAPH view provides a high-quality, user-defined graph for display.

USE: The /View Graph command is invoked by typing

/VG

Javelin asks you for the name of the graph to use in the GRAPH view. You can select a graph in two different ways:

1. Type the name of the graph to view, followed by Enter. Javelin assumes a graph name of *GRAPH* if no other name is given.

2. Use the SPELL key (Tab) to highlight the desired graph name, then press Enter.

Window Commands

/Window 1

PURPOSE: Javelin displays two active views at startup; each of these views occupies a window. The /Window 1 command tells Javelin to present a single view in one full-screen window.

USE: The /Window 1 command is activated by typing

/W1

Javelin does not prompt further. The active view expands to become a full-screen window.

/Window 2

PURPOSE: The /Window 2 command splits a full-screen Javelin window into two windows. The two windows can then be used to study different aspects of the model or different views of the same aspect of the model.

USE: The /Window 2 command is activated by typing

/W2

Javelin does not prompt further. The current view is shown in two windows. The single view that existed in the one-window mode is resized to fit into a two-window mode.

/Window Switch

PURPOSE: The /Window Switch command moves the cursor from one view to another when Javelin is in two-window mode. This command is identical to pressing the WINDOW key (F6). Javelin can only switch windows in two-window mode.

USE: The /Window Switch command is activated by typing

/WS

You can also switch windows by pressing the WINDOW key (F6). Pressing this key has the same effect as typing /WS.

/Window Adjust

PURPOSE: The /Window Adjust command lets you use the Up- and Down-arrow keys to move the center double bar up and down the screen (see fig. B.4), changing the portion of screen that each window occupies.

USE: The /Window Adjust command is activated by typing

/WA

Javelin then prompts you to adjust the center double bar by pressing the Up- or Down-arrow keys to indicate direction. When the bar is placed where you like, press Enter to end the process. Note that any two views can be active (except QUICK GRAPH and GRAPH) when adjusting window size.

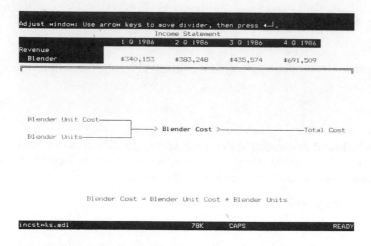

Fig. B.4. /Window Adjust command is used to expand the bottom window.

Print Commands

/Print Graph

PURPOSE: The /Print Graph command is used to print any Javelin graph defined with the /Define Graph command. The graph is not displayed on the screen unless you issue the /View Graph command or press the GRAPH key (F10).

USE: The /Print Graph command is activated by typing

/PG

Javelin responds by asking for the name of the graph to be printed. You can select a graph in three different ways:

1. Type the name of the graph, then press Enter. Javelin assumes a graph name *GRAPH* if no name is given.

2. Press Enter. This method works only if a graph has been previously displayed with either the GRAPH key (F10) or the /View Graph command.

3. Use the SPELL key (Tab) to highlight the name of the graph you wish to print and then press Enter.

/Print Current View

PURPOSE: The /Print Current view command is used to print the current Javelin view. The current view is the *active* view (the view with the cursor).

Javelin prints all the information in the current view, even data extending beyond the screen boundary. You could, for example, print all the formulas listed in the /View Formulas All command although all the formulas cannot be displayed on screen at the same time. In the DIAGRAM view, however, the /Print Current view command prints only what is visible in the active window.

USE: The /Print Current view command is activated by typing

/PC

Javelin does not prompt any further unless the current view is a WORKSHEET view. When you use /Print Current view in the WORKSHEET view (see fig. B.5), Javelin asks if you want to print out the worksheet borders.

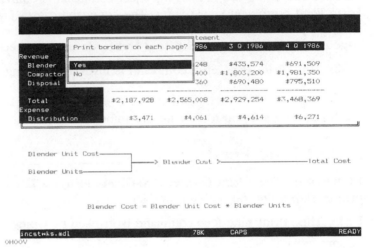

Fig. B.5. Javelin asks if you want to include worksheet borders when you use the /Print Current view command.

/Print Screen

PURPOSE: The /Print Screen command is used to print the Javelin screen, and is similar to using the PrtSc (print screen) key on the computer keyboard. Javelin prints all the information on the screen but does not print extended views.

USE: The /Print Screen command is activated by typing

/PS

Javelin does not prompt any further.

/Print Align Page

PURPOSE: The /Print Align page command tells Javelin that you have manually adjusted the paper in the printer to the top of a page. The command resets the top of the page but retains any special printer settings, such as boldfacing, expanded print, and so on. This command lets you move the printer platen until the top of the page is properly aligned with the print head. The command can also be used to align the first page of continuous-feed paper.

USE: The /Print Align page command is activated by typing

/PA

Javelin doesn't prompt you for any further information.

/Print Page Eject

PURPOSE: Using the /Print Page eject command is equivalent to pressing the Form Feed button on your printer. The command causes Javelin to issue a printer command to move to the top of the next page. The printer ejects the page currently under the print head and loads another sheet of paper.

USE: The /Print Page eject command is invoked by typing

/PP

Javelin doesn't ask you for any further information.

/Print Line Feed

PURPOSE: The /Print Line feed command instructs Javelin to have your printer skip a line on the current page.

USE: The /Print Line feed command is invoked by typing

/PL

Javelin doesn't prompt you for any further information.

File Commands

/File Load

PURPOSE: The /File Load command reads a Javelin model from a disk file into the computer's memory.

USE: The /File Load command is invoked by typing

/FL

Javelin then prompts you for the name of the model to load. You can enter the name of the desired model in three ways:

1. If the model you want to load is the current model in the Javelin system, press Enter. (This method only works if a model name has been defined with the /Define Settings command or the model was loaded earlier in the work session.)

2. Type the name of the model and press Enter. Javelin tells you if the specified file doesn't exist in the current data directory (specified with /Define Configuration).

3. If your model is in a different drive or subdirectory, you may enter the drive designator and/or the subdirectory name and then use the SPELL key (Tab). Javelin lists the models in that drive or subdirectory.

4. Use the SPELL key (Tab) to highlight the name of the desired model, and then press Enter.

Javelin warns you if modifications have been made to the current model before it loads in the requested model so that you can save the current model if you want. If you do not save the current model, the /File Load command effectively wipes out all the work you have done prior to loading in the new file (see fig. B.6).

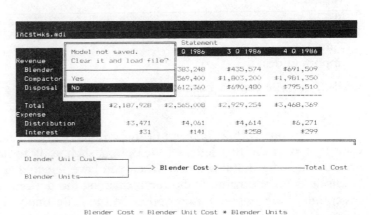

Fig. B.6. You can abort loading a new file if you need to save work in the current file.

/File Save

PURPOSE: The /File Save command is used to save a Javelin model to disk.

USE: The /File Save command is invoked by typing

/FS

Javelin responds by prompting for the name to save the model under. You can enter the name of the model to be saved in three different ways:

1. If you want to save the active model, simply press Enter. This method only works if a model name was defined previously with the /Define Settings command or was loaded earlier in the work session.

2. Type the name of the model and press Enter. Javelin tells you if the named model already exists in the current data directory.

3. Use the SPELL key (Tab) to highlight the name of the desired model, then press Enter. Javelin tells you if the named model already exists in the current directory.

/File Import

PURPOSE: The /File Import command transfers parts of other Javelin models into the active file. This command is useful when other models and files contain worksheets, data, variables, or other material needed in the current model. The /File Import command lets you move the following items into the current model:

Another Javelin model
Variable
Macro
Building block
Time period
Import values

USE: The /File Import command is activated by typing

/FI

Javelin responds with a submenu of the various options. Choose the option you want by typing the first letter of the option, such as *W* to import a worksheet or *B* to import a building block. When you have selected an item to import, Javelin asks for the name of the file containing the desired item. The only exception is the *Import values* option on the /File Import submenu.

There are two ways to select a file to import from:

1. Type the file name at the prompt, then press Enter. Javelin warns you if the desired file doesn't exist on the search path.

2. Use the SPELL key (Tab) to highlight the desired file name, then press Enter.

Once a file has been selected, Javelin asks you for the name of the item to import. There are two ways to select the item:

1. Type the name of the worksheet, building block, variable, etc., at the prompt, then press Enter. Javelin warns you if the desired item doesn't exist in the named file (see fig. B.7).

2. Use the SPELL key (Tab) to highlight the desired item, then press Enter.

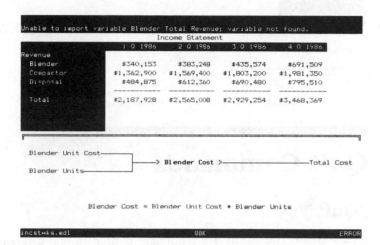

Unable to import variable Blender Total Revenue; variable not found.

Income Statement

	1 Q 1986	2 Q 1986	3 Q 1986	4 Q 1986
Revenue				
Blender	$340,153	$383,248	$435,574	$691,509
Compactor	$1,362,900	$1,569,400	$1,803,200	$1,981,350
Disposal	$484,875	$612,360	$690,480	$795,510
Total	$2,187,928	$2,565,008	$2,929,254	$3,468,369

Blender Unit Cost——
                    ——> Blender Cost >————————Total Cost
Blender Units——

Blender Cost = Blender Unit Cost * Blender Units

incstwks.mdl   88K   ERROR

Fig. B.7. The /File Save command asks you to rename the file if a file with a similar name exists.

The one exception to these procedures is the **/File Import Import values** command. This command imports only the variables and data defined in the **/Define Building block Rollup** and **/Define Building block Import data** commands.

/File Delete

PURPOSE: The **/File Delete** command removes a Javelin file from the current data directory. Warning: Javelin allows you to delete any file in the directory, not just files containing Javelin models. Javelin models are identified by the four characters *.MDL* after the model name.

USE: The **/File Delete** command is invoked by typing

/FD

Javelin responds by prompting for the name of the file to delete. There are two ways to enter the name of the desired file:

1. Type the name of the file and press Enter.

2. Use the SPELL key (Tab) to highlight the name of the desired file, then press Enter. Before the file is deleted, Javelin asks you to confirm that you want to remove the file from the disk.

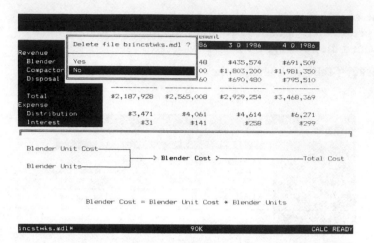

Fig. B.8. Javelin gives you a chance to stop the /File Delete operation.

Quit Commands

/Quit Yes

PURPOSE: The **/Quit Yes** command is used to end a Javelin work session (see fig. B.9).

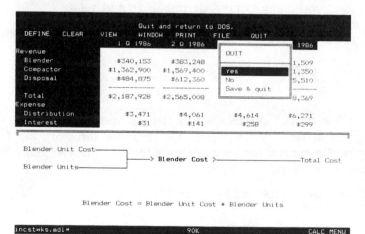

Fig. B.9. Options available after beginning the /Quit operation.

USE: The **/Quit Yes** command is executed by typing

/QY

Before complying with your request, Javelin warns you if the current model has not been saved to disk (see fig. B.10).

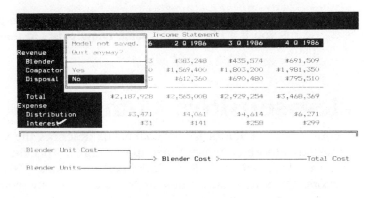

Fig. B.10. Javelin gives you a
chance to save the current model
before quitting.

/Quit No

PURPOSE: The /Quit No command is used to return to Javelin after invoking
the /Quit Yes command by accident.

USE: The /Quit No command is executed by typing

/QN

Javelin returns you to the current view when the /Quit No command is
executed.

/Quit Save & Quit

PURPOSE: The /Quit Save & quit command is used to save the active model
and exit to DOS.

USE: The /Quit Save & quit command is executed by typing

/QS

Javelin prompts you for a file name when exiting with the /Quit Save & quit
command. There are three methods of giving the current work session's model
a name when saving it with the /Quit Save & quit command:

1. To save the last model loaded (or the name given by the /Define
   Settings command if no other name is given), simply press Enter. If
   there is no name currently active, Javelin aborts the quit-save process
   and returns to the session.

2. Type a name and press Enter. Javelin warns you if a file with the same
   name exists in the current data directory.

3. Use the SPELL key (Tab) to highlight a name, then press Enter. Javelin warns you if a file with the same name exists in the current search path.

View-sensitive Commands

The following section of Javelin commands describes the view-sensitive commands—those commands that appear only in specific views. Javelin's view-sensitive commands include /*Worksheet, /*Formulas, /*Roots, /*Branches, and /*Errors. All view-sensitive commands are accessed by typing /*.

*Worksheet Commands

Whenever the WORKSHEET view is the current view, Javelin makes available the commands described in the following sections. Accessed by typing /*, the following /*Worksheet commands provide capabilities for copying, deleting, and sorting worksheet data; changing the worksheet borders or display of data; changing variable names; performing calculations on ranges of cells; and importing data into a Javelin worksheet.

/*Worksheet Copy

PURPOSE: The /*Worksheet Copy command copies a range of information from one part of the worksheet to another part of the same worksheet or to a separate worksheet in the same model. This command copies logic as well as data.

USE: Activate /*Worksheet Copy by typing

/*C

Copying a range for transfer can be done in three steps:

1. Define the range you want to copy. The range can be anything from a single cell to an entire block.

2. Place the cursor in the *anchor* position (the upper leftmost cell) of the new range.

3. Press Enter to complete the operation.

Keep in mind that a range is a rectangular block of information as large as an entire worksheet or as small as a single cell. As long as the range remains rectangular, you can define a range to be any portion of the worksheet.

Define the range to be copied by following the prompts. After you enter the /*Worksheet Copy command, Javelin asks you for a starting point. Move the cursor to the starting point of the range, and either press Enter to complete the range definition or press the period key (.) to tell Javelin you will define another corner of the range (see fig. B.11). If you are defining a range larger than one cell and you have pressed the period key, Javelin asks you for the other corner of the range (see fig. B.12).

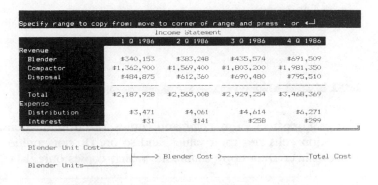

Fig. B.11. Javelin asks you for the starting point of the range to copy.

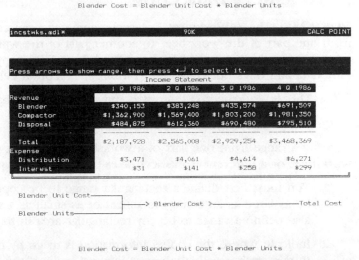

Fig. B.12. Javelin asks you for the end point of the range to copy.

When you copy data from one range to another, you must indicate a destination for the copied material. After you define the range, Javelin asks for the upper left cell of the destination range (anchor cell). Move the cursor to the anchor cell and press Enter (see fig. B.13).

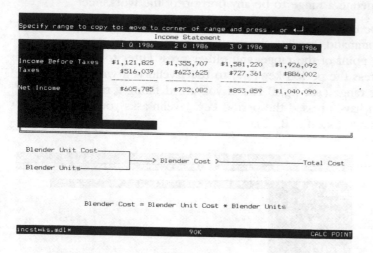

Fig. B.13. Javelin highlights the anchor cell and outlines the range.

The /*Worksheet Copy command copies formulas, relationships, names, exception cells and their values, and so on. Do not confuse this with the /*Worksheet Data copy command, which copies only data.

/*Worksheet Data Copy

PURPOSE: The /*Worksheet Data copy command can copy a range of data from one part of the worksheet to another part of the worksheet or to another worksheet in the same model. The /*Worksheet Data copy command copies only data and does not copy logic, formulas, exception cell names, and so on.

USE: The /*Worksheet Data copy command is invoked by typing

/*D

Copying a range from one part of a worksheet to another part of the same worksheet or a different worksheet takes place in two steps:

1. You must first define a rectangular range to be copied. The range may be as large as an entire worksheet or as small as a single cell. You can also define a range to be any rectangular area in the worksheet.

2. Indicate where the copied information is to go by moving the cursor to the *anchor* cell (the upper leftmost cell) of the destination.

Define the range to copy by following the prompts. After you select the /*Worksheet Data copy command, Javelin asks for a starting point. Move the cursor to the starting point of the range, and either press Enter to complete the range definition or press the period key (.) to tell Javelin you will be defining another corner of the range (see fig. B.11). If you are defining a range of more than one cell, Javelin asks you for the other corner of the range after you have typed a period.

Once the range is defined, Javelin prompts you for the upper leftmost cell (the *anchor* cell) of the destination range. Move the cursor to the anchor cell and press Enter. Javelin moves the ranges as you instruct.

/*Worksheet Border Dates

PURPOSE: The /*Worksheet Border Dates command is used to fill the worksheet borders with dates. The worksheet borders are the areas of the screen where you specify which variables and dates you want to display values for in the worksheet. The dates can be the default dates of the model as defined with the /Define Settings command. You can also enter the dates when Javelin prompts you to do so.

USE: Start by placing the cursor on a border cell on either the left or top border. Once the cursor is on a border cell, activate the /*Worksheet Border Dates command by typing

    /*BD

Javelin's prompt also shows Javelin's default setting of the model's starting date; you can accept this date by pressing Enter. You can override the default by typing in the date you want (see fig. B.14).

```
Begin date (February 1986):
                                  Income Statement
                          1 Q 1986     2 Q 1986     3 Q 1986     4 Q 1986
Revenue
  Blender             $340,153     $383,248     $435,574     $691,509
  Compactor         $1,362,900   $1,569,400   $1,803,200   $1,981,350
  Disposal            $484,875     $612,360     $690,480     $795,510
                    -----------  -----------  -----------  -----------
  Total             $2,187,928   $2,565,008   $2,929,254   $3,468,369
Expense
  Distribution         $3,471       $4,061       $4,614       $6,271
  Interest                $31         $141         $258         $299
```

```
Blender Unit Cost----
                      ----> Blender Cost >----------------Total Cost
Blender Units--------
```

Fig. B.14. Javelin asks you for the beginning date in the /*Worksheet Border Dates command.

```
Blender Cost = Blender Unit Cost * Blender Units
```

```
incstwks.mdl*                              90K                    CALC READY
```

Javelin then asks for an ending date. You can accept Javelin's default ending date (the last date defined in the model) by pressing Enter (see fig. B.15). You can also override the default, type your own ending date, and then press Enter.

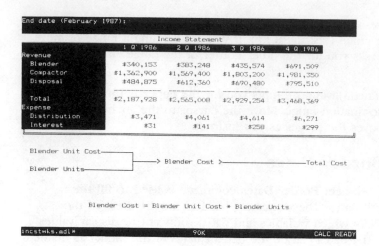

Fig. B.15. Javelin asks you for the ending date for the borders in the /*Worksheet Border Dates command.

Note that you do not have to move the cursor to enter a series of successive dates. With /*Worksheet Border Dates, Javelin places a succession of dates in the border, starting at the cursor. Also note that Javelin does not lock you into the new time periods. For example, you can use the /*Worksheet Border Dates command to fill in the border with monthly dates and then add quarterly dates within the same border.

/*Worksheet Border Variable Names

PURPOSE: The /*Worksheet Border Variable names command is used to fill in the worksheet border with variable names.

USE: Activate the /*Worksheet Border Variable names command by typing

/*BV

If the border is empty, Javelin fills it with all the variables listed in alphabetical order. If you move the cursor to a word in a border and press Enter, Javelin fills the border with variable names containing that word. For example, Blender Sales, Compactor Sales, and Disposal Sales all contain the single word Sales. Placing the cursor on the word Sales and entering the /*Worksheet Border Variable names command causes Javelin to fill in the border with the words Blender, Compactor, and Disposal.

/*Worksheet Border Insert Border

PURPOSE: The /*Worksheet Border Insert border command is used to add a border to the current worksheet.

USE: Start the */Worksheet Border Insert border command by entering

/*BI

Three different borders can be inserted, depending on where the cursor is when you enter the command. You can create another column border, another row border, or another worksheet (the intersection of a new column and row border).

To insert row or column borders, place the cursor at the row or column cell where you want to place the new border and enter the /*Worksheet Border Insert border command. To create a *subworksheet* within the borders of another worksheet, choose a cell somewhere in the main worksheet as the home cell (the cell in the upper left corner) of the new worksheet and then enter the /*Worksheet Border Insert border command.

/*Worksheet Border Remove Border

PURPOSE: The /*Worksheet Border Remove border command is one of the options on the WORKSHEET view. This command is the opposite of the last command, /*Worksheet Border Insert border. This command removes any borders previously inserted with the /*Worksheet Border Insert border command except for the two main worksheet borders. Although the results are the direct opposite of the insert command, the procedure is similar.

USE: Issue the /*Worksheet Border Remove border command by typing

/*BR

Begin by choosing the border you'd like to have removed. Move the cursor to the topmost part of a column border, the leftmost part of a row border, or the home cell (the cell in the upper left corner) of a subworksheet. Javelin automatically removes the border at the cursor and resizes the remaining worksheet to fill the screen.

/*Worksheet Border Expand Border

PURPOSE: The /*Worksheet Border Expand border command is used to expand row borders (the borders that run horizontally, usually at the top of a worksheet).

USE: To start the /*Worksheet Border Expand border command, type

/*BE

Wherever the cursor is in the worksheet, typing */BE* causes the nearest row border above the cursor to expand by one row. If no subworksheets or row borders are between the cursor position and the top border, typing the command will increase the width of the top border from one row to two rows, from two rows to three rows, and so on.

/*Worksheet Border Shrink Border

PURPOSE: The /*Worksheet Border Shrink border command is active only in the WORKSHEET view. This command is used to shrink row borders (the borders that run horizontally, usually at the top of a worksheet).

USE: To activate the /*Worksheet Border Shrink border command, type

   /*BS

No matter where the cursor is on the worksheet, typing /*BS shrinks the nearest upper row border by one row. If no subworksheets or row borders are between the cursor position and the top border, typing /*BS will reduce the width of the top border from two rows to one row, from three rows to two rows, and so on.

A Note on /*Worksheet Range Commands

Javelin's /*Worksheet Range commands perform operations on ranges of worksheet cells. These operations include commands for creating four types of worksheet formulas, a command for deleting a range of cells, and a command for printing a range of cells. The first four options available through the /*Worksheet Range command (Sum, Average, Low/Min, High/Max) let you create formulas for a range of cells and are similar in the following ways:

1. All four commands work only on a target cell—that is, a cell with a variable name assigned in one border and a date in the other border. The entries in the cell's borders determine whether the /*Worksheet Range command defines a single cell, a row, or column in the worksheet and whether the command defines a constant or time-series variable in the model.

2. Once you have defined a range for any of the commands, you can highlight the range as follows: place the cursor on the target cell, then press and hold down the Ctrl key while you press Enter.

3. Whenever you use any of the first four /*Worksheet Range commands, Javelin indicates in the FORMULAS view that a variable has been defined with the command and displays the variable as a building block in the DIAGRAM view.

4. If you delete a worksheet containing a formula created through /*Worksheet Range Sum, Average, Low/Min or High/Max, the formula is also deleted.

/*Worksheet Range Sum

PURPOSE: The /*Worksheet Range Sum command, which is active only in the WORKSHEET view, is used to sum the contents of a range of worksheet cells. Summing is a unique worksheet function. Although Javelin's SUM function has a similar effect, the /*Worksheet Range Sum command creates a building block in the DIAGRAM view. A formula defined through the worksheet differs from a normal Javelin formula. The worksheet-defined formula cannot be edited or removed from other views. Deleting a worksheet where this function is used also undefines all variables defined using the worksheet sum.

USE: Using the /*Worksheet Range Sum command involves four steps:

1. Place the cursor in the target cell.

2. Issue the /*Worksheet Range Sum command by typing

   /*RS

3. Define the range to which the command applies (see the introduction to the *Worksheet Range commands for directions on defining ranges).

4. Now press the CALC key (F9) to have Javelin calculate the values of the range formula.

/*Worksheet Range Average

PURPOSE: The /*Worksheet Range Average command is active only in the WORKSHEET view. This command, a unique arithmetic worksheet function, finds the average value in a range of cells in the worksheet. Although Javelin has a similar function (AVG), the /*Worksheet Range Average command has the advantage of being able to define the average over a range of values already gathered together in a worksheet. A formula defined through the worksheet differs from a normal Javelin formula. The worksheet-defined formula cannot be edited or removed from other views.

USE: Using /*Worksheet Range Average command involves four steps:

1. Place the cursor on the target cell.

2. Issue the /*Worksheet Range Average command by typing

   /*RA

3. Define the range to which the command applies (see the introduction to the *Worksheet Range commands for directions on defining ranges).

4. Press the CALC key (F9) to have Javelin calculate the values of the range formula.

/*Worksheet Range High/Max

PURPOSE: The /*Worksheet Range High/Max command, which is active only in the WORKSHEET view, is used to find the maximum value in a range of cells in the worksheet. Note that the /*Worksheet High/Max command is a unique arithmetic worksheet function. Although the Javelin function MAX is similar, this command creates a building block in the DIAGRAM view. A formula defined through the worksheet is different from a normal Javelin formula. The worksheet-defined formula cannot be edited or removed from other views.

USE: The /*Worksheet Range High/Max command involves four steps:

1. Place the cursor in the target cell.

2. Call up the /*Worksheet High/Max command by typing

    /*RH

3. Define the range the command is to work on (see the introduction to the *Worksheet Range commands for directions on defining ranges).

4. Press the CALC key (F9) to have Javelin calculate the values of the range formula.

/*Worksheet Range Low/Min

PURPOSE: The /*Worksheet Range Low/Min command, which is active only in the WORKSHEET view, finds the minimum value in a range of cells in the worksheet. This command is a unique worksheet function. Although Javelin's MIN function is similar, the /*Worksheet Low/Min command creates a building block in the DIAGRAM view. A formula defined through the worksheet is different from a normal Javelin formula. The worksheet-defined formula cannot be edited or removed from other views. Deleting the worksheet where this function is used also deletes the formula created by using the /*Worksheet Low/Min command.

USE: Using the /*Worksheet Range Low/Min command involves four steps:

1. Place the cursor on the target cell.

2. Issue the /*Worksheet Low/Min command by typing

   /*RL

3. Define the range to which the command applies (see the introduction to the *Worksheet Range commands for directions on defining ranges).

4. Press the CALC key (F9) to have Javelin calculate the values of the range formula.

/*Worksheet Range Delete

PURPOSE: The /*Worksheet Range Delete command, which is active only in the WORKSHEET view, is used to delete a range of the worksheet. Deleting a worksheet range doesn't remove the data from the Javelin model, only from the WORKSHEET view. Even if the data has not been entered elsewhere, the data remains in the model although it is deleted from the worksheet.

USE: The /*Worksheet Range Delete command is invoked by typing

   /*RD

Javelin responds by prompting you for the starting point of the range to be deleted. Place the cursor in a corner cell of the range to be deleted. If you just want to delete one cell, simply press Enter. If you want to delete more than one cell, press the period key (.) to indicate that a range is to be deleted, then move the cursor to the cell in the opposite corner of the range. Javelin highlights the range as it is defined. When you have defined the range, press Enter.

/*Worksheet Range Print

PURPOSE: The /*Worksheet Range Print command is active only in the WORKSHEET view. This command is used to print selected ranges of the worksheet. You are given the choice of having borders included on the printed page.

USE: The /*Worksheet Range Print command is invoked by typing

Javelin responds by asking you for the starting point of the range to be printed. Place the cursor in a corner cell of the range. If you want to print one cell, simply press Enter. If you want to print a range, press the period key (.) to indicate that a range is to be printed and move the cursor to the opposite corner cell of the range, and then press Enter. The range is highlighted as it is defined.

/*Worksheet Import File Wks

PURPOSE: The /*Worksheet Import file WKS (worksheet) command is active only in the WORKSHEET view. This command is used to bring a Lotus 1-2-3 file into a Javelin worksheet.

USE: The /*Worksheet Import file WKS command is issued by placing the cursor in the *anchor* cell (the upper left corner of the range where you want the imported data to appear) of the range that is to contain the imported data, then typing

/*IW

Javelin then prompts you for the name of the Lotus 1-2-3 file to be imported. Javelin will only import 1-2-3 files with the *.WKS* extension. You can use the SPELL key (Tab) to list available files.

Javelin issues an error message if no file can be found that matches your request.

/*Worksheet Import File Text

PURPOSE: The /*Worksheet Import file Text command is active only in the WORKSHEET view. This command is used to bring any ASCII text file into a Javelin worksheet.

USE: Activate the /*Worksheet Import file Text command by placing the cursor in the anchor cell (the upper left corner of the range where you want the imported data to appear) of the range that is to contain the imported data, then typing

/*IT

Javelin then prompts you for the name of the ASCII text file to be imported. Javelin will import any ASCII file, but you can use the SPELL key (Tab) to list available .PRN files only.

Javelin issues an error message if no file that matches your request can be found.

/*Worksheet Name Change

PURPOSE: The /*Worksheet Name change command, which is active only in the WORKSHEET view, allows rapid changes of variable names throughout the model. Other sections of this book have shown how to rename a variable using the /Define Variable command. Javelin's WORKSHEET view provides a quick way, using a single command, to rename several variables displayed in the worksheet.

USE: Begin the /*Worksheet Name change command by placing the cursor on the variable whose name you want to change. Then type

/*N

Javelin prompts you now for the new variable name (see fig. B.16). After you enter the name, press Enter.

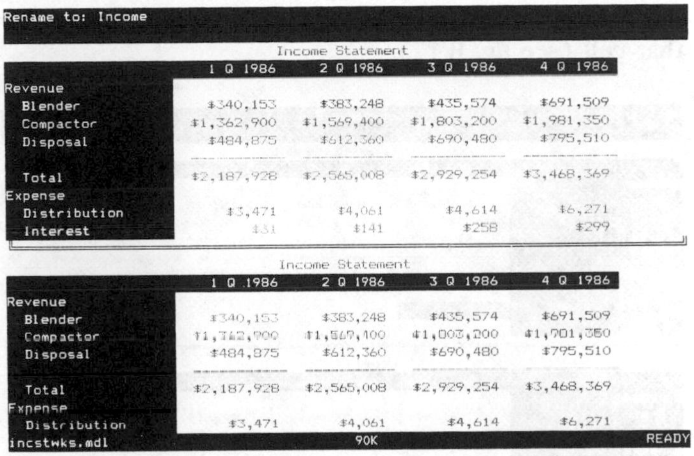

Fig. B.16. The /*Worksheet
Name change prompt.

/*Worksheet Name change can be used with either complete variables or parts. If you have divided variable names into parts, you can change any part and have that change reflected in the full name in the model. This command can be used with the cursor on the home cell (the cell in the upper left corner), a name in either border, or an exception cell; the results happen in a greatest-to-least pattern. Changing the name in a home cell changes all variable names on a worksheet. Changing the names in a border changes only those variable names in that border reference. Changing the name of an exception cell changes only the name of the variable in that exception cell.

Note that this operation also inserts the new variable name in any formulas that reference the old variable name.

/*Worksheet Exception

PURPOSE: The /*Worksheet Exception command is available only in the WORKSHEET view. This command is used to create a worksheet cell that is

independent of border references. An *exception cell* is a location on a
worksheet that is not bound by the definitions of other cells. You can have
as many exception cells on a worksheet as you wish, but too many can
confuse the documentation of your worksheet. If you plan on using several
exception cells in a worksheet, help yourself by assigning a NOTES view to each
exception cell.

USE: Use the /*Worksheet Exception command by positioning the cursor on
the cell you wish to single out and typing

    /*E

Javelin responds by prompting you for the variable and value to be placed in
that cell (see fig. B.17).

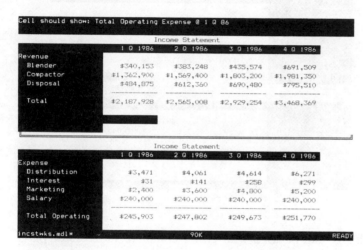

Fig. B.17. The /*Worksheet
Exception cell prompt.

/*Worksheet Sort

PURPOSE: The /*Worksheet Sort command is active only in the WORKSHEET
view. This command lets you sort the alphabetic and numeric values in rows of
the worksheet. This command works only on rows; there is no way to sort
through columns in a Javelin worksheet.

USE: Begin the /*Worksheet Sort command by typing

    /*S

Javelin responds with another submenu of options. You can use this command
to sort in either Ascending (least to greatest) or Descending (greatest to least)
order. Enter an *A* for *ascending* or *D* for *descending* sort. Javelin then prompts
you to place the cursor on the cell where sorting is to start.

Define the range to be sorted by pressing Enter at the first cell in the range, pressing the period key (.), moving the cursor to the last cell in the range, and then pressing Enter again.

Some things to know before attempting to sort:

1. Javelin rearranges groups of variables with the sort command, but does not rearrange variables from one grouping to another.

2. Javelin will not sort dates.

3. Javelin sorts alpha and numeric data in the same sort, but places the alpha data after the numeric data.

/*Worksheet Format

PURPOSE: The /*Worksheet Format command is available only in the WORKSHEET view. This command is used to format selected parts of a Javelin worksheet. Formatting cells, rows, and columns in the Javelin worksheet is similar to using the /Define Settings, /Define Variable, and /Define Worksheet commands listed earlier. The advantage of using the /*Worksheet Format command is the precision it gives you in displaying worksheet data.

USE: Begin by placing the cursor on the item to be formatted. To format the entire worksheet, place the cursor on the home cell (the cell in the upper left corner). To format a column or row, place the cursor on the column or row border. Format a cell by placing the cursor on that cell. To begin formatting, place the cursor in the appropriate location and type

/*F

Javelin allows you the usual formatting options. You can select a format option by moving the cursor to it and pressing Enter. You can change the number of displayed decimal points by moving the cursor to Decimal places, entering the number of decimal numbers you want to have displayed, and pressing Enter (see fig. B.18). These options go into effect when you press Esc.

Note that Javelin formats the worksheet on a "smallest-to-greatest" basis:

1. Model

2. Variable

3. Worksheet

4. Row

5. Column

6. Cell

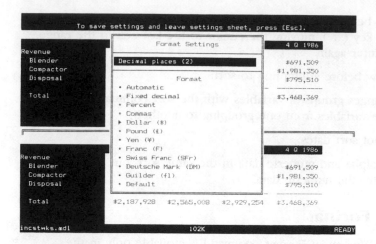

Fig. B.18. Using the Format settings sheet to change worksheet format.

/*Worksheet Width

PURPOSE: The /*Worksheet Width command, which is active only in the WORKSHEET view, allows you to change individual column widths. The command also lets you change the width of the left border.

USE: To change a column's width, place the cursor in the column to be changed and type

    /*W

Javelin then prompts you to enter the new width, which you can enter in either of two ways. The quickest method is to enter the number of characters you want shown in the column and then press Enter. Another method is to use the Right-arrow and Left-arrow keys to change the displayed width of the column (see fig. B.19). When the column is the width you want, press Enter. If you decide to return the width to its original size, press Del.

*Formulas Commands

/*Formulas All Formulas

PURPOSE: The /Formulas All formulas command restores the display of all formulas as first issued by the /View Formulas All formulas command.

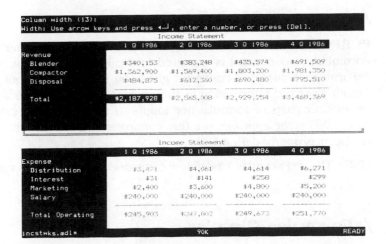

Fig. B.19. The /*Worksheet
Width command asks you for the
new column width.

USE: Activate the /*Formulas All formulas command by typing

/*A

/*Formulas Inputs

PURPOSE: This view-sensitive command is active only when the /View
Formulas All formulas command has been issued and the cursor is active in the
FORMULAS view. The /*Formulas Inputs command gives you model information;
you cannot alter the information in this view. The command gives you a
comprehensive listing of all input variables (variables defined with values, not
formulas). The command does not list formulas.

USE: The /*Formulas Inputs command is issued by typing

/*I

/*Formulas Results

PURPOSE: This view-sensitive command is active only after execution of the
/View Formulas All formulas command in the FORMULAS view. The /*Formulas
Results command provides model information; you cannot alter the information
in this view. This command lists all the variables that are not used in any other
variables. If your model concludes with one result from its calculations, that
result is displayed by this command. But if your model contains multiple results,
all those results will be listed.

USE: The /*Formulas Results command is activated by typing

/*R

/*Formulas Undefined

PURPOSE: This view-sensitive command is active only after the /View Formulas .All command is executed in the FORMULAS view. The /*Formulas Undefined command gives you information about the model; you cannot alter the information in this view. This command lists all variables that are neither parts of formulas nor inputs to the model. If a calculation results in an #UNDEF error message, use this command to see what variables have not been yet been properly defined.

USE: The /*Formulas Undefined command is activated by typing

   /*U

/*Formulas Circular

PURPOSE: This view-sensitive command is active only after the /View Formulas All command has been executed and the cursor is active in the FORMULAS view. The /*Formulas Circular command gives you information about your model; you cannot alter the information in this view. This command produces a listing of all variables that reference themselves directly or indirectly in their formulas and produce the #CIRC error message.

USE: Activate the /*Formulas Circular command by typing

   /*C

/*Formulas Notes

PURPOSE: This view-sensitive command is active only after the /View Formulas All command has been executed in the FORMULAS view. The /*Formulas Notes command gives you model information, but you cannot alter that information in this view. This command produces a listing from all views of all variables for which you've created notes. This FORMULAS view command is handy to use in the two-window mode with the NOTES view. As you move the cursor in the FORMULAS view, the notes listed for each variable are displayed in the NOTES view.

USE: Activate the /*Formulas Notes command by typing

   /*N

/*Formulas Time Spans

PURPOSE: This view-sensitive command is active only after the /View Formulas All command has been executed in the FORMULAS view. The

/*Formulas Time spans command gives you information about your model; you cannot alter the information in this view. This command provides a comprehensive listing of all variables and their time periods.

USE: The /*Formulas Time spans command is activated by typing

/*T

*Roots Commands

/*Roots All Roots

PURPOSE: This view-sensitive command is active only after the /View Formulas Roots command has been executed in the FORMULAS view. /*Roots All roots is identical to the /View Formulas Roots command: they both list all variables that are roots of the designated variable. /*Roots All roots is used to restore the list of all roots after /*Roots Input, /*Roots Undefined, /*Roots Notes, or /*Roots Timespans.

USE: The /*Roots All roots command is activated by typing

/*A

/*Roots Inputs

PURPOSE: This view-sensitive command is active only after the /View Formulas Roots command has been executed in the FORMULAS view. /*Roots Inputs lists all the input variables that are roots of the designated variable.

USE: The /*Roots Inputs command is activated by typing

/*I

/*Roots Undefined

PURPOSE: This view-sensitive command is active only after the /View Formulas Roots command has been executed in the FORMULAS view. This command lists all variables that are roots of the designated variable and are not defined elsewhere in the model.

USE: Activate the /*Roots Undefined command by typing

/*U

/*Roots Notes

PURPOSE: This view-sensitive command is active only after the /View Formulas Roots command has been executed in the FORMULAS view. This command lists all variables that are roots of the designated variable with associated notes from any view.

USE: Activate the /*Roots Notes command by typing

/*N

/*Roots Time Spans

PURPOSE: This view-sensitive command is active only when the /View Formulas Roots command has been executed in the FORMULAS view. This command lists all the time spans for every variable that is a root of the designated variable.

USE: Activate the /*Roots Time spans command by typing

/*T

*Branches Commands

/*Branches All

PURPOSE: This view-sensitive command is active only when the /View Formulas Branches command has been executed in the FORMULAS view. This command, identical to the /View Formulas Branches command, is used to restore the view of all branches after execution of one of the other *Branches commands. The command also lists all variables that are branches of the designated variable.

USE: Activate the /*Branches All command by typing

/*A

/*Branches Results

PURPOSE: This view-sensitive command is active only when the /View Formulas Branches command has been executed in the FORMULAS view. The /*Branches Results command lists all the variables that are branches of the designated variable and also have no other variables depending on them.

USE: Activate the /*Branches **Results** command by typing

   /*R

/*Branches Notes

PURPOSE: This view-sensitive command is active only after the /View Formulas Branches command has been executed in the FORMULAS view. This command lists all variables that are roots of the designated variable with associated notes from any view.

USE: The /*Branches Notes command is activated by typing

   /*N

/*Branches Time Spans

PURPOSE: This view-sensitive command is active only after the /View Formulas Branches command has been executed in the FORMULAS view. This command lists all the time spans for every variable root of the designated variable.

USE: The /*Branches Time spans command is activated by typing

   /*T

*Errors Commands

/*Errors All

PURPOSE: This command can be used only in an active ERRORS view. The /*Errors All command lists all errors in the model, regardless of their type. The /*Errors All command is identical to the /View Errors All command. You use the /*Errors All command to restore the view of all errors after executing the /*Errors Undefined or /*Errors Time span commands.

USE: The /*Errors All command is activated by typing

   /*A

/*Errors Undefined

PURPOSE: This command can be used only in the ERRORS view. The /*Errors Undefined command lists all variables in the model that are not the products of a formula and have no data associated with them. This command is only useful after a calculation has resulted in an #UNDEFINED# error message.

USE: The /*Errors Undefined command is activated by typing

/*U

/*Errors Time Period

PURPOSE: This command can be used only in the ERRORS view. The /*Errors Time period command lists all time discrepancies in formulas throughout the model. An elaborate model with several different time periods can result in such errors as attempting to perform arithmetic with data from different time periods or summing monthly and yearly data together. This command lists variables with inconsistencies in time.

USE: The /*Errors Time period command is activated by typing

/*T

C

A Javelin versus
1-2-3 Comparison

Javelin is a powerful new program for financial analysis and modeling. Because it was designed specifically for financial modeling, it is considerably different from 1-2-3, which is basically an electronic spreadsheet.

This appendix covers the differences and the common ground between Javelin and 1-2-3. The discussion will help you to make the transition quickly from 1-2-3 to the advanced financial modeling capabilities of Javelin.

Size and Memory Requirements

Javelin is a complex program that requires more main memory to run than does 1-2-3. A PC with 640K of main memory will be sufficient for most applications. For very large applications you can use an extended memory board.

	Javelin	*1-2-3*
Minimum memory requirement	512K	256K*
Program size	386K	181K*
Maximum model size in 640K	209K	414K*
Can utilize expanded memory	Yes	Yes*
Can utilize AT extended memory	No	No
Can utilize numeric coprocessor	Yes	Yes*

* 1-2-3 Release 2 feature

Recalculation

Javelin is always in manual recalculation mode. When you change a Javelin model, the CALC indicator comes on. However, the model is not recalculated until you press the CALC key (F9).

Data Types and Data Views

The key difference between Javelin and 1-2-3 is the way Javelin handles data and formulas. One aspect of this difference is Javelin data types. The other aspect is Javelin's use of a central Information Base to store data and formulas.

Data Types

The basic data type in Javelin is time series, a set of data with a defined periodicity (that is, daily, monthly, yearly) and time span. (Javelin also recognizes constants—variables that have the same value in every time period.) Javelin time-series data and constants are referred to by their variable names in all calculations and report definitions.

In contrast, the basic data type in 1-2-3 is the spreadsheet cell. All 1-2-3 operatic s are defined in terms of spreadsheet cells or ranges of cells. Time-series variables are handled by replicating data and formulas across spreadsheet rows or columns. In Javelin, time-series variables are created automatically.

Data Types	Javelin	1-2-3
Constants (single cells)	Yes	Yes
Labels	Yes(1)	Yes
Ranges	Yes(1)	Yes
Daily time series	Yes	No
Weekly time series	Yes	No
Monthly time series	Yes	No
Quarterly time series	Yes	No
Yearly time series	Yes	No
User-defined time series	Yes	No

(1) WORKSHEET view

The following is a simple Javelin model:

Sales Revenue = Unit Sales * Price Per Unit
Unit Sales = Grow(100 @Jan 1986, .01)
Price Per Unit = 10.95

The time-series variable *Sales Revenue* is defined for each time period as *Unit Sales* times *Price Per Unit*. *Sales* is defined as 100 in January, 1986, and growing by 1 percent in each subsequent month (assuming *Unit Sales* is a monthly variable). *Price Per Unit* is the constant amount $10.95. The time span of *Sales Revenue* is the same as the time span of *Unit Sales* (equals the default time span for the model unless defined otherwise).

A corresponding 1-2-3 model:

	A	B	C	D	E	F
1		Jan	Feb	Mar	Apr	May
2						
3	Sales		+C4*C5	+D4*D5	+E4*E5	+F4*F5
4	Units	100	+B4*1.01	+C4*1.01	+D4*1.01	+E4*1.01
5	Price	10.95	10.95	10.95	10.95	10.95

The Javelin model avoids the duplication of formulas required to model data over time in 1-2-3. Javelin formulas are also defined in terms of variable names. The resulting model is more readable, less likely to have errors in functions, and requires less space in main memory and on disk than the corresponding 1-2-3 model.

Views of the Data

Javelin maintains all data and formulas in an Information Base that is accessible in 10 different views. 1-2-3, in contrast, stores its data directly in the spreadsheet cells.

Storing data in a central information base offers two main advantages. First, the same data can be used in different reports without copying or rearranging. Second, all data and formulas are available in one place for debugging, verifying, or modifying the model.

View	Function
WORKSHEET	View data for selected variables and time periods in a row-column spreadsheet format. Prepare formatted reports.
FORMULAS	View formulas that define Javelin variables.
DIAGRAM	View a flow diagram showing the relationships between variables in the model.
NOTES	Display notes made to document the model.
TABLE	View data for a variable in a tabular format.

GRAPH   View a presentation graph of specified variables. Same
                    graph types as 1-2-3 Release 2 plus horizontal bar
                    graphs.

CHART   View a bar graph of a variable.

QUICK GRAPH   View a line graph of a variable.

MACROS   Display script of a Javelin macro.

ERRORS   Display formulas that contain errors.

1-2-3, in contrast, offers only two ways to look at data you have entered into
the spreadsheet cells:

View	*Function*
Spreadsheet	All data, formulas, and macros are displayed in a row-column format. Each cell in the spreadsheet is independent, requiring an individual definition. Different report formats require copying or rearranging the data.
Graph	View a graph of specified ranges of cells.

Data and Formula Entry

Javelin data and formulas can be entered in several different ways depending on
the current view. This contrasts to data entry directly into spreadsheet cells in
1-2-3.

View	*Method*
WORKSHEET	Enter or modify formulas and constants in the current worksheet.
FORMULAS and DIAGRAM	Enter or modify formulas and constants.
TABLE	Enter time-series data in a tabular format.
CHART and QUICK GRAPH	Enter time-series data in a graphical format.

Windowing

Javelin can display two windows on screen with the same or a different view in each. Although 1-2-3 lets you split the screen to view two different parts of the worksheet, Javelin's windowing capability goes much further. With Javelin, you can, for example, display two different worksheets, and changes you make while working in one window can be reflected immediately in the other window.

Number Formatting

Javelin number formatting capabilities correspond to those in 1-2-3 Release 2, including international currency formats but excluding date formats, which have no meaning in Javelin. Formats can be specified for the entire model, for an individual variable or constant, for an entire worksheet, for a row or column in a worksheet, or for a specific cell in a worksheet.

Information Exchange

Javelin can read data from 1-2-3 worksheets and ASCII text files, and can print to a file although Javelin does not have the extensive file translation capabilities available with 1-2-3 Release 2.

Consolidation Capabilities

Javelin's consolidation commands are much more advanced than 1-2-3's /File Combine command. The Javelin Rollup and Import data building blocks retrieve specified data from other Javelin models by variable name and time period instead of merely combining corresponding spreadsheet cells by position. Consolidation by name is important because it is self-documenting and reduces the possibility of errors in the consolidation.

Consolidation Method	Javelin	1-2-3
Positional (corresponding cells)	No	Yes
By variable name and period	Yes	No

Consolidation Hierarchy

Defined in rollup command	Yes	No
Manually specified file by file	Yes	Yes

Consolidation Commands with Javelin

Rollup building block   Defines consolidation hierarchy, imports data from other Javelin models, and calculates consolidated variables.

Import data building block   Import specified data from another Javelin model.

Macros and Command Language

Javelin's macro language is comparable to the macro language in 1-2-3 Release 1A, with the addition of a learn mode to make macro creation easier. The Javelin macro commands allow you to conveniently automate any Javelin application.

	Javelin	*1-2-3*
Keyboard macros	Yes	Yes
Macro command language	Yes	Yes
Learn mode	Yes	No
Autoexec macro	Yes	Yes
Branch	Yes	Yes
Subroutine call	Yes	Yes
Subroutine call with parameters	No	Yes*
User menus	Yes	Yes
If. . .Then	Yes	Yes
For loop	No	Yes*
Error branch	Yes	Yes
Commands to allow user input	Yes	Yes
Commands for storing and deleting strings or values in a cell	No	Yes*
File manipulation commands	No	Yes*

* 1-2-3 Release 2 feature

Function Comparison

The function comparison presents each Javelin function and its nearest 1-2-3 equivalent. This comparison is a useful way to bridge the gap between your knowledge of 1-2-3 functions and the equivalent Javelin functions.

Arithmetic Functions

Javelin has all the common arithmetic functions except a random number generator and a base 10 logarithm function.

Function	Javelin	1-2-3
Absolute value function	ABS(expr)	@ABS(expr)
Exponential function	EXP(expr)	@EXP(expr)
Integer part function	INT(expr)	@INT(expr)
Natural logarithm	LN(expr)	@LN(expr)
Base 10 logarithm	none	@LOG(expr)
Remainder function	MOD(expr)	@MOD(expr)
Random number generator	none	@RAND
Round to n decimal places	ROUND(expr,[n])	@ROUND(expr,n)
Square root function	SQRT(expr)	@SQRT(expr)

Trigonometric Functions

Javelin has no trigonometric functions. This doesn't, however, affect the true functionality of the program because trigonometric functions are seldom used in financial modeling.

Simple Statistical Functions

Because of its time-series orientation, Javelin has one set of statistical functions for comparing different variables and another for comparing different time periods within a variable.

	Javelin	1-2-3
Defined across variables:		
Average of items in list	AVG	@AVG
Maximum value in list	MAX	@MAX
Minimum value in list	MIN	@MIN
Sum of values in list	SUM	@SUM

Defined across time periods:

Number of observations	COUNT	@COUNT
Standard deviation	STDEV	@STD
Variance	VAR	@VA R
Average over time	TAVG	@AVG
Minimum value over time	TMIN	@MIN
Maximum value over time	TMAX	@MAX
Sum of values over time	TSUM	@SUM

Trend and Regression Analysis

Javelin's regression functions let you build trend line forecasts and simple regression forecasts into models. The corresponding 1-2-3 function is the /Data Regression function in 1-2-3 Release 2.

Javelin's trend analysis functions have no counterparts in 1-2-3, although their functions can be performed using the appropriate formulas.

	Javelin	*1-2-3*
Simple Regression vs. Time:		
Regression line	TREND	
Serial Correlation Coeff.	TRENDCORR	**/Data Regression**∗
Slope of regression line	TRENDSLOPE	
Intercept	TR ENDSTART	
Simple Regression Between Series:		
Y Intercept	INTERCEPT	
Simple correlation coeff.	CORR	**/Data Regression**∗
Predicted values of Y	PREDICT	
Slope of regression line	SLOPE	
Trend analysis functions:		
Cumulative sum of series	CUM	none
Rolling average	RAVG	none
Rolling maximum	RMAX	none
Rolling minimum	RMIN	none
Rolling sum	RSUM	none

∗ 1-2-3 Release 2 feature

Financial Functions

Javelin has all the common financial functions plus two specialized functions for calculating bond prices and bond yields.

	Javelin	*1-2-3*
Bond price function	BONDPRICE	none
Bond yield to maturity	BONDYTM	none
Declining bal. depr.	DEPRDECL	@DDB*
Straight line depr.	DEPRSL	@SLN*
Sum of years digits depr.	DEPRSOYD	@SYD*
Future value of expr	FV	@FV
Compound growth function	GROW	none
Compound growth rate	GROWRATE	@RATE*
Internal rate of return	IRR	@IRR
Net present value	NPV	@NPV
Mortgage loan payment	PMT	@PMT
Present value	PV	@PV
Number of periods to accumulate future value	none	@TERM* and @CTERM

* 1-2-3 Release 2 feature

Logical Functions

Javelin's logical functions correspond to the logical functions in 1-2-3 Release 1A.

	Javelin	*1-2-3*
IF statement	IF	@IF
Logical AND function	AND	#AND# Operator
Logical NOT function	NOT	#NOT# Operator
Logical OR function	OR	#OR# Operator
Choose from list of arguments	SELECT	@CHOOSE
Lookup table	LOOKUP TABLE (building block	@VLOOKUP, @HLOOKUP
Select value from two-dimensional table	none	@INDEX*

* 1-2-3 Release 2 feature

Data Type Conversion

Javelin type conversion functions allow time-series data to be converted from one periodicity to another by one of several methods. There are no corresponding functions in 1-2-3.

Time Period	Javelin	1-2-3
Daily	DAILY	none
Weekly	WEEKLY	none
Monthly	MONTHLY	none
Quarterly	QUARTERLY	none
Yearly	YEARLY	none
Custom period A A		none
Custom period B B		none

Lead and Lag Functions

Javelin's lead and lag functions allow values in past or future periods to be referenced in formulas. The corresponding functions can be performed by cell references in 1-2-3 formulas.

	Javelin	1-2-3
Value from past period	PREVIOUS	none
Value from future period	NEXT	none
Value from specified period (abs. cell ref.)	VALUE	none
Distributed lag function	Time delay (building block)	none

Date Functions

Given Javelin's superior capabilities for linking data to time, it has a number of date functions that have no comparable functions in 1-2-3.

	Javelin	1-2-3
# periods between dates	BETWEEN	none
# periods of data for variable	LENGTH	@COUNT
# periods since date	SINCE	none
# periods until date	UNTIL	none

# days in current month	MDAYS	none
# days in current quarter	QDAYS	none
# days in current year	YDAYS	none
Cumulative month-to-date	MTD	none
Cumulative quarter-to-date	QTD	none
Cumulative year-to-date	YTD	none
Time span begins on date	BEGIN	none
Time span ends on date	END	none
Time span between dates	RANGE	none
System date and time	@DATE,@TIME (reports only	@NOW*, @TO DAY

* 1-2-3 Release 2 feature

Miscellaneous Javelin Functions

Four special functions are available to calculate differences in values over time, to interpolate missing values, or to tell Javelin not to calculate a particular value.

	Javelin	1-2-3
Difference function	CHANGE	none
Percent difference	PCT	none
Interpolation function	INTERP	none
Null function	F	none

Javelin Building Blocks

Javelin building blocks provide you with a simple and effective way to define complex relationships between variables within a model or variables in different models. As such, these building blocks are some of Javelin's most powerful and useful functions.

	Javelin	1-2-3
Graphically define the relationship between two variables	Curve	none
Define a consolidation hierarchy	Rollup	none

	Javelin	*1-2-3*
Define delayed effect of one variable on another (Distributed Lag)	Time delay	none
Lookup table (such as a tax table)	Lookup table	@HLOOKUP, @VLOOKUP
Load data from another Javelin model	Import Data	/File Combine command
	Javelin	*1-2-3*

Index

More Computer Knowledge

LOTUS SOFTWARE TITLES

1-2-3 Business Formula Handbook 19.95
1-2-3 for Business 18.95
1-2-3 Financial Macros 19.95
1-2-3 Macro Library 19.95
1-2-3 Tips, Tricks, and Traps 19.95
Using 1-2-3, 2nd Edition 19.95
Using 1-2-3 Workbook and Disk 29.95
Using Symphony 23.95
Symphony: Advanced Topics 19.95
Symphony Macros and the Command Language 22.95
Symphony Tips, Tricks, and Traps 21.95

IBM TITLES

IBM PC Expansion & Software Guide 29.95
IBM's Personal Computer, 2nd Edition 17.95
Networking IBM PCs: A Practical Guide 18.95
Using PC DOS 21.95
PC DOS Workbook 14.95

APPLICATIONS SOFTWARE TITLES

dBASE III Plus Application 19.95
dBASE III Advanced Programming 22.95
dBASE III Handbook 19.95
Multiplan Models for Business 15.95
R:base 5000 User's Guide 19.95
Using AppleWorks.. 16.95
Using Dollars and Sense 14.95
Using Enable 17.95
Using Excel... 19.95
Excel Macro Library 19.95
Using Javelin 19.95
Using Paradox 19.95
Using Reflex 19.95
Using Smart 22.95

Que Order Line: **1-800-428-5331**
All prices subject to change without notice.

Books from Que

MORE COMPUTER KNOWLEDGE FROM QUE

Using PC DOS
by Chris DeVoney

A superior work, this first-rate book hit the best-seller list within one week of its publication. In the lucid, easy-to-understand style that made him a best-selling author, Chris DeVoney describes both the common and not-so-common operations of PC DOS. DeVoney guides users—both novice and intermediate—through basic and advanced DOS commands. A Command Reference defines every DOS command, gives examples, and tells how to handle common problems. *Using PC DOS* is two books in one—a concise tutorial and a valuable reference you will refer to over and over again.

Using 1-2-3, 2nd Edition
by Douglas Cobb and Geoffrey LeBlond

Nationally acclaimed, *Using 1-2-3* is "the book" for every 1-2-3 user. Whether you are using Release 1A or 2, you will find *Using 1-2-3,* 2nd Edition, your most valuable source of information. Spreadsheet, database, graphics, and macro capabilities common to both Release 1A and 2 or new to Release 2 are all covered in depth. Notations in the text and a tear-out command chart help you locate quickly the differences between Release 1A and 2. Like thousands of other 1-2-3 users, you will consider this book indispensable.

"A valuable text. Should be part of every PC library."—*PC BookSource*

Using WordPerfect, Revised Edition
by Walton Beacham and Deborah Beacham

Revised and updated, this popular book explains in detail the expanded capabilities of Version 4.0 and discusses those features common to all versions of WordPerfect. A clear and informative user's guide, *Using WordPerfect* covers the basics of this popular program and provides many practical applications. Special attention is given to WordPerfect's file management features and report generation capability. If you rely on the power of WordPerfect, this book is an excellent resource.

IBM PC Expansion & Software Guide

"This may well be the most comprehensive software directory of its kind. The *IBM PC Expansion & Software Guide* is a directory to be trusted."—*PC Magazine*

Containing descriptions of nearly 8,000 products for the IBM and PC compatibles, Que Corporation's expanded guide has grown with each publication. Published annually, this popular directory provides major listings for hardware, software products, supplies and services, and IBM PC dealers. Company and product questionnaires give readers the opportunity to contribute information and ask questions.

Mail to: Que Corporation • P. O. Box 50507 • Indianapolis, IN 46250

Item	Title	Price	Quantity	Extension
180	Using PC DOS	$21.95		
130	Using 1-2-3, 2nd Edition	$19.95		
11	Using WordPerfect, Revised Edition	$18.95		
189	IBM PC Expansion & Software Guide	$29.95		
		Book Subtotal		
	Shipping & Handling ($1.75 per item)			
	Indiana Residents Add 5% Sales Tax			
	GRAND TOTAL			

Method of Payment:

☐ Check ☐ VISA ☐ MasterCard ☐ American Express

Card Number _____ Exp. Date _____

Cardholder's Name _____

Ship to _____

Address _____

City _____ State _____ ZIP _____

If you can't wait, call **1-800-428-5331** and order TODAY.

All prices subject to change without notice.

FOLD HERE

‾‾‾‾‾‾‾‾‾‾‾‾‾‾‾‾‾‾‾‾‾‾‾‾‾‾‾‾‾‾

‾‾‾‾‾‾‾‾‾‾‾‾‾‾‾‾‾‾‾‾‾‾‾‾‾‾‾‾‾‾

‾‾‾‾‾‾‾‾‾‾‾‾‾‾‾‾‾‾‾‾‾‾‾‾‾‾‾‾‾‾

‾‾‾‾‾‾‾‾‾‾‾‾‾‾‾‾‾‾‾‾‾‾‾‾‾‾‾‾‾‾

Place
Stamp
Here

Que Corporation
P. O. Box 50507
Indianapolis, IN 46250

FOLD HERE

Que Publishing, Inc.
P. O. Box 50507
Indianapolis, IN 46250